The Problem of Social Inequality

Within and among nations, rising levels of social inequality threaten our collective future. Currently, upwards of 80% of people's life chances are determined by factors over which they have absolutely no control. Social inequality threatens the democratic project because it destroys the trust on which governments depend, and it gives rise to corrupt political and economic institutions. How can we get out of the traps we have created for ourselves? We need to *reboot capitalism*. Drawing on diverse examples from a range of countries, McNall explains the social, economic, and ecological traps we have set for ourselves and develops a set of *rules of resilience* that are necessary conditions for the creation and maintenance of democratic societies, and a set of rules essential for creating a sustainable future.

Scott G. McNall is Emeritus Provost and Professor at California State University (CSUC), Chico and currently an affiliated Professor in the Department of Sociology at the University of Montana. He was the founding Executive Director of the Institute for Sustainable Development at CSUC. He lives with his wife, Sally, in Missoula, Montana.

Scott McNall has written a lucid, comprehensive, and compelling account of economic inequality, its intersections with other forms of social inequality, and the threats it poses to democracy and the planet. His recommendations for reforming the current neoliberal capitalist regime suggest a sustainable path to a more democratic future.
Robert J. Antonio, *Professor of Sociology, University of Kansas*

Scott McNall's book moves effortlessly from big-picture to ground-level issues as he assesses the entrenched nature of inequalities. This readable treatment helps student readers see how Marx and Weber can illuminate their own struggles to pay for college, find jobs, establish relationships, and escape or avoid debt. McNall strikes exactly the right tone as he patiently excavates the global from the local. His brand of applied critical theory works.
Ben Agger, *Professor of Sociology and Humanities and Director, Center for Theory, University of Texas at Arlington*

McNall provides a sophisticated analysis of growing degrees of inequality in the world, as well as its causes, consequences, and solutions. As one's life chances are increasingly determined by irrelevant moral criteria such as gender, ethnicity, religion, and family, the trust on which a democracy depends is quickly eroded. The book offers a wise and plausible message for success: create high levels of human capital. By joining together the issues of climate change, social inequality, corruption, trust, and democracy, McNall offers the beginnings of a road map to a much-improved world.
Tom Kando, *Professor Emeritus of Sociology, Sacramento State University*

The Problem of Social Inequality provides essential insights into the causes of social inequality and why inequality serves as a major barrier [to] creating a sustainable and resilient future. The author argues that we need to *reboot* capitalism by maximizing human talent and creativity in order to adapt to an unknown future. For students and practitioners, this work is a significant contribution to discussions about global progress and should be required reading in both the social and environmental sciences.
Jim Pushnik, *Director of the Institute for Sustainable Development at California State University, Chico*

At a time when inequality has become the catchword for all that ails the globalized world, we are nevertheless ignorant of its sources, dynamics, and consequences. McNall's book is the go-to text for redressing these grievous inadequacies in current scholarship. Its central virtue is in pushing well behind the parochial fixation on income differentials. Instead, he views equality in all its various dimensions—and especially the catastrophic causal consequences of the drastic imbalance in political power at the local, national, and global level, the consequently lethal mal-distribution of health care and material well-being, and the often unobserved but brutal consequences of cultural inequality. And, within this, McNall harnesses his global focus to underscore, diagnose, and analyze the less-than-mediocre performance of the United States in addressing these issues within our national boundaries.
Michael Schwartz, *Distinguished Professor of Sociology, Stony Brook University*

The Problem of Social Inequality

Why It Destroys Democracy, Threatens the Planet, and What We Can Do About It

Scott G. McNall

NEW YORK AND LONDON

First published 2016
by Routledge
711 Third Avenue, New York, NY 10017

and by Routledge
2 Park Square, Milton Park, Abingdon, Oxon, OX14 4RN

Routledge is an imprint of the Taylor & Francis Group, an informa business

© 2016 Taylor & Francis

The right of Scott G. McNall to be identified as author of this work has been asserted by him in accordance with sections 77 and 78 of the Copyright, Designs and Patents Act 1988.

All rights reserved. No part of this book may be reprinted or reproduced or utilised in any form or by any electronic, mechanical, or other means, now known or hereafter invented, including photocopying and recording, or in any information storage or retrieval system, without permission in writing from the publishers.

Trademark notice: Product or corporate names may be trademarks or registered trademarks, and are used only for identification and explanation without intent to infringe.

Library of Congress Cataloging in Publication Data

McNall, Scott G., author.
The problem of social inequality: why it destroys democracy, threatens the planet, and what we can do about it / Scott G. McNall.
    pages cm
    1. Equality. 2. Democracy. 3. Social problems.
    4. Social action. I. Title.
HN18.3.M3995 2016
303.3—dc23   2015023241

ISBN: 978-1-138-95971-2 (hbk)
ISBN: 978-1-138-95970-5 (pbk)
ISBN: 978-1-315-65923-7 (ebk)

Typeset in Adobe Caslon and Copperplate Gothic
by codeMantra

Contents

LIST OF ILLUSTRATIONS IX
PREFACE AND INTRODUCTION XI
ACKNOWLEDGMENTS XXIII

1 THE NATURE OF SOCIAL INEQUALITY 1
   DEMOCRATIC SOCIETIES   2
   HUMAN NEEDS   4
   MAINTAINING SOCIAL INEQUALITIES   12
   STATUS AS AN INDEPENDENT FORCE   14
   DEMOCRACY, INEQUITY, TRUST, AND RESILIENCE   21
   SUMMARY   21
   THROUGH A SUSTAINABILITY LENS   22
   NOTES   22

2 A WORLD DIVIDED BY INCOME AND WEALTH 26
   THE NATURE OF POVERTY   28
   IS GLOBAL INEQUALITY GROWING OR DECLINING?   32
   WHO ARE THE 1%?   36
   HOW THE WEALTHY KEEP THEIR MONEY   40
   SOCIAL MOBILITY   43
   IS EDUCATION THE GREAT LEVELER?   45

MARRIAGE AND FAMILY STRUCTURE   50
THE EROSION OF THE SOCIAL CONTRACT   52
SUMMARY   53
THROUGH A SUSTAINABILITY LENS   54
NOTES   57

3   CAPITALISM AND INEQUALITY   63
THE ENLIGHTENMENT AND THE RISE OF THE SCIENTIFIC REVOLUTION   66
THE RISE OF A WORLD SYSTEM   73
THE OPTIMISTS: SMITH AND RICARDO   75
THE PESSIMIST: MARX   80
SUMMARY   85
THROUGH A SUSTAINABILITY LENS   86
NOTES   87

4   THE CONTINUING CRISES OF CAPITALISM   91
WAS MARX RIGHT?   92
WHY DOESN'T CAPITALISM COLLAPSE?   95
WILL CAPITALISM SURVIVE?   97
WHAT CAUSES INEQUALITY TODAY?   101
THE ECOLOGICAL CRISES OF CAPITALISM   106
CAPITALISM AND GLOBALIZATION   109
SUMMARY   110
THROUGH A SUSTAINABILITY LENS   111
NOTES   112

5   TRUST, INEQUALITY, AND DEMOCRACY   115
JAPAN: BONDS OF TRUST   115
INEQUALITY IS DESTABILIZING   118
HAITI: INEQUALITY, CORRUPTION, AND MISTRUST   120
TRUST, EQUALITY, AND SOCIAL CAPITAL   124
CREATING SOCIAL CAPITAL   126
THE NATURE OF BRIDGING SOCIAL CAPITAL   129
HISTORICAL CONDITIONS THAT GENERATE LOW LEVELS OF TRUST   133
THE FRAGILITY OF SOCIAL CAPITAL   134
SQUANDERING OF HUMAN TALENT   136

Inequality, Corruption, and Democracy   139
The Rise of the Ethnic State   140
Institutions and Trust   143
Declining Trust in the United States   145
Summary   151
Through a Sustainability Lens   152
Notes   153

6   Corruption and Social Inequality   160
Social Instability and the Rise of Corruption   163
The Costs of Corruption   168
Normative Corruption   169
The Worst of the Worst   176
Challenges to Democracy   178
Summary   183
Through a Sustainability Lens   185
Notes   187

7   Narratives of Power: How They Drive Inequality   192
The Great Society Versus the Free Market   193
Hardwired for Narratives   197
Ignoring Inconvenient Truths   198
The War on Unions   200
The Erosion of the Social Contract   208
The Debate over the Minimum Wage   210
The Political War Against Equality   216
Incompatible Narratives   219
Summary   223
Through a Sustainability Lens   223
Notes   224

8   Rebooting Capitalism to Create a Resilient Future   230
Where are we Headed?   232
Complexity, Energy, and Inequality   237
Resilience   242

SUSTAINABILITY   243
GUIDEPOSTS TO THE FUTURE   246
RULES OF RESILIENCE   248
CREATIVE ADAPTATION   250
SOLUTIONS   255
SOLUTIONS UNIQUE TO THE UNITED STATES   257
REBOOTING CAPITALIST SOCIETY   267
THE ELEVATOR SPEECH   273
NOTES   274

INDEX   279

LIST OF ILLUSTRATIONS

FIGURES

5.1	HOW MUCH OF THE TIME DO YOU TRUST THE GOVERNMENT IN WASHINGTON?	148
5.2	TRUST IN LOCAL GOVERNMENT BY RACE IN DETROIT	150
8.1	THE ECONOMY IS A SUBSET OF THE BIOSPHERE	244

TABLES

1.1	DIFFERENCES IN PERCEPTIONS OF WHY PEOPLE ARE RICH OR POOR BY POLITICAL PARTY	18
2.1	INTERNATIONAL COMPARISON OF STUDENT PERFORMANCE IN MATHEMATICS, READING, AND SCIENCE FOR SELECTED COUNTRIES: SCORES AND RANKINGS	46
4.1	DIFFERENCES IN INEQUALITY AS MEASURED BY THE GINI COEFFICIENT	102
4.2	PERCENT OF WEALTH HELD BY TOP 10% AND THE BOTTOM 90% OF THE U.S. POPULATION	104
5.1	COMPARISON OF COUNTRIES WITH LOWEST AND HIGHEST LOSSES OF HUMAN CAPITAL DUE TO INEQUALITY	137
5.2	CORRUPTION AND FREEDOM IN THOSE COUNTRIES DEMONSTRATING HIGH LEVELS OF INEQUALITY	138

5.3	Countries That Exhibit the Highest and Lowest Levels of Trust with Degree of Ethnic Fractionalization and Observation of the Rule of Law	141
5.4	Readiness for Climate Change	152

Preface and Introduction

In the spring of 2006 I was sitting on the roof of a house in St. Bernard Parish, Louisiana, with a student from California State University, Chico. Students in the Construction Management Program, along with some of the faculty, had gone to help rebuild people's homes in New Orleans about six months after Hurricane Katrina had struck. I went along for a short time to offer encouragement and help. They pulled a trailer 2,400 miles from Chico, California, to New Orleans loaded with the tools and equipment needed and when they arrived went to work immediately replacing electrical wiring, repairing plumbing, hanging sheet rock, reroofing houses, and repairing floors. They were repairing and rebuilding the homes of people who were living temporarily in trailers provided by FEMA, sometimes parked in the yard of their homes waiting for the crew to finish so they could move what possessions they still had back in.

The power and intensity of the storm was driven by the warming waters of the Gulf, a result of the growing effects of climate change.[1,2] When the levees gave way, 80% of the city of New Orleans was flooded with water, completely submerging the homes of some. In St. Bernard Parish, where the students were working, not all homes in a block were being repaired, because their owners could not be found. Many, especially the poor, never came back. In fact, five years after Katrina the population of St. Bernard Parish had dropped by almost 50%.[3]

So, sitting on the roof of a home being repaired, we saw scores of others that were not. What struck me was not just the destruction of homes and property but the furious remark made by the student sitting on the roof with me. "This is not America," he said. "How *could* this happen, here?" He had never before seen or imagined what it meant to be poor and helpless in one of the richest nations on earth.

It was clear that the poor in New Orleans had fewer options than those with economic resources. Some had no insurance on their homes and depended on volunteer labor to repair them. Some were trapped in the city because they did not have a car to get out and, even if they could leave, had no place to go. They had neither friends nor relatives who could take them in, nor money for a motel room. They lived in some of the most vulnerable areas of the city, below the levees. They suffered the greatest from the toxic sludge that leaked from damaged petrochemical facilities in their neighborhoods and into the waters inundating their homes.

In the storm's aftermath there were numerous schemes offered by think tanks and corporations for rebuilding the city that seemed to privilege the wealthy white community and disadvantage the poor, primarily Black, population. It was suggested that it was time to "re-create" New Orleans by closing poorly performing public schools and replacing them with charter schools, (which has now happened). Public housing should be abandoned in favor of private development, and public parks should be created where homes once stood whose owners had fled. Not all of the ideas advanced for dealing with the trauma were bad ideas, but most of them proved to be dead ends because there was such a lack of trust among the city's poor in their government, fostered by gross and long-standing social inequities. There was no civic capacity to respond, no trust to build on, only a legacy of corruption, incompetence, and inequity. In short, New Orleans was not a resilient community, one that could easily bounce back from a natural disaster.

The case of New Orleans and Katrina brings into focus a number of factors that relate to one another—climate change, social inequity, corruption, trust, and ultimately the very nature of a democratic society. If a society limits the ability of its citizens to participate based on their income, ethnicity, religion, or gender, it is not by any definition a democratic society. When climate change puts at risk the most vulnerable humans and further exacerbates their struggles to feed, shelter, and clothe themselves, it can give rise to political instability in many forms. Social, economic, and environmental problems and their solutions are tightly bound together. And to solve these linked problems we must rely on human ingenuity and develop human talent to do so.

Creative Adaptation

Before leaving a discussion of New Orleans I want to return to the people who went to help because they teach an important lesson about response to disaster. First, a number of those students who went were, in the parlance of construction management, "hammer swingers." They were people who had worked in the building trades and were now enrolled in an academic program to enhance their skill set so they could manage large construction projects. They went to New Orleans with significant human capital and with the knowledge and skills to complete the task at hand. However, virtually every home presented a unique set of problems that could not be anticipated ahead of time. Some homes had been pushed off their foundations by the flood waters so that, before plumbing and electricity could be reconnected and repaired, the students had to find ways to shift them back onto their foundations. Sometimes they had to repair the foundations. The students and the two instructors were engaged in constant problem solving. In addition to having a set of high-level skills, they also had permission to act and a clear set of goals. They were free to innovate and needed to do so. Here, then, is an important message for success: *Create high levels of human capital, clearly identify the problem or problems to be solved, and let people innovate to do so.*

In preparing for the future, we cannot anticipate all of the outcomes of three vastly complex systems (the economy, the environment, and human social systems) all of which affect one another. We have to prepare for unanticipated outcomes; ones we may never have seen before. The way to do this is to create sufficient human capital that people can innovate within the nations and communities in which they live. We are going to have to figure out how to solve some problems as they emerge. To innovate and to be creative people need to have permission to act; and they need to live in democratic societies that allow them to act. In other words, we need to create societies that are resilient. What stands in the way? Social inequality.

Concepts: Resilience, Human and Social Capital, Social Equity

Let me briefly note the central concepts with which I will be working. The first is resilience. In the environmental sciences resilience refers to the ability of an ecosystem to respond to exogenous shocks and to return to its previous state. An example could be a grassland fire that, if intense enough, could eliminate populations of snakes, mice and voles living in a field. But eventually, if the field is left undisturbed, seeds that had lain dormant would sprout, take root, and grow; the grass would spring up again from its deep root systems; and, the snakes, mice and voles would return. There are cities and counties using this model to prepare for climate change. It's the wrong model.

King County, Seattle has well-developed plans for how to prepare and recover from weather-related disasters. New York is developing plans to create barriers to prevent storm surges and power outages should a new Sandy strike the East Coast. In these cases the goal is to restore the county and the city to a *previous* state. I want to think about resilience differently. It must be *more* than the ability to respond to exogenous shocks (hurricanes, tornadoes, or acts of terrorism); it must be the ability to *adapt* to unanticipated shocks. I am not arguing that we should not prepare for anticipated disasters; if the weather channel says a tornado is headed your way, you should probably take shelter.

A second concept is that of *sustainability*. Briefly, the concept of sustainability refers to the need to balance environmental, social, and economic concerns and to meet the needs of people today without putting at risk the ability of future generations to meet their needs. This is easier said than done. To take but one example, many believe we need to stop burning coal to generate electricity, because it contributes to climate change. Yet India and China are committed to using coal in the coming decades to boost their economies and raise the standard of living for their citizens. Because of the challenges involved in trying to create sustainable and resilient societies are considerable, and because these link directly to issues of social equality, each chapter will include a discussion of sustainability.

Human creativity will receive its due also. I put great stock in the creative ability of human beings. We have adapted to every ecological niche on the planet, as well as every variety of political and economic regime. Since the time of the Enlightenment we have used science to improve the general lot of humankind. The constraints we face are only those imposed on us by the science of the known world. We can sequester the daemon of climate change—CO_2. We can achieve greater efficiencies in the use of irreplaceable natural resources. I am not arguing for a miracle of technological fixes for all of the problems we humans have created. What I am saying is that we humans are the only option. Nobody else is going to solve our problems; we must and can do it ourselves. But the circumstances under which we can do so require that we free up human capital in order to create resilient societies.

As the terms "human capital" and "social capital" are used so frequently, let me clarify how I will use them. *Human capital* here will refer to the knowledge and skills possessed by an individual. When I write about the need to acquire human capital I am referring to education, as well as to whether or not basic human needs are met within the society in question. Every human needs food, shelter, health care, clean water, and so forth. How societies provide these resources differ widely, and some meet only a minimal number of these needs. But for humans to achieve their full human potential (their human capital) it is essential that societies work systematically to provide for these needs.

I reserve the term *social capital* for the sum of the networks, connections, and assets in common available to people. Like others, I see social capital as central to the creation of a democratic society; its presence enhances the possibility of developing a civic culture, while its absence suggests the opposite. Social capital is what people draw on when they mobilize to demand more inclusive political and economic systems. Unfortunately, as data from the developed and developing world clearly show, opportunities to move beyond born-into economic and social circumstances are dwindling. Gaps between the wealthy and poor within and between nations are expanding. Today, the best predictors of your social and economic chances are the circumstances of your birth parents, the country and even town in which you grew up, as well as your race, gender, and religion. There is something wrong when outcomes depend on these morally irrelevant criteria, things over which we have no control. In other words, systems of social inequality limit the development of social capital and thereby limit people's ability to change their circumstances.

When I use the concept *social inequality* I intend it to mean not just differences in income or wealth but all of those conditions that affect our ability to participate in the societies in which we live. In Afghanistan or Saudi Arabia, gender is a determinant of a woman's ability to participate in her society. In the United States, wealth and income affect the extent to which we can be full participants. Economic power becomes political power, which in turn produces a system of economic and political exclusiveness. Anything that moves a society in the direction of closure, as opposed to openness, is a form of social inequality. I am not building an argument for the leveling of incomes. What I intend to show is that societies in which inequalities driven by irrelevant moral criteria (gender, ethnicity, religion, family) predominate are undemocratic, weak, and unstable societies, which will ultimately fail. *Unequal societies are by nature unstable societies.*

A Systems Approach

The approach in this work is grounded in systems theory and the simple idea that there are recursive and reinforcing links between all of the spheres that affect our lives. For example, economic challenges and environmental challenges are tightly linked. Poor countries, counties, states, or nations that are making efforts to develop frequently imperil the environment, as is happening in China and India today. This is not a new phenomenon. Over 2,500 years ago, Plato in *Critias* bemoaned the ecological destruction taking place in his own time.[4] He said that, whereas once the land of Greece was the best in the world there remained only the "bones of the body. All the richer parts of the soil having fallen away, the mere skeleton is left." He further said that, whereas there had been an abundance of wood in the mountains there was now only "sustenance for the bees." The land, he explained, could no longer hold the annual rainfall because the hills were denuded and it simply "flows off the bare earth into the sea." Today's visitor to Greece has no idea that the denuded hillsides of Athens were once wooded. What is invisible, and needs to be made visible, is the economic system that has laid land bare in support of commerce.

Complex Systems and Why Inequality Doesn't Work

Complex societies, organizations, or machines require significant amounts of energy to maintain them. Energy, whatever its form (kinetic, thermal, chemical, or electric) is a way of getting work done. And, when a complex system (human or otherwise) contains significant imbalances or inequities, it takes even more energy to maintain those inequalities. The proposition I want to advance is that whenever a system is pushed to a high level of inequity or inequality, greater and greater amounts of energy will be spent on maintaining that inequity. If this is a strategy for economic growth or development, it is one that is doomed.

To start with a simple example, a pattern emerges among the nations of the world where those with greater inequities or inequalities spend more resources or energy in keeping populations in line by spending on prisons, police, and paramilitary forces. The same pattern holds true for states within the United States. The greater the degree of income inequality within a state, the greater will be the expenditures on prisons. California has one of the highest degrees of income inequality in the nation and, consequently, one of the highest per capita expenditures spent on locking people up.

Now imagine a field of corn or potatoes that is a monoculture crop. A monoculture is a single-state system maintained by enormous amounts of energy: tilling, planting, harvesting, spraying against diseases from other plants, and so forth. If you simply planted a field of corn, using only one kind of seed, and left the field alone, it could devolve into a completely different state. Also, to prevent it from devolving to another state, you have to create significant barriers to isolate it.

In the same way, complex human systems, over time, require greater and greater investments with declining rates of return just to stay in one place. The eventual result is collapse followed by centuries of economic and social decline.[5] Inequalities have consequences in physical as well as social systems. Human actions are driving the planet toward tipping points. We are using up resources faster than they can be replenished, with the result that we are fast approaching the point at which the Earth's systems may tip out of balance. And we are driving human systems toward instability because of growing inequalities.

The Power of Narratives

The narratives we use to frame and understand the problems facing us matter, because they determine what we do about them. The struggle over the narrative regarding social inequality in the United States takes a variety of forms. One narrative suggests that glaring inequities in wealth and income are unfair, while another suggests they are due solely to individual effort and that people deserve what they get because they've worked hard for it. In Western European countries, on the other hand, the narrative is that the rich are rich because they were born to it or got lucky and not because of individual effort. The result in Europe is a greater willingness to invest in human capital and provide a social safety net. In some African countries, when a newly elected official who is a member of an ethnic group that has been struggling to obtain power finally succeeds and takes office, one may hear the refrain, "Now it is our turn to eat!" It is assumed that whoever is in power will enrich themselves, their friends, and their tribal or ethnic group. That's the point of having power. Our narratives ensnare us in the lives we live and prevent us from challenging the circumstances that freeze us into a particular position in life. As I will explain, narratives that assume people should all be self-reliant and stand on their own two feet prevent them from overcoming major catastrophes when the solutions depend on people working together. I will both explore the kind of narratives we use to frame existential dilemmas as well as suggest that a narrative of resilience could be a more effective one for facing immediate and future issues.

The Problem of Equity

Not only do the stories we tell matter in terms of the social policies we develop, they matter in terms of how we handle adversity and whether or not we feel we belong to our own societies. There is a growing body of evidence that identifies the pathologies that come from differentials in power.[6] To this we will add in Chapter 1 a discussion of status, which has been somewhat ignored in contemporary studies of inequality. It is important to make status part of the discussion, because it relates so closely to the social-psychological effects of differences in wealth and power. Even poor Americans living below the poverty line have many material goods compared to poor people living in a rural village in India or Afghanistan, though they may not have comparable status. *Equity is a matter not just of wealth and income, but of whether or not people have the ability to participate fully in the societies of which they are members.*

Social, economic, and environmental problems and their solutions are tightly bound together. Climate change will exacerbate existing inequalities because of its differential impact on women, children, the poor, and those who live on marginal lands trying to eke out a living. Existing global inequalities are politically destabilizing, as we saw in the Arab Spring of 2010–2012 and its aftermath. They will continue to serve as a catalyst for change, but not all changes result in more equitable or democratic societies. As of 2015, the number of failed states has grown throughout the Middle East and in Africa. Libya is now divided by warring factions and tribal groups. The war in Syria alone has lead to 200,000 civilian deaths and almost 40% of the entire population is homeless or living in refugee camps in neighboring countries. Political and economic instability has allowed the Islamic State to control large portions of the land mass in Iraq and Syria, and the United States and Western allies are spending significant resources bombing their positions.

Countries are positioned very differently to deal with the threats of climate change and the attendant problems of rising sea levels, droughts, and extreme weather events. They are also positioned differently to deal with the issues posed by inequality, including the loss of human potential and the squandering of resources used to maintain inequalities. If, like the United Nations, the World Bank, and the International Monetary Fund, you had to make a bet on which countries would benefit most from aid, it should be those countries that are making a transition to democracy, as evidenced by their investment in human capital, and where it is clear that people express a desire to move toward a more egalitarian society.

I intend to pull together in this book several different threads in order to provide a richer understanding of the world we humans have created, what has gone wrong, and how we might fix it. My goal is to identify how we might balance economic, social, and environmental needs to craft a pathway to the future. In the last chapter, I will lay out "rules of resilience." Those rules grow directly out of the evidence and arguments presented in the preceding chapters. They are intended to be a set of rules that apply in all times and in all places. The more of the rules present in any society, the more likely it is to be democratic. The caveat is that these are principles that we humans have to work constantly to implement.

The argument goes like this:

Chapter 1. All human beings have the same basic needs, which are objective and subjective. For people to be full participants in the society in which they live, all of their needs must be met.

Chapter 2. However, people are increasingly locked into place by virtue of where they were born, to whom, and by what their gender, ethnicity, and religion is.

Chapter 3. Capitalism is a unique political and economic system, as well as a system of ideas, that grew out of the Enlightenment. Personal freedom, private property rights, and equality before the law are all an extension of ideas rooted in the Enlightenment and provide a basis for the success of capitalism.

Chapter 4. Capitalism by its very nature creates economic inequality. If capitalism and the free market work efficiently, then wealth will concentrate in the hands of the few.

Chapter 5. Democracy depends on trust, and trust depends on social equality.

Chapter 6. Corruption is characteristic of "new" societies and stems from power being rooted in irrelevant moral criteria such as clan, tribe, ethnic group, or religion.

Chapter 7. The stories we tell one another matter because they shape action, but not all of the stories we tell are compatible. A narrative of market fundamentalism is at odds with a narrative about what we all owe to one another and about the nature of community.

Chapter 8. To create a sustainable future we must develop both human and social capital to free up human creativity, which will be essential for dealing with unanticipated shocks to our political, economic, and environmental circumstances.

Notes

1. Union of Concerned Scientists. 2015. "Hurricanes and Climate Change: Exploring the Potential Causes of Increased Storm Intensity." Retrieved on January 27, 2015 at: http://www.ucsusa.org/global_warming/science_and_impacts/impacts/hurricanes-and-climate-change.html.
2. Safa Motesharrei, Jorge Rivas, Eugenia Kalnay. 2014. "A Minimal Model for Human and Nature Interaction." In Joseph A. Tainter. 1988. *The Collapse of Complex Societies*. Cambridge, UK: Cambridge University Press.
3. Campbell Robertson. 2011. "Smaller New Orleans after Katrina, Census Shows." *The New York Times*. February 3. Retrieved on January 27, 2015 at: http://www.nytimes.com/2011/02/04/us/04census.html?pagewanted=all&_r=0.
4. Plato. 360 BCE. "Critias." Translated by Benjamin Jowett. Accessed at: http://classics.mit.edu/Plato/critias.html.
5. Safa Motesharrei, Jorge Rivas, Eugenia Kalnay. 2014. "A Minimal Model for Human and Nature Interaction." In Joseph A. Tainter. 1988. *The Collapse of Complex Societies*. Cambridge, UK: Cambridge University Press.
6. S.L. Johnson, L.J. Leedom, and L. Muhtadie. 2012. "The Dominance Behavioral System and Psychopathology: Evidence from Self-Report, Observational, and Biological Studies." *Psychological Bulletin* 138: 692–743; and Kate Pickett and Richard Wilkinson. 2011. *The Spirit Level: Why Equality Makes Nations Stronger*. London, UK: Bloomsbury.

Acknowledgments

I want to thank my colleague and friend, George Basile of Arizona State University, with whom I began a discussion of resilience and what we needed to do to create a sustainable future. I also want to thank those I prevailed on to read chapters and the manuscript as it developed: Ben Johnson, Tom Kando, Andrea Lerner, James McManus, Miles McNall, Jim Pushnik, Kay Schaffer, and of course my wife, Sally McNall, whose critical eye has informed all of my work. Special thanks are also due to my colleagues who agreed to review the entire manuscript: Ben Agger, Bob Antonio, and Michael Schwartz.

1
THE NATURE OF SOCIAL INEQUALITY

Consider:

- Out of a world population of 7 billion, 3 billion people live on less than $2.50 a day.[1]
- Thirty million people live in slavery due to forced marriage, sex trafficking, debt bondage, and the exploitation of children, including child soldiers.[2]
- One billion of the world's children live in poverty.[3]
- Twenty-five thousand people die from hunger each day.[4]
- The world's wealthy 10% accounted for 60% of all world consumption in 2014.[5]
- The world's poorest 20% accounted for just 1.5%.[6]
- The richest 1% own 50% of all the world's wealth.[7]
- The poorest 50% of the world's population hold just 1% of the world's wealth.

The consequences of growing inequality are considerable, for they affect social cohesion, levels of trust, the ability of countries to maintain or move toward a democratic form of government, and the ability of a country or people to adapt to new and changed circumstances. This leads directly to the question: What would a fair and just society be like? The American philosopher, John Rawls (1921–2002), sought to answer this question in his book, *A Theory of Justice*.[8] He argued that a just society was a fair society, which is not the same thing as an equal society. Rawls asks us to imagine a society into which we will be born and to decide what the rules of the game will be. We get to make up our own imaginary society but we must operate under a "veil of ignorance," which means we have no idea whatsoever what our own attributes will be. We don't know if we will be born male or female, black or white, rich or poor, Muslim or Christian, or any number of other things. The only thing we know about ourselves is that we have the capacity to participate in an enduring system of cooperation and we know we will be a member of the society we choose to create. Rawls assumes humans are rational, and therefore we would design a society that would secure for us maximum advantage at birth.

> What would a fair and just society look like?

We would not design a society that would privilege someone on the basis of their race or gender because that would be irrational. Would a just society be one in which inherited wealth was passed from one generation to the next according to religious status? Would we design a system in which people were denied food and shelter based on their gender? Probably not. This would not mean, however, that all differences would disappear, because each of us would be born with different characteristics and abilities. As the cognitive scientist Steven Pinker noted in commenting on Rawls, we are not born as blank slates. Some of us might be dealt a lousy genetic hand so we would want to guard against that possibility by designing a social system that provided protection in the form of a social safety net. Even if we assumed that genetics explained 100% of the differences between people, we could still get a just and fair society if it were designed along the lines Rawls suggested.[9] We would have to design a system that met universal human needs, regardless of our genetic endowments, and correct injustices when they are found. We would want to create a democratic society.

Democratic Societies

A democratic society does not need to be an equal society, but it needs to be a fair society. By "fair," I mean that it provides an opportunity for all of its citizens to meet their needs, regardless of their ethnicity, gender, religion, and regardless of their opinions, the amount of property they own, or whether they were born to rich or poor parents. As the Universal Declaration of Human Rights, adopted by the United Nations in 1948, spells out, "recognition of the inherent dignity and of the equal and inalienable rights of all members of the human family is the foundation of freedom, justice, and peace in the world."[10]

The nations of the world fall along a continuum in terms of whether their citizens are treated equally before the law and whether they are provided equality of opportunity, freedom of speech, freedom of assembly, and the right to individual liberty. Some nations do a much better job than others in terms of these goals. At one end of the spectrum, the "worst of the worst," we find countries like North Korea, Uzbekistan, South Sudan, and despotic African regimes. And at the other end we find countries like Denmark, Norway, Sweden, and New Zealand. However, no country is a perfect democracy. Let's look at what a lack of civil liberties can mean.

In 2012, a 14-year-old girl in Pakistan was shot in the head for being an advocate for the right of girls to an education. In Cambodia, a 70-year-old protesting the government's policy of seizing land for powerful corporate interests was sent to jail for twenty years. In Honduras a human-rights lawyer was killed because he opposed the development of special economic zones that would have benefited multinational corporations. It is best to understand democracy not as a final stage but as a continued effort to achieve and protect political and civil rights, to meet universal human needs, and to press continually for the development of open, rather than closed, political and economic systems.

Democracy involves far more than the being able to vote. Democracy can be fragile.[11] Freedom House, which tracks the progress of the nations of the world in granting their citizens full civil and political rights, reported in 2015 that for the ninth year in a row there were democratic reversals in the world.[12] While 33 countries showed gains, 61 showed reversals. Among the causes of these reversals were Russia's invasion of Ukraine; a rollback of democratic gains in Egypt by the president and former Army General, Abdel Fattah al-Sisi; the campaign of the Turkish president, Recep Tayyip Erdoğan, against freedom of the press; and China's continued centralization of power and authority. At the end of the day, democratic societies are ones that consistently work to assure the civil and political rights of all their citizens and to meet their needs.

Human Needs

Karl Marx once posited that we humans are creatures of need, and our needs are infinitely expandable.[13] We have both physical and emotional needs which, as we struggle to meet them, will be transformed over the course of our own life history as well as our collective human history. Marx hoped that at later stages of social development our higher needs, for instance, our need for time for creative and intellectual activities, would supersede our need to struggle simply for survival. Billions of people around the world are, however, still struggling to meet what we think of as basic human needs.

There is considerable debate that has extended over decades about whether or not all human beings in all places and all times have the same needs. I believe that *what it means to be human in a society is universal* although, again, how a specific need is met will vary. We all need sustenance to survive, but whether I eat pork depends on my culture and values. The approach I will sketch out differs from that of someone like Abraham Maslow, who outlined a hierarchy of needs. In Maslow's scheme our needs begin with the most fundamental. These needs are at the physiological stage and include such things as breathing, food, water, and sex. The highest need in Maslow's hierarchy is self-actualization, which is realized through creative and spontaneous acts.[14] A hierarchy of needs clearly suggests some needs are more important than others. And while it seems to make intuitive sense to argue that it is more important to eat, breathe, and procreate than to engage in creative problem-solving activities, the reality is that human beings *need to do all of these things and more.* There isn't a simple hierarchy of human needs; rather, there is a panoply of needs, all of which interact with one another, and all of which must to be met in order to be *human in one's own society.*

> There isn't a simple hierarchy of needs; rather there is a panoply of needs, all of which interact with one another and all of which must be met in order to be human in one's own society.

This perspective differs from that found in the work of those who focus on developing countries and who ask: What, at the most fundamental

THE NATURE OF SOCIAL INEQUALITY

level, is essential for people to survive? This approach, sometimes referred to as the basic needs approach, focuses on the concept of *absolute* poverty, which is a set standard in all societies and does not change over time.[15] The idea of *basic needs* grew out of a 1976 conference of the International Labor Organization and has shaped the development policies of agencies such as the United Nations.[16] Under this framework resources are provided to a country in order to meet basic physical needs, as opposed to providing resources to develop human potential or transform the economic and social structures of a country. The Urban Institute estimates that just to cover basic, subsistence household expenses (rent or mortgage, utilities, food, and so forth), a family of four in the United States needs an income of $42,000 a year.[17] While meeting basic needs of subsistence is of critical importance, it alone will not allow people to develop the potential to transform their lives and that of their society or to be a *full participant human in their own society or to live a decent life.*

Another important and useful concept for any discussion of inequality is relative poverty. Relative poverty recognizes that what it takes to meet basic needs will vary from society to society and can change over time. The British sociologist Peter Townsend (1928–2009) provided a good definition of relative poverty that has been used by many.

> Individuals, families, and groups in the population can be said to be in poverty when they lack the resources to obtain the diet, participate in the activities, and have the living conditions and the amenities [that] are customary, or at least widely encouraged or approved in societies to which they belong. Their resources are so seriously below those commanded by the average family that they are in effect excluded from the ordinary living patterns, customs, and activities.[18]

Many of the men and women who engage in low-wage work in cities such as New York, London, Hong Kong, or San Francisco, where housing costs are extremely high, experience relative poverty. They can meet their subsistence needs but find it difficult to be active in the cultural and political life of the cities they where they live.

The concept of relative poverty is important when considering whether poor Americans are really poor. If we look at the bottom 20% of the U.S. population in terms of income, 69% have a washer, 45.5% have a dishwasher, and 53.3% have a computer.[19] The bottom 20% also own televisions, refrigerators, cell phones, and microwaves.[20] However, they also have problems with paying their rent or mortgage as well as their utility bills and do not see a doctor or dentist when needed. Having a lot of low-priced things, then, is not an adequate measure of whether or not one can be fully active in society. It is irrelevant that somebody living in the slums of Mumbai doesn't have it as good as somebody living in Louisiana. What is relevant is whether or not a poor person in Louisiana can meet what are universal needs. We clearly need a richer understanding of universal human needs and how they are met in any society.

> There are nine needs of equal importance: subsistence, protection, affection, understanding, participation, leisure, creation, identity, and freedom. All must be met for a decent life.

Without reprising all of the debates about exactly how many human needs there are, I want to draw on two primary bodies of work to expand upon the position that there are basic, universal human needs that *must* be met. There is a moral argument embedded here: societies and organizations that do not meet basic human needs are unjust and undemocratic. As I also intend to demonstrate, undemocratic societies are unstable and unsustainable.

Manfred Max-Neef, a Chilean economist, and his colleagues developed a classification of human needs based on what it means to be human. There are nine needs of *equal* importance: subsistence, protection, affection, understanding, participation, leisure, creation, identity, and freedom.[21] In this list there are both objective needs (subsistence and protection) and subjective needs (affection, understanding, participation, leisure, creation, identity, and freedom). We all understand the objective need of subsistence—a person must have food, shelter, and clothing to survive—but they also need protection. Virtually all human groupings, whether bands, tribes, clans, or nation-states, have to protect their members.[22] It is fundamental to the very essence of the group. They do this, of course, in different ways.

In a modern, industrial state we expect the state to provide for the daily security of its members by providing an army and/or a police force and to take care of its people through such mechanisms as universal health care and social security. The United States has been a laggard among developed democracies in providing for all of its citizens. Most European societies provide robust social safety nets which include universal health benefits, mandated parental leave, and extended unemployment benefits. Societies that fail to meet these basic human needs—to provide subsistence and to protect its members—usually prove to be inherently unstable. For example, in 2014 the Central African Republic could not protect its Muslim citizens from its Christian citizens or Christians from reprisals by Muslims. The Rwandan state did not protect Tutsi and Hutu moderates during the genocide that occurred in 1994. As of this writing, the current war in Syria has put the entire civilian population at risk, whether they are on the side of the rebels or the Assad government. In early 2014 over 300 young high school girls were seized in Nigeria by the Muslim rebel group Boko Haram (which in the Hausa language means "Western education is a sin.") and government forces failed to respond. Though fifty escaped, it was reported that those held captive were being auctioned off at twelve dollars each to become "wives" of the militants.[23] The list of those countries that are unable to protect their citizens is long, and all are nondemocratic regimes. But a community must do more than protect its members.

> The freedom to achieve well-being is a fundamental need, and the freedom to achieve well-being is determined by people's capabilities, which a democratic society must develop.

Like Max-Neef, the British researchers Gough and Doyal approach human needs in terms of the *costs of being human in a given society*.[24] They provide a compelling case, based on empirical research, that there are two universal human needs: a need for health, broadly defined, and a need for autonomy, and there is an inherent *right* to the satisfaction of these two needs in a *democratic society*. What does it take, for example, for human beings to meet all of their needs in a democracy? Not just those for food, water, shelter, clothing, and safety but also those for economic security, autonomy, and the ability to develop significant and meaningful relationships with others? One way is for people to develop their capacities or capabilities. The more capabilities people have, the more likely they are to make choices that will allow them to meet all of their needs and lead a better life. This perspective, sometimes referred to as the *capability approach*, was first developed by the Indian economist Amartya Sen and elaborated by the philosopher Martha Nussbaum.[25]

Sen's work, for which he received a Nobel Prize, was intended to bring attention to the plight of the poor and shift the emphasis from a focus on pure economic growth to a focus on the conditions of the poorest of the poor and the need to improve their lot. His case study of the Bengal Famine of 1943, when between 1.5 and 4 million people died, demonstrated that starvation could occur even during a time of robust economic growth in British Colonial India. He reasoned that if nations are to prosper over the long run, development must focus on increasing the capacity of human beings through education and productive work so they have the freedom to make choices that will benefit them. The capability approach makes two normative or moral claims. First, the freedom to achieve well-being is a fundamental need or right, and second, freedom to achieve well-being is determined by people's capabilities, which a democratic society must develop. Human subsistence needs must be met, but so too must our needs for freedom and for a sense of self-worth.

Subjective needs must be realized for a society to maintain stability and to make progress toward or to maintain a state of democracy. If human needs such as understanding, participation, creation, and identity—the need to feel we count in the eyes of others—are universal, then societies that do not meet these needs are not stable and will not make a transition to democracy. In some patriarchal societies, village elders wield considerable power and authority, which means among other things that young men are not autonomous; they cannot fulfill a need for participation, freedom, or identity. Jihad and war are ways to gain respect and autonomy in a society in which other avenues for meeting basic needs are

> Morally irrelevant criteria—gender, ethnicity, religion—give rise to durable inequalities. One problem in developing democratic forms of government in some Middle Eastern and African countries is that resources are allocated on the basis of tribal and ethnic groupings.

closed off. We need to feel we matter and that others matter, or we will develop contempt for both ourselves and for them.

The failure to meet the needs of other humans can be an unconscious process. We can harm others not just by employing violence but by engaging in what have been termed *microaggressions*.[26] These are the small acts of discrimination that serve to remind people of their subordinate status. They can be subtle, as when somebody does not get an invitation to a party. People can lose "face" in Asian societies if they are made to appear foolish, uneducated, or unsophisticated. The Chinese inhabitants of Hong Kong became irate when a child from mainland China urinated in public, leading to claims that mainland Chinese were uncivilized.[27]

Microaggressions can be overt. New York has basically two classes of renters—those who pay market-based rates for apartments and co-ops and those who live in rent-controlled apartments. The law regarding rent control is complicated, but it sets strict limits on the rent that can be charged to a person who has lived in the same unit continuously since 1970, and on the amount the rent can be raised in any given year. Building owners dislike the law because they would prefer to charge market-based rates on all units. An apartment building will sometimes have remodeled, high-end, apartments in the same building as rent-controlled apartments. In an effort to attract those willing to pay higher prices, landlords offer amenities such as pools, storage space, and gyms. The law allows landlords to exclude tenants in rent-controlled units from these facilities and even from enjoying the view from a building's rooftop garden. New buildings, built with public funds that require 20% of the units be reserved for low-income tenants, sometimes have separate doors for those paying less.[28] Microaggressions give rise to *micro-inequities*, when people are discounted on the basis of some unchangeable characteristic such as age, gender, race, or social class.[29]

There is a difference between social *inequities* and *inequalities* that we need to spell out, because it gets to the heart of what we humans consider to be fair. Remember Rawls contention that *a fair society does not need to be an equal society*. We all recognize inequalities; some people are better looking than others, and some seem to be smarter. Some people have jobs that pay well and lots of friends, others do not. There are many inequalities in any society and many differences in how we experience these inequalities. In 2014, the average height of an NBA player was 6 feet 7 inches. If I am

5 feet 5 inches tall, it is unlikely that I can even expect to play in the NBA. We don't think of it as unfair in modern societies if a person who graduates from the top of his or her class in electrical engineering earns more than the person who failed to graduate from high school. However, if individuals' positions in the social order, measured by earnings or wealth, are determined by factors over which they have no control—the parents to whom they are born, their gender, race, or religion—this would be a *social inequity*. Take gender as an example: In the United States, being born female means you are likely to earn 19% less than your male counterpart. In Saudi Arabia women are not been allowed to drive, work, or participate in sports. Charles Tilly referred to these kinds of categorical differences as durable inequalities and noted that societies based on such inequities are inherently unstable because they set up a persistent struggle between the haves and the have-nots.[30] The anthropologist Deborah Rogers has also noted that unequal access to a society's resources is inherently destabilizing. It not only leads to social conflict, but it drives people out of a society in search of better conditions elsewhere.[31] Illegal migration out of Central and South America into the United States and from northern African countries such as Algeria and Morocco into Spain and France serves to mitigate conflict within the states that "send" immigrants, but it increases conflict inside of those states that receive them.

> Fairness may be something for which we are hardwired.

Unequal access to scarce goods is a driver of religious and ethnic tensions in the Middle East. As the sociologist Michael Schwartz has noted, Shia and Sunni lived together for at least 1,000 years without conflict. Only after the U.S. occupation of Iraq (2003–2011), when we tried to use one side against the other, did genocide occur. By the time the U.S. began drawing down its forces in 2009, employment stood at close to 60%, electric service was erratic, agricultural production had fallen, and the educational and medical systems were a disaster.[32]

South Sudan was created as an independent state in 2011 after years of conflict with Sudan over oil resources. In 2013, war broke out between rival forces in South Sudan who represented the two dominant ethnic groups—the Dinka and the Nuer. These two groups had lived in peace until two political rivals, both from different ethnic groups, fell out with one another. They fell out over the issue of which ethnic group would benefit from new-found oil revenue. The result pitted Dinka against Nuer, leading to the loss of thousands of lives and the displacement of upwards of one million people.[33] By 2014, South Sudan was facing catastrophic famine and U.S. Secretary of State, John Kerry, warned of genocide.[34]

Driven by social inequities and a struggle over resources, people can be mobilized against one another on the basis of ethnicity, gender, or religion. These struggles have long-term negative consequences for the development of democratic societies. *People have historical memories*, and if resources were once allocated to others on the basis of class, ethnicity, race, or gender, they want their group to benefit when they take the reins of power. Politics in Kenya has been a contest between ethnic and tribal groupings seeking an opportunity to loot state resources. Elected leaders are expected to serve as patrons and deliver the goods to those who supported them. The saying is, when one ethnic group replaces another, that "now it is our turn to eat."[35] We can't get to or maintain democracies when resources are allocated in ways people believe is unfair. Likewise, when wealthy American corporations are able to lobby legislators to craft legislation that privileges their economic position, people can come to believe the system is rigged.

Children playing games don't like cheaters and may call out, "That's not fair." Fairness may be something for which we are hardwired. In 2008, an Austrian team of researchers led by Friederike Range, worked with dogs trained to respond to the command, "give me a paw."[36] At first the dogs simply, and apparently happily, responded to the command. Then, the researchers introduced a treat that was given when the dogs offered their paw. After that, things, as they say in science, got weird. One dog was given a treat while the other was not. For a time the dog that got nothing continued to respond to the command, but shortly after seeing its companion get food while it got nothing, it stopped raising its paw. Did the dog without the treat feel cheated? Would

> Categorical inequalities based on characteristics such as race, gender, and religion can be maintained through exploitation, opportunity hoarding, and legislation. All of these processes lead to a closed economy and a closed political structure, which leads to instability.

we feel cheated? We do not know how the dogs felt, but a previous study of monkeys, with whom we share more genetic material, provides some insight. Monkeys were trained to give a researcher a rock in exchange for a piece of cucumber and seemed content with the exchange. However, the researchers then gave some of the monkeys a better treat, grapes, while continuing to give just cucumber to the others. The fact that some monkeys were getting better treats caused those getting the lesser treat to grow extremely agitated and throw their rocks at the lab wall instead of handing them over for a piece of cucumber. Eventually those monkeys getting unequal "pay" quit.[37] Dogs made no distinction between "good" treats and "bad" treats; they just wanted to be rewarded.[38]

Sarah Brosnan, who headed up the study of unequal pay among the monkeys, reasoned that human behavior is very similar because we do not live in a world of absolute values but one in which we are constantly comparing ourselves with those about us and, like a [monkey] we can tell when we are being shortchanged.[39] If we are so averse to inequality, then how is it maintained?

Maintaining Social Inequalities

Charles Tilly argued that we need to understand how categorical differences are maintained between groups of people, as opposed to individual differences, because the differences between categories of people are greater than individual differences.[40] In other words, differences between the individual human abilities of men and women may be small or nonexistent, but the differences between the gender categories of female and male are substantial. Inequalities based on categorical differences such as race, gender, and religion are maintained through exploitation, and opportunity.[41] Exploitation is the process by which those who have control over the means of production and distribution—factories, industrial farms, retail outlets—use that control to withhold the full value of people's contributions to the enterprise. This, of course, is the basis of capitalism.

The capitalist must realize a profit if he or she is to stay in business and does so through a variety of means, including legislation and, in some countries, the use of force. The early history of the labor movement in all developed democracies is replete with instances of force being used to coerce people to work under unsafe conditions and to keep the cost of labor down. In the early twentieth century in the United States, coal miners who tried to form unions found themselves thrown out of company housing and beaten by hired thugs. New Zealand, regarded as a progressive and democratic country, also witnessed labor battles in the early twentieth century. Farmers with the support of the government clubbed dock workers who were striking for higher wages and closed the docks, which meant New Zealand's farm products could not make it to world markets.

Opportunity hoarding is usually practiced by elites and people with close ties to one another.[42] One mark of a corrupt regime is the extent to which scarce resources and opportunities are allocated on the basis of a categorical inequality or on the basis of dense friendship networks. Hosni Mubarak, the former president of Egypt, allocated business opportunities to his cronies and family members, and the military upheld this arrangement because they benefited from it. Ferdinand Marcos, president of the Philippines 1965–1986, looted the country of billions of dollars for his family and friends. Graft and corruption are an issue for developing countries, as we will explain in Chapter 6. The weekly magazine, the *Economist*, calculated the wealth accumulated by billionaires in the developing world due to graft. Crony capitalists benefited from casinos; natural resources such as oil, diamonds, coal, and timber; defense contracts; ports; steel; and telecommunications services.[43] Opportunity hoarding creates a closed economy and a closed political structure leading away from democracy.

> Status is a form of inequality based on perceived differences in honor, esteem, and respect.

I would add another means by which systems become closed and that would be the *systematic legislative attempts to maximize profit and limit the rights of workers*. I will discuss such attempts at length in Chapter 7. To take but two examples for now, in 2011 the State of Wisconsin eliminated almost all bargaining rights of all public employees, with the exception of police and firemen. Following the same script, the Governor of Illinois introduced legislation in February 2015 to curb the power of all public sector unions in the state. Exploitation, opportunity hoarding, and legislative efforts are not the only ways in which systems become closed and a chance for individuals to escape categorical boundaries becomes limited. Status differences also help to solidify social structures and maintain inequalities.

Status as an Independent Force

The German sociologist, Max Weber (1864–1920) sketched out a system of social stratification with three essential components: class, status, and party.[44] Briefly, class is seen by Weber as being determined by one's market position or one's differential access to the scarce goods of a society. The possession of property or wealth, made up of investments, ownership of the means of production, land, and so forth, was the main determinant of class position. Class translates into power in all its forms—political, social, legal, and economic—because people with money can shape political and legal outcomes in their favor by hiring lobbyists and making campaign contributions to people who will support their goals. Parties, in Weber's model, are the organized means by which classes struggle for political power. Classes for Weber are not, however, communities of like-minded people who act together on the basis of their economic position in society. Status groups are.

In German, the term *Ständ* ("status") has its origins in the concept of medieval guilds, professions, and ethnic identities.[45] Status groups are communities with a common style of life and social restrictions to maintain their boundaries. They possess an important resource: honor. Status groups reveal their presence in different ways.[46] The first is endogamy, or marrying within the status group. When Chelsea Clinton, the only child of President Bill Clinton and Secretary of State Hilary Clinton, wed the investment banker Marc Mezvinsky in 2010, it was not a random match. Mezvinksy was the son of Marjorie Margolies, a former Democratic Congresswoman from Pennsylvania who was a supporter of President Clinton, as well as the son of former Iowa Democratic Congressman Edward Mezvinsky. Second, status groups share benefits. Faculty who teach at private universities in the United States usually are able to send their children to the same private university, or another with exchange privileges, without paying the cost of tuition. Surgeons often perform without cost operations on the family members of other surgeons. A third way a status group reveals itself is when economic opportunities are provided to members of the group, at the exclusion of others. A drug cartel could be compared to a medieval guild in which production and distribution of goods is rigidly controlled and benefits accrue only to members of the guild or cartel. The investment firm Goldman Sachs seeks recruits from a small number of elite universities, which enroll a disproportionate number of the children of men and women of wealth.

Status is thus a form of inequality based on perceived differences in honor, esteem, and respect. It differs from power and class because it is grounded not in material assets but in cultural beliefs about the worth of people in a particular category, such as race or sex. It is an independent mechanism, as the sociologist Cecilia Ridgeway has noted, by which inequality between individuals and groups is maintained.[47] Status understood in this way brings into the discussion an important psychological dimension of inequality; that is, do we feel *valued* by the societies to which we belong? Status, unlike material wealth, is grounded in cultural beliefs that work their effects on inequality at the social relational level—interactions between individuals and groups. As Ridgeway notes, the research literature demonstrates that status beliefs about what people are like develop quickly when material inequality and categorical differences are consolidated. This destructive combination has been found in virtually all colonial empires, whether Belgian, British, French, or English. Africans and Southeast Asians, regardless of their tribe or ethnic affiliation, were deemed by the colonizers to be of lower status, not as "worthy" as the whites. Contemporary status beliefs in the United States reinforce the assumption that people who hold positions of power are necessarily more competent than those who do not. It is felt to be shameful to be poor and to need to ask for help.

The *New York Times* reporter Jennifer Medina interviewed a California couple who had been without work for three years.[48] Previously, they earned in excess of $100,000 a year making and selling jewelry. They thought of themselves as wealthy. They took trips, bought their children toys, and owned a five-bedroom home in a suburb east of downtown Los Angeles. When they were laid off, they had to sell their house for less than they paid for it and move to a low-cost rental unit in Moreno Valley, sixty miles inland. To make ends meet they made ice pops, known as *paletas*, and sold them in parking lots around the Inland Empire (Ontario, Riverside, and San Bernardino Counties). If they were lucky, they made enough money to buy food but still needed help from public programs to pay their rent.

They could no longer afford to buy clothes for themselves or for their children. And when their son wanted to get hamburgers at In-N-Out Burger, he was reminded that he needed to sell $25 worth of ice pops for that to happen. "The hardest part is the shame," said the father. "People say to me, 'Why don't you find a job over there, or at that factory, or that place?' First of all, they aren't there. I've tried. But even if they have a job it's going to pay me eight dollars an hour." To buy his son pizza, he pawned a silver bracelet he had made for his wife because he was too embarrassed to tell his son he could not afford a pizza. As the mother said, "We have to be really good actors," around the children. "There is never enough."

To be poor in an advanced modern society like the United States, England, France, or Germany is equivalent to being in prison. This more than a metaphor. The family in California is trapped in the Inland Empire; they cannot move to where there might be jobs because they could not afford the rent in a better area. They cannot take their children to the coast, because they don't have money for gas. They rely on food stamps, but need to get toilet paper at Catholic Charities, because you can't use food stamps to buy toilet paper. People juggle two jobs and sometimes more to make ends meet. In my home town of Missoula, Montana, the local paper, the *Missoulian*, runs weekly appeals from people who need help. One woman needs gas money because she has a part-time job as a housekeeper in Drummond, Montana, 50 miles distant from her home. One woman needs diapers for her new child. Another asks for new tires for the family car, because it was the only way they have to get to work on snowy and icy roads. There are frequent requests for furniture, money for groceries, clothes for the children, money to buy prescription medications, and so forth. But whatever help they receive, most people remain embedded in circumstances from which there seems to be no escape. Why should we care?

Because it means that *inequities, including durable inequities such as race, gender, or religion, constrain everyone's ability to fully participate in their own societies.* The costs of inequality are high. Inequality reduces trust, limits civic engagement, and erodes the basis of a democratic society. Inequality determines whether or not political and economic systems are rigid or open. Inequality leads to a waste of human and material resources and reduces the ability of an organization or nation-state to adapt to radical changes in the environment or changes in our political, social, and economic systems. Inequality also costs more to maintain in terms of human energy and material resources than equal systems. Inequality is not only unfair; it cannot work.

Respect, as the sociologist Richard Sennett has explained, is difficult to maintain in a world divided by ethnicity and class.[49] Sennett argues that we get respect in three ways: by developing our talents, by looking after ourselves, and by helping others. As we know, there are limits imposed on our ability to develop our talents if our parents are poor, because we may go to poor schools and have little opportunity for enrichment, which of course affects our ability to take care of ourselves and to help others. The need for respect and belonging is as much a primary factor driving people into urban gangs or into terrorist cells as ideology or religion.

Once status differences take root, they deepen material inequalities. Numerous studies have shown that even when educational level and quality of education is equal, women are paid less than men and Blacks are paid less than Whites.[50] If you bargain hard for goods in a Moroccan *souk*, people may refer to you as "more stubborn than a Berber." It is a backhanded compliment at best. Traditionally, Berbers were herders who migrated across the northern Sahara in search of water and food for their flocks. Today they are hemmed in by political borders and their status is now associated with rural poverty, a lack of education, and a lack of opportunity. A website devoted to fighting discrimination against the Berbers notes that their children need access to education and the men need jobs.[51] Biased expectations of what Berbers are like affect their material chances and, as with other low-status groups, are self-reinforcing.

Most Americans believe inequality is increasing, but there is a huge gap between people's perceptions of why some people are rich and others are poor, as a 2014 poll from the PEW Research Center/USA Today reveals. Democrats consistently report that some are rich because they have had advantages others did not and that the economic system favors the wealthy. Republicans, on the other hand, see poverty as stemming from lack of work ethic and say that people could get ahead if they wanted to. These gaps reveal two radically different views of the causes of poverty and inequality, and result in very different views about the need to provide social safety nets. As Charles M. Blow, an opinion columnist for *The New*

Table 1.1 Differences in Perceptions of Why People Are Rich or Poor by Political Party

	Total %	Rep. %	Dem. %	Ind. %	R-D Gap
Opinions about the rich and poor					
Which has more to do with why a person is rich?					
Because he or she worked harder	38	57	27	37	+30
Because he or she had more advantages	51	32	63	52	-31
Which is more to blame if a person is poor?					
Lack of effort on his or her part	35	51	29	33	+22
Circumstances beyond his or her control	50	32	63	51	-31
Fairness of the economic system in this country					
The system is generally fair	36	53	25	35	+28
The system unfairly favors the wealthy	60	42	75	60	-33
Hard work and determination are no guarantee of success for most people	38	20	48	39	-28

Source: Adapted from the "Most Republicans Say the Rich Work Harder than Others, Most Democrats Say They Had More Advantages." PEW Research Center, Washington, DC/USA Today (January 2014). Accessed at: http://www.people-press.org/2014/01/23/most-see-inequality-growing-but-partisans-differ-over-solutions/.

York Times, wrote, the poor are not poor because they reject traditional values, but because they started life with less. Nobody sets out to be poor.

> Poverty is a demanding, stressful, depressive and often violent state. No one seeks it; they are born or thrust into it. In poverty, the whole of your life becomes an exercise in coping and correcting, searching for a way up and out, while focusing today on filling pots and plates, maintaining a roof and some warmth, and dreading the new challenge tomorrow may bring.[52]

> We judge people according to their status, and the multiple interactions people have with others reinforce their sense of either belonging or being excluded.

Why try, if everyone expects you to fail? Children born to parents without material resources have a double handicap. They not only have to overcome a lack of material resources, they have to overcome other's perception of their abilities and their own feelings of negative self-worth. A low-status job shapes the unspoken perception of others that a worker does not have the talent for higher status-jobs. Some of the rhetoric that supports paying workers the minimum wage, rather than a living wage, focuses on the supposed lack of talent and motivation of those who take the work, rather than on bad luck or economic necessity. In addition, those who work in a low-status job are not embedded in the kind of social networks that make it easy to find other work, or acquire the *human capital* (education, knowledge, skills) and *social capital* (social networks) that would allow them to escape their status. This is why the poor, and not the rich, play the lottery. It's a rational choice for the poor; it gives them a chance they would not have otherwise.

The polymath Herbert A. Simon developed the theory of bounded rationality to explain why rational people make what sometimes seem to be irrational decisions. Our decisions are bounded by the knowledge we have at any given time; we do the best with the information we have available to us.[53] This is why a capabilities approach is an important way to approach the problem of inequity. You increase people's capacity to make decisions that will benefit them in the long run, so that the lottery doesn't seem the only option to advancement.

The Harvard business professor and sociologist Rosabeth Moss Kanter once advised that if you wanted to succeed in life you needed to hang out with winners, not losers.[54] Whom we associate with makes a difference in the eyes of others. Status is like a virus spreading among members of a group; all members derive status and benefits from associating with their particular group. If I hang out with soccer hooligans from the English football team Manchester United, my status will be derived from the group in the same way it will for somebody who socializes only with the colleagues from a prestigious law firm. She will go out for drinks with these colleagues, take vacations with them, and likely marry within their circle.

Status groups tend to be self-regulating and move toward closure simply because we want to associate with people who are like us. If we are in a high-status group, we also have higher levels of social capital, or networks that have "cash" value, in the sense that we can translate it into good jobs and "hoard" opportunities for the in-group. It is difficult for members of low-status groups to try to network with members of high-status groups. The Montana writer Walter Kirn came from a small town and a family of limited means. He graduated from both Princeton and Oxford and described what it was like to be an impoverished student among wealthy friends. He was well liked and invited to go on vacations and trips but found it embarrassing to explain his circumstances and therefore turned down opportunities to connect with the rich.[55] Minority students who attend prestigious schools are faced with the dilemma of whether or not to try to network with the social and economic elites to which they aspire, since it can mean turning their backs on the communities and friends who have supported them.[56]

We judge people according to their status, and the multiple interactions people have with others reinforce their sense of either belonging or being excluded. Those with low social status find it difficult to challenge the assumptions or ideology of those who have power. For example, the children of some families living next to a petrochemical complex in Buenos Aires were suffering from lead poisoning. They deferred to the company doctors' explanations of what the problem was. The parents were not prepared, because of a lack of knowledge and of status, to question doctors or to explain in detail their child's symptoms. The doctors, employed by the chemical companies, were quick to provide an irrelevant explanation for the children's illnesses and prescribe pills, which the parents could not always afford.[57]

Inequality in social status also gives rise to a lack of trust. Lower status individuals seeking some form of government benefit will be judged on the basis of individual criteria and only receive a benefit if they are seen as badly off, or more "defective," than others. A government representative will want to know about all forms of income, about relatives who might or might not be able to help, about all material assets, about level of education, about whether or not somebody has been looking for work and if so, when and where, and so on. These interactions are not empowering; they erode a sense of self-worth. It is one reason why people who receive benefits express anger and hostility toward government agencies, rather than gratitude. As the Swedish political scientist Bo Rothstein found in his study of Swedish welfare applicants, this process of qualifying for benefits greatly decreases people's trust in public institutions, thereby decreasing the social capital necessary for a strong civic sector.[58]

> Inequality in class and status gives rise to a lack of trust.

Democracy, Inequity, Trust, and Resilience

I am arguing that the nine basic human needs I identified earlier are not just what is necessary for a decent life; they are the very basis of a democratic society. Democracy is a *necessary* political form to address problems of inequity and to create open political and economic systems that can meet the full range of human needs. It is through democracy that people have a structured opportunity to express their demands.

In the chapters that follow we will see there is a strong relationship between the values that support democratic institutions and the values that support self-expression, or political and civil rights. However, support for these rights kicks in only after people's basic needs for subsistence and security are met. This is important because much of what the Western press records as demonstrations or revolutions for democracy, as in the case of the Arab Spring (2010–2011), are in fact only an expression of demands to have these basic needs met. The protests in Egypt that lead to the fall of Hosni Mubarak were more about opposition to decades of oppression and corruption, as well as economic chaos, than a vote for democracy.[59] For power to be transferred from elites to majorities, modernization, which focuses on education and improving human capacity, is essential; without this there will not be a democratic society. You expand choices when you expand human capacity rather than by setting boundaries on choice. We will also see that a number of societies "waste" human talent, which erodes trust and undermines support for democracy.

Summary

Inequity is a social malignancy. As others such as Kate Pickett and Richard Wilkinson have documented, a healthy society is one in which equity, not inequity, is the norm.[60] Durable inequalities, grounded in differences in class, ethnicity, gender, and religion, are a barrier to the creation of open and democratic societies. Societies where there are gaps between the wealth and incomes of various groups of citizens see more of them imprisoned, more of them in poor health, more of them suffering from depression, and more of them facing infant and maternal mortality. Inequities do not cause people to struggle to overcome their situations; *in fact the reverse is the case*, because inequities stigmatize people and cause them to lose hope. We cannot be fully human in societies characterized by durable inequalities. How we untangle this snarl of inequity will be explored in the following chapters as we detail the reasons for our current circumstances and how we can and must change them.

Through a Sustainability Lens

Sustainable societies must balance economic, social, and environmental needs, but often we focus on just the environment when discussing sustainability. Doing so will not get us to where we need to be. Social inequality constitutes an existential challenge. If we don't address the issue, we will never have fair or just societies that make use of the full range of human talent and creativity. We also need to make use of humans' capacity to deal with two other major challenges facing humankind: climate change and energy poverty.[61] Energy poverty means that people have no access to clean or reliable energy of any sort. Presently, 1.3 billion people, or 20% of the world's population have no access to electricity which means they cook over coal or wood fires increasing their risk of respiratory disease.[62] Climate change, which will differentially affect women, the poor, those who make a living from subsistence agriculture, is destroying the biosphere on which we depend for life. We need to work on all of these related problems (climate change, energy poverty, and social inequity) simultaneously in order for humanity to have a future.

Notes

1 Global Issues. 2013. Poverty Facts and Stats. Accessed on May 15, 2014 at: http://www.globalissues.org/article/26/poverty-facts-and-stats.
2 Walk Free Foundation. 2013. Accessed on October 22, 2013 at: http://www.globalslaveryindex.org/.
3 Statistics Brain. 2013. "World Poverty Statistics." Accessed on October 22, 2013 at: http://statisticbrain.com/world-poverty-statistics/.
4 Share the World's Resources. 2014. Accessed on May 19, 2014 at: http://www.stwr.org/.
5 World Bank. "Development Indicators." 2014. Accessed on May 25, 2015 at: http://wdi.worldbank.org/table/2.9.
6 Ibid.
7 Oxfam. 2015. "Wealth: Having It All and Wanting More." Retrieved on September 26 at: https://www.oxfam.org/sites/www.oxfam.org/files/file_attachments/ib-wealth-having-all-wanting-more-190115-en.pdf.
8 John Rawls. 1971. *A Theory of Justice*. Cambridge, MA: Harvard University Press.

9 Steven Pinker. 2002. *The Blank Slate: The Modern Denial of Human Nature.* New York, NY: Penguin.
10 The United Nations. "The Universal Declaration of Human Rights." Retrieved on February 9, 2015 at: http://www.un.org/en/documents/udhr/.
11 See Charles Tilly. 2007. Ch. 1, "What is Democracy?" In *Democracy.* New York, NY and London: Cambridge University Press.
12 Freedom House. 2015. "Freedom in the World, 2015." Retrieved on February 10, 2015 at: https://freedomhouse.org/report/freedom-world/freedom-world-2015#.VNpFmubF_To.
13 Karl Marx. 1844/1927. *Paris Manuscripts.* Moscow: International Publishers.
14 Abraham H. Maslow. 1943. "A Theory of Human Motivation." *Psychological Review.* 50(4): 370–396.
15 The Poverty Site. Definition of relative and absolute poverty. Retrieved on May 2, 2014 at: http://www.poverty.org.uk/summary/social%20exclusion.shtml.
16 Richard Jolly. 1976. "The World Employment Conference: The Enthronement of Basic Needs." *Development Policy Review.* 9(2): 31–44.
17 The Urban Institute. 2015. "Racial and Ethnic Disparities Among Low-Income Families." Retrieved on February 9, 2015 at: http://www.urban.org/publications/411936.html.
18 Peter Townsend. 1979. *Poverty in the United Kingdom: A Survey of Household Resources and Standards of Living.* Harmondsworth, UK: Penguin, p.31.
19 Julie Siebens. 2013. "Extended Measures of Well-Being: Living Conditions in the United States: 2011." United States Census Bureau. Accessed on May 2, 2014 at: http://www.census.gov/prod/2013pubs/p70-136.pdf?eml=gd.
20 Annie Lowrey. 2014. "Changed Life of the Poor: Better Off, but Far Behind." *The New York Times.* April 30. Accessed on May 2, 2014 at: http://ntyi.ms/1rQEue1.
21 The list of needs and how they are met can be found at: http://en.wikipedia.org/wiki/Manfred_Max_Neef; see also Manfred A. Max-Neef, Antonio Elizalde and Martin Hopenhayn. 1991. *Human Scale Development.* Oman: Apex Press.
22 Charles Tilly has made the point that protection is central to the integrity of all stable social groupings in several publications. See in particular: Charles Tilly. 1998. *Durable Inequality.* Berkeley, CA: University of California Press; Tilly. 2007. *Democracy.* New York, NY and London: Cambridge University Press.
23 Nicholas Kristof. 2014. "Bring Back Our Girls." *The New York Times.* May 4, 2014: Sunday Review, p.11.
24 Ian Gough. 1994. "Economic Institutions and the Satisfaction of Human Needs." *Journal of Economic Issues.* 28(1): 25–66; Len Doyal and Ian Gough. 1991. *A Theory of Human Need.* London: Palgrave Macmillan.
25 Martha Nussbaum. 1988. "Nature, Functioning Capability: Aristotle on Political Distribution." *Oxford Studies in Ancient Philosophy.* 6(Supplement): 145–184; Nussbaum. 1992. "Human Functioning and Social Justice: In Defense of Aristotelian Essentialism." *Political Theory.* 20(2): 202–246. See also the Stanford Encyclopedia of Philosophy. "The Capability Approach." http://plato.stanford.edu/entries/capability-approach/; Amartya Sen. 1984. "Rights and Capabilities." In *Resources, Values and Development.* Cambridge: Cambridge University Press; Sen. 1999. *Development as Freedom.* Cambridge: Oxford University Press; Sen. 2005. "Human Rights and Capabilities." *Journal of Human Development.* 6(2): 151–166.

26 Chester M. Pierce, J.V. Pierce-Gonzalez and D. Wills. 1970. "An Experiment in Racism: TV Commercials." *Education and Urban Society*. 10(1): 61–87.
27 Gerry Mullany. 2014. "Call of Nature Becomes a Call to Arms in Hong Kong." *The New York Times*. May 4: International, p.10.
28 Ronda Kaysen. 2014. "What's Next, Bouncers?" *New York Times*. May 18: Business, p.8.
29 The term "micro-inequities" comes from the work of Mary Rowe. 1974. "Saturn's Rings: A Study of the Minutiae of Sexism Which Maintain Discrimination and Inhibit Affirmative Action Results in Corporations and Public Institutions." *Graduate and Professional Education of Women*. Washington, DC: American Association of University Women, pp.1–9.
30 Charles Tilly. 1998. *Durable Inequalities*. Berkeley, CA: University of California Press.
31 Deborah Sanders. 2012. Interview in *New Scientist*. July 28.
32 Michael Schwartz. 2014. "It's the Oil, Stupid." TomDispatch. Retrieved on February 10, 2015 at: http://www.tomdispatch.com/post/175860/tomgram%3A_michael_schwartz%2C_the_new_oil_wars_in_iraq/. (Michael Schwartz, February, 2015, private communication with author.)
33 Isma'il Kushkush and Michael R. Gordon. 2014. "South Sudan Fighting Rages as Kerry Appeals to Rebel Leader." *The New York Times*. Retrieved on May 6, 2014, at: http://www.nytimes.com/2014/05/06/world/africa/kerry-south-sudan-fighting.html.
34 *New York Times*. "South Sudan in Peril." Sunday Review Editorial. May 18: 10.
35 Michela Wrong. 2010. *It Is Our Turn to Eat: The Story of a Kenyan Whistle-Blower*. New York, NY: Harper.
36 Friederike Range, Lisa Hoen, Zsosfia Virangi, and Ludwig Haber. 2008. "The Absence of Reward Induces Inequity Aversion in Dogs." *Proceedings of the National Academy of Sciences*. The article was first published online. The printed version appeared 2009, 106 (1): 340–345. This is available online at: http://www.pnas.org/content/106/1/340.full.
37 Sarah F. Brosnan and Frans B.M. de Waal. 2003. "Monkeys Reject Unequal Pay." *Nature*. 425: 297–299. September 18. See the online abstract: http://www.nature.com/nature/journal/v425/n6955/abs/nature01963.html.
38 Apparently, nobody has yet tried these experiments with cats.
39 Brosnan and de Waal, "Monkeys Reject."
40 Tilly, 1998. Charles Tilly (2008). *Durable Inequalities*. Berkeley, CA: University of California Press.
41 Tilly also introduces two other processes, emulation and adaptation, to explain how inequalities become durable in organizations. Organizations emulate successful organizations. Only 25% of software firms in California have female employees, and most major administrative positions are held by males, because that is what "works." Adaptation refers to the fact that people conform to the rules and expectations of the workplace and replicate structures of domination in doing so. Tilly has been criticized for his focus on the how inequality has been maintained, rather than why it exists in the first place. See, for example, Kim Voss. 2010. "Enduring Legacy? Charles Tilly and *Durable Inequality*." *The American Sociologist*. December. 41(4): 368–374.
42 Charles Tilly. 2000. "Relational Origins of Inequality." *Anthropological Theory*. 1(3): 355–372.
43 *The Economist*. 2014. "Planet Plutocrat." March 15: 57.
44 Max Weber. 1946. *From Max Weber*. Translated and edited by Hans Gerth and C.W. Mills. New York, NY: The Free Press.

45 Tony Waters and Dagmar Waters. 2010. "The New Zeppelin Translation of Weber's Class, Status, Party." *Journal of Classical Sociology*. 10: 153–158.
46 Charles Hurst. 2007. *Social Inequality: Forms, Causes, and Consequences*, 6th ed. Boston, MA: Allyn & Bacon.
47 Cecilia L. Ridgeway. 2014. "Why Status Matters." *American Sociological Review*. 79(1): 1–16.
48 Jennifer Medina. 2014. "Hardship Makes a New Home in the Suburbs." *The New York Times*. May 10. Accessed on May 14 at: http://www.nytimes.com/2014/05/10/us/hardship-makes-a-new-home-in-the-suburbs.html?_r=0.
49 Richard Sennett. 2003. *Respect: The Formation of Character in an Age of Inequality*. New York, NY: Penguin.
50 Sarah Jane Glynn and Audrey Powers. 2012. "The Top 10 Facts About the Wage Gap." *Center for American Progress*. https://www.americanprogress.org/issues/labor/news/2012/04/16/11391/the-top-10-facts-about-the-wage-gap/; U.S. Department of Labor. 2011. "The African - American Labor Force in 2011." http://www.dol.gov/_sec/media/reports/blacklaborforce/.
51 Accessed on May 13, 2014 at: www.tamazirth.com.
52 Charles M. Blow. 2014. "Poverty Is Not a State of Mind." *New York Times*. May 19, 2014. Accessed online at: http://www.nytimes.com/2014/05/19/opinion/blow-poverty-is-not-a-state-of-mind.html?comments.
53 Herbert A. Simon. 1990. *Reason in Human Affairs*. Palo Alto, CA: Stanford University Press; Herbert A. Simon, Massimo Egidi, Riccardo Viale, Fondazione Rosselli, and Robin Marris. 2008. *Economics, Bounded Rationality and the Cognitive Revolution*. New York, NY: Edward Elgar Publishing.
54 Rosabeth Moss Kanter. 2004. *Confidence: How Winning Streaks and Losing Streaks Begin and End*. New York, NY: Crown.
55 Walter Kirn. 2014. *Blood Will Out: The True Story of a Murder, a Mystery, and a Masquerade*. New York, NY: Liveright, W.W. Norton.
56 Tamika Jackson. 2010. "The Lived Experience of Economically Disadvantaged Black Students Attending Predominantly White, Elite Private Boarding Schools." Dissertation. Atlanta, GA: George State University. Accessed on May 13, 2014 at: http://scholarworks.gsu.edu/cgi/viewcontent.cgi?article=1050&context=cps_diss.
57 Javier Auyero and Débora A. Swistun. 2009. *Flammable: Environmental Suffering in an Argentine Shantytown*. New York, NY: Oxford.
58 Bo Rothstein. 2005. *Social Traps and the Problem of Trust*. Cambridge, UK: Cambridge University Press.
59 Freedom House. 2015. "Freedom in the World, 2015." https://freedomhouse.org/report/freedom-world/freedom-world-2015#.Vd9KByVVhHw.
60 Kate Pickett and Richard Wilkinson. 2011. *The Spirit Level: Why Greater Equity Makes Societies Stronger*. New York, NY and London: Bloomsbury.
61 The links between trust, climate change, global inequality, and energy poverty have been made by the authors of *The Hartwell Paper*. Retrieved on February 10, 2015 at: http://www.lse.ac.uk/researchAndExpertise/units/mackinder/theHartwellPaper/Home.aspx.
62 International Energy Agency. 2015. "Percentage of world population without electricity." Accessed on February 10, 2015 at: http://www.worldenergyoutlook.org/resources/energydevelopment/accesstoelectricity/.

2
A World Divided by Income and Wealth

Consider:

- Poverty causes pain and humiliation.
- Currently, just 85 individuals own 50% of the world's wealth.
- Where you are borne determines 80% of your annual income. The rest is determined by things over which you have no control.
- Social policies determine the extent to which wealth and income concentrate in the hands of the few.
- Gaps in income and wealth are growing wider both between and within nations.
- The 400 richest individuals in the United States together have more wealth than the bottom 150 million.
- High-income families pass their advantages on to their children.
- Low-income families pass their disadvantages on to their children.
- Social mobility in developed countries has slowed.
- Great differences in wealth and income are eroding the social contract.
- Pursuing economic growth as the sole means of reducing poverty will imperil the biosphere.

Right before Thanksgiving 2014 in Missoula, Montana, bulldozers flattened the three remaining trailers at what had formerly been Hanson's

Trailer Park and scooped them into dumpsters. Gone already was the pet cemetery. The 41-lot park, one of the oldest in Missoula, Montana, was being cleared for an AutoZone store and a ninety-unit apartment complex. Some of the 150 residents had lived in the park for decades, raising their children there. For many it was the only home they had ever owned, and some thought they would live there forever. When they were told they had to move, most did not know what to do. They were poor, worked primarily at minimum wage jobs, or relied on their Social Security or disability benefits. They literally had no place to go. Some of the trailers had been in place for decades and the wheels had sunk into the ground. Even if the trailers could have been moved, few owners could find a place to move them. There were few vacant lots in the city, and even where there were spaces, landowners were reluctant to rent to those with trailers that were 20–30 years old.

Ken Nettleton and his partner, Tammy Valentine, lived in a forty-foot vintage camp trailer, but could find no place to put it. Ken had a prison record, which meant many places would not rent to him. Their only option was to demolish the trailer and sell the frame for $90 to a scrap metal dealer. They ended up buying a derelict Winnebago motor home for $500 and had it towed to an RV lot outside of town, where they live with their six cats and two dogs. There is no place to shower, they have no water, and can't afford to buy propane. They must make do with Ken's $721 a month disability check and the occasional minimum wage work Tammy finds jobs cleaning motel rooms when she can find a ride to work. Like others in the park, Ken and Tammy lost neighbors, friends, and the sense of belonging to a community.

Cathleen Redfern, another resident of the park, understood her trailer was run down but noted that four generations of her family had lived in it off and on. She was not only distressed by the notice of eviction but depressed by the fact that her son and his family had just moved out after Cathleen's unemployment benefits ran out. Like Ken and Tammy, she had no place to go and was being helped by a social services worker to find something, as she had absolutely no income. Cathleen wanted to work but had trouble finding a job because she had a genetic disorder that caused her head to shake, and at the age of 59 she was missing teeth. As she said, "People take one look at me and don't want to hire me." One of the places she was shown by her caseworker had no kitchen; another had a bathroom down the hall. Subsidized housing was not an option for her because in Missoula there is a five-year waiting list. Cathleen may become homeless.

Her neighbor Harry Matt, a former appliance repairman, was living on $600 a month in Social Security benefits. Half of it went for the $300 a month rental of his lot. At age 79, Harry could not imagine moving; his whole life and all his possessions were wrapped up in his trailer. He said he was scared. "The thought of losing everything I've worked for, everything I've saved—they can just wipe it out." Harry got lucky. After detaching his rotten wooden porch, and jacking up his fifty-foot, 1963 mobile home, he was able to move it to a new place people had helped him find. His cat, "Go-Go," went with him.[1] Others in the park who could move their trailers found places outside of town, and others simply seemed to have disappeared.

> Poverty is pain and humiliation.

The Nature of Poverty

What does it mean to be poor? The World Bank has portrayed poverty as pain.

> Poor people suffer physical pain that comes with too little food and long hours of work; emotional pain stemming from the daily humiliations of dependency and a lack of power; and the moral pain from being forced to make choices such as whether to pay to save the life of an ill family member or to use the money to feed their children.[2]

Poverty puts people at risk. Simple things can tip them from relative security to absolute hopelessness, as happened at Hansen's Trailer Park. The inability to participate in society can lead people to commit desperate acts. Shonelle Jackson, a young man from Montgomery, Alabama, explained how he ended up in the criminal justice system. It started because he and his sisters had no food and he was too embarrassed to ask his neighbors for help.

> I stole food ... because I hated going to ask the next-door neighbors do they have some bread—a boy like that be the laughing

stock of the school the next day. I went from stealing one pack of bologna to two packs. I used to go from apartment to apartment, trying to steal perfume, sell it on the street. Me and my sisters go to Burger King and eat. That make you feel special, to be able to do that for your sisters. I was 11 [at the time].[3]

Does poverty look the same and have the same consequences everywhere? Is it the same in Afghanistan as it is in the United States? Are villagers who live in Vietnam's Mekong Delta poor because they live in open-walled, thatch-covered homes and engage in subsistence agriculture? Depending on the society in which they live, people will have different ideas about what it means to be poor or rich and about what it takes to be a full participant in their society. There are significant differences between the developed and the developing countries of the world in terms of their citizens' income. Income alone doesn't tell us much about what it would be like to live in another country.

Poverty is multidimensional; it is defined by many more things than income. It also includes poor people's experiences of deprivation resulting from poor health, lack of education, inadequate living standards, the threat of violence, dangerous or poor quality work, and disempowerment.[4] Poverty exists in every society. A poor person living in the South Bronx in the United States lives with the fear of violence from drug gangs, from a lack of job opportunities, and suffers poor health, just like somebody living in the developing world.

Yet poverty needs to be understood within the context of a particular country. Staff from the World Bank interviewed over 60,000 people in sixty different countries and asked them to explain the difference between being rich or poor in their particular country.[5] When poor people in Vietnam were asked to describe the differences between a rich family and a poor family they described a rich family as one that had a solid and stable house which did not need frequent repairs, owned a motorcycle or bike, owned a television, could afford to send their children to school, and had money left over after the harvest. A poor family was described as having a home that needed to be repaired frequently, no radio or television, no money to send their children to school, nothing left over after the harvest to sell, and no well or access to fresh water.[6] The daily problem the poor must solve is hunger, and their efforts are bent to solving it. In Vietnam's rural areas, not having enough to eat is captured by the saying:

> In the evenings, eat sweet potatoes, sleep
> In the mornings, eat sweet potatoes, work
> At lunch, go without[7]

In all societies, to be hungry is to be poor. This can be a temporary situation. When the Soviet Union broke apart in 1991, many suffered as pensions were cut, people were laid off work, and the value of the ruble plunged. A Ukrainian woman said, "Often I [had] to decide who [would] eat, me or my child." People sold household goods and other personal possessions to buy food, the price of which shot upwards. In the freezing cold of the winter of 1991 in St. Petersburg, I saw a woman standing outside a private market, trying to sell her winter gloves to buy food—another, her winter boots. Some offered jewelry, rugs, and furniture. Hunger for the vast majority of Russian citizens was, fortunately, a temporary shock from which they were able to recover.

People can be stuck in poverty because they have neither physical capital (machinery, a shop, or land [which they could farm]) nor human capital, which would include education and training. The way most people survive in the world is through their labor power; they work. The illness of the person with a job or even the sickness of a child can threaten the economic stability of the entire family. In the West African nation of Togo, when children were asked to draw a poor person, they would frequently draw somebody who was sick or disabled.[8]

The case of Ziem Der from Ghana illustrates how the lack of human capital and unexpected setbacks can trap people in poverty. Ziem Der lives in a small village in northern Ghana, where the per capita income averages about $2 a day, or $730 a year. Ziem was one of sixteen children, four of whom attended school, but Ziem was not one of these. Ziem describes himself as "blind," meaning he is illiterate, which prevents him from getting a job in town, where average wages are much higher. His father was "rich" by village standards because he owned land on which to farm as well as herds of sheep, goats, and cattle. Ziem has two wives and eight children, and when his brother died, as was customary, his two wives and seven children became part of Ziem's household, bringing the number to twenty. The four wives' "job" is to cook, garden, and search for firewood they can trade for food. When his father died, the animals were divided among Ziem and his brothers and for a while Ziem lived well. But in 1997, twelve of his cattle were stolen in one night, and the next year fourteen more were taken. His goat herd got dysentery and erratic rainfall coupled with depleted soils means he can no longer realize the yields from the land that he once did. Ziem's community has few resources, so there are no social networks to which he can turn to help his family survive.[9] Without outside help, Ziem and all of his family members are likely to remain poor, living from day to day, hoping that no further catastrophes are visited upon them.

Drought, heavy rainfall, a sick child, or the death of a spouse can quickly tip a family from security to poverty. How do people cope? According to the men in Ghana, a family copes by borrowing money, defrauding others, stealing, depending on a family member, or collecting remittances from those who have migrated. The women may look for boyfriends with money, engage in prostitution, or use witchcraft to obtain money. In times of need people will sell their cows or goats, take their children out of school to work, sell firewood and charcoal, offer themselves as day laborers to others, and try to borrow money.[10] They do everything they can to keep their families together.

Malawi is one of the world's most populous and most underdeveloped countries. The annual per capita income is $320 a year. Fifty percent of the population lives on $1.25 a day or less. Most people live in rural areas and make their living from agriculture. Early marriage, high fertility rates, and competition for land all contribute to the high poverty rates. People are trying to raise large families of ten or more on less than half an acre. Depleted soil means they need to buy expensive fertilizer. Village women noted:

> In the past we were able to harvest at least four full oxcarts without using fertilizer, and we could sell the excess to buy things like bicycles. But now the price of fertilizer has gone up and the

soils have lost their fertility; we harvest just enough for home consumption and not enough to sell.[11]

> The consequences of poverty are the same worldwide.

The effects of poverty identified by Malawians are not just hunger and the lack of money but also crime, social exclusion, debt, stress, death, diseases such as AIDS, alcoholism, suicide, imprisonment, and stunted growth of children.[12] As for government agencies like the police, they are seen as corrupt and unhelpful.

The consequences of poverty listed by Malawians—abuse by those in power, social exclusion, crime, poor health—are remarkably the same worldwide. Those who live in poverty in developing countries may also suffer from the effects of civil war, hostile neighbors, and openly corrupt governments. Of course, not everyone who lives in Vietnam, Ecuador, Ghana, or Malawi is poor; many are wealthy. So we have to talk about the degree of social inequality within a country or the differences in levels of consumption by different members of the population. Inequality within a country can be a source of instability and give rise to such results as crime and mental illness, which stem from groups being excluded from participation. *The outcomes of inequality and poverty are primarily the same across both the developed and developing world, although the reasons for poverty and inequality differ*, as we will see.

Is Global Inequality Growing or Declining?

At this time, the richest 1% of the world's population controls half of all the wealth.[13] A 2013 Gallup Poll survey of reported household income across 131 countries worldwide revealed wide gaps between and within countries. Based on its findings, 22% of the world's population has a household income of less than $1.25 a day, which the World Bank considers the threshold for extreme poverty. Using the standard preferred by other academics—less than $2.00 a day[14]—34% of the world's population should be classified as living in extreme poverty. Extreme poverty is concentrated in Sub-Saharan Africa, South Asia, and Southeast Asia. In Sub-Saharan Africa 69% of the population is living on $2.00 a day or less; the figure for South Asia (including Afghanistan, Bangladesh, and Pakistan) is 60%, and that for Southeast Asia (including Cambodia, Laos, Thailand, and Vietnam) is 50%.[15] These raw data do not tell us whether or not things are getting better or worse for the world's poor. The answer depends, in part, on how we add things up.

The World Bank issued a report in 2013 emphasizing that there had been significant declines in global poverty, using $1.25 as its standard. However, it also noted that in Sub-Saharan Africa the actual number of those living in poverty had *increased* since 1981, from 205 million to 414 million in 2010, a doubling of the numbers.[16] The reason for this doubling during this time period (1981–2010) was that the population of the African continent doubled. The poor in Sub-Saharan Africa were still poor; there were just more of them.

The reason for the World Bank's claim that things are getting better—that there is a decrease in the number of individuals living on $1.25 a day or less—is the rapid growth of the economies of China and India. In India the drop has been equally impressive from a high in 1981 of 60% living on $1.25 a day or less to 33% in 2010.[17] They tilt the scale, because together they account for 2.7 billion people, or 37% of the world's population. Economic progress in China has been particularly rapid. In 2007, 26% of people living in China lived on $1.25 a day or less per person, but by 2012 that number had fallen to 6% and is projected to fall even further. Had China and India's economies not expanded, the rate of global inequality would have remained relatively stable.[18] Are China and India catching up with the developed world?

The economic historian, Angus Maddison, has provided data that allow us to answer the question about whether inequality is growing or declining between countries.[19] In 1820, before the Industrial Revolution, Britain and the Netherlands were the two richest countries in the world, but they were only three times richer than the most populous countries at the time, China and India. Today, in spite of China's rapid growth, Britain (although no longer the wealthiest country) is now six times richer than China, a doubling of the difference between 1820 and 2012. Even greater is the increase in the ratio of the world's richest and poorest countries, which has risen to more than 100:1.[20] These extremes can be best exemplified by considering differences in annual incomes. For example, the average annual per capita income of someone living in Luxemburg is $90,000 a year, while that of someone living in the Central African Republic is $600 a year; a ratio of 150:1. The income differences among the countries that made up the Roman Empire in 117 CE, at the height of its greatest expansion, were much smaller than they are today, because most people made their living from agriculture. Today per capita purchasing power parity (PPP) varies widely among these countries. (PPP takes into account the fact that the same dollar will buy more in a country with a lower cost of living. This concept is used by international agencies in place the currency exchange rate method of calculating GDP.) The difference in PPP between an oil-rich country like the United Arab Emirates ($63,000) and Egypt ($11,000) is now 6:1, whereas 2,000 years ago there was virtually no difference between these two areas.

China's economy (with a GDP of $17.6 trillion) overtook that of the United States ($17.4 trillion) as the world's largest economy in 2014 after adjustments were made for the lower cost of living in China. But this does not mean that China is catching up to the United States. Branko Milanovic, the World Bank's expert on global inequality, calculated that in 1980, U.S. per capita income was PPP $25,500 while China's was PPP $525, for an absolute difference of about PPP $25,000 per person. By 2007, China's PPP had grown to $5,050 per capita and that of the United States to PPP $43,200 for a difference of PPP $37,000.[21] Just to stay even with the United States and not lose ground, China's economy would need to expand at a rate of 8.6% per year (a very high rate), and the United States would have to experience a growth of only 1%. As of 2014, the U.S. economy was growing at the rate of about 2.6% annually.

Rich people today are also richer than before. The Roman Emperor Marcus Crassus (115 BCE–53 BCE) had a fortune of 200 million sesterces or an annual income of around 12 million sesterces. This meant that his income was equivalent to that of 32,000 Romans put together. Andrew Carnegie had an income of $1.35 million a year, which was equivalent to that of 48,000 Americans, who had annual incomes of $280 a year. The richest man in 2013, Carlos Slim of Mexico, is worth close to $80 billion, and his annual earnings are equivalent to those of 300,000 Mexicans.[22] What is happening to cause these trends?

> The rich are getting richer.

When globalization of the world economy began around 1980, rich countries grew faster than poor countries, since countries like the United States and the Euro-bloc countries were selling knowledge, technologies, and machinery to developing countries and benefiting from importing consumer goods from countries with low wages like Haiti, China, Vietnam, and Thailand. Rich countries were better positioned to benefit from the expansion of trade and the integration of markets because they had more capital to invest and thus grow their wealth as well as a more educated and productive work force. The benefits of globalization and the inequality that resulted from it tapered off around 2000, but the gaps between rich and poor countries remained.

If you wanted to predict a stranger's income, you would want to know where they lived, because *citizenship explains 80% of a person's income; 20% is due to things over which people have no control, such as their gender or ethnicity.*[23] The poorest person born in America is better off than two-thirds of everybody else in the world. A comparison offered by Milanovic between India and the United States illustrates this point. Only the top 3% of the Indian population has an average income greater than that of the bottom 10% of Americans, who live in poverty.[24]

But why do the growing wealth and income gaps between countries matter? These differences drive immigration, both legal and illegal, and they give rise to political instability within poor countries. Somalia is one of the largest sources of refugees in the world after Syria, Iraq, and Afghanistan. Jamac Said was interviewed by a UN team in Mogadishu about his attempts to flee Somalia:

> I was very jealous of young diaspora guys who visited … the country and got married to young, beautiful women in the locality. As local boys, we cannot marry because we do not have jobs and good education. Then I and six of other friends (four boys and two girls) decided to migrate to Europe through Ethiopia, Sudan, and Libya to Italy. We were arrested in South Sudan by rebels … who harassed us and took everything and raped the girls. After two days we started our journey to Khartoum where again the Sudanese army imprisoned us for nineteen months, after which we came back to Mogadishu.

Jamac did not give up in his attempt to flee Somalia with his friends. They next tried to flee through the Kenyan border but were again captured, imprisoned and beaten. Finally released Jamac said, "I feel so lucky just because I am alive, while many of my peers died in the high seas, in prisons in Africa, or from attacks by wild animals [while they were] on their way to Europe, the Arab States, or Southern Africa."[25]

The Harvard economist Dani Rodrik has raised the question of whether or not developed nations have a moral obligation to open their borders to those seeking jobs and security.[26] After all, wealth—in the form of money, labor power, and natural resources—has flowed from developing to developed countries for well over a century. There is a danger in keeping people bottled up in countries where there are few opportunities. As a report from the United Nations Development Agency has suggested: "When a large pool of young people are uprooted, intolerant, jobless, and have few opportunities for positive engagement, they represent a ready pool of recruits for ethnic, religious, and political extremists seeking to mobilize violence."[27]

In the case of Somalia, lack of jobs and devastation of the fishing industry by foreign trawlers gave rise to piracy. As one former Somali pirate indicated, it was the only employment option left to him. He borrowed money to buy bazookas, a machine gun, and an AK-47. After many failed attempts he and his team finally captured a ship far from Somalia in the Indian Ocean. His share of the $4 million ransom was $70,000, which he used to pay back the borrowed money. The rest he spent on drugs, alcohol, sex workers, and when the money was gone he went back with his crew to capture another ship. Arrested, he went to vocational school and became an employee of the government. His conclusion: "Now I am happy and believe that job creation for the youth is the answer to stopping young people from joining piracy."[28]

Differences between countries in terms of per capita income clearly matter and so do differences between income groups within countries. There are several questions of interest when it comes to income differences within a country. Who are the super-rich and how did they get their money? How do they keep it and what are the chances that their fellow citizens might one day ascend into their ranks?

Who Are the 1%?

The 1% in America is made up of three primary groups: sports and media stars; star professionals like doctors and lawyers; and CEO's of large corporations. LeBron James, the 6 foot 8 inch basketball player who stars for the

Cleveland Cavaliers, had a net worth of $325 million in 2014. His annual earnings in 2014 totaled about $73 million, $20 million for playing basketball and $53 million from endorsements and sponsorships. The actor Robert Downey Jr. has a total net worth or about $170 million. He made $50 million in one year alone for starring in the *Iron Man* franchise. The golfer Tiger Woods has a net worth of $600 million. He earned $61.2 million in 2014, $6.2 million from tournaments, and $55 million from endorsements and sponsorships. That made him the second richest African-American in the United States. Oprah Winfrey was first, with a net worth of $2.9 billion and an annual salary of $300 million in 2014 from her media empire. The singers Bruce Springsteen, Taylor Swift, and Beyoncé each make in excess of $10 million a year, sometimes much more. The earnings of these performers and athletes put them in the top 1% of income earners in the United States. One explanation for their wealth and earnings is that their influence extends to a global audience, magnifying the impact of their individual efforts. They are not, however, typical of the top 1%.[29]

To be in the top 1% of U.S. earners in 2012, a person needed a taxable salary of $380,000, which would not make them rich in a city like New York, San Francisco, or Chicago. To be in the top 1% in San Francisco you would need an income of $558,000 a year and in Manhattan it would be $790,000.[30] College presidents, cardiologists, neurosurgeons, and lawyers with top firms make up about 25% of the top 1%. People who own their own businesses, such as a convenience store franchise, an independent insurance agency, or a car dealership, make up another part of this top group. The rest of the 1% is made up of people who profit primarily from gains realized from stocks and bonds, those who work on Wall Street for financial firms, and the CEOs of large corporations. The picture of who is making the most changes dramatically when we consider just the top 0.1% of income earners. One study found that executives, managers, supervisors, and financial professionals account for about 60% of the top 0.1%, and they accounted for a full 70% of the national income that went to the top 0.1% between 1979 and 2005.[31] The big winners have been the CEOs of large corporations.

> The 1% in the United States are sports and media stars, entrepreneurs, and the CEOs of large corporations.

Larry Ellison, chief of Oracle Corporation, a software company, received compensation worth $153 million in 2014. Daniel R. Hesse of Sprint received $49 million, and the heads of T-Mobile, Ralph Lauren, Lockheed Martin, Chevron, ExxonMobil, and Chipotle Mexican Grill each averaged around $25 million.[32] There are several reasons for these high salaries. One is that wages and bonuses are linked directly to increases in the value of the company's stocks, and the overall value of stocks has been increasing since 2011. According to the *Wall Street Journal*, the average compensation for the CEO of a top 300 firm in 2013 was $11.4 million a year.[33] A related reason is that often stock options (where a stock is offered at a discounted price) are part of the compensation (pay) package, and frequently the largest part of annual compensation. Third, the salaries of company CEOs are not set by stockholders but by boards or salary committees who might compare the salaries of their CEO to those of CEOs in other large corporations and seek to achieve equity.

The top 1% of income earners in the United States take home about 20% of all pre-tax income, double the amount they took home just thirty years ago.[34] Income, though, tells only part of the story. We need to consider the wealth, or assets (stocks, bonds, real estate, etc.), a person owns. As noted, Larry Ellison's income in 2014 was $153 million but his wealth totaled upwards of $56 billion. The economists Emmanuel Saez of the University of California, Berkeley, and Gabriel Zucman of the London School of Economics looked at capital income—dividends, interest, rents, and business profits.[35] Using this method, they found that wealth inequality has followed a U-shaped distribution over the past 100 years. From the Great Depression of the 1930s all the way through the 1970s, there was a democratization of wealth, but between 1970 and 2012, the share of wealth owned by the very rich, the 0.1%, increased to 22%. There are only 160,000 families in this category, each with an average net worth of $73 million. But this small group collectively possesses as much wealth as the entire bottom 90%. The concentration of wealth becomes even starker when we look at the wealth of the 16,000 families who make up the 0.01%, or the one-hundredth of 1%. The net worth of each of these families was $371 million, which means that these 16,000 families, who constitute just a tiny fraction of all households, control 11.2% of America's total wealth.[36]

The outsized fortunes of the few have grown rapidly in large part because they are fueled by the growth of stocks; earnings are put into savings and more investments, which generate more wealth. Wealth begets wealth. Thomas Piketty and Gabriel Zucman, both of the Paris School of Economics, have calculated the assets held by different sectors of the population for eight of the largest economies—the United States, Japan, Germany, France, the UK, Italy, Canada, and Australia.[37] They found that for the four decades from 1970 to 2010, wealth has been steadily concentrating in the hands of the few. What do the ultra-rich do with all of their money?

Those with children hire tutors to help them get into elite private schools and pay their tuitions so they graduate debt free. They pay for private lessons for their children and give them rich cultural experiences, all of which, plus good health, give them a head start in life. They also buy themselves toys. Billionaires are now competing with one another to purchase the $65 million G650 from Gulfstream. Demand for this plane is currently so great that one buyer was able to flip his for $72 million after owning it for just a few weeks. Some are buying the new Boeing 777–300ER, which normally carries 400 passengers, and outfitting it for personal use.[38]

Other countries have their own 1%. Karen Dawisha, a political scientist at Miami University in Oxford, Ohio, has estimated that 110 individuals in Russia control 35% of the country's wealth.[39] To be in the top 1% of earners in Great Britain you would need an income of $260,000 a year, but in Britain the top 1% does not include, as it used to, doctors or professors. The top 1% is now made up principally of financiers, managers, accountants and attorneys. London, which is an international financial center, now has more individuals with a net worth of $30 million than any other city in the world. The wealthy elite of London also includes the largest collection of Russian millionaires outside of Moscow. Gains in labor productivity have gone, as they have in the United States, to those at the top of the income ladder. If Britain's national minimum wage of $10.17 had kept pace with the salaries of CEO's since 1999 it would now be $29.56 an hour.[40]

Though China has done much to lift people out of extreme poverty ($1.25 a day or less), incomes are highly skewed. In fact, the degree of inequality in China, as measured by the Gini coefficient, is now higher in China (0.55) than in the United States (0.45) (The Gini is a measure of income concentration; the higher the number, the greater the concentration). Researchers from the University of Michigan and Peking University, who teamed up to analyze income inequality in China, noted significant regional variations in income inequality.[41] They concluded that "the rapid rise in income inequality can be partly attributed to long-standing government development policies that effectively favor urban residents over rural residents and favor coastal, more developed regions, over inland, less developed regions." The top 10% in China took home 60% of all income in 2013.[42] China's new millionaires and billionaires have derived much of their wealth from their class positions, which were determined by whether or not their relatives and parents fought alongside Mao Zedong and supported the Chinese Revolution of 1949. They were privileged by having access to a superior education, by living in urban areas, and by connections to the Communist Party, which provided capital for their investments.

How the Wealthy Keep Their Money

We understand how wealth magnifies itself, but why is it that the wealthy are able to hang on to their money, barring worldwide economic collapse? One way is to hide money from the tax man. In a study sponsored by the Tax Justice Network, James Henry, a former chief economist for the global consulting firm McKinsey estimated that wealthy families have hidden financial assets of between $21 trillion and $32 trillion in offshore accounts to avoid taxes in their home countries.[43] To put this in perspective, the conservative estimate of $21 trillion is as much money as the entire annual economic output of the United States and Japan combined.[44] The wealthy are aided in these efforts by banks such as HSBC Holdings PLC (a British multinational), UBS (a Swiss financial company), Crédit Suisse, and Goldman Sachs. A third to a half of all offshore wealth ($10 trillion) is held by only 100,000 people, or 0.000014% of the world's population of 7 billion people.[45] Where does the money come from? It is not all from rich countries. Corrupt elites in developing countries hide money that should

> Tax increases do not decrease economic growth.

have gone to the public purse. Henry calculated the amount of capital flowing out of developing countries in Sub-Saharan Africa, the Middle East, and Southeast Asia, and estimated that about a third of the $21–32 trillion hidden in offshore accounts comes from corrupt elites, who are basically robbing their fellow countrymen. It is not just individuals but also corporations that seek to avoid taxes. According to the calculations of the French economist Gabriel Zucman, 20% of all corporate profits in the United States have been shifted offshore.[46]

Virtually any discussion about whether to cut or lower taxes creates a furor, regardless of the country in which it occurs. A study in the Netherlands, which found that 10% of Dutch households owned 60% of the country's wealth, sparked debates in 2014 about whether or not wealth taxes needed to be increased. At the present time all Dutch must pay a tax of 1.2% on assets valued at over $26,500.[47] One argument, offered by the Labor Party, was that it is very difficult in today's world to get rich by one's labor, and therefore the distribution of wealth should be smoothed. The opposition party argued that raising taxes on wealth would be "punishment for good behavior." Do high taxes really affect entrepreneurial behavior (whether that is "good" or not) or, put another way, do high taxes limit economic growth?

In 2012, Thomas Hungerford of the Congressional Research Service was asked to look at two competing theories: does cutting taxes on the wealthy boost the economy or does cutting taxes on the wealthy simply makes the rich richer and the poor poorer?[48] He looked at two taxes: the marginal tax rate which is the amount of tax paid on each additional dollar earned; and, the capital gains tax, which is the tax paid on the gain realized from the sale of some asset like a stock. *He found no relationship between cuts in the top marginal tax rate or in the top capital gains tax and economic growth. Cutting taxes on the wealthy does not stimulate economic growth.* In Germany and Switzerland the top tax rate has not changed in fifty years, yet their economies have continued to grow and create jobs. In Britain, where top tax rates have fallen and the ranks of the wealthy have grown, economic growth has slowed and jobs have been lost.[49] Two economists, Sebastian Vollmer of the University of Göttingen and Dierk Herzer of Harvard, found in an analysis of nine high-income countries between 1961 and 1996 that *the greater the share of national income going to the top 10%, the slower the rate of economic growth.*[50] Modern economies are driven by consumption, and concentration of wealth means less consumption for a majority of the population. Why do tax laws continue to benefit the 1%? They remain in place because the wealthy are able to translate their economic power into political power and influence legislation. (See Chapter 7, "Narratives of Power," [this volume] for an elaboration of this point.)

Some tax deductions clearly benefit the well-off. For example, being able to deduct the interest paid on mortgages up to $1 million clearly benefits the wealthy, rather than the poor. And being able to deduct payments for gold-plated health insurance plans also benefits them. According to the weekly business magazine, the *Economist*, more than 60% of all tax preferences flow to the wealthiest 20% of Americans, and only 3% go to the bottom 20%.[51] What most benefits top income earners has been steep cuts in federal income tax rates. In 1960 the top 1% paid 44.4% on their earnings, but by 2004 the marginal tax rate had dropped to 30.4%. And if earnings came from dividends and capital gains, which is where the majority of annual earnings come from for those worth $30 million or more, the top rate paid on capital gains was 15%. As the billionaire Warren Buffett noted in 2011, the way the tax code is written, his secretary paid a higher tax rate on her income than he did.[52] When all of these exclusions—itemized deductions for charitable expenses, mortgage interests, capital gains on home sales, and so forth—are added up, they cost the federal government about $751 billion a year. The bottom 20%'s share of these collective tax breaks is 0.7%, or $55 billion. The top 20% got $597 billion.

Low-income workers benefit primarily from the earned income tax credit (EITC), which is a refundable tax credit determined by one's salary and the number of children in the home. Only those who work can receive an EITC, as it was designed to reward those who worked, rather than those who relied on welfare. Presently around 30 million low- and moderate-income families, or 25% of all families, receive these benefits.[53] To put this in perspective, all refundable credits (including the EITC and child credit) cost the federal government around $122 billion a year. The bottom 60% of all income earners received 72.7% of these benefits or $89 billion out of the $122 billion spent. Yet this remains a tiny share of the value ($597 million, as noted above) of all of the tax breaks and loopholes available to those in the top 20%.[54]

Many wealthy families want to pass their estates on to their children. The conservative Harvard economist N. Gregory Mankiw claims this is due to "intergenerational altruism." People naturally want to take care of their children, he says.[55] In 2014, it was possible to avoid paying the 35% federal tax rate on estates valued at less than $5.34 million; this figure will rise to $5.43 million in 2015.

Those with the means to do so can also escape estate taxes by setting up an irrevocable trust. An irrevocable trust provides parents with income during their lifetime and allows the wealth and its appreciation to be passed on to heirs without paying taxes. As we will see in the next two chapters, this process of keeping fortunes intact is recreating the kind of class structure that existed in the United States and Western Europe in the 1920s, when the wealthy lived off of their inheritances rather than working. One of the most important factors in reducing the wealth gap has historically been education, but even here a gap is widening between the children of wealthy and poor families.

Social Mobility

The degree of social mobility that exists in a society generates controversy because it may be part of a society's narrative or myth. Why don't Americans support redistributive policies? Because they believe that someday they or their children will climb the income ladder.[56] For Americans there are plenty of iconic figures to stoke the myth of mobility. There is Andrew Carnegie who started out in a cotton factory making $1.20 a week and rose to become one of the richest men in the world, as well as contemporary figures like Bill Gates of Microsoft, Steve Jobs of Apple, or Mark Zuckerberg, the Facebook billionaire. But they are the exception rather than the rule. There are two ways to think about mobility. Absolute mobility compares the earnings of one generation to the next. There has been absolute mobility in most countries simply because the economy has grown. A 2012 survey found that 84% of adult Americans had income higher than

> Our social fates are determined primarily by factors over which we have no control.

their parents.[57] However, even though people make more money, they still can be in the same class position, or income category, as their parents. What we want to know is their relative mobility, or whether they moved up or down, relative to their parents. We care about relative mobility because it best reflects the value of social inclusion and equality of opportunity. If we look at income data in the period after the Civil War, there was considerable mobility—both relative and absolute—in the United States, compared to a country like Britain.[58] But a study by the Harvard economist Raj Chetty and his colleagues have shown that over the last 30–40 years mobility has slowed greatly in the United States. If we break incomes down into quintiles (five categories of 20% each), we find that 70% of those born into the bottom quintile have *never* made it into the middle class, and only 10% have ever made it into the top quintile. Many (40%) have remained poor over the course of their lifetimes.[59] Compare this to Canada, where there is more mobility both up from and out of the bottom tier of incomes as well as downward mobility from the top tier.[60]

In another mobility study the economic historian Gregory Clark looked at the degree to which our economic fates are determined by our parents and grandparents. He tracked family surnames over 800 years to measure relative mobility in different nations, including the United States, China, Sweden, and England. What he found was that *there never has been much mobility*. Today's elites are the children and grandchildren of yesterday's elites. The advantages and disadvantages we inherit stick with us for generations unless governments intervene to raise the standard of living for everyone.[61] Patrick Egan, a professor of politics at New York University, also sees rates of mobility directly tied to government policy. People are more mobile in those states with bigger governments and more progressive systems of taxation, such as California, than in states with smaller governments and less progressive tax systems, such as West Virginia. However, Egan calculated that *the things for which each of us cannot be held accountable—religion, ethnicity, gender, country of origin, parents' educational and occupational levels, or the town in which we were born—explain roughly half of overall social inequality.*[62]

The relationship between parents' socioeconomic status and that of their children is significant in all of the world's developed countries.[63] In France, Italy, the United Kingdom, and the United States, at least 40%

of the economic advantage of high-earning parents is passed on to the children, whereas in Australia, Norway, Finland, and Canada, only 20% of a parents' advantages are passed along to the children, meaning that these are much more open societies than is the United States.[64] Generally, the higher a country's degree of social inequality among its citizens, the lower its economic and social mobility.[65] There are few "rags to riches" stories to be found in the United States. Those who are born into the lowest economic tier have a slim chance of making it into the top income spectrum.[66]

Is Education the Great Leveler?

Education has been seen to be a great leveler, and there is considerable evidence that going to pre-school and graduating from college can boost one's income over a lifetime. Sabino Kornrich, a sociology professor from Emory University, studied the expenditures of families from all income levels during the Great Recession (2007–2010). All parents either spent the same or cut down slightly on expenses such as childcare, food, books, toys, and clothing.[67] However, one group, the top 10% of income earners, doubled down on their children's futures. Average spending per child for education went up 35% during the recession.[68]

There are numerous ways for wealthy parents to improve their child's life chances. One is to provide them with access to top-quality medical and dental care. Another is to buy a house in a top public school district. Living in a district with high-quality schools can boost a child's chance of mobility.[69] That is, districts with smaller class sizes, lower drop-out rates, and higher expenditures for education make it more likely that children will not be trapped in the class into which they were born. But if public school budgets are slashed, as they were during the Great Recession, the rich can send their children to private elementary and secondary schools, where enrollments increased by 36% between 2007 and 2011.

According to studies by Sean F. Reardon of Stanford University, the education achievement gap has been growing for at least forty years. Compared to 1970, when educational achievements were less influenced by income, he estimates that now *differences in family income account for between 30 and 60% of the differences in educational achievement*.[70] SAT test scores, used by many colleges for admission and even by some employers when it comes time to hire, are directly related to parental income. The gap in SAT scores between the lowest 10% and the highest 10% income groups is almost 400 points (1324 to 1722). For each $20,000 increase in family income there is an increase in student SAT scores.[71]

Parental education is, along with level of income, an equally important factor in whether or not children go on to college and succeed. So is getting married to another college graduate. The income gap, as the Harvard labor economists Claudia Goldin and Lawrence Katz have demonstrated, between a family with two college graduates and one with two high school graduates grew by $30,000 between 1979 and 2012, adjusting for inflation.[72] America's educational system helped it become the richest nation in the world but, beginning around 1970, the system began to stagnate at the very time that the rate of return on educational investments began to climb.

> The educational system in the United States privileges children from wealthy families.

A 2014 study by the Organization for Economic Cooperation and Development (OECD), which is made up of the world's richest countries, showed that the United States now trails nearly all other industrialized nations when it comes to educational equality, even though it spends more (7.31% of its GDP in 2010) on education that most other wealthy countries.[73] In 2010, the United States spent more than $11,000 for each elementary student, more than $12,000 for each high school student, and $15,171 for those in college or vocational training programs.[74] *Educational equality, however, is not determined by the amount of money spent but by the outcomes achieved.*

U.S. students routinely do less well than students in other industrial countries on standardized tests that measure ability in mathematics, reading, and sciences, as Table 2.1 indicates.

Table 2.1 International Comparison of Student Performance in Mathematics, Reading, and Science for Selected Countries: Scores and Rankings

	Math Score/Rank	*Reading* Score/Rank	*Science* Score/Rank
Shanghai	613 1	570 1	580 1
Singapore	573 2	542 2	551 2
Korea	554 5	536 5	538 11

	Math Score/Rank	Reading Score/Rank	Science Score/Rank
Japan	536 8	538 3	547 3
Switzerland	531 9	509 19	515 18
Germany	514 12	508 20	524 9
Poland	518 13.5	518 16	526 14
Canada	518 13.5	523 9	525 12
Finland	519 15	524 7	545 4
Average score	**494**	**496**	**501**
United States	481 35	498 24	497 27

Source: OECD (2014), *PISA 2012 Results: What Students Know and Can Do – Student Performance in Mathematics, Reading and Science* (Volume I, Revised edition, February 2014), PISA, OECD Publishing. Accessed at: http://dx.doi.org/10.1787/9789264201118-en.

On a test of math literacy, 15-year-olds in the United States came in 35th in international rankings, 24th in reading, and 27th in science. The story of high school graduation rates is bleak by comparison. Portugal, Slovenia, Finland, Japan, and the United Kingdom report graduation rates of between 92 and 96%. The high school graduation rate in the United States is 76%, giving it a ranking of 21st, right below Canada.[75] Every year 3 million students in the United States, or 8.1% of the total high school population, drop out of school. On average the person who drops out will earn $20,000 a year while the person who graduates from high school will earn $36,000 a year.

Fewer than 30% of American adults have a better education than their parents, compared to Finland, where more than 50% of adults are better educated than their parents. The chance that a young person in the United States will be enrolled in a university if their parents do not have a college education, is only 29%. Further, for those whose parents did not graduate from high school, only one in twenty (5%) will manage to graduate from college. Compare this percentage to that of the twenty richest countries of the world, where it is one in four (25%). While graduation rates from four-year colleges have slowed in the United States, the rest of the developed world has begun to catch up. One reason is that *the cost of higher education in the United States has put it out of reach of those in the lowest income categories.* Starting in the late 1980s many states faced increased pressures on the public purse due to the expansion of prison systems, growing social welfare needs, and so forth. Some reasoned that that because a college graduate was the personal beneficiary of their education, they should pay for it. The result was that tuition even in public universities, like the University of Michigan and the University of California, Berkeley, shot up. Tuition and fees at private universities were already high. (In 2014, the average yearly cost to attend an Ivy League school like Brown, Harvard, Princeton, or Yale was about $45,000.[76])

Writers for the Bloomberg Report estimated that since 1978, college and tuition fees have increased by 1,120%, four times faster than the consumer price index and faster than expenditures for food, shelter, and medical expenses.[77] And while the United States provides many of its poorest students with aid to attend college, the OECD nations charge students far less to go to school, meaning students can graduate with little or no debt compared to middle-class students in the United States.[78] A telling comparison between the United States and the OECD countries is that in the U.S. taxpayers paid 36 cents of every dollar spent on high school and higher education; in OECD countries taxpayers picked up 68 cents of every dollar spent.[79] *The cost of educating a child has shifted to the individual family in the United States, magnifying the importance of the family's income.*

Suzanne Mettler, a professor of government at Cornell University, calculated the percentage of family income necessary to send a child to school. Breaking income groups down into five categories, she found that in 1971 it took 42% of the annual income of members of the poorest fifth of families in America to send a child to school; this number had climbed to 114% by 2011, more than their total annual earnings. At the other extreme, for the wealthiest 20%, the share of household income needed to attend college went up only three percentage points, from 6% to 9%.[80] The result of these high costs is to push low-income students into community colleges, where the rate of transition to a four-year college remains low, and to make exclusive colleges the enclaves of the children of the wealthy and privileged. College, instead of being a great leveler, is now rigidifying the social structure in the United States. Anthony Carnevale, director of Georgetown University's Center on Education and the Workforce, has noted that only 5% of students from the bottom quartile of income distribution are enrolled in one of the nation's 200 most prestigious universities. And of the entire lower 50% of the income distribution, just 14% are enrolled in these schools. Carnevale argues that elite universities have become "passive agents for the intergenerational reproduction of elites." Elite schools, with their high endowments, spent more per student than public schools. Those who go to elite colleges have a better chance of getting into elite graduate schools and professional programs than those who go to public universities, and those from elite schools who get their first job after earning their baccalaureate have a starting salary that averages $17,000 a year more than students who went to a nonselective school. Elite universities also give their students more social capital, connecting them to key positions of power and influence.[81]

The failure of schools to reduce gaps in inequality has been, interestingly, laid at the feet of public school teachers. A number of writers have looked at the data on student performance and concluded there was and is an educational crisis.[82] The first report to capture the public's attention was in 1983: *A Nation at Risk,* commissioned by President Ronald Reagan. Public schools were identified as the main culprit for student failings. The authors of the 1983 report claimed that "the educational foundations of our society are presently being eroded by a rising tide of mediocrity that threatens our very future as a Nation and people." It was unimaginable that other countries were matching and surpassing America's educational achievements. The boldest statement began: "If an unfriendly foreign power had attempted to impose on America the mediocre educational performance that exists today, we might well have viewed it as an act of war ... [W]e have in effect been committing an act of unthinking, unilateral educational disarmament."[83] A mantra developed that continues to this day: schools are broken, teachers lack rigor and have low expectations for their students—*and* we need to test everyone. It seemed to some that the educational system was being redesigned to make education "teacher proof." Teachers were clearly in the crosshairs that came with the pressure in 2002 generated by President George W. Bush's No Child Left Behind Act, which mandated standardized examinations that were supposed to bring every child to "proficiency" by 2014. There was significant pressure for teachers to teach to the test and for the teachers and their schools to be graded in terms of how well their students did. In New York and

California teachers' names are published beside their students' test scores and in others their pay is directly linked to student performance.[84]

Wealthy and educated parents have learned how to use the public school system to their advantage by creating charter schools where they can control who teaches, who attends, and what gets taught. Creating charter schools requires financial and political resources. Charter schools are also partly funded from the public school budget, draining resources for the most needy and weakening public school systems in general.[85]

The United States commits significant resources to attempting to overcome the effects of poverty, including spending for early childhood education, free lunch and breakfast programs, English as a Second Language (ESL) programs, after-hours programs, parent programs, gang prevention programs, and extra resources for tutoring and counseling. But all of these efforts do not trump the lasting effects of coming from an impoverished background or of living in a community where there are limited cultural resources, no jobs, and where violent crime threatens the safety of children. Why do Finnish children do so much better in school than U.S. students? Less than 5% of children in Finland live in poverty, while 23% of American children do. Our urban schools are in trouble, says Ravich, because of concentrated poverty and racial segregation.[86] Why do students drop out of high school? One study found that 32% left because they needed to get a job and make money, 26% because they had become a parent, and 22% because they needed to take care of a family member.[87]

Marriage and Family Structure

Between the 1950s and 1970s in China, if your parent had been the member of a "counterrevolutionary" class, that is, a landlord or a "rich" peasant, it would have been impossible to marry, except perhaps another person with a "bad" class background. Things have changed somewhat in China, but marriage between people who have the same backgrounds continues. This is partly due to the fact that in China and other Asian countries marriages are as much between families as they are between individuals, so the family frequently gets involved. However, the sex ratio in China provides a twist on marrying

> Whom you marry matters in terms of your mobility.

somebody of the same class background. Because of China's 1980 one-child policy and the sex-selected abortions that occurred because of it, there are fewer women than men. The result is that today there are 120 men for every 100 women. This means women have more options than men and some will move up the class ladder through marriage. However, in China, as elsewhere, educated women want to marry educated men, and this has resulted in an increase in the number of single, college-educated women. Overall, 55% of Chinese college-educated men will marry women who are less educated but only 32% of college women will do the same.[88] Marital patterns, driven by changes in the role of women, heavily influence social mobility.

Among college-educated adults in America, 71% of men are married to women with a college degree and 64% of college-educated women are married to a man with a college degree. The lower tally for women is driven in part by the fact that there are 7% more women with college degrees than men.[89] In 2012, the median income for a household in which both people were married and working was $91,779. Compare this to the household income of a family where the wife stays home ($50,881) or a where there is a single father ($42,358) or a single mother ($30,686). Being single carries with it significant economic penalties, and single mothers and fathers now constitute 26% of all U.S. households, double the number in 1950.[90]

The decline in marriage has been steepest among minorities, the poor, and the least educated.[91] As the Brookings Institute reported, marriage is now "another mechanism through which advantage is protected and passed on from one generation to the next. Affluent, committed parents tend to get married, stay married, and raise their children together."[92] The rationale for marriage is no longer income sharing but rather child rearing. As the economists Shelly Lundberg and Robert Pollak put it:

> The primary source of the gains in marriage shifted from the production of household services ... to investment in children ... Marriage is the commitment to a mechanism that supports high levels of investment in children and is hence more valuable for parents adopting a high-investment strategy for their children.[93]

Though cohabitation has become a more common and acceptable living arrangement for many, the cohabiting college-educated couple often waits until after marriage to have children, while the poor and less educated do not.

A strong predictor of a child's mobility is family structure.[94] The reasons poor children suffer goes beyond the fact that their parents don't get married. They suffer because they are frequently trapped in communities where there are no jobs, where the schools are problematic, and where the neighborhood is dangerous. Children do escape such circumstances—there are single parents who make a good life for their children—but they often do so under extraordinary circumstances. To break out of these ever-continuing cycles, there needs to be a social compact that provides a robust social safety net for both children and parents. In many European countries, the weight of one's family does not press down as heavily on children as in the United States.

The Erosion of the Social Contract

The British historian Tony Judt wrote extensively about the nature of the social contract, that is, about what we owe to one another. As he has explained, in the aftermath of World War II, Western European countries and the United States engaged in a grand social experiment. They asked what it would take to achieve lasting peace, stimulate economic growth, create a safety net for a society's most needy citizens, and deal with the complexities of a mass society.

> The grand bargain of democracy is threatened by rising inequality.

Their answer was to create strong, high-taxing, activist nation-states. They did so because they had lived with the consequences of weak states and inflation that had ruined economies and given rise to war. It was reasoned that some institution, in this case the state, was essential to mediate between the needs of citizens and the marketplace. Sound social policies were needed to save capitalism from itself and its Cold War enemies. The economies of Western Europe rebounded, that of the United States grew at a record pace, and working men and women benefited from rising standards of living. Judt argued that this grand bargain fell apart with the beginning of the Reagan Era (at its peak in the 1980s; covering a similar time period at the Thatcher Era in Britain), which generated a phobia regarding state intervention, with the result that protections against unfettered capitalism were whittled away.[95]

In the United States, the Gini coefficient (the measure of income inequality) jumped from 35 to 40 between 1980 and 1990. Gaps between wealth and income have now reached levels that are socially devastating and politically destabilizing. These gaps are growing, not just within developed countries, but *between* the countries of the world. Though economic growth is supposed to be the panacea that cures all ills, it will not, unless the benefits of this growth are directed so that everyone has an opportunity to develop their full human potential. Inequality washes away the foundations of trust that allow us to create and maintain democratic societies.

Summary

Poverty exists in all societies. Sometimes it is temporary, but when it is not the consequences are devastating not only to the individuals involved but also to the societies in which the poor live. Poverty is pain and humiliation; it limits the ability of people to participate in their own societies. Poverty that cannot be escaped locks people into place in the same manner as other irrelevant social criteria such as gender, religion, or ethnicity. The evidence is clear that divisions between rich and poor nations are growing, which drives people across national borders as they seek to find food, jobs, and security.

So, too, do we find that within the developed world, gaps are continuing to grow between those at the bottom of the economic pyramid and those at the top. Upward mobility has slowed. The hope that education would be a path out of poverty for many has not been realized. Education in the United States is reinforcing existing class barriers. College graduates marry college graduates, stay married, and have children in whom they invest, thus amplifying the advantages of children raised in such households. Parents pass both advantages and disadvantages on to the children. The more unequal a society, the greater the advantages that the wealthy pass on to their children, magnifying even further the gaps between the wealthy and poor.

Though the outcomes of poverty are similar in all societies, solutions to the problem of poverty in the developed world and the developing world differ somewhat. For citizens to be able to participate in their society in the developing world, the United Nations has spelled out a set of goals that include: (1) eradicate extreme poverty and hunger, (2) achieve universal primary education, (3) promote gender equality and empower women, (4) reduce child mortality, and (5) improve maternal health.[96] Achievement of these goals will create the human capital needed for people to make their own choices about the kind of societies in which they wish to live. For the developed world, social policies must reduce the growing gaps in wealth and income among various groups in society.

Through a Sustainability Lens

In 2014, China announced for the first time that it would set a goal for reducing carbon dioxide emissions. However, it will wait to set this goal until 2030, when its emissions are expected to peak. In the meantime, China will continue to build coal-fired plants to fuel its economic growth. China also plans to expand by 2030 the amount of energy it gets from zero-emissions sources such as nuclear, wind, and solar power. Climate scientists, like John Sterman of MIT, believe this will not be of much help in responding to the most pressing environmental issues of the near future, namely rising sea levels, extreme weather events, water shortages, and reduced agricultural output.[97] India, with its population of 1.2 billion, has no intention of setting a limit on its emissions. As India's power minister, Piyush Goyal, said, "India's development imperatives cannot be sacrificed at the altar of potential climate changes many years in the future." To meet the needs of India's poor, he promised to double India's use of domestic coal by 2019.[98] The irony, if it is one, is that India will suffer from toxic air, rising sea levels, and the degradation of its environment as a result. The goal of reducing global poverty runs headlong into the goal of reducing greenhouse gas emissions (GHGs).

> Economic growth alone cannot solve the problem of poverty.

As the International Energy Agency has noted, "Energy alone is not sufficient for creating the conditions for economic growth, but it is certainly necessary."[99] Energy poverty limits people's ability to transform their lives. Only 42% of Africa's 1 billion people have access to electricity. South Asia is also a region where universal access to electricity is a problem. In November 2014, a transmission line carrying power to Bangladesh failed and the entire country was blacked out for a day. This did not pose a problem for the 38% who had no electricity to begin with! Worldwide, almost 20% of the population, or 1.4 billion, is without electricity.

World energy use is highly skewed, with the rich and developed world consuming the bulk of the world's energy. For example, the United States with only 5% of the world's population, consumes close to 20% of all energy and, next to China, is the major emitter of GHGs. The *New York Times* journalist Nicholas Kristof provided an interesting comparison when he noted that the Dallas Cowboys football stadium consumes three times as much power at peak time as Liberia can produce at any given time.[100] The small city (120,000) of Evansville, Indiana alone consumes three times as much power during peak use as Liberia can produce. [101]

Poverty is a driver of climate change. The poor person without access to clean energy sources must search for wood and other forms of fuel, sometimes leading to the collapse of entire ecosystems. The family in Ghana with many mouths to feed is often farming depleted land and has no other choice but to continue doing so. The fisherman who takes whatever finds its way into his net to eat or sell is not worried about the environment, even when the catch diminishes. People desperate for a job and a way to feed their families find multiple ways to cope, including illegal poaching, overgrazing of herd animals, logging, and mining. And many of these means of coping imperil the biosphere upon which human life depends.

Affluence, of course, is also a driver of climate change. As economies modernize, as people become more affluent, and as consumption increases, so will GHGs if nothing else changes. The evidence for this is not that people use less energy or use fewer resources when they move beyond the subsistence level; it is that they use more. As an example, China's growing affluence has created a spike in the worldwide demand for pork, fish, poultry, and grains. China's economic growth requires the continued use of coal. The affluent world has been shielded from many of the effects of its consumption because the environmental effects and the human costs are felt elsewhere. The polluted air in Beijing does not immediately affect the person in California who buys a sweater or a pair of socks made in China. The developed world imports energy, pollution, and low-wage labor in the form of cars and car parts, aluminum water bottles, lumber, and oil from the developing world. We do not see the link between income poverty, energy poverty, and climate change, because we don't have to yet.

George Marshall, a British expert on climate change communication, has spent a good part of his career trying to understand why people will not accept simple facts about climate change, which seem indisputable to those who believe the climate is changing: that humans are responsible and that if we do nothing, then civilization as we know it will come to an end. Marshall explains that we convert information about climate change into stories that embody our own values. When people were asked about the weather in their area, if they believe in climate change they are likely to say, "it's warmer." In the same area and with the same weather, those who do not believe in climate change say, "it's colder."[102] We do the same thing with poverty. If we believe poverty is the consequence of people not working hard enough to find a job, then we are not likely to support an expanded social welfare net, even when the evidence is clear that most of those who are poor are actually working; the problem is they are working in low-wage jobs.

Making poverty visible is essential, because we must solve the conjoined issues of climate change, poverty, and the fact that 20% of the world's population still has no access to electricity. We must also develop a narrative that reminds us of what our answer is to the question, What kind of a world would you want to be born into?

Bolivia's ambassador to the World Trade organization, Angélica Navarro Llanos, explained to a United Nations climate conference what needed to be done.

> We need a Marshall Plan for the Earth. This plan must mobilize financing and technology transfer on scales never seen before. It must get technology onto the ground in every country to ensure we reduce emissions while raising people's quality of life. We have only a decade.[103]

However long we have, it is indeed critical that developing countries must be helped to overcome poverty. But technology transfers will only go so far in solving the problem of poverty. The argument here is that we need to help create human capital so that those most likely to suffer the consequences of climate change can make their own decisions about the kinds of lives they wish to live and how best to escape the confines of poverty. We need to unlock human creativity, because the problems we face will require that we find new ways to solve what now appear to be intractable problems.

Notes

1. Based on David Erickson. 2014. "Residents of Hansen's Trailer Park Losing Hope, Homes." *Missoulian.* July 20: A1, 12; Kim Briggeman and Alice Miller. 2014. "City's Growth Spurs Purchase of Lots, Displacement of Residents." *Missoulian.* July 20: A1,11; Martin Kidston. 2014. "Last Residents of Trailer Park on Missoula's Third Street Makes Unbearable Move." *Missoulian.* October 12: A1, 11.
2. Deepa Narayan. 1999. "A Review of World Bank Participatory Poverty Assessments: Consultations with the Poor." *Poverty Reduction Strategy Paper.* Washington, DC: World Bank Poverty Group, PREM.
3. Paige Williams. 2014. "Double Jeopardy." *The New Yorker.* November 17: 65.
4. Oxford University Poverty and Human Development Initiative. 2014. "Policy – A Multidimensional Approach." Accessed on November 11, 2014 at: http://www.ophi.org.uk/policy/multidimensional-poverty-index/.
5. World Bank. 2012. "Voices of the Poor." Retrieved on November 29, 2014 at: http://web.worldbank.org/WBSITE/EXTERNAL/TOPICS/EXTPOVERTY/0,,contentMDK:20622514~menuPK:336998~pagePK:148956~piPK:216618~theSitePK:336992,00.html.
6. Deepa Narayan, et al. 1999. *A Review of World Bank Participatory Poverty Assessments: Consultations with the Poor.* Washington, DC: World Bank, p.28. Accessed on November 11 at: http://www. participatorymethods. org/resource/review-world-bank-participatory-poverty-assessments-consultations-poor.
7. Ibid.
8. Ibid., p.42.
9. Ernest Y. Kunfaa and Tony Dogbe with Heather J. MacKay and Celia Marshall. 2002. "Ghana: Empty Pockets." in Deepa Narayan and Patti Petesch, eds., pp.17–49. *Voices of the Poor: From Many Lands.* Washington, DC: World Bank, 23670.
10. Ibid., pp.22–29.
11. John M. Kadzandira, Stanley W. Khaila, and Peter M. Mvula. 2002. "Malawi: Tangled Web." In Narayan and Petesch, eds., *Voices of the Poor,* p.58.
12. Ibid., p.70.
13. Oxfam. 2015. "Wealth: Having It All and Wanting More." Retrieved on February 11, 2015 at: http://www.oxfam.org/en/research/wealth-having-it-all-and-wanting-more.
14. United Nations. 2015. "Hunger: Vital Statistics." http://www.un.org/en/globalissues/briefingpapers/food/vitalstats.shtml.
15. Glenn Phelps and Steve Crabtree. 2013. "More than One in Five Worldwide Living in Extreme Poverty." Gallup Poll. Retrieved on November 11 at: http://www.gallup.com/poll/166565/one-five-worldwide-living-extreme-poverty.aspx.
16. World Bank. 2013. "Remarkable Declines in Global Poverty, But Major Challenges Remain." Retrieved on November 12 at: http://www.worldbank.org/en/news/press-release/2013/04/17/remarkable-declines-in-global-poverty-but-major-challenges-remain.
17. World Bank. 2013. "The State of the Poor: Where Are the Poor, Where Is Extreme Poverty Harder to End, and What Is the Current Profile of the World's Poor?" http://siteresources.worldbank.org/EXTPREMNET/Resources/EP125.pdf.
18. Branko Milanovic. 2012. "Global Income Inequality by the Numbers: in History and Now—An Overview." Washington, DC: World Bank Policy Working Paper 6259.

19 Angus Maddison. 2007. *Contours of the World Economy, 1–2030: Essays in Macro-Economic History.* Oxford, UK: Oxford University Press. See Branko Milanovic (2011) for the technical details of how Maddison's data can be manipulated for comparison purposes.
20 Milanovic. 2011, p.100.
21 Ibid., p.103.
22 Some of the figures are from Milanovic, ibid., pp.42–45.
23 Ibid., pp.112–123.
24 Ibid., p.118.
25 United Nations. 2012. *Somalia Human Development Report: Empowering Youth for Peace and Development.* New York, NY: United Nations, p.66.
26 Dani Rodrik. 2011. *The Globalization Paradox: Democracy and the Future of the World Economy.* New York, NY: W. W. Norton.
27 Ibid., p.39.
28 Ibid., p.41.
29 The U.N. report, footnote xxiv. United Nations. 2012. *Somalia Human Development Report: Empowering Youth for Peace and Development.* New York, NY: United Nations, pp.39–41.
30 Shaila Dewan and Robert Gebeloff. 2012. "Among the Wealthiest One Percent, Many Variations." *The New York Times.* January 14. Retrieved on November 17 at: http://www.nytimes.com/2012/01/15/business/the-1-percent-paint-a-more-nuanced-portrait-of-the-rich.html?pagewanted=all&_r=0.
31 Jon Bakija, Adam Cole, Bradley T. Heim. 2012. "Jobs and Income Growth of Top Earners and the Causes of Changing Income Inequality: Evidence from U. S. Tax Returns Data." Retrieved on November 17 at: http://web.williams.edu/Economics/wp/BakijaColeHeimJobsIncomeGrowthTopEarners.pdf.
32 *Forbes.* 2015. "The World's Highest-Paid Celebrities." http://www.forbes.com/celebrities/list/.
33 *Wall Street Journal.* 2014. Accessed on November 17 at: http://graphics.wsj.com/executive-salary-compensation-2014/.
34 Shaila Dewan and Robert Gebeloff. 2012. "Among the Wealthiest One Percent, Many Variations." *The New York Times.* January 14. Retrieved on November 17 at: http://www.nytimes.com/2012/01/15/business/the-1-percent-paint-a-morenuanced-portrait-of-the-rich.html?pagewanted=all&_r=0.
35 Emmanuel Saez and Gabriel Zucman. 2014. "Wealth Inequality in the United States, 1913–1998." *Quarterly Journal of Economics.* 118(1): 1–39.
36 *The Economist.* 2014. "Forget the 1%; It is the 0.01% who are really getting ahead in America." November 8: 79.
37 Thomas Piketty and Gabriel Zucman. 2014. "Capital is Back: Wealth-Income Ratios in Rich Countries, 1700–2010." *Quarterly Journal of Economics.* 129(3): 1155–1210.
38 Robert Frank. 2014. "Another Widening Gap: The Haves vs. the Have-Mores." *The New York Times.* November 16: 4BU.
39 Karen Dawisha. 2014. *Putin's Kleptocracy: Who Owns Russia?* New York, NY: Simon and Schuster.
40 Danny Dorling. 2014. "How the Super Rich Got Richer: 10 Shocking Facts about Inequality." *The Guardian.* September 15. Retrieved on November 18 at: http://www.

theguardian.com/society/2014/sep/15/how-super-rich-got-richer-10-shocking-facts-inequality.
41 Yu Xie and Xiang Zhou. 2014. "Income Inequality in Today's China." *Proceedings of the National Academy of Sciences*. 111(19): 6928–6933.
42 Oxfam. 2013. "The Cost of Inequality: How Wealth and Income Extremes Hurt Us All." Retrieved on November 18 at: http://www.oxfam.org/sites/www.oxfam.org/files/cost-of-inequality-oxfam-mb180113.pdf.
43 James S. Henry. 2012. "The Price of Offshore Revisited." Tax Justice Network. Retrieved on November 18 at: http://www.taxjustice.net/cms/upload/pdf/Price_of_Offshore_Revisited_120722.pdf.
44 Amy Goodman. 2012. "Exhaustive Study Finds Global Elite Hiding Up to $32 Trillion in Offshore Accounts." Democracy Now. Retrieved on November 17 at: http://www. democracynow. org/2012/7/31/exhaustive_study_finds_global_elite_hiding.
45 See Gabriel Zucman, 2013, for another estimate of how much of global wealth in held in offshore tax havens. Zucman believes it is as much of 8% of the global financial wealth of all households. "The Missing Wealth of Nations: Are Europe and the U.S. Net Debtors or Creditors?" *The Quarterly Journal of Economics*. 2013: 1321–1364. Retrieved on November 18 at: http://gabriel-zucman.eu/files/Zucman2013QJE.pdf.
46 Ibid.
47 *The Economist*. 2014. "Inequality in the Netherlands: A Capital Issue." June 28: 46.
48 Thomas L. Hungerford. 2012. "Taxes and the Economy: An Economic Analysis of the Top Tax Rates Since 1945." Washington, DC: Congressional Research Service. Retrieved on November 18 at: http://www.dpcc.senate.gov/files/documents/CRSTaxesandtheEconomy%20Top%20Rates.pdf.
49 Danny Dorling. 2014. "How the Super Rich Got Richer: 10 Shocking Facts about Inequality." *The Guardian*. September 15. Retrieved on November 18 at: http://www.theguardian.com/society/2014/sep/15/how-super-rich-got-richer-10-shockingfacts-inequality.
50 Dierk Herzer and Sebastian Vollmer. 2013. "Rising Top Incomes Do Not Raise the Tide." *Journal of Policy Modeling*. 35(4): 504–519.
51 *The Economist*. 2012. "Makes and Takers: America's Government Redistributes, but Not Well." October 13. Retrieved on November 18 at: http://www.economist.com/node/21564407.
52 Warren Buffett. 2011. Cited in *News*. Retrieved on November 21 at: http://www.usnews.com/debate-club/should-the-buffett-rule-become-law.
53 Center on Budget and Policy Priorities. 2014. "Earned Income Tax Credit Promotes Work, Encourages Children's Success at School, Research Finds." Retrieved on November 19 at: http://www.cbpp.org/cms/?fa=view&id=3793.
54 Calculated from data presented by David Leonhardt and Bill Marsh. 2012. *The New York Times*. April 15. SR: 1, 6–7.
55 N. Gregory Mankiw. 2014. "Why Inheritance Is Not a Problem." *The New York Times*. June 22. SR: 4.
56 Roland Bénabou and Efe A. Ok. 2011. "Social Mobility and the Demand for Redistribution: The POUM Hypothesis." *The Quarterly Journal of Economics*. 116(2): 447–487.

57 Pew Charitable Trusts. 2012. "Pursing the American Dream." Retrieved on November 24 at: http://www.pewtrusts.org/en/research-and-analysis/reports/0001/01/01/pursuing-the-american-dream.
58 Joseph P. Ferrie. "The End of American Exceptionalism? Mobility in the U.S. Since 1850." Retrieved on November 25 at: http://faculty.wcas.northwestern.edu/~fe2r/papers/Exceptionalism.pdf. See also: Markus Jäntii et al. 2006. "American Exceptionalism in a New Light: A Comparison of Intergenerational Earnings Mobility in the Nordic Countries, the United Kingdom, and the United States." Bonn, Germany: Institute for the Study of Labor. Retrieved on November 25 at: http://ftp.iza.org/dp1938.pdf.
59 Raj Chetty, Nathaniel Hendren, Patrick Kline, and Emmanuel Saez. "Where Is the Land of Opportunity?" Retrieved on November 24 at: http://obs.rc.fas.harvard.edu/chetty/website/IGE/Executive%20Summary.pdf.
60 Miles Corak. 2013. "Income Inequality, Equality of Opportunity, and Intergenerational Mobility." *Journal of Economic Perspectives.* 27(3): 79–102.
61 Gregory Clark. 2014. *The Son Also Rises: Surnames and the History of Social Mobility.* Princeton, NJ: Princeton University Press.
62 Patrick J. Egan. 2014. "Measuring Inequality of Opportunity and Assessing Its Political Causes." Paper retrieved on November 24 at: http://politics.as.nyu.edu/docs/IO/4819/egan.equality.of.opportunity.entire.apr.2014.pdf.
63 Markus Jäntti et al. 2006. "American Exceptionalism in a New Light: A Comparison of Intergeneration Earnings Mobility in Nordic Countries, the United Kingdom, and the United States." Institute for the Study of Labor.
64 Orsetta Causa and Asa Johansson. 2010. "Intergenerational Social Mobility in the OECD Countries." *OECD Journal: Economic Studies.* Retrieved on November 21 at: http://www.oecd.org/eco/growth/49849281.pdf.
65 Jason DeParle. 2012. "Harder for Americans to Rise from Lower Rungs." *The New York Times.* January 4. Retrieved on November 24 at: http://query.nytimes.com/gst/fullpage.html?res=9C07E5D61E3FF936A35752C0A9649D8B63.
66 Pew Charitable Trusts. 2012. "Pursuing the American Dream: Economic Mobility across Generations." Retrieved on November 21 at: http://www.pewtrusts.org/en/research-and-analysis/reports/0001/01/01/pursuing-the-american-dream.
67 Megan McRainey. "Wealthy Parents Increased Spending on Children During Recession." Atlanta, GA: Emory University. Retrieved on November 20 at: http://news.emory.edu/stories/2014/10/upress_kornrich_parent_spending/campus.html.
68 Josh Boak. 2014. "School Spending by Affluent Is Widening Wealth Gap." Associated Press, October 1. *Missoulian.* October 1: A8.
69 Raj Chetty, Nathaniel Hendren, Patrick Kline, and Emmanuel Saez. 2013. "The Economic Impacts of Tax Expenditures: Evidence from Spatial Variation across the U.S." Cambridge, MA: Harvard University. Retrieved on November 19 at: http://obs.rc.fas.harvard.edu/chetty/tax_expenditure_soi_whitepaper.pdf.
70 Sean F. Reardon. 2011. "The Widening Academic Achievement Gap between the Rich and the Poor: New Evidence and Possible Explanations." In Richard J. Murane and Greg J. Duncan, eds., *Whither Opportunity? Rising Inequality and the Uncertain Life Chances of Low-Income Children.* New York, NY: Russell Sage Foundation.
71 Josh Zumbrun. 2014. "SAT Scores and Income Inequality: How Wealthier Kids Rank Higher." *Wall Street Journal.* October 7. Retrieved on November 20 at: http://blogs.wsj.com/economics/2014/10/07/sat-scores-and-income-inequality-how-wealthier-kids-rank-higher/.

72 Claudia Goldin and Lawrence Katz. 2010. *The Race between Education and Technology.* Cambridge, MA: Harvard University Press.
73 Organization for Cooperation and Economic Development. 2014. PISA. "Country Educational Comparisons." Retrieved on November 20 at: http://www.oecd.org/statistics/compare-your-country.htm. See also: Eduardo Porter. 2014. "A Simple Equation: More Education = More Money." *The New York Times.* September 10. Retrieved on November 20 at: http://www.nytimes.com/2014/09/11/business/economy/a-simple-equation-more-education-more-income.html.
74 OECD. 2014. Education. Retrieved on November 21 at: http://www.oecd.org/edu/eag.htm.
75 Aneki.com. 2014. "High School Graduation Rates." Retrieved on November 21 at: http://www.aneki.com/oecd_countries_high_school_graduation_rates.html?number=25.
76 UnivStats. 2014. Ivy League College Comparison. Retrieved on November 21, 2014 at: http://www.univstats.com/compare/ivy-league.
77 Michelle Jamrisko and Ilan Kolet. 2012. "Cost of College Degree in U.S. Soars 12 Fold: Chart of the Day." *Bloomberg.* August 15. Retrieved on November 20 at: http://www.bloomberg.com/news/2012-08-15/cost-of-college-degree-in-u-s-soars-12-fold-chart-of-the-day.html.
78 Edward N. Wolff, William J. Baumol, and Anne Noyes Saini. 2013. "United States vs. Other OECD Countries." *Economics of Education Review.* 39: 1–21.
79 OECD. 2012. Education at a Glance. Retrieved on November 21 at: http://www.oecd.org/edu/eag.htm.
80 Suzanne Mettler. 2014. "College, the Great Unleveler." *The New York Times.* March 2: SR5.
81 Anthony P. Carnevale. 2013. "Lifelong Benefit: Access to Money and Power." *The New York Times.* Retrieved on November 24 at: http://www.nytimes.com/roomfordebate/2010/11/29/does-it-matter-where-you-go-to-college/lifelong-benefit-access-to-money-and-power.
82 See for example, John M. Bridgeland, John J. Dilulio, Jr., and Karen Burke Morison. 2006. "The Silent Epidemic: Perspectives of High School Dropouts." Washington, DC: Peter D. Hart Research Associates; Ronald Reagan's Commission on Excellence in Education. 1983. *A Nation at Risk: The Imperative for Educational Reform.* Washington, DC: U.S. Government. Accessed on November 21 at: http://www2.ed.gov/pubs/NatAtRisk/risk.html.
83 Ibid., p.1.
84 Diane Ravich. 2013. *Reign of Error: The Hoax of Privatization Movement and the Danger to America's Public Schools.* New York, NY: Alfred A. Knopf.
85 Diane Ravich. 2010. "The Myth of Charter Schools." *The New York Review of Books.* November 11. Retrieved on February 11 at: http://www.nybooks.com/articles/archives/2010/nov/11/myth-charter-schools/.
86 Ibid.
87 John M. Bridgeland, John J. Dilulio, Jr. and Karen Burke Morison (2006). "The Silent Epidemic: Perspectives of High School Dropouts." Washington, DC: Peter Hart Research Associates.
88 *The Economist.* 2013. "The Hypergamous Chinese." July 14. Retrieved on November 25 at: http://www.economist.com/blogs/freeexchange/2013/07/chinas-marriage-market.
89 Pew Research Center. 2010. "Women, Men, and the New Economics of Marriage." Retrieved on November 25 at: http://pewsocialtrends.org/files/2010/11/new-economics-of-marriage.pdf.

90 Richard V. Reeves and Joanna Venator. 2013. "The Marriage Crisis Hurts Social Mobility." Washington, DC: The Brookings Institute. Retrieved on November 25 at: http://www.brookings.edu/blogs/social-mobility-memos/posts/2013/10/03-marriage-crisis-social-mobility-reeves-venator.
91 The Hamilton Project. 2014. "The Marriage Gap: The Impact of Economic and Technological Change on Marriage Rates." Washington, DC: The Brookings Institute. Retrieved on November 25 at: http://www.hamiltonproject.org/papers/the_marriage_gap_the_impact_of_economic_and_technological_change_on_ma/.
92 Richard V. Reeves and Joanna Venator. 2013. "The Marriage Crisis Hurts Social Mobility." Washington, DC: The Brookings Institute. Retrieved on November 25 at: http://www.brookings.edu/blogs/social-mobility-memos/posts/2013/10/03-marriagecrisis-social-mobility-reeves-venator.
93 Shelly Lundberg and Robert A. Pollak. 2013. "Cohabitation and the Uneven Retreat from Marriage in the U.S., 1950–2010." Bonn, Germany: The Institute for the Study of Labor. Retrieved on November 25 at: http://www.nber.org/papers/w19413.
94 Raj Chetty, Nathaniel Hendren, Patrick Kline, and Emmanuel Saez. 2014. "Where is the Land of Opportunity? The Geography of Intergenerational Mobility in the U S." Retrieved on November 21 at: http://obs.rc.fas.harvard.edu/chetty/website/IGE/Executive%20Summary.pdf.
95 Tony Judt with Timothy Snyder. 2012. *Thinking the Twentieth Century*. New York, NY: Random House. See also: Tony Judt. 2011. *Ill Fares the Land*. New York, NY and London: Penguin.
96 United Nations. 2014. Report on Millennium Development Goals. Retrieved on November 26 at: http://www.un.org/millenniumgoals/2014%20MDG%20report/MDG%202014%20English%20web.pdf.
97 Seth Borenstein. 2014. "Warming Won't Slow: Scientists Say Agreement by U.S., China Only a Start." Associated Press, November 13. *Missoulian*. November 13: A2.
98 Gardiner Harris. 2014. "Coal Rush in India Could Tip Balance on Climate Change." *The New York Times*. November 17. Retrieved on November 26 at: http://www.nytimes.com/2014/11/18/world/coal-rush-in-india-could-tip-balance-on-climate-change.html?_r=0.
99 International Energy Agency. 2014. "World Energy Outlook: Access to Energy." Retrieved on November 13 at: http://www.worldenergyoutlook.org/resources/energydevelopment/accesstoelectricity/.
100 Nicholas Kristof. 2014. *The New York Times*. October 22. Retried on November 13 at: http://www.nytimes.com/2014/10/23/opinion/nicholas-kristof-how-to-defeat-ebola.html.
101 Jon Greenberg. 2014. "Kristof: Dallas Cowboys Stadium Draws 3 Times More Power than Liberia Can Produce." Political Fact, October 30. Retrieved on November 13 at: http://www.politifact.com/punditfact/statements/2014/oct/30/nicholas-kristof/kristof-dallas-cowboys-stadium-draws-3-times-more-/.
102 George Marshall. 2014. *Don't Even Think about It: Why Our Brains Are Wired to Ignore Climate Change*. New York, NY and London: Bloomsbury.
103 Cited in Naomi Klein. 2014. *This Changes Everything: Capitalism vs. the Climate*. New York, NY: Simon & Schuster. Introduction.

3
CAPITALISM AND INEQUALITY

Consider:

- Capitalism is not "natural": it grew out of specific historical circumstances.
- Capitalism is both an economic and a political system, as well as a system of ideas.
- Capitalism is *one* solution to the question of how to meet basic human needs.
- All democratic countries are capitalist.
- But not all capitalist countries are democratic.
- Capitalism subordinates the biosphere to the economy.
- You can have economic growth while vast economic inequalities develop.
- Capitalism contains no built-in checks against the concentration of wealth.
- Capitalism creates inequality.

In the summer of 2013, my son and I traveled to the Peruvian Amazon and stayed at an eco-lodge located sixty miles from the nearest city, Iquitos. Iquitos, a city of 400,000, is itself isolated in that it can only be reached by boat or plane. I had not really given much thought ahead of time to where our food at the lodge would come from, what villages in the Amazon were like, or how people made a living there. The lodge purchased vegetables, fruit, chicken, eggs, and fish from a local village, and some villagers worked at the lodge for wages as kitchen help, cleaned the cabins and grounds, or provided security at night. The income villagers earned made it possible for them to stay, if they chose, rather than migrating to Iquitos or Lima to make a living.

Though many Amazonian villages were self-sufficient in the past, and still could be, they no longer are. As we traveled by boat with our guide up and down the tributaries that fed into the Amazon, we passed larger villages that served as central locations for schools, something the current Peruvian government has recently been quite good at creating and supporting. Yet sending one's children to school requires that their parents sell something—their labor, foodstuffs, or something they have made—since going to school requires modest expenditures for appropriate clothing, pencils and paper. Villagers put fish, bananas, and rice on the ferries that ply the routes between their homes and Iquitos to sell in the market. The Amazon basin, rich as it is in biological diversity, imports a majority of its food rather than exporting it. People thus take the ferries to town on shopping trips to buy food and other sundry items.

A feature of the villages with schools is that they all have soccer fields used for competition between villages. How do you get a soccer ball? You buy it. Sometimes you get the money by selling trees to loggers, who are found throughout the region. The young men who ran the speedboats between Iquitos and the lodge used their wages to buy watches, cell phones, and they dressed pretty much like young urban men dress anywhere. We went by one village during the evening and could see most villagers sitting on wooden benches in a thatch-covered open-walled room watching the glow of a television set. Electricity for the television was provided by a diesel powered generator, the fuel for which was purchased in Iquitos and transported up the river. A tall antenna above the village captured signals beamed into the jungle.

Capitalism intrudes into the Amazonian rainforest in others ways. Thousands of acres are cleared each year for farming and ranching operations and by multinational timber companies such as Georgia Pacific. There are currently over thirty multinational companies searching for oil and gas in the Amazon. Peru has opened up 75% of its Amazon territory for oil exploration, and in many cases the areas targeted for exploration are the most species-rich. The areas are also home to indigenous communities. The need for cheap energy and raw materials is thus leading to dramatic and irreversible environmental changes.

The outmigration from the Amazonian basin is continuous, with immigrants heading for the town of Iquitos or the capitol city, Lima. Once they reach their destination, they will most likely live in shantytowns with relatives who have made the trip before them. They will work in low-wage jobs and be fully enmeshed in the world of capitalism. This also means that they will live in a class-based society with significant differences in income and life chances from others.

What struck me about the circumstances of these villagers was how deeply capitalism had penetrated their lives, formed their consumption patterns, required them to sell their labor power to participate in their own society, and shaped their ideas about a good life. Our guide, called "Machete" by the other guides because of the energy he displayed in slashing down anything green in his path, wanted to leave. Though he had grown up in the Amazonian rainforest, he told us, "I want to leave. I'm tired of the mosquitoes." Others, like "Machete," leave because no matter how hard life will be in an urban environment, they expect it to provide them or their family members with more opportunities. They leave with hope, and for some, life will be better.

One of the many questions I was left with was, "Why did things have to be this way?" That is, how and why had capitalism penetrated into these remote regions and began to reshape the way in which people lived and worked? One answer is that once you need cash to buy the goods produced by others, you have to sell something, most likely, your labor. And once you have done that, you are enmeshed in the capitalist economy and web of systems that give rise to it and support it. All economic systems, whether modern, pre-modern, capitalist, or socialist, have to solve the problem of how to meet basic human needs, and all economic systems have to deal with the problem of production, distribution, and consumption of goods. Any given economic system is comprised of values, culture, legal and political systems, as well as such factors as available natural resources and environment.

Capitalism is an evolving economic system as well as an idea system about what we are like as human beings, the proper role of government, and the purpose and meaning of work. It is also a system by which human labor power is harnessed to generate wealth for the owners of capital. Why did capitalism take root and why does it have such a powerful influence on our ideas of how an economic system should work? Because capitalism is rooted in the Enlightenment (Age of Reason), and Enlightenment ideas still shape how we think about the world in which we live. The Enlightenment gave rise to: (1) the scientific revolution, (2) the idea that science and technology could infinitely improve humankind's lot, (3) ideas about the proper role of the state, and (4) the recognition and protection of private property rights. We would not want to jettison this set of values and ideas, nor abandon science and technology, but we need to recognize that we are now facing a shortage of natural resources, weakening the resilience of the biosphere on which human life depends and deepening inequalities between nations and people. A better understanding of capitalism may help us solve these problems.

The Enlightenment and the Rise of the Scientific Revolution

To understand how radical the transformations ushered in by the Enlightenment were, it is useful to take a quick step back to examine the social and economic conditions of the European feudal period, from the thirteenth to the fifteenth centuries. *Capitalism, which grew out of the Enlightenment in Europe, was a direct response to the crises of feudalism and the need to solve a specific set of problems.* By the beginning of the thirteenth century, agricultural production had stagnated because fertile soils had been used up and some food crops were replaced by others, such as flax, that could meet a growing industrial demand. Populations had soared during the Medieval Warm Period (950–1250 CE) at the same time that agricultural productivity had been falling, which drove food prices higher.

In the spring of 1315, heavy rains began to fall in Europe and continued on into the summer. These cool, wet conditions caused widespread crop failure and made it impossible to harvest and cure hay for the winter, leaving no fodder for cattle and horses. Poverty was already widespread, so when the price of wheat and other grains shot up, in some cases by 320%, people starved. They turned to gathering edible roots, plants, and nuts in the forests.[1] With the onset of spring in 1316, the rains began again. Peasants, who made up 95% of the population, had few options. They ate up their remaining grain, slaughtered draft animals, and sometimes abandoned children to their own fates. Rain and bad weather followed in 1317 and it is estimated that upwards of 25% of the population of Europe died in the Great Famine of 1317.[2]

Populations grew back slowly, but in 1348, a plague spread over the entire continent. The Black Death, brought on an Italian ship to Genoa from Asia, struck the cities especially hard; at the end of two years (depending on location), 25–50% of the population had died. An Italian writer, Giovanni Boccaccio, who lived through the plague, described its effects on ordinary citizens.[3] One was to sow confusion about divine laws.

> Capitalism's roots can be traced to the Enlightenment.

> In this suffering and misery of our city, the authority of human and divine laws almost disappeared for, like other men, the ministers and the executors of the laws were all dead or sick or shut up with their families, so that no duties were carried out. Every man was therefore able to do as he pleased.[4]

Social order broke down. "One citizen avoided another; hardly any neighbor troubled about others, relatives never or hardly ever visited each other." Family members abandoned one another; dead bodies filled up homes and lay rotting in the streets. "Such was the multitude of corpses brought to the churches every day and almost every hour that there was not enough consecrated ground to give them burial." Many turned away from the church, seeking explanations for their suffering in what we would understand as witchcraft and superstition.

Continued pressure on peasants led to sporadic but ineffectual uprisings throughout Europe. Life expectancies were low, even for Kings. Between the years 1000 and 1600, the average ages at death for the Kings of Scotland and England were respectively 51 and 48 years. One-third of children born did not live past the age of 5, and close to 20% of women died in childbirth. People were vexed with poverty, hunger, and disease and were being pushed off the land as nobles decided to raise sheep on what had once been tillable land.

Later, in the early sixteenth century, the corruption of the Catholic Church and the power of the Pope to legitimate the "Divine Right of Kings" was being challenged. Pope Alexander VI (1492–1503) was accused of keeping mistresses, theft, simony, and murder. Monasteries under the control of the Church often concentrated on amassing wealth and stoking superstition as a means of controlling the peasantry, rather than saving souls. Not all monarchs wished to cede authority to any Pope, nor did they wish to put up with their political intrigues, which pitted one monarch against another. Best known of the strong monarchs may be Henry VIII (1509–1547) who broke with the Church of Rome, seized monasteries, and replaced the Roman Catholic Church with his own Church of England. The Catholic Church was also challenged by the newly formed of Protestant Sects, which grew in numbers after Martin Luther (1483–1546) taught that the Bible, not the Church, was the central religious authority and that people can achieve salvation by faith alone.

Great gaps of wealth were also seen as a problem during this period of time, although concerns about the wealth of kings and queens needed to be carefully disguised. Sir Thomas More (1478–1535), or, as he is known by Catholics, Saint Thomas More, wrote in 1516 of a perfect place (which he called Utopia) where there was no private property, goods were stored in an unlocked warehouse, and people could ask for what they needed. The economy was primarily agricultural and everyone had to learn to farm and had to work for two years in the fields. Men and women all performed the same jobs, and all needed to learn a trade in addition to farming. The workday consisted of six hours, and citizens were encouraged to engage in study during their free time. To make things easier, every household was allocated two slaves, who were usually those who had committed criminal acts. Utopia was a true welfare state, with free hospitals. No one went hungry and everybody ate in a communal dining hall, with families taking turns cooking for the collective.

There is controversy about the meaning of More's *Utopia*, whether it is simply a satire or a biting critique of life in sixteenth-century England. It is most likely a critique of the new order that was beginning to take shape[5]. One line of thought sees *Utopia* as a direct attack on the rise of capitalism and the passing of the ideal of feudal collectivism. Another interpretation is that More was drawing on a Renaissance notion of Virtue, which meant honor should be accorded only to those who devoted themselves to the good of the community as a whole. The rich, said More, were "the least rather than the most deserving of our respect, since their anxiety to protect and add to their possessions generally [meant] that they worry only about their own self-interest, not about the interests of society as a whole." More expressed great bitterness about nobles who believed their merit resided in their inherited position and wealth.[6]

Challenges to received wisdom also came from other arenas. The move from a religious world view to a human-centered universe begins with Sir Francis Bacon (1561–1626), regarded as the father of modern science.[7] Bacon argued that it was on the basis of empirical and careful observations of the real world that we would come to understand the laws and principles by which it operated and learn to use that world to our maximum advantage. Bacon wanted us to free ourselves of false ideas or idols. Free of these idols we would be rational humans

> The scientific revolution ushered in a change in the way we thought about the world; armed with the tools of science we could overcome the limits of the physical world.

who used science to improve our lives. When Bacon wrote in 1605 that "necessity is the mother of all invention," he made the optimistic assumption that creative humans, armed with the tools of science, could overcome the limits imposed by the physical world.

The one man who was perhaps more than any other responsible for the scientific revolution that characterized the Enlightenment was a man born prematurely on Christmas Day in the year 1642 in a small farming town in Lincolnshire, England. Sir Isaac Newton (1642–1727) is remembered as a physicist, mathematician, astronomer, and natural philosopher (one who studies the natural sciences through the method of observation).[8] In his *Principia Mathematica* (1687) he laid the foundations for classical physics, described how gravity worked, and laid out three laws of motion. He demonstrated that whether on earth or in the heavens, all bodies were governed by the same laws.[9] The scientific revolution he helped to usher in depended on a shift in our ability to *discover the ways in which the world worked, as opposed to accepting the received wisdom of the church or kings*. This revolution turned on the notion that we were rational actors who, with the aid of science and technology, would shape the world to our satisfaction.

While Bacon and Newton laid out the principles of science, Thomas Hobbes (1558–1697) wondered how humans, given their nature, would govern themselves in a changing world. Hobbes is often best remembered for a sentence from his book *Leviathan* (1651) in which he characterized the nature of men in their "natural" state, without any form of government. Left to our own devices and our "natural" competitive nature, he said, we would be in a constant war of all against all and would have no arts, letters, or society. We would live in constant fear and danger of violent death. Summed up, he said the life of man without a government would be "solitary, poor, nasty, brutish, and short."[10] The solution to this problem was to enter into a commonwealth to protect ourselves from constant warfare. We would understand that it was in our best, or our rational, interests to form a state, but what Hobbes proposed was an absolute sovereign with whom we would form a covenant, or social contract. The sovereign would make war and peace as he saw fit, be a judge in all matters, and prescribe the rule of law.

John Locke (1632–1704) had a different idea about the role of government.[11] Locke started with the assumption that people are inherently reasonable and tolerant, not programmed for a war of all against all. Rational men entered in a contract to form civil society as a means of resolving conflict. In Locke's *Second Treatise of Government* (1690), he made clear that men have the freedom to live under the rule of government but will do so when there are clear rules to live by, commonly agreed upon, and not "subject to the inconstant, uncertain, unknown, arbitrary will of another man." Only a "government with the consent of the governed," is a legitimate government. However, his most important idea for our purpose was his concept of private property and his ideas about how the value of a good or commodity was determined.

In the *First and Second Treatise of Government*, Locke challenged the Divine Right of Kings and argued for a complete separation of church and state. He argued for the rights of the individual and for the *right to have and protect private property*. We have a right to the efforts of our labor, Locke maintained. Locke understood that it is human labor power that transforms natural or raw materials and underlies the value of all goods. This early form of the "labor theory of value" would inform the later work of Adam Smith, David Ricardo, and Karl Marx. That is, goods or commodities have no intrinsic value; their value is due to the labor power embedded in them.

In France, the ideas of Voltaire (1694–1778), along with those of Locke and other Enlightenment thinkers, had a catalytic effect. A strong advocate for the separation of church and state, Voltaire also championed the right to a fair trial and denounced a system of taxation that placed an unfair burden on ordinary citizens while sparing the clergy and nobility. The French Revolution of 1789 drew heavily on Enlightenment ideas of freedom. In overthrowing the old order the French took as their slogan, "Liberty, Equality, and Fraternity," and drew on Voltaire, who used sarcasm, wit, and his prolific pen to make fun of government, religious intolerance, and superstition.

The Enlightenment had a powerful hold on people's imaginations. Opposing ideas about environmental, economic, and resource limits were largely cast aside in the centuries that followed. William Goodwin (1756–1836) saw a future in which "There will be no war, no crimes, … and no government. Besides this, there will be no disease, anguish, melancholy, no resentment … Men will see progressive advancement of virtue and good."[12] The notion that the future would be bountiful was widely shared. Even Karl Marx, whose ideas we will explore below, believed that we had arrived at the point in history when all of our basic human needs could be met because of discoveries in science and technology and increased efficiencies in the production of food and material goods.

The Enlightenment gave rise not only to the scientific revolution but also: (1) capitalism, (2) the expansion of world trade or globalization, and (3) the development of banking and modern monetary systems. These revolutions, the French Revolution and similar developments in Europe, as well as the industrial revolution that followed, are intimately bound up with one another. For example, capitalism required a banking system, as did globalization, and globalization eventually expanded because of capitalism. New inventions stimulated by the scientific revolution made it possible for factory owners to expand productivity and ship goods to new markets. The Enlightenment was also a source of new ideas including freedom and democracy. The sociologist, Milan Zafirovski, has suggested that the establishment of a contractual basis of rights would lead to the market mechanism and capitalism.[13]

Capitalism did not and could not spring up everywhere. It required specific historical conditions for it to arise and flourish. As the financial writer and physician William Bernstein noted in *The Birth of Plenty*, there were four linked reasons why economic progress boomed in England and capitalism first took root there.[14] First was the recognition of private property rights and a legal system that guaranteed that people could keep what they created (Locke). Second was the scientific revolution that encouraged intellectual inquiry (Bacon and Newton). Third was a robust capital market that allowed entrepreneurs to take risks and to acquire the money needed to mass produce goods. Finally, there were fast and safe means for bringing goods to the public. Sailing and shipping became much safer in the late nineteenth century and, when it did, trade expanded in Europe from her colonies around the world. Bernstein's argument is similar to that of the Harvard historian, David Landes, who argued in *The Wealth and Poverty of Nations* that the reason why countries like England and the United States flourished was because of their ability to exploit science and develop technology and because they were cultures that rewarded hard work, thrift, and patience.[15] In short, a unique confluence of events led to the development of capitalism and created real economic growth.

Capitalism was both a new idea system, a revolt against tradition, and new ideas about the value and importance of work, as Landes suggested. The German philosopher and sociologist Max Weber (1864–1920) set out to understand why capitalism emerged within particular societies in the West and not within countries like China or within Islamic countries.[16] His answer in one short word: Calvinism. He noted that followers of a Calvinist tradition had a different work ethic than followers of other religions and were more successful at accumulating wealth and material goods than those who were Buddhists, Catholics, Hindus, or Muslims. John Calvin (1509–1564), like Martin Luther, was responsible for a radical alteration in how people understood their relationship with God; it was *not* mediated through Church authorities. According to Calvin's doctrine of total depravity, man was born into sin and could only be saved because of God's mercy. You could be saved only if God chose to save you. This doctrine of predestination led, argued Weber, to a state of psychological uncertainty; you never knew if you were one of the elect and could only deal with this uncertainty by following Calvin's doctrines that preached strict obedience to moral laws and hard work. This often led to worldly success. Worldly success, therefore, became a means by which people could assure themselves they were among the righteous. Being a good capitalist was a step on the road to salvation. And, for those countries to which Calvinist doctrine spread (Switzerland, Scotland, the Netherlands, Hungary, France, England and eventually, with the Puritans, to America) there was ample evidence that capitalism had taken root there.[17]

The Rise of a World System

The focus on individual nations and their fortunes distorts somewhat the picture of what was happening on a global level at the same time capitalism was taking off. The growth and spread of capitalism was not even and it did not create balanced economic growth. In fact, as world system analysis argues, *the growth of the capitalist world system automatically created global inequalities within and between nations* that persist until this day. These inequalities were rooted in the fact that some countries had navies and armies that could be used to enslave native populations and take their natural resources. This process, beginning in the fifteenth century, deepening throughout the sixteenth and continuing into the nineteenth, determined the relationships between the regions (Western Europe, Asia, Africa, and Latin America), as well as the political and economic systems that developed within them. The sociologist Immanuel Wallerstein, who developed world system analysis, saw the world as divided mainly between core and peripheral economic regions.[18] The core economies of Western Europe "developed strong central governments, extensive bureaucracies, and large mercenary armies."[19] This combination allowed merchants and industrialists to control international commerce for their own benefit. On the other hand, in the peripheral regions that were colonized by countries such as England, France, Portugal, and Spain, there were weak governments and production was organized around the exportation of raw materials to the core and coercive labor practices from which the core benefited. One can explain current income inequalities in Latin America as the result of the process of colonization.

> The Spanish and Portuguese conquests destroyed indigenous authority structures and replaced them with weak bureaucracies under the control of these European states. Powerful landlords of Hispanic origin became aristocratic capitalist famers. Enslavement of the native populations, the importation of African slaves, and coercive labor practices such as the *encomienda* and forced mine labor made possible the export of cheap raw materials to Europe.[20]

This meant that even in the periphery a few people grew rich, rigid class structures developed, and the economy as a whole remained anchored in the past. One can explain the income inequalities that exist today in Argentina, Mexico, and Peru as a result of these historic processes: when and how a country became embedded in a capitalism world system. Core nations came to dominate in three areas as a result of their jump-start on development: (1) dominance in productivity, (2) dominance in world trade, and (3) financial dominance.[21] By the nineteenth century virtually every major European power had put a stake down somewhere for the purpose of extracting riches from the labor of others. In 1800, the European core had colonized 35% of the world's territory and by 1914 it claimed 85%.[22] The United States was a latecomer to this process of colonization, and it took a somewhat different form. In 1823, we declared, under the Monroe Doctrine, that any further efforts of European nations to colonize land in North or South America would be regarded as acts of aggression requiring U.S. intervention. We then took California, New Mexico, and Texas from Mexico in the U.S.–Mexican War of 1846–1848.

One of the more egregious cases of exploitation of the periphery by the core occurred when King Leopold II of Belgium (1835–1909) simply seized what we now know as the Democratic Republic of Congo. Like other European leaders he saw overseas colonies as key to a country's wealth and greatness. Using a mercenary army, he forced native populations to collect sap from rubber plants. Villages were given quotas to meet and if they failed in their efforts, people had their hands cut off. A missionary was so upset by what he saw that he wrote to Leopold's agent saying, "I have just returned from a journey inland to the village of Insongo Mboyo. The misery and utter abandon is positively indescribable. I was so moved, Your Excellency, by the people's stories that I took the liberty of promising them that in the future you would only kill them for the crimes they commit."[23] Leopold was responsible for the death of at least 2 million people and some estimates are as high as 15 million Congolese. Because of the legacy of colonialism, the Democratic Republic of the Congo, while rich in natural resources such as oil, iron ore, and precious metals, still remains one of the poorest countries of the world.[24]

This new and emerging capitalist world system was, and still is, driven by three primary factors:

A search for cheap energy.
A search for cheap raw materials.
A search for cheap labor.[25]

All of them would have long-term environment impacts.

Capitalism was an evolving and adaptable system, which meant that putting one's finger on its pulse to explain how it worked and how it shaped relations between people was not easy. Those who wrote about it in the late eighteenth and early nineteenth centuries had a limited set of experiences on which to draw, but they were quite optimistic about its future. The views of the benefits and the downsides of capitalism would change as the historical circumstances of those writing about it changed. The point I wish to underscore is that our theories of the economy, sometimes even expressed as laws, are grounded in specific historical moments.

The Optimists: Smith and Ricardo

One of the first to write about this newly emerging economic order was the Scottish moral philosopher and economist Adam Smith (1723–1790). When Smith wrote *The Wealth of Nations* (1776), capitalism had not yet been recognized for what it was. The colonization of half the globe and the grim industrial centers that would pack people into unhealthy and dangerous environments were yet to come. Smith believed that the division of labor was a good thing because it increased production, wealth, and well-being. Everyone would be their own merchant and specialization would allow each person to do what he did best, pursuing his own rational self interest, whether it was making pins or mining coal. Said Smith, "It is not from the benevolence of the butcher, the brewer, or the baker that we expect our dinner, but for their regard to their own self-interest." Some see Smith as the godfather of capitalism: a system in which—theoretically—people end up better off because they follow their own self-interest. The *invisible hand of the market* supposedly channels people's competitive instincts in order to improve production and lower prices, which can be beneficial for everyone. He opposed restrictions on free trade because he believed that trade opened up new markets for the excess goods that would be produced by a high division of labor and it would provide commodities from other nations at a lower cost at home. If there were differences in wages, it was because some jobs took longer to learn or were especially odious, like the hangman's. Thus, if there were differences in incomes, they were "meritorious," not based on the exploitation of one class by another. In fact, in Smith's system you really do not have classes but groups of laborers with different specializations.

However, Smith also noted in his writings that this system would not work unless it could be guarded from abuse. It could work in societies in which all people knew the worth of what they produced, and where cartels and monopolies did not exist. It worked when all people who traded, bargained, and entered into contracts had the same information. Thus *Smith's capitalism relied on moral restraint and human rationality.* Smith, like others at the time, had no conception of what could happen when constraints on growth occurred because of the shortage of raw materials or the energy needed to drive the emerging industrial system. He assumed the system would just continue to grow and provide more for everyone. *Smith's ideas about the benefits of the division of labor and the ways in which a*

> Adam Smith's ideas about the ways in which a free market would work are a theory, not a statement of fact.

"free" market would work is a theory, not a statement of fact. It was an important *theory* and an important *story* about how we organize our economy, but it was and is not the only theory or story.

It is reported that David Ricardo (1772–1823), another member of the pantheon whose works gave rise to modern economics, read Adam Smith's *Wealth of Nations* at the age of 27 and decided to become an economist. He is important for our discussion because of his notions about how wealth is created, how wages are set, and his idea, which would be appropriated by Marx, that as industrialists expand their businesses, the rate of return will inevitably fall. That is, as more and more resources such as machinery are used to increase the efficiency of labor, returns on capital will diminish. Marx took this idea to its next step, which was to assert that capitalism would suffer constant crises of overproduction as industrialists in competition with one another increased their investments in plants and machinery and ramped up production in order to deal with falling rates of profit. (I'll return to the question of whether or not crises are endemic to capitalism in the following chapter.)

Like Smith, Ricardo believed people were rational economic actors and took Smith's idea of the single-minded pursuit of self-interest a step further and developed a theory of competitive advantage that suggested that each nation, not just each individual, could pursue those industries that are internationally most competitive, trading with those countries that produced something of value that the home nation did not. Ricardo argued, as many do today, that international free trade would eliminate inefficiencies and produce positive results for everyone. Today, this drive for efficiency and lower prices has been dubbed the Walmart effect. By one calculation, the opening of a Walmart in a community drives down the cost of food by 25%; 20% is the direct result of paying Walmart's lower prices, and 5% comes from stores seeking to match Walmart's prices.[26] What Ricardo did not anticipate, as Marx did, was that cheap prices would come at the expense of laboring men and women. To deal with the falling rate of profit, industrialists would not just need to improve efficiencies, but find ways to lower wage costs.

Ricardo, drawing on Thomas Malthus's theories of population growth, developed an unusual idea of how wages would and should be determined. Malthus had argued in *An Essay on the Principle of Population* (1798) that population growth would outstrip the food supply and that one effective way to limit population growth was to keep population equal to the means of subsistence. That is, you would pay workers no more than they needed to survive, even if this meant workers lived in misery and vice.[27] Ricardo was not alone in his view that the way to control workers and keep wages down was to starve them. The Reverend Joseph Townsend noted in 1817 that "legal constraint (to labor) is attended with too much trouble, violence, and noise ... whereas hunger is not only a peaceable, silent, unremitted pressure but, as the most natural motive to industry and labor, it calls forth the most powerful exertions."[28]

Wages were thus a result of the supply of workers. If the labor market worked "correctly," too many workers would allow the capitalist to pay lower wages and expand their profits. However, if capitalists were to pay workers above the cultural subsistence level, workers would simply have more children. Then, increased population would result in falling wages. Wages and profits would thus vacillate "naturally" as populations expanded and contracted.

For Ricardo, the wealth of a nation was not represented by the efforts of laboring men, women, and children but by the profits and investments of the capitalist or merchant. Merchants and capitalists would grow the economy by investing in new technologies and expanding the means of production. Workers in Ricardo's model are not members of a productive class. They have nothing to invest in growing the economy, because they must eat up all of their wages simply to live. And in fact this is pretty much the case now in the United States. In 2012, for example, 46.5 million Americans were living at or below the poverty level and had virtually no savings.[29] Ricardo was the champion of the new emerging industrial classes and argued against the interests of landlords.

In his view it wasn't just workers who were members of the nonproductive classes, but landlords. As far as he was concerned, they were virtual parasites, because they lived off of inherited wealth and did not expand the wealth of the country. Ricardo's views about the nature of capitalism, as well as those of Marx, were sharpened in debates over Britain's Corn Laws in the early nineteenth century. The Corn Laws were a tax or tariff placed on the importation of grain into England, which had the effect of raising the value of agricultural land (or rents) and reducing the profits of the industrialists. The new, emerging class of capitalists or manufacturers wanted to eliminate tariffs that would cause the price of bread to fall, enabling them to pay their workers even less. There were clear and strong divisions between free traders (who were against the Corn Laws) and protectionists in the debates. One member of the Anti–Corn Law League, Dr. Bowring, laid out the free trade position by asserting in 1848: "Jesus Christ is Free Trade and Free Trade is Jesus Christ."[30] The debates about whether to keep or repeal the Corn Laws have a remarkably contemporary flavor to them, with capitalists and merchants portrayed as the "job creators," and everyone else portrayed as a burden on the progress of capitalism.[31]

Ricardo was against tariffs, for they limited free trade and the ability of all to profit from the competitive advantage people in one country or region might enjoy over another. In his ideal system, the role of government would be to create favorable conditions for trade. Labor markets, within a nation, would be driven by what brought the greatest competitive advantage and the greatest gain in profit whether it was spinning cotton, mining coal, or building sailing ships. The profits realized by the capitalist were seen as a *natural* result of the production process. Laborers would migrate to where they could gain the greatest advantage. Today we see the logical consequence of this, as jobs are outsourced to other countries where labor is cheaper. Ricardo saw total profit as a result of the amount of capital invested. The greater the amount invested, the higher the overall gain, even if the rate of profit fell.

Ideas about how the economy *should* work, as I noted earlier, stem from the Enlightenment faith that science and technology will be used for the common good. Private property is sacrosanct. A division of labor in which each person, as a rational actor, pursues his or her own self-interest is celebrated. The role of government is to facilitate trade, not interfere in commerce. It is the capitalist who creates the conditions for economic growth. Wages are determined by the size of the labor pool and the assumption is that labor will migrate to where there are jobs. The U.S. Chamber of Commerce's list of policy priorities for 2014 embeds many of these ideas.

> The agenda includes expanding trade, producing more domestic energy, ... modernizing the regulatory process, making essential changes to entitlements, fixing the flaws in Obamacare, curbing lawsuit abuse, and advancing American innovation by protecting intellectual property. The agenda also focuses on revitalizing capital markets ... and improving education and training, which will expand opportunity, address inequality, and create jobs.[32]

Here we find encouraging free trade, limiting government regulation, pushing innovation, protecting private property, and improving the environment for creating jobs—all elements of Enlightenment thinking. But not everyone has believed that capitalism would usher in a utopia.

The Pessimist: Marx

Karl Marx (1818–1883) had a very different understanding from those of Smith and Ricardo of the new economic system that was emerging, even though he shared their beliefs that labor costs underlay the value of all commodities, that investments in agriculture would produce diminishing returns, and that humans were rationally calculating actors. He saw competition as driving efficiencies that would benefit all of humankind, provided *workers and* not *capitalists* were the ones to benefit from new technologies, and provided *workers owned the products of their labor*. He believed that capitalism would collapse and a new socialist order would arise. (I'll note the reasons why Marx thought this in the next chapter.)

Marx also wrote about the Corn Laws but, unlike Ricardo, framed the discussion as an argument about who would benefit from the efforts of workers, regardless of whether they worked in factories or labored on farms. In a speech to the Democratic Association of Workers in 1848, Marx noted that English workers "[knew] very well that the price of bread was to be reduced [by eliminating tariffs] in order to reduce wages, and that industrial profit would rise [accordingly]."[33] In the same speech he laid out ideas that would provide the framework for *Capital* ("*Das Kapital,*" 1885). He understood that labor was not only the source of value but that *labor itself was a commodity, like any other.*

Smith, Ricardo, and Marx all understood labor to be a key factor in establishing the value of commodities.[34] Borrowing from Adam Smith, Marx made a distinction between use value and exchange value. The term use value means just what it says; it refers to the usefulness of an object. If someone knits a sweater and wears it, it has *use value* to the owner but it doesn't have a price. It would have a price (or *exchange value*) only if it were traded for something else. The owner of the sweater might exchange it for six bushels of wheat, in the kind of world imagined by Adam Smith, where the person who knit the sweater and the farmer who harvested and planted wheat each knew how much time and effort it took the other person to produce the good in question. Marx reasoned, then, that if a commodity has no intrinsic value, the value realized in exchange must be determined by something else. That something else was the amount of human labor embedded in it. This was the essence of the labor theory of value.[35]

As Marx explained, "Commodities, therefore, in which equal quantities of labor are embodied, or which can be produced in the same time, have the same value ... [A]ll commodities are only definite masses of congealed labor time."[36] This doesn't mean that sweaters confront bushels of wheat in the marketplace. It means that humans confront one another through the products of their labor. Relations between people become, in a market system, relationships between things. While using our laptop computer, we do not see the labor of the Taiwanese worker who spent long hours assembling parts that were made by robots, or the workers who built the robots in Germany, or the labor of those who dug tantalum, tungsten, or gold out of the ground in the Congo for the circuit boards, or the steel workers in South Korea who made the metal for the robots. Virtually everything we use and consume in the modern world has labor power *as a commodity* embedded in it.

In a capitalist system everything is a commodity that can be bought and sold, including labor power. Production is not for the purpose of meeting human needs but for making a profit. As the conservative, Nobel Prize–winning economist, Milton Friedman, once said, the sole purpose of a business in a system of free enterprise is to increase its profits.[37] Marx argued that capitalists extract surplus labor power, or value, by not paying the worker for the full value of what the worker produces. This is how they stay in business. The capitalist, depending on the nature of the business, will have an investment in plants and machinery, distribution and transportation of goods, research and development expenditures, and so forth. For example, the owner of a Subway sandwich franchise has to pay the upfront costs for a franchise (around $200,000+), pay for a business license, utilities, the annual cost of the franchise, the ingredients for the sandwiches, the wages of the workers, and so on. Workers must be sufficiently productive and make enough sandwiches in a year to pay for the owner's annual expenses and leave the owner with a profit—the surplus. For a Subway franchise owner to realize $60,000 in yearly profit he or she would need to sell $1,000 worth of food every day.[38] Unless you have a very good location, that is hard to do; you might go bankrupt.

This is the basis of capitalism, or the free enterprise system. You benefit from the risks you take. This division between worker and owner was seen by Marx as the fault line in capitalism and gave rise, automatically, to inequalities in income and wealth. Few would argue about this principle, although they sometimes try to disguise the logic behind the inequities that result as due to the *invisible hand of the market*. For it to be invisible you would have to wear blinders.

Theoretically, there are two ways for the capitalist to increase surplus value or profit. One, which is *absolute surplus value*, is to simply increase the numbers of hours worked, or the number of days or weeks in a year. When Marx wrote, men worked upwards of at least 12 hours a day for 6 days a week. Women and children were pressed into work in factories and they, too, put in long hours in miserable working conditions. In Marx's words, "It is in the absolute interest of every capitalist to press a given quantity of labor out of a smaller, rather than a greater number of laborers," as a means of increasing surplus value.[39] During the worldwide economic crisis of 2007–2011, some businesses cut the number of employees and let the remaining workers shoulder the burden of their departed colleagues with no additional compensation. As of 2015, profit margins remain high for corporations while the size of the workforce has not been restored to pre-crisis levels in the United States or in Western Europe.[40] What did increase was the number of part-time workers. The Bureau of Statistics for England showed that between September 2012 and September 2013, the number of part-time workers jumped by 100,000 for a total of nine million. In the United States, between 2007 and 2013 the percentage of those working part-time rose from 16.9% to 19.2%, an increase of 2.8 million people.[41] The exploitation of workers giving rise to surplus value or profits occurs in both the developed and developing world, or the core and periphery, to use the terms introduced above.

Leslie T. Chang, a former Beijing correspondent for the *Wall Street Journal*, followed two young women for three years. They were part of the exodus of 130 million migrants from rural villages to urban centers in China, looking for work in 2008.[42] One of the young women, Min, applied for work at Carrin Electronics, a Hong Kong firm that makes clocks, calculators, and electronic calendars. When she went for an interview, she was not allowed inside the factory. When she was hired and started work, she found that women were required to sleep twelve to a dirty room in bunks next to the toilets. A thousand women worked in the factory, either teenagers newly arrived from the countryside or married women over the age of 30 with no other prospects. Workers ate in the company canteen where a meal often consisted of rice, one meat or vegetable dish, and watery soup. A working day lasted 13 hours with two breaks for meals. Bathroom breaks were limited to ten minutes every four hours and required a sign-up list. Talking on the job resulted in small fines deducted from wages, as were costs of clothing when winter clothes were switched for summer ones. Min wanted to quit, but quitting was not an option, because the factory held back two months of a worker's pay until they had completed their six-month contract. The exploitation of immigrant workers, whether from other countries or domestic rural areas, is common. If they are refugees, as are Syrians and Iraqis who have fled to Turkey and Jordon and who are now trying to make their way to Western Europe because of civil war ….

There are even more dire ways to increase profits. Thailand is now listed by the U.S. State Department as one of the worst violators of human rights in the world because of its involvement in human trafficking, especially the sex trade. In addition, as reported in the *New York Times* in 2014, men from Myanmar, Cambodia, and Thailand who have paid brokers to help them find work have been literally sold to ship owners. "Under threat of jail or deportation and desperate for income, they are forced to work 18–20 hours a day, seven days a week, for very low wages and are often threatened and beaten."[43]

Another way to increase value—in this case *relative surplus value*—is to replace workers with machinery to speed up production. It can also be done by lowering wages or reducing the cost of the materials used by the workers to produce commodities. Something Marx did not anticipate was the migration of workers across international borders in search of work, regardless of the low pay. Nor did he anticipate companies moving across borders. Cheap labor was the reason Carrin Electronics set up their factory in China, why Apple has its iPods manufactured there, and the reason garment manufacturers locate in countries as diverse as Haiti, Vietnam, and Bangladesh. Because of a lack of opportunity at home, Pakistani workers labor in the oil fields of Kuwait; Philippine women are working in the United Arab Emirates as maids, and men from the Horn of Africa are working in Saudi Arabia as agricultural laborers.

> Marx understood that the social relations of production determined the social distribution of profits.

Marx's genius was to demystify how capitalism worked and how it would evolve. As for how it worked, he sought to answer the question, How is it that capitalists can increase the hours labored, speed up the production process, and cut workers' pay? His answer lay in his analysis of the social relations of production. It is worth quoting Marx at length to understand what he meant by this concept.

> In the social production of their existence, men inevitably enter into definite relations, which are independent of their will, namely relations of production appropriate to a given stage in the development of their material forces of production. The totality of these relations of production constitutes the economic structure of society, the foundation, on which arises a legal and political superstructure and which correspond to definite forms of social consciousness.[44]

The point to be emphasized is that *the way in which production is organized determines how distribution occurs*. It cannot be otherwise. The point of capitalism is to produce a profit and how this profit gets distributed is determined by ownership of production and by legal and political systems designed to assure how profits get distributed.[45] *Social power thus reinforces economic inequality.* As Max Weber also understood, economic power could be translated into political power to maintain the status quo. I will expand on this topic in Chapter 7, which deals with the "war" against working men and women, but I want to emphasize that the issue of distribution is by no means one-sided or settled once and for all. Capitalists don't always get their way. For example, the Koch brothers, David and Charles, who have become the poster boys for free enterprise in the United States, have poured literally millions of dollars into political campaigns designed to elect pro-business, anti-union sympathizers to public office at the state and national level. They put $400 million of their own and others' money toward defeating Barak Obama in the 2012 Presidential Election, only to have their candidate, Mitt Romney, defeated soundly.[46]

As economic inequality increases, political and economic systems move from openness to closure. Openness is what characterizes democracies. *Inequality thus threatens democracy itself.* Kenneth Vogel, who has written extensively about campaign financing, noted in *Big Money* that in the 2012 Presidential election in the United States, 5.7 million small donors contributed a total of $370 million to the campaigns of Obama and Romney, but another $470 million was given by just 100 people.[47] In addition, close to $7 billion was spent on all races in 2012, much of it coming from groups shrouded in the secrecy made possible by the U.S. Supreme Court's ruling in 2010—the *Citizens United* case—that megadonors can now make contributions in unlimited amounts. The Koch brothers have indicated they intend to spend $889 million in support of various conservative issues in the run-up to the 2016 Presidential Election.

Summary

The ideas and values that gave rise to capitalism and still serve to undergird it grew directly out of the Enlightenment. These are ideas about the kind of government that best allows for human freedom and expression as well as ideas about our ability to solve the problems we confront using science and technology. Capitalism arose in the West because of a unique confluence of events: the crises of feudalism, the scientific revolution, the liberating ideas of the Enlightenment, technological innovations, and a culture that valued work. Early writers like Adam Smith and David Ricardo sought to understand the nature of this emerging order and assumed that economic and social progress would be harmonious and that everyone would be better off as a result. The cautionary note that Smith offered—that enterprise would need to be guided by moral restraint—has been largely ignored.

The optimistic views offered by Smith and Ricardo were challenged by Marx, who understood that the way in which work was organized in a capitalist society *automatically* determined the distribution of profits. It could be no other way. Once people sold their labor power, the capitalist used that labor power to create a surplus; they had to take a greater share than the worker so they could realize a profit. Marx saw capitalism not as a system designed to meet human needs but to make a profit. It thus wasted human potential and wasted material resources.

Through a Sustainability Lens

Ecological systems, social and political systems, and economic systems are tightly woven together but not always to the benefit of everyone or to the benefit of the planet. As I noted in the case of the Amazon, an entire ecosystem is being altered and the damage is not reversible. Because of our need for cheap raw materials, energy, and human labor, we have wrecked and continue to wreak havoc on the environment that sustains us. Growing populations and a desire for an improved quality of life for those in developing countries will increase these pressures. So far, we have met these crises in energy, food, and labor by mastering the environment, inventing new technologies, finding new energy sources, or picking up and moving someplace else, especially to cities. We created a green revolution with the use of chemical fertilizers and genetically modified organisms (GMOs) that have allowed us to feed many more people, and some of them very well. Every new crisis has meant a transformation in how we relate to the natural world. One critique of capitalism is that it externalizes environmental costs and leads to the systematic degradation of ecosystems across the planet.[48]

We can and must change this because *we are running up against what appear to be hard ceilings*. As the historian Ian Morris has said, we may have thought we solved the crises of famine, state failure, migration, and disease, but they are back in a different form.[49] Today's Horsemen of the Apocalypse are climate change, inequity, and energy poverty. There are answers that do not require jettisoning the values of the Enlightenment and that underscore humans' creative ability. If we can determine the kind of future we wish to create—and it will have to be a sustainable one—we can then make progress toward that future. What stands in the way are institutions, which we created, that push toward closed economic and political systems. Our final chapter describes how we can and must free up human capital to use the science of the known world to manage our future and create new institutions.

Notes

1 *Medieval Sourcebook*. 2014. "Famine of 1315." Fordham University. Accessed on July 10, 2014 at: http://www.fordham.edu/halsall/sbook.asp.
2 Teofilo F. Ruiz. 2014. *Medieval Europe: Crisis and Renewal*. Lecture 5. "An Age of Crisis: Hunger." The Great Courses. Retrieved on July 10, 2014 at: http://www.thegreatcourses.com/tgc/courses/course_detail.aspx?cid=863; see also, John Aberth. 2009. *From the Brink of the Apocalypse: Confronting Famine, Plague, War and Death in the Later Middle Ages*. New York, NY: Routledge.
3 Giovanni Boccaccio. 1348 (1930). "The Black Death, 1348: Eyewitness to History." Translated by Richard Aldington. Accessed on July 10, 2014 at: http://www.eyewitnesstohistory.com/plague.htm.
4 Ibid.
5 Quentin Skinner. 1978. "The Lesson of Thomas More." *The New York Review of Books*. October 12. Accessed on July 8, 2014 at: http://www.nybooks.com/articles/archives/1978/oct/12/the-lesson-of-thomas-more/.
6 Ibid.
7 Sir Francis Bacon. 1597 (1875). Published as *The Essays of Sir Francis Bacon*. London: Longman and Green.
8 For an exceptional story about Newton, his life, and his role in the Enlightenment, see Thomas Levenson. 2009. *Newton and the Counterfeiter*. New York, NY: Houghton Mifflin.
9 The three laws of motion follow. First, there is the law of inertia, which means that everything stays the same unless something acts on it, for instance, an external force. Second, there is a relationship between the mass of an object and the rate of acceleration. For an object to move there must be a force with a greater mass acting on it. Third, for every action there is an equal and opposite reaction.
10 Hobbes. 1678. *Leviathan*. Chapter 13, paragraph 9.

11 For an overview of Locke's philosophy see *The Stanford Encyclopedia of Philosophy*. Accessed on November 16, 2011 at: http://plato.stanford.edu/entries/locke/.
12 William Godwin. 1793. *Enquiry Concerning Political Culture and Its Influence on Morals*. Vol. 2: 528. London: G.G.J. and J. Robinson. Spelling has been changed to reflect current usage. Retrieved on June 17, 2014 at: http://knarf.english.upenn.edu/Godwin/pj87.html.
13 Milan Zafirovski. 2010. The Enlightenment and Its Effects on Modern Society. New York, NY: Springer.
14 William J. Berstein. 2010. *The Birth of Plenty: How the Prosperity of the Modern World Was Created*. New York, NY: McGraw Hill.
15 David S. Landes. 1999. *The Wealth and Poverty of Nations: Why Some Are Rich and Some So Poor*. New York, NY: W.W. Norton.
16 Weber, Max. 1905/2002. *The Protestant Ethic and the Spirit of Capitalism*. Trans. Peter Baehr and Gordon C. Wells. New York, NY: Penguin.
17 There have been challenges to Weber's idea that capitalism grew in the West because of the doctrine of Calvinism. Our position is that Calvinism was part of a total package (ideology, globalization, exploration, environmental challenges) that led to the development of the West.
18 Immanuel Wallerstein. 1974. *The Modern World System I: Capitalist Agriculture and the Origins of the European World-Economy in the Sixteenth Century*. New York, NY: Academic Press.
19 Paul Halsall. 1997. *Modern History Sourcebook: Summary of Wallerstein on World System Theory*. New York, NY: Fordham University. Accessed on July 7, 2014 at: http://www.fordham.edu/halsall/mod/Wallerstein.asp.
20 Ibid., p.2.
21 Immanuel Wallerstein. 1980. *The Modern World System II: Mercantilism and the Consolidation of the European World-Economy, 1600–1750*. New York, NY: Academic Press.
22 Paul Kennedy. 1987. *The Rise and Fall of the Great Powers: Economic Change and Military Conflict from 1500 to 2000*. New York, NY: Random House.
23 Mark Dummett. 2004. "King Leopold's Legacy of DR Congo Violence." BBC Report. Retrieved on July 7, 2014 at: http://news.bbc.co.uk/2/hi/africa/3516965.stm.
24 Central Intelligence Agency. 2014. *World Fact Book*. Accessed on July 8, 2014 at: https://www.cia.gov/library/publications/the-world-factbook/geos/cg.html.
25 World systems theory sees the evolution of capitalism as driven by these three factors.
26 Charles Fishman. 2006. *The Wal-Mart Effect: How the World's Most Powerful Company Really Works—and How It's Transforming the American Economy*. New York, NY: Penguin reprint edition.
27 Thomas Robert Malthus. 1798. *An Essay on the Principle of Population*. Depending on the edition accessed this citation comes at the end of Chapter 7.
28 Cited in Mick Brooks. 2002. "An Introduction to Marx's Labor Theory of Value—Part One." Retrieved on June 11, 2014 at: http://www.marxist.com/marx-marxist-labour-theory-value.htm.
29 United States Census Bureau. 2014. Accessed on June 4, 2014 at: http://blogs.census.gov/2012/06/18/changes-in-household-net-worth-from-2005-to-2010/.
30 E.A. Bowring and V.H. Hobart. 1848. *Free Trade and Its So-Called Sophisms: A Reply*. Accessed on June 4, 2014 at: http://books.google.com/books/about/Free_trade_and_its_so_called_sophisms_a.html?id=aogDAAAAQAAJ.

31 John Boehner, former Republican Speaker of the House, has portrayed his party as the one most interested in job creation. The supposed proof of this is the Party's opposition to "Obamacare," climate change regulation, and their opposition to increasing the Federal Minimum wage, which they claim all limit the ability of businessmen and women to make a profit and create jobs. John Boehner. 2014. Speech in House. Accessed on June 4, 2014 at: http://www.newsmax.com/Newsfront/john-boehner-gop-job-creation/2014/04/26/id/567883/.

32 U.S. Chamber of Commerce. 2014. *Policy Priorities for 2014*. Accessed on June 17, 2014 at: https://www.uschamber.com/about-us/us-chamber-policy-priorities-2014.

33 Karl Marx. 1848. "On the Question of Free Trade." Speech before the Democratic Association of Brussels. Accessed on June 11, 2014 at: http://www.cooperativeindividualism.org/marx-karl_on-the-question-of-free-trade-1848.html.

34 There are debates within Marxist theory and in modern economic theory about whether or not the labor theory of value has meaning. Many economists argue, for example, that marginal utility determines price. Wikipedia, for example, has a good summary of criticisms of the theory. See: http://en.wikipedia.org/wiki/Criticisms_of_the_labour_theory_of_value. There are also Marxist explications of why the labor theory of value is important as a means of understanding the logic of contemporary capitalism. See, for example, Samir Amin. 2013. *Three Essays on Marx's Value Theory*. New York, NY: Monthly Review Press.

35 There are numerous objections raised about the labor theory of value and whether it is a "law" or a "tendency." For example, the profit realized by Microsoft from its monopoly on an operating system has created great wealth for the firms' founders. There is little labor cost involved in reproducing the disks that contain, say, Office 7 or Windows. In the case of intellectual property, it is difficult to identify the labor involved or to see a tight link between price and labor costs. As many Marxists would note this misses the point, which is that labor power is a commodity.

36 Karl Marx. 1867. *Capital*, Vol. 1—Part 1: Commodities and Money. Chapter 1: Commodities. Retrieved on June 11, 2014 at: http://marxists.org/archive/marx/works/1867-c1/ch01.htm.

37 Milton Friedman. 1970. "The Social Responsibility of Business Is to Increase Its Profits." *The New York Times Magazine*. September 13, 1970. Retrieved on June 11, 2014 at: http://www.colorado.edu/studentgroups/libertarians/issues/friedman-soc-resp-business.html.

38 Average profit of a Subway franchise owner. Retrieved on July 17, 2014 at: http://www.ask.com/question/how-much-does-the-average-owner-of-a-subway-franchise-make-annually.

39 Karl Marx, 1867. *Capital*, Vol. 1, Chapter 25. Retrieved on June 11, 2014 at: http://en.communpedia.org/Reserve_army_of_labour.

40 Sam Ro. 2014. "Here's the Big Tailwind to Corporate Profit Margins That Everyone Has Forgotten." *Business Insider*. Retrieved on June 11, 2014 at: http://www.businessinsider.com/pension-cost-profit-margin-tailwind-2014-1.

41 Catherine Rampell. 2013. "The Rise of Part-Time Work." *The New York Times*. March 8. Retrieved on July 17, 2014 at: http://economix.blogs.nytimes.com/2013/03/08/the-rise-of-part-time-work/.

42 Leslie T. Chang. 2008. *Factory Girls: From Village to City in a Changing China*. New York, NY: Random House.

43 The Editorial Board, *The New York Times*. 2014. "Slavery and the Shrimp on Your Plate." June 22. Retrieved on June 23, 2014 at: http://readersupportednews.org/opinion2/277-75/24383-slavery-and-the-shrimp-on-your-plate.

44 Karl Marx. 1859. Preface to *A Contribution to the Critique of Political Economy*. Retrieved on June 16, 2014 at: http://www.marxists.org/archive/marx/works/1859/critique-pol-economy/preface.htm.

45 These points are made by Marx in *Grundrisse*. 1858.

46 Daniel Shulman. 2014. *Sons of Wichita: How the Koch Brothers became America's Most Powerful and Private Dynasty*. New York, NY: Grand Central; see also Michael Tomasky. 2014. "The Billionaire Koch Brothers." *The New York Review of Books*. June 19: 22–24.

47 Kenneth P. Vogel. 2014. *Big Money: 2.5 Billion Dollars, One Suspicious Vehicle, and a Pimp—on the Trail of the Ultra-Rich Hijacking American Politics*. Washington, DC: Public Affairs.

48 Fred Magdoff and John Bellay Foster. 2011. *What Every Environmentalist Needs to Know about Capitalism*. New York, NY: Monthly Review Press.

49 Ian Morris (2011). *Why the West Rules—For Now: The Patterns of History, and What They Reveal about the Future*. New York, NY: Macmillan (Picador).

4
THE CONTINUING CRISES OF CAPITALISM

Consider:

- A free market increases inequality.
- Capitalism runs on cheap energy, labor, and raw materials.
- The values that gave rise to capitalism can serve to undermine it.
- The concentration of wealth and income leads to a concentration of political power.
- Only the modern state can play an active role in creating the conditions for economic growth and mitigating the effects of income concentration.
- Capitalism has not yet collapsed because it continually reinvents itself; however, it must solve the problems of inequity, destruction of the biosphere, and energy inequality to endure.

Karl Marx's understanding of capitalism was that it would ultimately implode and give rise to a new economic and political system. This has not happened but it is important to understand why Marx thought that capitalism "contained the seeds of its own destruction." There are at least two primary and related reasons he did:

- The tendency of the rate of profit to fall.
- The crisis of overproduction.

Was Marx Right?

Let me start with the falling rate of profit. It is important to recall how the value of goods is created. Goods acquire value, as Adam Smith and David Ricardo noted,[1] when they are transformed by labor. However, Marx realized that under capitalism there were two kinds of labor embedded in all commodities. Every commodity that gets sold—car, television set, or smart phone—contains two forms of labor time: necessary labor time (the time it takes to transform something into a commodity) and surplus labor time (the time taken by the employer in order to realize a profit). Ford Motor Company has to sell its popular pickup, the F-150, for more than the labor time it takes to make it, or it would go out of business.

It is logical for the capitalists do whatever they can to increase surplus value, and they can do this by driving down wage costs, speeding up production, making people work longer hours, or simply not paying them for all the hours they work. This logic applies whether they are flipping hamburgers or processing insurance claims. After the capitalist has squeezed out all of the surplus value possible from the production process, they then need to find new ways to magnify their profits or return on their investment.

> Addiction to growth is part of capitalism's DNA. There can be no steady-state capitalist economy.

To increase productivity, they can invest in machinery and equipment to amplify labor power and increase surplus value. However, the greater the investment in plants and machinery, the lower will be the rate of profit. Consider this simple formula of $R = L/C$, where R is the rate of profit, C represents fixed capital investment (machinery, plants, and so forth), and L represents the costs of labor. Even if labor costs are constant or driven to the lowest level possible, and the denominator (C) increases because of investments in capital equipment, then R, the rate of return, *must* decrease. Hence, the "law" of the falling rate of profit gives rise to the second source of crisis, overproduction.

The capitalist must sell the commodities produced in order to realize the surplus value—the unpaid labor—embedded in them. According to Marx, the sole purpose of capitalism is to produce a profit rather than to meet human needs. To offset a falling rate of profit, more must be produced and sold. The enterprise must be continually expanded in order to just maintain the same level of wealth or capital. Marx reasoned that competition among capitalists would further erode profits, as each searched for new and cheaper ways to reduce the cost of labor and maximize efficiency.[2] But each would need to sell more goods, which would lead to overproduction and warehouses full of goods. As the saying goes, capitalism must grow or die. *Addiction to growth is in capitalism's DNA.* There can be no steady-state economy, but only one that lurches from boom to bust.

Add up all of these elements and they point toward collapse. Why? Workers will always be paid less than the value of their work, which means that workers cannot pay for all the goods consumed. So capitalists need to find new buyers in other countries. Coca-Cola and Pepsi, for example, have opened up bottling plants for carbonated drinks, bottled water, flavored waters, and "vitamin" drinks throughout Latin America, Asia, and Africa. They could instead create new "products." Coca-Cola is also trying to expand its share of the market for drinks in the United States by packaging milk, and marketing it as a healthy choice.

At a certain point, however, world markets are saturated with goods and competition and price-cutting lowers the rate of profit. The "solution" to the falling rate of profit is to capture a larger share of the market, which often occurs through consolidation and centralization. Google, had it existed when Marx was writing, would have been an example of the concentration of capital. Since 2010, Google has been acquiring more than one firm a week, and as of 2013, had bought over 100 companies, including Motorola, for which it paid $12.5 billion.[3]

Big companies buy out small companies. Walmart and Target replace corner grocery stores, and Walgreen's and CVS replace the local pharmacy. Airlines and insurance companies outsource work to developing countries, and manufacturers shift fabrication to Taiwan, Vietnam, and Thailand. This also means that workers get laid off, which means again they cannot buy all of the goods produced, which then leads to economic stagnation. This is not just as theoretical issue. We can see it happening today.

As the political economists John Bellamy Foster and Robert W. McChesney have demonstrated in *The Endless Crisis*, stagnation has set in, not just in Western industrialized countries but also in China.[4] There is a worldwide crisis of overproduction, resulting in an overaccumulation of capital. For example, manufacturing capacity in the United States has dropped from a high of about 84% in 1970 to around 77% today. Plants are sitting idle. One reason for the decline is that manufactured goods from low-wage countries substitute for high-wage manufactured goods. But even though manufacturing capacity has dropped, overall profits for major multinationals have not fallen, in part because the price of goods has remained high. If you can cut wages and still maintain your rate of profit by marking up the price of goods, you can temporarily deal with the problem of the falling rate of profit. As the Council of Economic Advisors noted in 2012, the "price markup is the highest in postwar history," and the benefits of those price markups have gone to the owners of capital.[5] Since 1980, for example, worker productivity driven by mechanization has increased by 240%. However, workers have not shared in the growth of capitalism. Wages have stayed flat, while the income of the top 1% has gone up by 80%.[6] This is exactly the type of scenario envisioned by Marx: Due to wage cuts and overproduction, there is nobody left who can afford the goods being produced. These contradictions have given rise to a new form of capitalism.

If the rate of profit falls and there is a crisis of overaccumulation, then where do capitalists put their money? Research by the French economist Thomas Philippon has shown that the financial sector now accounts for 8.4% of all the goods and services produced annually in the United States (Gross National Product; GNP), up from 2.8% in 1950.[7] This represents *a transformation of the form of capital that is dominant, though not a transformation of the logic of capitalism.* This shift in the share of growth of the financial sector is a process referred to as financialization, in which financial leverage overrides capital investments and dominates traditional industrial and agricultural economies. Financialization reduces everything that can be bought, sold, or traded to a *commodity*. For example, mortgage-backed securities are asset-backed securities; mortgages are commonly pooled into hundreds or thousands of mortgages which are then sold to a bank, which securitizes or bundles the mortgages into a security that can be sold to investors. Problems, such as in the financial collapse of 2007–2008, arise when the assets' values drops. Foster and McChesney have argued that the financialization of the accumulation process is seen as a way to offset stagflation and to stimulate consumption. Basically, the people with surplus capital have to find some means other than investing in industry to magnify their wealth, which means investing in the financial sector. *Consumption, made possible by extending credit, drives the economy in this model.*

Robert Reich, Berkeley professor and former Secretary of Labor under President Bill Clinton, focused in his book *Aftershock* on the effects of the economic crisis of 2007–2008 on the American middle class.[8] In his view, inequity helped to drive the collapse. When wages do not rise, but costs for medical care, sending a child to college, and household expenses increase, people need to find ways to cope. First, starting in the 1970s, with wage stagnation, women entered the workforce, giving some families second incomes. Parents put in longer hours, but finally they went into debt, borrowing on the equity in their homes or running up credit card debt. They also went into debt for psychological reasons: As noted in Chapter 1, people need to feel as though they can participate fully in the societies to which they belong. If others are spending, they also spend, although the poor and middle class cannot spend much relative to the 1%.

> Though the form of capitalism has changed over the centuries, the logic of capitalism remains unchanged.

Why Doesn't Capitalism Collapse?

One explanation for the resilience of capitalism is that each crisis leads to a reshaping and re-engineering of the capitalist system, like the financialization of capital. From the perspective of the Adam Smith Society, capitalism survives because it evolves in a Darwinian fashion, weeding out the weak from the strong.[9] As the political economist and geographer David Harvey has noted, "Much gets torn down and laid waste to make way for the new."

> Once productive landscapes are turned into industrial wastelands, old factories are torn down or converted to new uses, working-class neighborhoods get gentrified … Business parks, R&D [Research and Development], and wholesale warehousing and distribution centers sprawl across the land in the midst

of suburban tract housing, linked together with cloverleafed highways ... Golf courses and gated communities pioneered in the USA can now be seen in China, Chile, and India, contrasting with sprawling squatter and self-built settlements ...[10]

Each change, each crisis, and each stage of capitalism brings with it dramatic changes in the ways we understand how the world works. How one thinks about capitalism, its benefits, and its downside depends a great deal on specific historical conditions. The logic of capitalism remains, but how we think about capitalism has changed over the centuries.

There were good empirical reasons why men like Smith and Ricardo painted such a rosy picture of the new nineteenth century's emerging economic order. Democracy itself, the outcome of struggles between rulers and ruled, was neither smooth nor even, but it made it possible for growing numbers of people to express their social, political, and economic needs.[11] Capitalism had become part of the fabric of democratic societies, and democratic societies created the conditions for economic growth, which improved the lot of ordinary people.

The rise of capitalism and ideas about its advantages and disadvantages were often conflated with ideas about the value of industrialization itself. It would take until the 1800s before writers like Charles Dickens, depicted the filth, foul air, and economic hardships of the working poor in London. Friedrich Engels, Marx's collaborator, completed a survey published as *The Condition of the Working Class in England* (1845) in which he documented higher mortality rates from smallpox, measles, scarlet fever, and whooping cough among industrial workers in cities like Liverpool and Manchester compared to those who lived in the countryside. The French writer Émile Zola wrote in his novel *Germinal* (1885) about the violence, alcoholism, and misery that accompanied the rise of the Industrial Revolution in France and characterized the despair and anarchy that typified working-class communities. Somewhat later in the United States, writers like Frank Norris and Upton Sinclair would do the same. Today the focus on the downside of capitalism may shift to those sold as slaves, those living in their cars or "camping out," or those picking saleable trash out of rubbish heaps in Mumbai or Lagos.

Whatever one's perspective, one thing in the nineteenth century was clear: the world economy was changing dramatically, introducing radical new divisions of labor, and creating new classes whose interests were seldom compatible. Concerns about the nature of the evolving economic order would persist into the twentieth century. Was capitalism a system that would endure? The answers and economic theories that developed during the aftermath of the two world wars were driven in large part by the lived experiences of the theorists and the role they thought the state ought to play in stimulating growth and mitigating the excesses of an unchained market. Many of the ideas developed during this period of time still have significance and traction today.

Will Capitalism Survive?

Joseph Schumpeter's (1883–1950) answer to the question was an emphatic "No." His 1942 book *Capitalism, Socialism, and Democracy* is one of the most important and debated economic texts of all time.[12] In that work he champions the notion of creative destruction, which is the process by which spirited entrepreneurs drive long-term economic growth by destroying the value of the old through radically new innovations. Capitalism thus renews itself from within without the need for state intervention.

Schumpeter wrote that this situation would create a class of intellectuals who would want to replace capitalism with some form of socialism. The revolution could be a soft one in which social democratic parties, which would distribute wealth more evenly, would be voted into office. Where would these intellectuals come from? They would emerge out of the democratic societies that supported universal education, but the lack of appropriate work for these intellectuals would lead to their disaffection with, and the undoing of, capitalism. (There were countries, such as Sweden, Denmark, and Norway, in which social democratic parties became ascendant but not because there was no work for intellectuals.)

In the aftermath of World War II, Karl Polanyi, an Austro-Hungarian economist, also wrote that capitalism was inherently unstable. *The Great Transformation*, published in 1944, suggested that strong state systems were necessary for capitalism to grow. The state needed to push transformations in old social orders rooted in values like the family and community in order for capitalism to expand, and it needed to create "free" markets. In short, capitalism was a culture-busting system. *And because the operation of free markets produced radical social disruptions, the state would also have to act in order to mitigate the excesses of capitalism.* This balancing act between the needs of capital and the needs of humans would, Polanyi predicted, be the future function of the capitalist state.[13]

World events also informed the work of two other prominent economists, John Maynard Keynes and Friedrich Hayek, and their views on the proper role of government in a capitalist economy. John Maynard Keynes (1883–1946) outlined his main ideas in 1936 in *The General Theory of Employment, Interest, and Money*.[14] Before Keynes, economists drawing on the ideas of Ricardo had argued that the economy was generally in equilibrium and that full employment was the norm, not the exception. That is, the needs of consumers would always be greater than the ability of producers to meet those needs. Everything produced would be consumed. If there was overproduction, prices would drop to the point where the goods would be consumed.

Keynes, on the other hand, argued that demand was not driven simply by price, but by whether or not an economy was expanding or contracting and whether or not people were employed. The American industrialist, Henry Ford (1863–1947), figured out that he needed to pay his workers high wages so they could afford to buy the cars they were mass-producing. In the face of the Great Depression of the 1930s, Keynes argued it was up to governments to use their savings to stimulate demand and create employment opportunities through government spending. These ideas gained more traction during the global financial crisis beginning in 2007, when the U.S. Federal Reserve Bank poured close to $1 trillion into the economy to try to jump-start it and provided billions to stabilize the financial sector.

Another economist, whose ideas still resonate, but differently from those of Keynes, was the Austrian, Friedrich Hayek (1899–1992). Hayek fought for the Austro-Hungarian Army in World War I, which devastated his country and led to the breakup of the Austro-Hungarian Empire. The Austro-Hungarian Army suffered 1 million military casualties in World War I, and 500,000 civilians were killed. The aftermath of the war wreaked even more havoc. With the split of the Austro-Hungarian

Empire into four states (Austria, Czechoslovakia, Hungary, and Yugoslavia), many different groups—nationalists, socialists, and communists—competed to seize power, with nobody initially able to establish control. Civil wars broke out, people starved, and hyperinflation accelerated, making old currencies worthless. The terms of the victors (France, the United Kingdom, and the United States) added to people's miseries. They even wanted the losers to turn over their remaining cows. The young Hayek was determined to set out on a career that would make his world a better place.

Although Hayek and Keynes agreed about many things, they disagreed about the proper role of government in stimulating the economy. For Hayek the road to wealth and full employment was not through government spending but through private investment. Hayek may be best known for his 1944 work, *The Road to Serfdom*.[15] His main argument was that central planning leads to totalitarianism and that socialism and fascism had common roots in privileging the power of the state over the individual. Abandoning naked individualism leads to the loss of freedom, the rise of dictators, and the serfdom of the individual. On the other hand, liberation of the market from all state controls would result in a spontaneous and peaceful order. Both Margaret Thatcher, British prime minister from 1979 to 1990, and Ronald Reagan, American president from 1981 to 1989, embraced Hayek's ideas, which are today cited frequently by conservative and libertarian economists and politicians.

The extension of the ideas of Ricardo and Hayek into current economic thought takes the form of neoliberal economic theory. Erected in part to stand against the ideas of Marx, it is our dominant framework for explaining how markets work, how wealth is accumulated, and what the role of the state should be. Two fundamental components of neoliberal theory are the ideas that:

- A competitive capitalist economy left to itself and without an interfering government will generate full employment and prosperity. The Adam Smith Institute of Great Britain sees its role as fighting big government and championing free markets, free choice, competition, and enterprise. Big government is seen as the problem "interfering with lifestyle choices and undermining civil

liberties."[16] In the United States, these sentiments are echoed by the U.S. Chamber of Commerce and the Republican Party.
- Income and wealth are a result of the "marginal productivity" of people's contributions to their societies.[17] People get what they deserve.

As the Nobel economist Joseph E. Stiglitz noted, marginal productivity theory arose to explain inequality and exploitation from a non-Marxist perspective. Marginal productivity theory assumed that "… those with higher productivities earned higher incomes that reflected their greater contributions to society. Competitive markets, working through the laws of supply and demand, determine the value of each individual's contributions."[18] As we shall see, differences in wealth and income have today little relationship to education or skill levels.

The crises of capitalism are not just economic. Changes in the values systems that gave rise to capitalism can cause their own problems. The journalist and sociologist Daniel Bell thought that capitalism in the United States contained a major contradiction that would be its undoing. He argued that the Calvinist culture that gave rise to a robust form of capitalism would be diluted by the hedonism that characterized the 1960s and 1970s—a hedonism made possible by the wealth and leisure time created by capitalism. People would lose their entrepreneurial zeal and waste resources on non-productive activities. The solution would require a strong state to encourage continued economic growth. This would include assuring that workers develop new skills for the emergent post-industrial economy, which would demand scientific and technical knowledge and an ability to work with information.[19]

Economic theories and ideas grow out of the empirical problems faced by governments and people. They are an attempt to explain why a problem has arisen and what its solution should be. As circumstances change, so must our solutions. Capitalism has environmental, cultural, social, and economic consequences that have not, until recently, been clear. Growing disparities of wealth and income pose problems for a democratic society; the externalization of environmental costs is driving global warming; and the power of economic interests to set the agenda of the modern state must be addressed. A columnist for the *Wall Street Journal*, Al Lewis, said, "I love capitalism. I want the economy and our corporate system to run well." He then went on to provide an analysis of what stands in the way of success.

- Nothing grows forever. Why should anyone believe economic thinkers who pretend the economy should?
- Consumption isn't a virtue to be left unchecked.
- Corporations wield more power than individuals.
- Businesses externalize costs. They consume. They pollute. They exploit.
- The free market doesn't work without referees.[20]

I would add to Lewis's list the problem of growing inequality in wealth and income, because durable inequities make it extremely difficult for individuals to create the conditions under which corporate power and the ability of businesses to externalize costs can be checked. Likewise, inequity creates gaps in the level of human capital (e.g., knowledge, education, skills) people possess and therefore limits the ability to create a civic sector. Without a strong civic sector it is not possible to mount discussions about issues of distribution and the need to provide social safety nets in a society. *The reality is that inequity is increasing because the free market is operating perfectly, not imperfectly.*

What Causes Inequality Today?

Marx was clear: capitalism by its very nature creates inequity—the unequal distribution of income— because some must sell their labor power to others and they will always be paid less than its full value.[21] Levels of inequity as detailed in Chapter 2 vary greatly within and between countries. One way in which comparisons can be made between countries is to use the Gini coefficient, developed by the Italian statistician, Corrado Gini, in 1912 to measure income inequality. The Gini coefficient can vary between 0 and 100. If it were 100, it would mean that only one person received all of a country's income; if 0, it would mean incomes were equally distributed. Taking just a few of the world's democracies as examples, the Gini varies from a low of 24.0 for Denmark to a high of 63.1 in South Africa, meaning incomes in South Africa are more skewed than in Denmark, where they are more evenly distributed.

Table 4.1 Differences in Inequality as Measured by the Gini Coefficient

Country	Gini Index
Denmark	24.8
Sweden	24.9
Norway	26.8
Germany	27.0
Israel	37.6
USA	45.0
South Africa	62.5[22]

Source: Central Intelligence Agency. 2014. *World Fact Book.* Retrieved August 5, 2015 at: https://www.cia.gov/library/publications/the-world-factbook/fields/2172.html.

All countries in the world exhibit different levels of income inequality. The reasons vary, but one clear reason is that they vary because of differences in the culture, policies, laws, and social safety nets. As Joseph E. Stiglitz, has noted, *it is not the laws of economics that create inequality; it is our political policies.*[23] Denmark, Sweden, and Norway all have more equitable systems than the United States, because high taxes provide for more robust social safety nets. Some high Gini scores, as in the case of South Africa, are the result of a divide between the incomes of those living in rural areas as opposed to urban areas. Gaps in income, however, tell only part of the story. When we look at differences in wealth we find even greater disparities.

The French economist, Thomas Piketty, has demonstrated that wealth or capital has been increasingly concentrated in the hands of the few since the 1970s.[24] His definition of wealth is a robust one and includes all explicit or implicit assets on which returns can be realized: housing, land, machinery, and financial capital in the form of cash, bonds, stocks, and patents.[25] In the late nineteenth and early twentieth centuries, for example, wealth in Britain was primarily in land. The wealthy in France or Britain could simply live off of their incomes rather than engage in any form of productive activity. Piketty provides data for the developed economies of the world which suggests a return to this state of affairs, where people live off their investments rather than the efforts of their labor. We could call this the *Downton Abbey Syndrome.*

The television drama of the same name is set in post-Edwardian England during the reign of King George V and shows us what will come next in the evolution of capitalism. The first season opens in 1912, before the onset of World War I. We are introduced to the Crawleys, a rich family who socialize with their own kind, patronize the villagers and farmers who occupy the Crawleys' buildings and land and pay the Crawleys rent, as have their mothers and fathers before them. Lord Crawley, Earl of Grantham, presides over it all. It is not clear what exactly Lord Crawley does other than preside. His income and the estate were inherited, though as we learn later in the series, he needed to marry well—Cora, a rich American— to keep the enterprise going. And after running through Cora's money, the entire operation would have collapsed had not Matthew, the long-lost heir apparent, found that he was heir to still another fortune, which he pledged to commit to save Downton Abbey and the Crawleys, if Lord Crawley, Earl of Grantham, will start running the estate like a business; a prospect sniffed at by Crawley. The marital prospects of the daughters, especially Lady Mary Crawley, take center stage for several episodes and are weighted and evaluated in terms of income gained and lost or alliances formed with the right sort. Though the daughters are all well educated and "serve" the local community, only Edith, unlucky in love, sets out to find a job—much to the dismay of the family. One of the intended ironies of the series is that the fortunes of the estate are eventually saved by the chauffeur, who marries one of the daughters and then uses his practical skills to manage the estate.

In Ricardo's view, landlords serve no useful function; they do not save and invest; they do not increase the supply of capital goods; they are simply engaged in consumption. Today's wealthy no longer live off rent from their land, but they own stocks, bonds, cash, real estate, and art. So we may have arrived again at the point in history where a small class of people live off of inherited wealth, consume goods designed to maintain their status, and contribute little or nothing to the productive forces of society. In the United States, six out of the ten richest people all inherited their wealth.[26] This erodes the basis of a meritocracy and advantages those who are fortunate enough to be born to the wealthy and privileged. There are no brilliant chauffeurs waiting in the wings.

In the United States, the wealth of the top 10% of the population is held in stocks, bonds, and trust funds, as well as the ownership of businesses and land, as Table 4.2 makes clear.

Table 4.2 Percent of Wealth Held by Top 10% and the Bottom 90% of the U.S. Population

Investments:	Top 10%	Bottom 90%
Stocks and mutual funds	91.3	8.7
Financial securities	85.9	14.1
Trusts	81.0	19.0
Business ownership	91.9	8.1
Non-home real estate	79.1	20.9

Source: Table 9, "The Percent of Total Assets Held by Wealth Class," 2010. Edward N. Wolff. 2012. "The Asset Price Meltdown and the Wealth of the Middle Class." Cambridge, MA: National Bureau of Economic Research, Working Paper 18559.

Branko Milanovic, the lead research economist for the World Bank and an expert on income inequality noted in commenting on Piketty's work that there is a fundamental law of capitalism that boils down to this: If the rate of return on capital (cash, stocks, bonds, infrastructure) is greater than the rate of economic growth in a nation, then the share of capital incomes as a percentage of national income will increase.[27] Let's take the case of Larry Ellison, CEO and founder of Oracle, as an illustration. As of January 2015, Ellison's net worth was around $52 billion—that's his capital. If the rate of return on Ellison's capital or wealth (R) averaged 3% over the course of the year, he would gain $1.56 billion for a total of $53.6 billion at the end of one year, and would have even more money to invest to magnify his wealth year after year. His share of national income would grow simply by virtue of the mass of capital he controls. What Piketty adds to this analysis is his understanding, backed up massive data sets, that if the rate of return (R) is greater than the rate of growth (G), then the share of national income held by the wealthy automatically increases. In 2014, the growth rate for the U.S. economy was around 2.6% (growth is the sum of population growth and growth in the economy), while during the twentieth century the stock market returned on average 10.4% a year. In this case the rate the rate of return is 7.6 points higher than the growth rate.

> When the rate of return on capital exceeds the rate of economic growth (R>G), then the rich get richer.

Piketty demonstrates that the owners of capital absorbed a series of blows between 1914 and 1973. World Wars I and II destroyed physical capital (one of the bases of wealth) in Europe, while taxes were raised on the wealthy to pay for the wars. Inflation then ate away at the assets of wealthy creditors. Countries like the United Kingdom and France nationalized industries, while property and industrial assets during the post-colonial period were either ceded to or seized by new nations. In the United States, the Great Depression wiped out capital and gave rise to the New Deal coalition, which kept taxes on income high, empowered labor, and gave rise to Social Security and unemployment insurance.[28]

After World War II the economies of both the United States and Europe soared, while tax rates remained high and labor's share of income matched or exceeded growth rates. This situation held for at least thirty years in France, Germany, the United Kingdom, and the United States. During this period of time, economic growth exceeded the rate of return on capital.

This situation has now flipped and we are back to where we were before World War I. Labor's share of income as a portion of national wealth has dropped, economic growth is slowing, and the rate of return on capital has returned to historic highs.

One reason growth has slowed in developed countries is that populations (a factor in growth) are not growing there. One of Piketty's most controversial claims is that eventually China, India, and other developing countries will follow the same path as the developed countries of the world, with capital accumulating in the hands of the few and with growth slowing so that *the rate of return will always be greater than the rate of growth in the future*. This means that economic growth will be determined by technological progress calculated at between 1 and 1.5% a year, with population adding another 1% for an upper limit of 2.5% growth. This concentration of capital is socially destructive. Capitalism can deliver the goods but it does not have built-in safeguards against unsustainable inequality. A system that meets the current needs of only 20% of the world's population cannot sustain itself forever.

For Piketty, the central contradiction of capitalism is: r>g (rate of return > rate of growth). In his words:

> The inequality r>g implies that wealth accumulated in the past grows more rapidly than output and wages. This inequality

expresses a fundamental contradiction. The entrepreneur inevitably tends to become a rentier, more and more dominant over those who own nothing but their labor. Once constituted, capital reproduces itself faster than output increases. The past devours the future.

The implications are serious. *If capitalism and the free market work exactly as they should, then wealth will concentrate in the hands of the few.* The only thing that would prevent it, from the perspective of either Piketty or the Marxists, would be politics.[29] Is this likely? Many nation-states have passed laws to lower taxes on corporate revenue as a way of stimulating growth and attracting overseas corporations. As a result of Ireland lowering its corporate tax rate, Apple shields a significant share of its overseas income by parking it in Ireland. General Electric also shelters income from overseas operations in nations with lower rates. States like Tennessee, Alabama, and South Carolina have given generous tax breaks to foreign automobile manufacturers such as Mercedes, BMW, Honda, and Toyota.

Those who derived a substantial portion of their income from dividends on their investments were also rewarded through the political process. During the Presidency of George W. Bush, the top tax on dividends was cut and fell from 39.6% (because they were taxed as ordinary income) to 15%. As of 2015, the Republican House is advancing a plan that would eliminate taxes on interest, capital gains, dividends, and inheritance.[30] This would, of course, shift tax burdens to those with less means and greatly exacerbate inequality. The contradictions of capitalism are not just limited to how income and wealth are distributed; they also include the fact that capitalism is fueled by cheap energy, raw materials and, of course, cheap labor. These factors are bound tightly together and affect our ability to create a sustainable future.

The Ecological Crises of Capitalism

Capitalism runs on energy. The rise of an industrial society is normally traced to England and the invention of the steam engine in 1765 by Hargreaves. Its design was later improved and patented by James Watt, a Scottish instrument maker. This improved engine meant that power could be generated by burning coal, and the engine could be used to pump water out of mine shafts, a problem that had limited the use of coal. A coal-fired steam engine meant that textile mills were no longer dependent on water power, because it was now possible to situate a plant where it was most convenient—near ports and population centers—and have the coal transported to it.

Coal solved an energy crisis. The forests of England had been cut over centuries for buildings, for ships, and for warmth. Wood was used to produce charcoal, which was used in the production of pig iron. The shift from wood to coal was rapid and dramatic. The iron industry, which had been dwindling because of a lack of wood, could use coke, made from coal, to power blast furnaces. By 1800 coal could drive power looms propelled by steam to speed the manufacture of cotton, making Britain the world's leading textile producer. The iron and steel industry was boosted because railroads needed to be built to transport coal and raw materials and finished products to ports.

The historian Ian Morris has tackled a question that arises during those moments in which the dominance of a world power seems to be threatened, or waning.[31] Is China set to take the place of the United States as the world's dominant nation? In *Why the West Rules—For Now*, Morris outlined the processes that gave rise to capitalism and makes the important point that human history, whether in the East or the West, is simply the same story of the same kind of people solving the same kind of problems—famines, droughts, disease, state collapse, energy needs—over time.[32] As he said,

> ... East and West have gone through the same stages of social development in the last fifteen thousand years, in the same order, *because they have been peopled by the same kinds of human beings, who generate the same kind of history.* (Emphases added.)[33]

Morris's theory was that social change is driven by humans, who are inherently lazy, frightened, and greedy; who are short-sighted; and who are continually looking for more profitable and easier ways to do things. Leaving aside his assessment of human character, he has indeed carefully demonstrated his point that social development in all societies proceeds through fixed phases. He constructed a development index composed of four factors to illustrate these concepts:

- **Energy capture**, which he estimated to have been 4 kilocalories per capita per day in 14,000 BCE and to now be the 230,000 kilocalories we consume on a per capita basis every day in the West.
- **Urbanization**, which he saw as a proxy for the development of organizational capacity.
- **Information technology** and the means by which information was at that time spread—private letters, by sea, telegraph, telephone, and so on.
- **War-making capacity**.[34]

Morris shows that when we compare East and West on these factors although the West gets a jump on Asian countries in the development of capitalism, all countries eventually tread the same path. China and India are using more energy every day, continuing to urbanize, using information technology to speed connectivity among their cities, and building strong states and armies. Morris predicts that at some point China will surpass the United States in terms of its development index. This leads to the overall conclusion that a society's development score is a measure of:

> All countries tread the same path toward development with greater energy requirements at each stage of growth.

> its ability to master its physical and intellectual environment and get things done … [It] is the bundle of technological, subsistence, organizational, and cultural accomplishments through which people feed, clothe, house, and reproduce themselves, explain the world around them, resolve disputes with their communities, extend their power at the expense of other communities, and defend themselves against others' attempts to extend power.[35]

The implication is that energy is critical to the growth and development of all nation states and will continue to be so.

The sociologist, Jason Moore, has outlined this process of international economies staggering from one economic and ecological crisis to another.[36] Coming from a very different theoretical perspective than Morris, Moore sees history unfolding as the direct result of ecological crises and the need to solve them. This is by no means a process that unfolds in slow incremental steps; it is characterized by punctuated equilibria where one political or economic system is maintained for centuries, and then, because of a need for additional labor power (for example, slaves on sugar plantations), cheaper food (international agribusiness), or cheaper raw materials (oil from the Middle East or Africa), things change rapidly and dramatically. Ecological spaces are exhausted and then we move on. For at least 500 years we have been searching the globe for goods acquired cheap, to be sold dear elsewhere.

Capitalism and Globalization

Globalization refers to processes by which the people of the world are incorporated into a single world economy.[37] *Capitalism and its contemporary handmaiden, globalization, have transformed cultures.* As noted in the last chapter, the creation of a capitalist world system began as early as the fifteenth century, but the globalization of today involves somewhat different processes. The International Monetary Fund has identified four aspects of globalization: trade, the movement of capital and investments, human migration, and the dissemination of knowledge.[38] It has penetrated virtually every place on the planet in one form or another. It does so now for the simple reason that it takes cash to participate in modern society. As I noted at the beginning of Chapter 3, even those isolated in small villages in the Amazonian basin are linked to the global economy and are being overrun by it. Globalization has created a more complex world linking the production, consumption, and distribution of wealth and resources across the globe. It has caused worldwide shifts in employment and the centralization of economic power.

Hand in hand, capitalism and globalization cause inequality. Why? As the economic historian Jerry Muller has noted, though capitalism has opened up opportunities for human potential, not everyone has been able or is able to take advantage of these opportunities. "Some individuals, families, and communities are simply better able than others to exploit the opportunities for development and advancement that today's capitalism affords."[39] In addition, globalization often contributes to inequity, because a multinational corporation will need to negotiate with an elite group or tribe in order to extract resources such as tin, gold, diamonds, or oil. The income thus concentrates in the hands of those in power, who then use these assets to reward friends and punish enemies, as has happened in areas of Africa, the Middle East, and South America, and elsewhere.

The processes of capitalism, globalization, and industrialization have not been even. That is because human agents, living in different historical, environmental, and political conditions, have developed different solutions for the problems they face. We have not yet arrived at a good solution. There are, however, those who argue we are on the right track. In 1992, the Stanford University political scientist Francis Fukuyama argued that we had reached *The End of History*.[40] The Cold War was over, and we had reached the end point of mankind's ideological evolution with the triumph of liberal democracy. There has indeed been a steady increase over the twentieth century in the number of countries that can be considered liberal democracies.[41] *But there are many different forms of capitalism in existence*. As business professors Aldo Musacchio and Sergio Lazzarini have detailed, state capitalism has made a comeback.[42] In China, for example, the state is a majority stockholder in many companies. In Russia and Brazil, companies in which the state has a share account for 30–40% of capitalization.[43] For a time, the U.S. government "owned" shares of automobile and mortgage companies in the aftermath of the 2007–2010 financial collapse. We are not at the end of history if we continue to invent new ways to respond to the challenges and opportunities we face. For liberal democracies to become the end point, we must find ways to manage the three problems we previously identified: environmental issues related to climate change, global inequity, and energy inequality.

Summary

At each stage of capitalism's evolution, thoughtful writers like Polanyi, Schumpeter, Keynes, and Hayek have sought to explain how the system of capitalism works. The experience of the Great Depression of the 1930s convinced Keynes that the role of the state was to stimulate economic growth and full employment. Hayek, drawing on his experience of life in post-war Austria, believed it was private enterprise that was best positioned to stimulate economic growth and that centralized planning could only lead to serfdom. After World War II, Polanyi thought the state must deal with the contradictions between the needs of its citizens and the needs of capital. Today a major problem facing us globally is the continued concentration of wealth and growing inequalities between and within nation-states. Piketty argued that capitalism gives rise to inequity because the rate of return on capital will always be greater than the overall growth of the economy, a fact that historical data supports. So we find today that even though the world economy is eleven times greater than it was in 1820, prosperity is highly concentrated. If we define poverty, as living on less than $10 a day, then 80% of the world's population is poor and unable to participate in the societies in which they live. We are on a crash course with the future.[44]

Through a Sustainability Lens

Capitalism has derived its staying power from being rooted in the ideas of the Enlightenment and the revolutions that grew out of new ways of thinking about the world. One important new way of thinking was the optimism associated with the scientific revolution; the idea that science would usher in, as it has, numerous benefits. Capitalism also depended on being able to secure labor power, raw materials, and energy at low cost. One consequence has been global inequality and a division between those nations that control world finance and markets and those that have as their assets cheap labor power, raw materials, and energy to export. The complex problems of modern capitalist societies have been "solved" by using up human and material resources, finding new markets, and inventing new things to sell, be they laptops or iPhones. The environmental consequences of discounting the biosphere are now well known and need not be enumerated here. The human consequences are a different matter.

Climate change will hurt everyone, but the poor will suffer the most. In Nepal 60% of the population lives on less than $2.00 a day, and in India it is 70% of the population. Most of those living on so little depend on rainfall to irrigate their crops, and in Nepal more than 90% of electricity comes from hydropower. Both nations have already experienced climate-related disasters. In Nepal ice dams have melted and entire villages have been wiped out. In India, heat waves have killed crops and livestock. How are villagers coping? By reducing their already poor diets and cutting out crops that depend on a steady water supply. Climate suffering, to use the words of Paul Wapner, has come to the doorsteps of those living on marginal lands and in substandard structures. The suffering is not just economic. Many of those interviewed by Wapner in India and Nepal "expressed shame at not being able to provide for their families and those who had borrowed money felt hopeless in the face of dwindling economic opportunity."[45]

Our modern economies see the environment (including humans) as subordinate to the economy, rather than the reverse. A major challenge lies in convincing everyone that for there to be a future that works, we have to operate with the rule, "do no harm to the biosphere." We need to determine what is possible within the constraints of the physical universe. And, we need to be agile in our management strategies, because we cannot predict all of the ways in which a complex system will work or what new problems might emerge.

Notes

1. Https://en.wikipedia.org/wiki/Labor_theory_of_value.
2. For an explanation of Marx's falling rate of profit see: http://www.economictheories.org/2008/07/karl-marx-falling-rate-of-profit.html.
3. Google. Accessed on June 16, 2014 at: http://googlemergers.blogspot.com/2013/02/mergers-and-acquisitions-by-google.html.
4. John Bellamy Foster and Robert McChesney. 2012. *The Endless Crisis: How Monopoly-Finance Capital Produces Stagnation and Upheaval from the U.S.A. to China*. New York, NY: Monthly Review Press.
5. Council of Economic Advisors. 2012. *Economic Report of the President, 2012*: 64.
6. Lawrence Mishel. 2012. *The State of Working America*. Washington, DC: The Economic Policy Institute. Retrieved on June 17 2104 at: http://www.epi.org/publication/ib330-productivity-vs-compensation/.
7. Thomas Philippon. 2013. "Has the U.S. Finance Industry Become Less Efficient? On the Theory and Measurement of Financial Intermediation." Retrieved on June 17, 2104 at: http://www.epi.org/publication/ib330-productivity-vs-compensation/.
8. Robert B. Reich. 2010. *Aftershock: The Next Economy and America's Future*. New York, NY: Alfred A. Knopf.
9. Madsen Pine. 2013. "Why Marx Was Wrong about Capitalism." London: The Adam Smith Society. Retrieved on February 13, 2104 at: http://www.adamsmith.org/research/think-pieces/why-marx-was-wrong-about-capitalism/.
10. David Harvey. 2014. *17 Contradictions and the End of Capitalism*. London: Profile Books, p.ix.

11 Charles Tilly. 2007. *Democracy*. Cambridge, MA: Cambridge University Press.
12 Joseph A. Schumpeter. 1942 (1975). *Capitalism, Socialism, and Democracy*. New York, NY: Harper.
13 Karl Polanyi. 1944 (2001). *The Great Transformation: The Political and Economic Transformations of Our Time*. New York, NY: Beacon.
14 John Maynard Keynes. 1936 (2011). *The General Theory of Employment, Interest, and Money*. London: CreateSpace Independent Publishing Platform.
15 Friedrich von Hayek. 1944. *The Road to Serfdom*. Chicago, IL: University of Chicago Press.
16 The Adam Smith Institute (UK), "Blog." http://www.adamsmith.org/.
17 For an elaboration of the problems with neoclassical economic theory, see John Bellamy Foster and Michael D. Yates. 2014. "Piketty and the Crisis of Neoclassical Economics." *Monthly Review Press*. November. 66: 6. Retrieved from: http://monthlyreview.org/2014/11/01/piketty-and-the-crisis-of-neoclassical-economics/.
18 Joseph E. Stiglitz. 2012. *The Price of Inequality*. New York, NY: Norton, p.30.
19 Daniel Bell (1976), *The Cultural Contradictions of Capital*. New York, NY: Basic Books.
20 Al Lewis. 2014. "That's It. I Quit." *Wall Street Journal, Sunday*. July 13. Reprinted in the *Missoulian*. July. 14: D5.
21 To be correct, he said "surplus value."
22 Central Intelligence Agency. 2014. *World Fact Book*. Retrieved on June 25, 2014 at: https://www.cia.gov/library/publications/the-world-factbook/fields/2172.html.
23 Joseph E. Stiglitz. 2014. "Is Inequality Inevitable?" *The New York Times*. June 29: SR7.
24 Thomas Piketty. 2014. *Capital in the Twenty-First Century*. Cambridge, MA: Harvard University Press.
25 There have been objections to Piketty's operationalization of the concept of wealth. See, for example, David Harvey. 2014. "Afterthoughts on Piketty's Capital." Retrieved on June 25, 2014 at: http://davidharvey.org/2014/05/afterthoughts-pikettys-capital/; Michael Roberts. 2014. "Unpicking Piketty." *Weekly Worker*. Retrieved on June 25, 2014 at: http://sponsor.adverstitial.com/view/advertisement?loc=9419&adv=2861707&camp=668192&w=300&h=250&rnd=4267239215521592285; Michael Thompson. 2014. "Mapping the New Oligarchy." *Logos*. 14: 53-57. Most of the objections from the left argue that Piketty's analysis is not a Marxian analysis because he misunderstands the fact that capitalism is a process and fails to discuss how the social relations of production shape distribution.
26 Robert Frank. 2011. "Are We Entering the Age of Inherited Wealth?" *Wall Street Journal*. September 23. Retrieved on July 15, 2014 at: http://blogs.wsj.com/wealth/2011/09/22/are-we-entering-the-age-of-inherited-wealth/?mod=WSJBlog.
27 Branko Milanovic. 2013. "The Return of 'Patrimonial Capitalism': Review of Thomas Piketty's Capital in the 21st Century." Retrieved from: http://mpra.ub.uni-muenchen.de/52384/. What Milanovic specifically said was, "[T]he share of capital incomes in total national income (A) is equal to the rate of return on capital (R) multiplied by B, which is the capital/income ratio or K/Y."
28 Thomas B. Edsall. 2014. "Capitalism vs. Democracy." *The New York Times*. January 28. Retrieved on July 15, 2014 at: http://www.nytimes.com/2014/01/29/opinion/capitalism-vs-democracy.html.
29 Benjamin Kunkel. 2014. "Paupers and Richlings." *London Review of Books*. 36(13): 17–20.

30 Paul Ryan. 2014. House Budget Committee. Retrieved on July 15 at: http://budget.house.gov/.
31 See, in particular, the work of Giovanni Arrighi and his *The Long Twentieth Century: Money, Power, and the Origins of Our Times.* New York, NY: Verson, 1994. Arrighi traces in his work the rise of economic powers over time and draws the conclusion that American capitalism will ultimately succumb to collapse because of the internal contradictions that are inherent in capitalism.
32 Ian Morris. 2010. *Why the West Rules—For Now.* New York, NY: Farrar, Straus, and Giroux.
33 Ibid., pp.29–30.
34 Ibid., pp.628 ff.
35 Ibid., p.144.
36 Jason Moore. 2011. "Ecology, Capital, and the Nature of Our Times: Accumulation and Crisis in the Capitalist World-Ecology." *American Sociological Review* 42(1): 108–147; Jason Moore. 2009. "Ecology and the Accumulation of Capital." Paper prepared for the "Food, Energy, Environment: Crisis of the Modern World-System." Binghamton, NY.
37 Martin Albrow and Elizabeth King, eds. 1990. *Globalization: Knowledge and Society.* London: Sage, p.8.
38 International Monetary Fund. 2000. "Globalization: Threats or Opportunities." Retrieved on June 25, 2014 at: http://www.imf.org/external/np/exr/ib/2000/041200to.htm.
39 Jerry Muller. 2013. "The Hard Truth about Economic Inequality That Both the Left and Right Ignore." PBS News Interview. April 11. Retrieved on June 25, 2014 at: http://www.pbs.org/newshour/rundown/the-hard-nut-of-economic-inequality-what-the-left-and-right-both-ignore/.
40 Francis Fukuyama. 1992. *The End of History and the Last Man.* New York, NY: The Free Press.
41 Freedom House Index. 2014. Accessed on June 25 at: http://www.freedomhouse.org/.
42 Aldo Musacchio and Sergio G. Lazzarini. 2014. *Reinventing State Capitalism: Leviathan in Business, Brazil and Beyond.* Cambridge, MA: Harvard University Press.
43 *The Economist.* 2014. "Leviathan as Capitalist: State Capitalism Continues to Defy Expectations of Its Demise." June 21: 66.
44 Global Issues. 2015. "Poverty Facts and Stats."
45 Paul Wapner. 2014. "The New World of Climate Suffering." Washington, DC: The Woodrow Wilson International Center for Scholars. Retrieved on July 15, 2014 at: http://climateandsecurity.org/2014/06/25/the-new-world-of-climate-suffering-harsh-realities-explained-by-paul-wapner/.

5
TRUST, INEQUALITY, AND DEMOCRACY

Consider:

- Democracy depends on trust and trust depends on social equality.
- Corruption erodes trust.
- Winner-take-all systems destroy trust.
- Over the past decade trust in political institutions and trust in others has declined in the United States and Western Europe.
- People are more trusting of others in homogenous societies—those not divided by gender, ethnicity, religion, or social class.

Japan: Bonds of Trust

On the afternoon of Friday, March 11, 2011, tectonic plates off the east coast of Japan buckled deep under the Pacific Ocean, triggering a massive earthquake. The tremors were felt in Tokyo and immediately all radio and television stations went to coverage of the quake. Alarms sounded in schools and children ducked under their desks to avoid injury from falling debris, as monthly drills had prepared them to do. Those children who were outside playing gathered quickly in the center of pre-designated open spaces. Workers exited their buildings calmly, even as books fell from shelves and office furniture shifted and rumbled. No other country was better prepared to deal with a quake than Japan, having learned from the Kobe earthquake of 1995 that killed over 6,000 people. What they were not ready for was the magnitude of the tsunami generated by the 2011 quake.

The Japanese government had developed early warning systems to alert people to storms, torrential rains, heavy snow, tsunamis, tidal waves, high surf, and floods.[1] They had prepared evacuation maps for coastal areas likely to be affected by tsunamis and had built substantial seawalls, some 18–20 feet high, in key coastal cities. Generally, most people felt safe because of the care that had been taken to prepare for possible evacuation and because of the tall seawalls that guarded their homes and villages. But waves as high as 36 feet swept over the barriers, washing ships onto land, flattening homes, and sending docks, houses, and people adrift in the sea. Roads and bridges were destroyed and people were without power. Over 1 million buildings were damaged or destroyed. Twenty thousand people were dead or missing. A year after the storm, an additional 6,000 were injured, and estimates of the homeless ranged as high as 400,000 people.

In Fukushima, one of the prefectures hardest hit by the tsunami, another disaster quickly developed. Three of the four nuclear reactors at the Fukushima Dai-ichi power plant had been damaged by the quake and tsunami and were starting to melt down, as one backup system after another failed. There were sea walls, but they were not high enough; there were generators to provide backup power, but they were flooded; the containment domes were cracked by the quake and leaking radiation. Heroic efforts by workers prevented another Chernobyl, but they could not contain all of the damage. Radiation leakage forced the evacuation of 100,000 people and the government eventually established a 12-mile exclusion zone around the plant, where no homes can be built or food grown until the radiation levels are once again at a safe level.

> Whether or not a community recovers rapidly from a disaster depends on the level of pre-existing trust and the social resources on which people can draw.

The collective response to these multiple tribulations did not result in disorder or looting. Instead, long and orderly lines formed as people queued up seeking food and water. Lights were turned off in Tokyo in order to save power for others. Throughout the country people spontaneously organized to deal with the aftermath of the tsunami and quake. One small fishing village, Hadenya, serves as an example. The wave crushed homes, destroyed bridges, and cut off all links, including cell phones, to the outside world. Those who survived clustered together in a community center on the top of a hill. They did not wait for instruction about what to do. They quickly determined who would do what and who would help whom. The young would take care of the old. Men would forage for firewood and gasoline and women would take care of washing and cooking. A nurse set up an emergency clinic. Groups were organized to hunt for food in the rubble. Eventually help came from outside twelve days later, after a successful journey by three men across the mountain to make contact with the outside world.[2]

The villagers of Hadenya survived on their own in large part because they could draw on strong communal bonds that had been established over the centuries and because *they trusted one another*. Westerners, in fact, marveled at the discipline and order that was shown. Carol Gluck, a Columbia University professor of Japanese history, attributed the responses of the Japanese to a deep-seated collective commitment to maintaining community and the social order.[3] Given this history, it should come as no surprise that cooperation was the rule, not the exception. However, we should not conclude that it is Japanese culture alone that serves to explain people's responses to the earthquake and tsunami.

First, some Japanese communities bounced back more quickly than others and appeared to cope with their losses and psychological burdens more easily. Why? Daniel Aldrich, a professor of political science at Purdue, has demonstrated that *whether or not a community recovers rapidly from a disaster depends on the level of pre-existing trust and the social resources on which people can draw*.[4] The tsunami of 2011 provided him with a "natural" experiment so that he could compare not only the towns most heavily hit but the neighborhoods within them. So, even though the Japanese are generally cooperative, some neighborhoods exhibited more cooperation than others. Those Japanese communities in which social bonds were strong and people were engaged in community organizations recovered more quickly than those that did not have dense social networks. Our small fishing village, where generations of people had lived and worked together, is an example where interaction was extensive and trust and resilience high.[5]

When we compare Japan to other nations in the world we find that Japanese society is composed of more trust-building dimensions than simply a willingness to cooperate with one's neighbors. Japan is also a democratic nation and a relatively prosperous society with an effective government. People live long and healthy lives. The population is well educated, homogeneous, and has the resources to deal with natural disasters. Finally, in terms of income inequality or concentration of income, Japan is one of the most egalitarian countries in the world. The Gini coefficient, which measures income concentration, for Japan is 37.[6] By comparison it is 47 for the United States.[7] (If everyone received the same income, the coefficient would be 0; if just one person received all of the income it would be 100.) It may be that the resilience of the Japanese people to the earthquake is grounded less in their culture and more in the economic, political, and social institutions that shape their daily lives. A brief look at how social inequality affects people's response to disasters illustrates this point.

Inequality Is Destabilizing

When disasters strike, people frequently rise to the challenge, behaving in an altruistic fashion and caring for those around them. The writer Rebecca Solnit has detailed in *A Paradise Built in Hell* the many occasions when in the aftermath of hurricanes, fires, and earthquakes people have worked to create a small paradise in the face of some hellish disaster. As she notes,

> The image of the selfish, panicky, or regressively savage human being in times of disaster has little truth to it. Decades of meticulous sociological research on behavior in disasters, from the bombings of World War II to floods, tornadoes, earthquakes, and storms across the continent and around the world, have demonstrated this.[8]

Differences in wealth and power in a city or country contributes to "elite panic" or the belief that others will behave like savages, which in turn leads to repression by elites.

One of Solnit's examples was the San Francisco earthquake of 1906, which toppled buildings, cracked and shifted others, collapsed chimneys, and broke water and gas lines. What ultimately devastated the city were the fires that destroyed five square miles and 28,000 structures.[9] Citizens tried to fight the fire with water, shovels, and wet gunnysacks but were actively prevented from doing so by the city's firemen, and had to stand by while their homes and businesses burned down. The firemen were implementing City Hall's policy of dynamiting or blasting firebreaks, which only made things worse. Brigadier General Frederick Funston at the Presidio saw his job as protecting the city from its citizens and used his troops to drive volunteers away from scenes where fires could have been prevented.[10] The troops also took it upon themselves to shoot citizens who had been given permission by shop owners to take provisions before their businesses burned. In the words of Solnit, "A handful of men in power and a swarm of soldiers, National Guardsmen, and militiamen," destroyed San Francisco.[11]

In the meantime, those burned out of their homes set up improvised soup kitchens and shelters in Golden Gate Park and other places safe from the fire and improvised their own care. The city tried to step in and organize kitchens where people would need to provide a ticket to be served. This was seen by the hungry as degrading, so they went on running their own kitchens.

The Mayor set up a committee of fifty businessmen to deal with the aftermath of the quake and to look out for the interests of business. One of their first acts was to try to seize Chinatown in a real estate grab fueled by racism. Others tried to use the quake to reduce wages by arguing for the need for "mutual concessions"—$2.50 for nine hours of work, instead of $8.00—in the face of the crisis. Though San Francisco obviously recovered, it struggled in the immediate aftermath of the quake, because divisions of power and wealth within the community led to high levels of distrust and an inability to work together for common purposes.

When social inequality in a country or a community is high and this is coupled with free-market ideologies, the results can be disastrous for ordinary citizens. (See Chapter 4 for an elaboration of neoliberal economic theories.) In *Shock Doctrine*, the journalist Naomi Klein shows how current disasters have been seized upon to strengthen the power of economic elites. In New Orleans, elite panic led to the militarization of "relief" efforts and to the shooting of innocent civilians. In addition, those scattered after hurricane Katrina found that public housing, schools, and hospitals were never to be reopened, so many have never returned. When a tsunami hit the coasts of Southeast Asia in 2004, sweeping away fishing villages in Indonesia, Thailand, and Sri Lanka, the beaches were auctioned off for tourist resorts.[12] These incidents massively erode trust in public institutions. Further, deep inequalities in wealth, income, and social standing erode people's trust in one another. Haiti serves as a comparison with Japan to illustrate how powerful social inequality is in shaping outcomes.

Haiti: Inequality, Corruption, and Mistrust

On January 12, 2010, a massive 7.0 earthquake struck Haiti, devastating the capital of Port-au-Prince, where over 25% of the population lived. Thousands of homes were flattened and upwards of 2.3 million Haitians were left homeless. An estimated 200,000 people died as a direct result of the quake. The quake exacerbated long-standing problems. Even before the devastation, about 70% of the population were living in slums and 55% of Haiti's 10 million citizens were living on less than $1.25 a day.[13] Unlike Japan, Haiti was not prepared for a quake, and the government of Haiti left most of its citizens to cope on their own. Images of the devastation and suffering posted on social media sites as well as television coverage led to an outpouring of international support and pledges of up to $5 billion to help the Haitian people.[14] But things were slow to change.

One year after the quake, little of the $5 billion had been allocated to Haiti, primarily because donors worried about political corruption that would funnel the money to the elites, who continued to dine in elegance and live in splendor, while right outside their homes and restaurants people were living in tent cities and going hungry.[15] In 2014, four years after the quake, many of the temporary camps had been closed, although around 137,000 Haitians were still living in 300 tent cities. Conditions in the camps were miserable.[16]

One could easily argue that the difference between the ability of the Japanese to manage the twin crises of the earthquake and the tsunami and the Haitians' ability to cope after their earthquake was that Japan was a wealthier and more highly developed country than Haiti. It is, of course, true that Japan is an advanced industrial, democratic society and Haiti is not. However, it leaves open the question as to why Haiti is one of the least developed countries in the world and why its political and economic systems benefit only the few. To answer that question we need to consider the social and historical conditions that gave rise to modern Haiti.

When Columbus set out to search for a passage to China in 1492, he "discovered" an island in the Caribbean that he called *Hispaniola*, meaning "little Spain." The Spanish eventually settled in and built the town of Santo Domingo on the eastern side of the island, which became their base for colonization of the New World in their search for gold and silver. The eastern side of the island eventually became the Dominican Republic. The French arrived some time after the Spanish and colonized the western side of the island. Haiti became the center of a great Caribbean sugar empire. To meet their labor needs, the French enslaved native populations and imported thousands of additional slaves from Africa. The slave ships that brought human cargo returned to Europe with sugar and timber in their holds. Logging denuded steep hillsides, destroying entire ecosystems, affecting the fertility of the land, and limiting the ability of Haitians to make a living from agriculture.[17] By the end of the eighteenth century, Blacks were the dominant population in Haiti, which had 500,000 black slaves, 27,000 Black freemen, and 30,000 Whites.

Throughout the nineteenth century, Haitian slaves engaged in long and fierce battles to free themselves from French rule. The deepest divide, though, was between the Europeanized mulatto elites, who spoke French and adopted Catholicism as their religion, lived in the capital of Port-au-Prince, and came to dominate all aspects of Haitian social and economic life, and those who lived in the countryside, speaking Creole and practicing Vodou, a religion combining elements of several African religions and of Roman Catholicism (it is today one of the two official religions of Haiti). This divide between "sophisticated" urban elites and the "superstitious" rural poor still exists, and urban and rural populations have been played off against one another in elections. The violence that allowed Haiti to free itself of French rule would be used by future leaders to control dissent and pit Haitians against one another.

Haiti has been bedeviled by corrupt dictators. François ("Papa Doc") Duvalier, became president in 1957. Duvalier positioned himself as a populist, using Vodou and a cult of personality to draw support from the country's rural Blacks, playing them off against the mulatto elites of Port-au-Prince. Under Duvalier's dictatorial leadership (1957–1971) it is estimated that 30,000 Haitians were murdered, and those who could, fled the country. He was succeeded by his son, Jean-Claude Duvalier ("Baby Doc"), who ruled from 1971 until he was overthrown in a popular uprising in 1981. Since his overthrow and flight into exile, Haiti has lurched between democracy and tyranny, from democratically elected presidents to ones who seized power illegitimately, often with the backing of the armed forces or the police. For example, in 1994, the United States, in "Operation Uphold Democracy," sent combat forces to remove the military regime that took power in 1991 in a coup d'état that overthrew the democratically elected president, Jean-Bertrand Aristide. The current president of Haiti is Michel Martelly, known by his stage name as "Sweet Micky." He is a former musician and businessman. Martelly, who was associated with the Duvalier regime and supported the 1991 coup against Aristide, campaigned on the promise to bring back the military, which had been abolished under Aristide. Haiti serves as an almost perfect example of what MIT economist Daron Acemoglu and his colleague James Robinson, a Harvard economist and political scientist, have described as a society with closed political and economic systems, meaning that there are rigid inequalities based on what I referred to in Chapter 1 as irrelevant moral criteria. Haiti is poor not because of its culture but because of corrupt institutions.

> Haiti is impoverished because of its corrupt economic and political institutions.

Why do some nations fail and others succeed? Two cities provide a natural experiment: Nogales, Arizona and Nogales, Mexico, divided by a border fence. On the American side of the fence crime rates are lower, income and life expectancy are higher, the roads and infrastructure are better, and corruption is lower. There is nothing else to distinguish the two cities in terms of geography or culture. For years, people have spoken the same language, practiced the same religion, listened to the same music, and enjoyed the same food. What does differentiate the two cities are their political and economic institutions. As Acemoglu and Robinson say of Nogales, Arizona:

> Its inhabitants have access to the economic institutions of the United States, which enable them to choose their occupations freely, acquire schooling and skills ... They also have access to political institutions that allow them to take part in the democratic process. Those of Nogales, Sonora, are not so lucky.[18]

Haiti's neighbor, the Dominican Republic, is a much more prosperous and open society than Haiti, because it evolved different political and economic institutions.

The quake in Haiti was a human disaster that revealed the bones of a society that squanders human talent. The gross historical inequities, shored up by violence, had already destroyed Haitians' faith in democracy, in their government, and in one another. The quake made this toxic situation worse. A cholera epidemic spread throughout the makeshift tent cities. With a few exceptions, reconstruction efforts were grounded in the neoliberal economic assumption that growing businesses was the salve for the wounds. This meant rebuilding efforts were driven by elites, international businesses, and nonprofit organizations that decided what was best for the Haitians, not those whose lives were most dramatically affected by the quake.

Even before the quake, Haitians exhibited one of the lowest levels of support for democracy in the Americas at 70.5%, compared to a country like Costa Rica, at 80.4%.[19] After the quake hit, it fell to 65.8%, making it, along with El Salvador (64.1%), Paraguay (63.3%), Guatemala (62.8%), Honduras (62.6%), and Peru (60.1%), one of the six lowest countries out of 25 in the Americas in its support for democracy.

Only 32% of Haitians expressed faith in how their political institutions function.[20] Small wonder, given the fact that in 2009, 53.6% of Haitians reported they needed to pay a bribe to a government official whenever they needed help, whether it was public assistance or the need to get the police to respond to the report of a time.[21] In the aftermath of the quake only 14.2% of Haitians turned to their government for help; they turned instead to family, friends, or nongovernmental organizations providing aid.

How trusting are Haitians of their immediate neighbors? Sixty percent did not trust them before the quake and, after the dislocation caused by the quake, *78% of Haitians reported that they did not trust others*, the lowest ranking of all 25 countries in the Americas.[22] The comparable figure for Japan shows that 65% of all Japanese trust others, compared to the 22% of Haitians who do.[23]

We can see in this brief comparison of two countries stark differences in people's faith in their government, their support for democracy, their trust in one another, and their ability to respond to a major catastrophe. The argument I am laying out is that *there is a virtuous cycle whereby strong democratic states with effective institutions generate equality and trust, which further enhances the legitimacy and effectiveness of state institutions*. Further products of this virtuous cycle are the creation and fuller use of human capital, social capital, and civic engagement, all of which position citizens to respond more effectively to emerging social and environmental challenges such as climate change. What set limits on this virtuous cycle are differences in power, wealth, and income, which destroy trust.

Trust, Equality, and Social Capital

A lack of trust in other people and in the institutions that shape our lives threatens the survival of those very institutions that give human beings the best chance of maximizing their human potential. *I am also arguing that trust is eroded when inequities, based on irrelevant criteria, become the norm.* Nepal is another example of how an irrelevant moral criterion, in this case, caste, affects trust. Nepal is one of the poorest countries in the world, with a gross per capita income of only $730 in 2013.[24] Nepal has ten distinct ethnic groups and little income inequality, as virtually everyone is poor. Trust in the government had been affected by the Maoist insurgency of 1996–2006, but since the formation of a new government, trust in the government has improved as it focuses on meeting people's basic needs and providing security.[25] Trust of other Nepalese, however, depends on something else—ethnicity and caste.[26] Low status groups simply do not trust their fellow Nepalese. As the cultural anthropologist Kimber Haddix McKay has noted, in those regions where the Hindu caste system is in place, those of lower castes frequently express their distrust for those of higher castes.[27] *Trust, depends on equality.*

The phrase "I don't trust you!" is a powerful emotional statement. Whatever the reason for saying this, it means that a relationship is in danger. Trust is the basis of all human contact and institutional interaction.[28] Trust requires taking a calculated risk that others will play by the rules of the game and not cheat. Trust promotes social cooperation—the willingness to create and maintain social networks.[29] Being a member of a social network—be it a family, gang, or clan—requires a degree of cooperation and carries with it the expectation that there will be a benefit from being a member of the network. The benefit can be safety, prestige, or just the comfort of knowing that somebody has your back. Human capital—the resources each of us has as a human being—are also part of this mix. As noted in Chapter 1, human capital consists of such factors as the knowledge, skills, and attitudes each of us has. The less human capital people have, the less social capital they are likely to have.

Those who are economically disadvantaged or lack an education are less likely to trust their neighbors, less likely to trust people in general, and less likely to trust the government, whether local or national, that affects their lives. They do not trust because they don't have the economic or political power to change things; they are stuck with the way things are. The powerful and privileged have greater trust because they know from education and experience that, if something goes wrong, they can call on the resources of political, economic, and judicial elites to make things right.

Trust comes in many forms. There is the trust we have in public institutions or our governments; the trust we have in other people in general; and the trust we have in those to whom we are close. Whether we trust others or a government depends on concrete social experiences. Haitians do not trust their government because of its performance; they don't trust their neighbors because of high crime rates; but they do trust their family members to help out when there is a need. Sociologist James Coleman defines *social capital* as anything that facilitates individual or collective action, generated by networks of relationships grounded in trust and reciprocity.[30] In Coleman's definition, trust and social capital are equivalent. The implications of this are profound: Without trust, or social capital, you will not get a democratic society. *Democratic societies require people to work together for a common good.*

We can distinguish two kinds of social capital: bonding and bridging social capital. Bonding refers to the social capital we develop with people like us—same family, same tribe, and same ethnic group. Bridging social capital refers to the ties we develop between different groups and is, for purposes of creating a civic culture, the most important form. Social capital, acquired through membership in a network, can be used for positive or negative purposes. Members of Mexican drug cartels have well-developed networks used to accumulate wealth, provide benefits for their members, and solidify their economic power by bribing or murdering public officials. The person who volunteers to work at a local food bank will have social capital derived from the connections he or she makes with other volunteers, and these ties may be of benefit in another setting. Bonding and bridging capital are independent of one another. That is, close ties between members of an ethnic group or tribe do not necessarily give rise to bridging social capital. For example, ties between Sunni, Shiite, and Kurdish ethnic groups in Iraq were ruptured by the civil war that followed the invasion in 2003, which has prevented the formation of bridging social capital, making it extremely difficult to form a unified democratic state. As we shall see, when one ethnic or religious group is privileged over another, the potential for democracy dissolves. But how does any form of bridging social capital get created?

Creating Social Capital

In 1831, the young Frenchman Alexis de Tocqueville came to the United States to observe its prisons. However, his focus quickly shifted. Coming as he did from post-revolutionary France, he sought to understand how the American experiment in democracy was unfolding. Americans were the busiest people he had ever witnessed. They combined to "give fêtes, found seminaries, build churches, distribute books, and send missionaries to the antipodes." "Americans of all ages, all stations of life, and all types of disposition [were] forever forming associations."[31] This passion for joining groups brought people from different backgrounds together in a wide variety of settings to discuss political and social issues. Tocqueville reasoned that *American society would be a self-regulating society* that would not need the heavy hand of government to guide it. Norms of reciprocity and cooperation would grow out of collective interaction.

The greater the number of civic associations (or what we would today refer to as interest groups), the more deeply rooted are the cultural conventions that give rise to democracy. People learn to trust one another by working with one another. They learn the value of compromise by virtue of their involvement in voluntary associations and political organizations. Tocqueville's idea—that trust grows out of engagement—animates much of the literature on how democratic societies get created. I'll return to this point, but I want to note the observations of another visitor to America who was also fascinated by its ways.

The German sociologist and theorist, Max Weber (1864–1920), made his trip to America in 1904 to understand what would hold together a rapidly urbanizing and industrializing society when the kind of bonds of community and religion that had held European nations together had been dissolved. What Weber found was a nation focused on trade and commerce, with great geographic and social mobility. A fundamental of commerce is that you need to trust those with whom you sell and barter. Where does trust come from? You might be well known in your hometown and, as a result, people can trust you or not because they observe your actions and also know the character of your associates. Reputation is confined to the town's boundaries. But if the economy were to grow, it cannot be constrained by a town's boundaries.

Business dealings in the early twentieth century were not defined solely by laws and contracts; deals based on a handshake and trust were not uncommon. Businessmen thus needed some form of "moral currency" that would allow strangers to trust them. When you did business in communities different from your own, what mattered was your membership in networks that could be extended beyond the community. Weber's observations of America led him to believe that membership in fraternal organizations would

> Social networks are a form of bankable capital, no less important than cash, stocks, or bonds.

provide the bonds necessary for social harmony and the trust on which commerce depended. In the late nineteenth and early twentieth century many middle-class men were either members of some group like the Masons, Elks, Loyal Order of Moose, or they aspired to be. Being a member of the Masonic Brotherhood, whether you were from New

York City or Wichita, Kansas, opened doors for you with fellow Masons across the country. Members of fraternal organizations were members of networks that gave them *social capital*. Social capital was a real and bankable asset in that it could be used to facilitate business dealings. So, like Tocqueville, Weber saw social capital as arising through membership in organizations.

A caveat is in order here. Tocqueville thought that the associational behavior he witnessed was proof that Americans were a cooperative lot and their differences would be resolved by their coming together. What he ignored, because a class system was not yet well developed, was that differences in power, income, and wealth, would limit the development of trust and thus limit engagement. There were other divisions besides class. In many early American communities, particularly urban communities, people coalesced in distinct neighbors on the basis of their ethnicity. The holidays and celebrations Tocqueville witnessed were often ones that celebrated their inherent uniqueness. There were Irish Catholic enclaves, and Ulster Protestant Irish enclaves, as well as communities of Bohemians, Italians, Jews, and Cornish men and women. Riots broke out in New York between different Irish communities in 1871 when the Ulster Irish decided to organize a parade to celebrate their victory over the Irish Catholics. Bitter battles were fought between ethnic communities for jobs and political dominance. Certainly these diverse communities would become integrated in American society, but people continued to cast their votes, determine where they would live and which churches they would attend, based on their religion and ethnicity.

Weber was closer to the mark when he argued that fraternal organizations were a key to the integration of a diverse nation. A man could not, however, simply show up at the Masons or Loyal Order of the Moose, knock on the door and ask to join. Membership in most fraternal groups was by invitation, which meant that people asked those to join who were like them. And any prospective member could be "blackballed" by a single person. The result was that the voluntary associations and the networks being formed in nineteenth-century America brought together people of similar interests and backgrounds. In both the case of Tocqueville and Weber, the kind of social capital to which they were referring was *bonding social capital*, not bridging.

The child of wealthy parents who is sent to a private boarding school, then to an elite college, and who gets her first job at a company owned by one of her parents' friends certainly has economic capital, but it is her dense network of social connections, her social capital, which gives her a head start in life. Social capital allows those who possess it to gain access to positions of power and prestige and to maintain their privileges. The worker who loses his job and has to rely on friends and family for food or shelter also has bonding social capital—although it weighs more lightly on the scale than that of their wealthy counterpart. The differential allocation of social capital is one of the reasons why social mobility in a country like the United States is at an all-time low. *The concentration of wealth, the concentration of social capital, and social inequity are tightly coupled.*[32]

The Nature of Bridging Social Capital

The theorist who first popularized the idea of social capital was the political scientist Robert Putnam, perhaps best known for his 2002 work *Bowling Alone*.[33] He picks up where Tocqueville left off, seeing associations as key to democracy. The worry he expressed in that book was that the *number of horizontal connections (bridging social capital) between people was declining in America.* Focusing on the 1980s and 1990s, Putnam noted that even though there was an increase in the number of bowlers, people were not participating in leagues; they were bowling alone. He also found that membership in other forms of association, e.g., unions, trade organizations, symphony boards, the PTA, and the Boy Scouts, were down. But there are good reasons, rather than a disinterest in associating with other people, that membership in some associations is down. People are working more. When I asked leaders in the League of Women Voters and the American Association of University Women in my community, "Where is the younger generation?" the response was, "They're working." Changes in labor force participation by women and men have altered part of the neat equation whereby we can count on associations to provide the bonding agent for modern industrial societies. In addition, as I will discuss in Chapter 7, union membership, which used to bring together people for a common purpose, has dwindled significantly. And both men and women at the bottom of the income scale find themselves working two or more jobs to make ends meet.

Prior to his study of American society, Putnam had focused on Italy's economy and asked: Why did the southern Italian economy fail to launch, while that of the north served as the country's economic engine? His answer was that social capital was abundant in the north, while in the south it was in scarce supply.[34] He made the strong argument that associational behavior drove the economy. Putnam was provided with an exceptional natural experiment to study the effect that associations had on the creation of a democratic society. In 1970, Italy created twenty regional governments (five had existed previously and fifteen were added) to make policy decisions relevant to the citizens of each region. The central government thought it made good sense to let people govern themselves when the issues were not relevant to other regions or to the central government. Over time the twenty bodies gained significant governing power and they also received their fair share of national funds to spend. Twenty years later, Putnam noted what many others had: There was an economic divide between the north and south. The fact that all regional governments had the same powers and duties meant that something other than institutional design had to account for the differences he found. It was, he asserted, the vibrancy of associational life. In northern Italy people actively participated in sports clubs, literary guilds, service groups, and choral societies. In the north, regional governments were "efficient in their internal operation, creative in their policy initiatives, and effective in implementing those initiatives."[35]

In the south, associational ties were weaker than in the north, and the regional governments were corrupt and ineffective. The south was basically trapped by its own history. Vertical relations, such as those exemplified by middlemen or brokers, dominated economic transactions. The result was a form of debt peonage similar to that which existed in the U.S. South after the Civil War. The Mafia corrupted civil society, because it promoted norms of secrecy that limited social capital, such as it was, to members of one's immediate family. There were literally no political, social, or economic institutions that promoted trust and developed norms of reciprocity.

As Putnam concluded, "economics does not predict civics, but civics does predict economics."[36] The relationship between civic cooperation and social capital is circular.[37]

In an earlier study (1958), the political scientist Edward Banfield sought to answer the same question Putnam did. Why were southern Italian and Sicilian communities economically backward compared to those in northern Italy?[38] Banfield observed the "inability of the villagers to act together for their common good or, indeed, for any end transcending the immediate material interests of the nuclear family." He attributed this lack of cooperation to a culture of distrust, envy, and suspicion of others. People helped their neighbors only when they themselves could benefit from an "altruistic" act. Banfield labeled this complex of cultural behaviors amoral familism. In such a system, everything is a zero-sum game. Your good fortune must be my misfortune, even if I cannot figure out how. Though Banfield's focus was on a lack of trust, this lack of trust grew out of historic differences in power and influence.

A culture of mistrust is not something that evolves in isolation from political and economic institutions. In the case of southern Italy, Banfield noted that the presence of the Mafia in Sicily was one explanation for the rise of a culture of secrecy. In addition, Banfield saw the dominance and hierarchical structure of the Catholic Church as dampening down the growth of autonomous community-based groups. I believe a more accurate explanation for the rise of a culture of mistrust was that it was driven by gross economic inequities. The system of land tenure concentrated money in the hands of the few, leading to the impoverishment of small farmers and waged workers. An Italian, Carlo Conestabile, wrote to his local newspaper in 1881 explaining the poverty of his region:

> When wheat is grown the crop belongs entirely to the landlord, and the laborers are paid by the day; when maize is grown the landlord takes two-thirds of the crop and pays his workman with the other third. The grievance of this consists in this, that wages in money are very low, whereas wages in kind, if paid in maize, which is of very inferior value, are not sufficient for the proper maintenance of the laborer.[39]

And, when local farmers did own the land, the plots were so small as to make them unprofitable. This combination of circumstances—distrust that grows out of economic inequality—helps to explain why it is rational for people to take care of their families first and to assume the government is not there to help anyone, except those with power.

There are, then, different ways of looking at Putnam's data and his analysis. First, as Putnam himself acknowledges, there is a dark potential to social capital, even though it is essential to democracy. Shanker Satyanath and two of his colleagues at the National Bureau of Economic Research analyzed a cross-section of German cities and found that dense networks of civic associations such as bowling clubs, choirs, and animal breeders went hand-in-hand with a rapid rise of the Nazi Party. Whether the associations were bridging or bonding, their density in a city predicted the degree of support for the Nazi party.[40]

The second concern has to do with causal direction. There are other historical factors that could explain differences between the north and south in Italy. Italy is an industrialized nation, but industry and jobs are concentrated in the north, where clothes, shoes, furniture, automobiles, computers, and electronic equipment are now made. This industrialization is of long-standing, dating back to the late nineteenth and early twentieth century, and it bypassed southern Italy and Sicily. As early as the eleventh century, shipping, banking, commerce, art, and culture concentrated in northern cities like Florence, Rome, Milan, and Venice. It was in northern Italy that the Renaissance flourished. The trading links between Europe and northern Italy were established in the Middle Ages and deepened over the centuries. In other words, democratic institutions and industry were well in place by the time the Italian government gave greater power to regional governments.

In this view, Italy is simply playing its history out, with the economy, not associations, shaping the outcomes. As for good government, Italy has had 65 national governments in the 69 years since World War II.[41] Italians in general express less support for their government than other industrialized nations, and have a lower level of trust than other economically developed countries. Only 28% of Italians believe you can trust others, while 65% of Swedes do.[42] As I will later show, *the best predictor of trust and social capital within a nation state is not the degree of associational behavior but whether or not people see government institutions as effective.*[43]

Some believe that social capital and trust can be created *de novo*. If a country has a corrupt and ineffective government, the solution offered by many international aid organizations has been to encourage the creation of voluntary associations for which they sometimes provide the funding. Cities with high rates of unemployment, crime, or drug abuse have hoped they could solve those problems through the development of associations and social networks that would provide the necessary social capital. Some have argued we can solve the problem of climate change by creating more associations.[44] But it is not that simple, because *people have historical memories that determine what is possible in the future.* If people don't trust one another or their government, it closes off options for changing one's circumstances and dealing with emerging challenges.

Historical Conditions That Generate Low Levels of Trust

In a small Greek village where I was working in the 1960s, people got up early on a Monday mornings to go out to their fields, catch the bus for Athens, or go to school.[45] They turned on the tap to make coffee or tea or to wash up before the day began. But when they turned the faucet handle, nothing came out. In the late 1960s, the Greek government had decided they would run water from a spring-fed cistern at the top of a hill down to homes in a rural village, situated north of Athens. The new communal waterline, with pipes leading to individual homes, meant that the women and children of the village would no longer have to trek up to the top of the hill each day to fill buckets and other containers with water. With the help of some men in the village, a ditch was dug and red clay pipes were laid down the village's central street. The water flowed for a short time, but then the pipes were broken at night by some unknown person or persons. They were re-laid with the same result. This went on for over a month— the pipes would be repaired during the day and then destroyed in the dark—until people gave up. When I asked why people would deliberately break the pipes and deprive themselves the luxury of running water, the answer given was that the pipes were broken because only a few people, those whose homes were directly connected to the main line, were benefiting. The waterline should have come down every lane, and all families should have received the benefit. Waiting was not seen as an option, because, as many said, "How can we trust we will be allowed to connect to the main line in the future?"

The villagers who engaged in self-destructive behavior saw it as a reasonable way to protest what they saw as pervasive government corruption that seemed to benefit only the few, but not them. The explanation for who got what was grounded in power differentials between those with the right "connections" and those without. As an outsider, who was perceived to have power and connections, I was asked to help individual families seek revenge against other families. Distrust among villagers stemmed in part from the German occupation of Greece during World War II and its aftermath as different groups competed for power. Villagers still remembered who had fought for the resistance, who were communists, and who were royalists. Distrust had deep roots.

Beginning in the fifteenth century, Greeks had been part of the Ottoman Empire and did not receive their independence until the War of Greek Independence in 1825. *Their relationship with the Ottoman administrators taught corruption and mistrust.* For example, Greeks learned to hide their assets to avoid taxation and continue to hide them today from their own government. Trust or social capital is actually quite fragile. It can be destroyed by wars, economic downturns, and active discrimination.

The Fragility of Social Capital

Social capital is fragile. Both bridging and bonding social capital are subject to the vagaries of people's economic fortunes. The French social theorist, Pierre Bourdieu and nineteen of his colleagues undertook a major research effort to understand what they termed social suffering in contemporary French society.[46] They interviewed scores of people to grasp the social and psychological impacts people were suffering in the 1980s due to transformations in the French economy, high rates of unemployment, and the collapse of the steel industry.

Antonio Demoura and his wife migrated from Portugal to France in the mid-1960s, he to take up work as a mechanic and she as a janitor. With both of them working, they were able to buy a small home close to their places of work. Antonio was an exceptional soccer player and became part of the community by playing and eventually coaching for the local club. Everything was going well for Antonio until his wife had a stroke in 1985 at the age of 46. Then Antonio's toes were cut off by a lawnmower in 1990. Both of Antonio and his wife consequently had the usual set of problems that people living on the margins often have with social services. Antonio's doctor fitted him with orthopedic shoes that had open toes and told him he needed to return to work. At work he was told that he had to have safety shoes, so he was sent back to the doctor who eventually gave him the shoes he needed. This further delayed his going back to work. The delays in receiving services and long delays returning to work meant that they ran out of money. And that is when their integration—their *bridging social capital*— into French society came to an end. The soccer club dropped him after 19 years of service. As Antonio said:

> [I was] completely dropped ... I brought in a lot of support, I brought a lot of money... I gave money and trips, lost [work] time, paid for repairs to the clubhouse at the end of every season without getting a penny in return from the club. I paid out of my own pocket because it was my group, and today I have to pay to get into the stadium.[47]

The Demoura's hold on what they had thought of as "their" society was fragile and one that depended on money. Many middle-class Americans found themselves facing similar situations when the housing market began its collapse in 2008. Those people who lost their homes usually lost both bonding and bridging social capital. When they needed to move elsewhere, they lost connections to the neighborhoods in which they were raising their families, and their children lost friends at school.

The destruction of social capital limits people's abilities to participate in their own society, to make decisions on their own, and to create economically viable, democratic societies. The solution must be twofold. One way is create more effective governments that meet the needs of their people, creating trust and social capital. The second is to increase the level of *human capital*. As I noted in Chapter 1, there are fundamental needs or rights that all humans have, including subsistence, protection, affection, understanding, participation, freedom, and so forth. Whatever the society and however those needs are met, people must have the capacity to participate in the societies in which they live. Right now many countries squander human talent and thereby limit the creative potential people have to solve their nation's current problems, as well as emerging problems such as climate change. This squandering of talent reduces the resilience of any society.

Squandering of Human Talent

The United Nations created the Inequality-Adjusted Human Development Index (IHDI) to take into account not only how a country compares to others in terms of life expectancy, access to education, and standard of living, but to also measure and compare the *loss* of human development (what I have termed human capital) due to inequality.[48] Under perfect equality the Human Development Index (HDI) and the IHDI would be the same. But countries with equivalent HDI scores can vary considerably in terms of the IHDI when inequality is taken into account. For instance, the United States ranks as one of the world's ten most developed countries with an HDI score of 0.914, making it comparable to Norway, Australia, Switzerland, the Netherlands, and Germany in terms of levels of human development. However, when inequality (in income, education, and life expectancy) is taken into account, *the United States is an outlier among the most developed countries, wasting 17.4% of its human resources.*[49] Saudi Arabia, as another example, has a high HDI score (89%) but scores lower on the IHDI (32%), because it does not fully employ the talents of women.[50]

> Globally the average loss, in human development due to social inequality is 22.9%.

Worldwide, the average lost in overall human development due to inequality is 22.9%, ranging from a low of 5.5% in Finland to a high of 44.3% in Sierra Leone, even before the Ebola epidemic in the fall of 2014. Countries that waste human resources are often ones engaged in civil war. One reason for Sierra Leone's poor score on equality was that it was still recovering from a civil war that lasted for over a decade (1991–2002), led to the death of 50,000, and displaced upwards of 2 million people. Before civil war broke out in 1991, Sierra Leone's elected leaders had systematically perverted state agencies in the pursuit of private gain. So rapacious was the looting of public coffers that by the 1980s the state could no longer pay its civil servants; teachers were laid off, and schools were closed. Children whose parents could not afford private tutors wandered the streets, and some became child soldiers in one or more of the rebel forces that sought to take control of the country.

In spite of rich natural resources—diamonds, gold, and iron ore—by the time civil war broke out in 1991, Sierra Leone was one of the poorest countries in the world. People had suffered through years of poor governance, extreme poverty, corruption, and violent oppression by the military. The war drove more than 80,000 into refugee campus; many were children, most were starving or needed medical help. They proved to be ready recruits for the rebel armies. They were promised food and shelter, as well as a share in the spoils from looting and profits from gold and diamond mining. The atrocities visited on the general population by both rebel and government forces have been well documented and included forced abduction, murder, torture, rape, amputation, and sexual slavery.[51] It would take the help of United Nations and British forces to bring the war to an end. But years of ineffective governmental institutions have left deep scars on the body politic of Sierra Leone, including a lack of trust by members of different ethnic groups, just as is currently true in Iraq and will be true in Syria.

Internationally, the losses in human capital due to inequality reveal somewhat different patterns, depending on the region of the world. For example, the United Nations reports that in "Sub-Saharan Africa the losses are due to inequality in all dimensions, followed by South Asia and the Arab States and Latin America and the Caribbean. Sub-Saharan Africa suffers the highest inequality in health (36.6%), while South Asia has the highest inequality in education (41.6%). The region of Arab States also has the highest inequality in education (38%), Latin America and the Caribbean suffers the largest inequality in income (36.3%)."[52] The following tables will make clear how inequality destroys trust.

Table 5.1 Comparison of Countries with Lowest and Highest Losses of Human Capital Due to Inequality

High Loss		*Low Loss*	
Sierra Leone	44.3%	Finland	5.5%
Angola	44.0%	Norway	5.6%
Central African Republic	40.4%	Iceland	5.7%

(Continued)

High Loss		Low Loss	
Guinea-Bissau	39.6%	Slovenia	5.8%
Haiti	39.5%	Sweden	6.5%
Botswana	38.5%	Netherlands	6.7%
Guinea	38.0%	Denmark	6.9%
Chad	37.8%	Germany	7.1%
Lesotho	35.6%	Austria	7.2%
Djibouti	34.6%	Switzerland	7.7%
Benin	34.6%	Australia	7.8%
		[U.S. = 17.4]	

Source: Adapted from the United Nations. 2014. "Inequality Adjusted Human Development Index." Accessed August 20, 2014 from: http://hdr.undp.org/en/content/inequality-adjusted-human-development-index-ihdi.
Note: Average loss for all countries = 22.9%

The countries in the right-hand column (Finland to Australia) have similar traits. All of those countries most equitable in terms of life expectancy, living standards, and access to education are mature democracies. The rule of law also characterizes the developed countries and its absence characterizes those countries with the highest degree of inequality. *The rule of law is critical for either maintaining a democracy or creating a democracy, because it signals that people are not receiving special treatment or being discriminated against on the basis of irrelevant moral criteria.* (Table 5.2 looks at this relationship.)[53] Without a rule of law, corruption wins out.

Table 5.2 Corruption and Freedom in Those Countries Demonstrating High Levels of Inequality

	Level of Corruption Index	*Freedom Index*
Chad	163	6.5
Guinea-Bissau	163	5.5
Haiti	163	4.5
Angola	153	5.5
Central African Republic	144	7.0
Guinea	144	5.0
Sierra Leone	119	3.0
Benin	94	2.0

	Level of Corruption Index	Freedom Index
Djibouti	94	5.5
Lesotho	55	2.5
Botswana	30	2.5

Source: The World Bank. 2014. "Freedom House Index, 2014." Accessed at: http://www.freedomhouse.org/.
Notes: Range for *Level of Corruption Index* = 1–175, with 1 = least corrupt. Range for *Freedom Index* = 1–7, with 1 = most democratic. World Bank. 2014. "Governance Indicators." Accessed at: http://data.worldbank.org/data-catalog/worldwide-governance-indicators.

Inequality, Corruption, and Democracy

Using the Freedom House Index of Democracy to assess the degree of civil and political liberties in any given country, level of corruption, and those countries showing the highest degree of wasted human capital, we can find another pattern, shown in Table 5.2. Those countries with the highest levels of inequality (IHDI) are not democracies, and they all suffer from poor political institutions. That is, they tend toward closure as opposed to openness.[54] The measure of corruption comes from the World Bank, which ranks 175 countries in terms of levels of corruption or absence of good government.[55] The measure assesses whether or not the rule of law is upheld, meaning whether everyone is treated equally before the law. (It can also be seen as a proxy for democracy.) Sierra Leone, for example, is the nineteenth most corrupt state out of all 175 ranked and, with a score of 3.0 on the Freedom Index, is only a partial democracy. The Central African Republic has no civil or political liberties, yielding the lowest possible score of 7.0; it ranks 144th most corrupt out of 175 countries.

Why is there *a strong negative relationship between level of corruption and degree of democracy?* Virtually all of those countries with high levels of corruption (Sierra Leone, Angola, the Central African Republic, Chad, and so forth) have suffered through years, sometimes decades of civil war, military coups, ethnic conflicts, and, as we saw in the case of Haiti, natural disasters that exposed fault lines in the larger society. The winners in these conflicts, especially ethnic conflicts, saw the spoils of war as belonging to them. In Chad, for example, civil wars (2005–2010) sprung up sporadically between Arab Muslims and Christians. Whoever was in power, the other side would try to oust with the explanation that those in power were privileging their ethnic group. As of 2015, there is a genocidal war taking place between Christians and Muslims in the Central African Republic, and Angola is recovering from 27 years of civil war. On the other hand, Botswana, which is low on the corruption index and high on democracy, has had a civilian government for four decades. The reason it scores low on the inequality index (Table 5.1) is because it scores low on the indicator for health. It has one of the highest levels of AIDS in Africa, although one of the more progressive programs to deal with it.

The Rise of the Ethnic State

The Cambridge University historian, David Reynolds, has observed the rise of two types of nations—the civic nation and the ethnic nation. The civic nation is "a community of laws, institutions, and citizenship." A founding creed of the United States was that "We hold these truths to be self-evident, that all men are created equal, that they are endowed by their Creator with certain unalienable Rights, and that among these are Life, Liberty and the pursuit of Happiness." An ethnic nation, on the other hand, is a "community of shared descent, rooted in language, ethnicity, and culture."[56] The fragmentation of the Balkan states into Croatia (Catholic), Serbia and Montenegro (Orthodox Christian), and Bosnia and Herzegovina (Muslim) are clear examples of ethnic nations, and bloody wars were fought to establish their boundaries and to deprive members of opposing ethnic groups or religions of their rights. When people are discriminated against on the basis of durable inequities such as ethnicity and religion, they are unlikely to trust other people or their governments.

Table 5.3 looks at the relationship between trust, democracy, ethnic fractionalization, and the rule of law. *Countries with the lowest levels of trust are also characterized by ethnic fractionalization and the absence of the rule of law.* Column 1, "Democracy," comes from the Freedom House Index and level of trust comes from the World Value Survey. Ethnic fractionalization in Table 5.3 is determined by the number of languages spoken in a country, with 0 being the score for one language and 1 being the score for more than one. A score of 0 would mean that everybody spoke the same language. In Norway most people speak Norwegian giving it a score of .09 on ethnic fractionalization. At the other extreme there are 126 living languages spoken in Tanzania, giving it an ethnic fractionalization score of 0.95.[57] The average for all countries in the world in terms of ethnic fractionalization is 0.47. In those countries demonstrating the lowest levels of trust, 8 out of 10 are above the average. The rule of law data comes from the World Bank and the scores run from a high of 1.95 in Finland to a low of −2.45 in Somalia. The average for all nations in terms of the rule of law is 1.72, which means all of the low-trust societies are below the average for that variable.

Table 5.3 Countries That Exhibit the Highest and Lowest Levels of Trust with Degree of Ethnic Fractionalization and Observation of the Rule of Law

	Democracy	*Ethnic Fractionalization*	*Rule of Law*
Lowest trust levels			
Tanzania	3	.95	−0.58
Uganda	5	.93	−0.36
Ghana	1.5	.85	−0.03
Iran	5.5	.67	−1.50
Trinidad and Tobago	2	.65	−0.19
Peru	2.5	.64	−0.61
Malaysia	4	.60	+0.51
Brazil	2	.55	−0.11
Zimbabwe	5.5	.37	−1.62
Algeria	5.5	.32	−1.72
Highest trust levels			
Norway	1	.09	+1.95
Finland	1	.13	+1.94
Australia	1	.15	+1.75
China	6.5	.15	−0.49
Sweden	1	.19	+1.93
Switzerland	1	.19	+1.81
Vietnam	6	.23	−0.50
New Zealand	1	.36	+1.88
Saudi Arabia	7	.55	+0.24
Indonesia	3	.77	−0.60
Average	5.52	.47	+1.72

Sources: Measure of democracy, Freedom House, "Freedom in the World, 2015." https://freedomhouse.org/report/freedom-world/freedom-world-2015#.Vd-ODiVVhHw; Ethnic fractionalization comes from the CIA World Fact Book, "Ethnic Groups." https://www.cia.gov/library/publications/the-world-factbook/fields/2075.html; Data on the rule of law is derived from the World Bank, "Worldwide Governance Indicators." http://databank.worldbank.org/data/reports.aspx?source=Worldwide-Governance-Indicators; Level of trust is derived from the World Values Survey, "Wave 6, 2010–2014."

In summary, as Table 5.3, makes clear: *Trust is strongly related to ethnic homogeneity* (in, for instance, states such as Norway, Finland, Australia, and China) *and to the rule of law.* There are three exceptions among the high trust nations in terms of the rule of law. China and Vietnam are one-party dictatorships and Indonesia has experienced clashes between Muslims and Christians that have lead to the suspension of many civil rights. One reason for the relationship between ethnic homogeneity and trust is that when a country is ethnically homogeneous, there is likely to be less discrimination based on ethnicity. *Ethnicity, when coupled with inequality, reduces trust.* Trust is also reduced when a country suffers from crime or other forms of internal conflict. It should be no surprise that people in Trinidad and Tobago (Table 5. 3, column 1) do not trust one another because it is a country wracked by drug crimes and related violence. *Where crime and corruption are high, trust is low.*[58]

> Trust is strongly related to ethnic homogeneity and the rule of law.

The relationship between trust, rule of law, and democracy, and ethnic diversity is not invariable. There are many countries with diverse ethnic populations that are democracies or are on their way to becoming full democracies. For example, Indonesia has upwards of 300 different ethnic groups. Malaysia has twenty different ethno-linguistic groups and Indonesia's multi-ethnic population is made up of Chinese, native Malaysians and Indians. *Ethnic diversity does not in itself lead to a breakdown of democracy. It does so when people are excluded from government and economic opportunities because of their ethnicity.* Discrimination wastes resources and leads to conflict.[59]

The sociologist Andreas Wimmer and his colleagues have linked the outbreak of civil wars and political unrest to ethnic discrimination in multi-ethnic societies.[60] Halvard Buhaug of the Peace Research Institute in Oslo and others have also shown that differences in economic inequality between ethnic groups and political discrimination drives violence.[61] It should come as no surprise that when people are shut out of participation in societies that privilege some at the expense of others, the dispossessed will use violent and non-democratic means to acquire power.

Ethnic groups, tribal groups, and clan networks are *trust networks*. As the sociologist Charles Tilly has argued, *trust networks must be integrated into the state, if it is to assume a democratic nature.*[62] Ethnic groups and clans will resist being incorporated into the state unless they derive benefits from doing so or can see that all groups will be treated equally before the law. Political and economic systems that are closed, as we can see from the above tables, are ones where people do not trust one another. Trust can be easily destroyed by corrupt institutions.

Institutions and Trust

I argued earlier that people join organizations of like-minded people when they trust one another and that whether or not people trust one another depends in large part on whether or not their own government is seen as trustworthy. The World Bank has developed a World Governance Indicator (WGI) to assess the processes by which governments are chosen, monitored and replaced; the ability of the government to effectively formulate and implement policies; and the respect that citizens have for the institutions that govern social and economic interactions among them.[63] If I take those ten countries that score highest and lowest on the WGI index, with the exception of the Russian Federation and Moldova, the lowest scoring countries are in Africa: Burkina Faso, Rwanda, Ghana, Zimbabwe, Egypt, Ethiopia, Zambia, and Mali. Those scoring high on the WGI are all developed countries: Australia, Canada, Finland, Hong Kong, Japan, New Zealand, Netherlands, Norway, Sweden, and Switzerland. And, when I examined the relationship between scores on the WGI (good governance) and the IHDI (wasted resources due to inequity) for these countries good government and equality go hand in hand.[64] When government performs well—meets the needs of all its citizens—people are happy with their lives, their economic situations, and they trust one another. Good and effective government explains positive outcomes and, as we'll see in the case of the United States, it explains why trust in the government continues to drop.

When we look at those factors that give rise to trust across nations, the importance of good institutions comes more clearly into focus.[65] In the analysis advanced by Robert Putnam, participation in associations should relate to trust and democracy. To assess this claim I used data from the World Values Survey across all nations of the world (200+) for which data was provided and looked at specific forms of associations, e.g., sports, music, philanthropic organizations, religious groups, environmental groups, and so forth to see if membership related to trust. *There was no relationship between membership in associations of any kind and levels of trust.* Even when I added all forms of associational behavior together there was still no relationship.[66] What did relate to levels of trust in a society was the level of human development; satisfaction with one's economic lot; high personal income level; the rule of law; and perception of the quality of the government. This demonstrates a point made by others about good government and trust. There is a "rainmaker" effect, where the most effective governments create the conditions for generalized trust in others to flourish.[67]

> Trust depends on government acting in a fair and impartial manner.

In sum, democratic, equitable societies in which a rule of law predominates, and the government is effective in dealing with the needs of its citizens, show the highest levels of trust and the highest levels of engagement. To underscore the point, democracy is about far more than whether or not people can vote. *For social capital to develop there must be a political system that operates in an impartial manner.* Trust, however, has declined in recent years in the developed countries of Western Europe, because citizens perceive their governments as not meeting their immediate social and economic needs, which is exacerbated by the influx of immigrants. A poll of European Union citizens in 2014 clearly showed a significant drop in levels of trust in national governments since the onset of the financial crisis in 2007/2008. Only 24% of Europeans expressed trust in their national governments to solve the problems of unemployment, the economy, debt, and inflation.[68] Levels of trust in others and one's government was lowest in those European countries hardest hit by the global downturn of 2007, namely Greece, Ireland, Italy, Portugal, and Spain.[69]

As the Swedish political scientist Bo Rothstein has noted, corruption, ethnic conflicts, suspicion, treachery, opportunism, discrimination and deceit in societies all poison the atmosphere for cooperation.[70] What happens when people do not believe their government is meeting their needs and allowing them to reach their potential Let us consider the case of the United States, which has seen over several decades a long decline in trust in both political institutions and trust in others.

Declining Trust in the United States

As I noted earlier, the United States has a high degree of income inequality compared to other nations. Like other industrialized, democratic nations it has open institutions and, relatively speaking, an effective government. Nevertheless, public opinion polls reveal deep divisions within the country and declining trust in the Federal government. One of the most significant divides in the country remains the racial divide.

Divided by race

Equal and impartial treatment by government agencies is critical to the development of trust. On August 9, 2014, an unarmed Black teenager, Michael Brown, was shot six times, twice in the head, by a police officer outside an apartment complex in Ferguson, Missouri. Ferguson, a suburb of St. Louis, is a predominately African-American community, policed by a force that is almost exclusively White. Fifty of Ferguson's 53 officers were White. Rioting and looting continued for several days after the death of Brown and demonstrators were confronted by heavily armed policemen in battle gear acquired as surplus from the U.S. military. An Associated Press report on the conflict was filed by Jim Salter and posted on Yahoo's news site on August 16.[71] By August 27, the posting had generated 35,010 comments, a huge number. Virtually 99% of them were racist in tone. Blacks were portrayed as lazy leeches supported by hard-working White taxpayers. Looting by Blacks was blamed on President Obama. The media were seen to be biased in favor of minorities and clearly hated Whites. Michael Brown was described as a thug who got what was coming to him.[72]

The PEW Research Center conducted interviews August 14–17, 2014, of 1,000 adults and found, to use their words, that there were "Stark racial divisions in reactions to Ferguson police shooting."[73] Eighty percent of Blacks who were interviewed said that the shooting of Michael Brown raised important racial issues, whereas only 37% of Whites did. Conversely, 47% of Whites thought race was getting too much attention in the coverage of the shooting, while only 18% of Blacks did. Sixty-five percent of Blacks thought the police had gone too far in shooting the teenager, but only 33% of Whites felt that way. Blacks indicated they had little confidence (18%) that the investigations of the shooting would have any positive results, while 52% of Whites believed that "justice should take its course." The racial divide was also reflected in political party membership. Sixty-eight percent of Democrats thought the shooting raised important racial issues, but only 22% of Republicans agreed. Republicans tended to see the police response as appropriate and expressed confidence that "justice would be done."

African-Americans have very different experiences with the judicial system than Whites. In cases of fatal police shootings in cities like Las Vegas, New York, Los Angeles, and San Diego, Blacks represent a disproportionately high number of the victims.[74] Years of discrimination have caused African-Americans to be distrusting of their fellow Americans.[75] In a 2012 survey by the National Opinion Research Center (NORC) at the University of Chicago, 80% of Black Americans said you "can't be too careful" in terms of trusting others. This figure has remained remarkably steady since 1972. Erik M. Uslaner, professor of government and politics at the University of Maryland, attributes this lack of trust to poverty. "People who believe the world is a good place and it's going to get better and you can help make it better, they will be trusting," according to Uslaner. On the other hand, "If you believe it's dark and driven by outside forces you can't control, you will be a mistruster."[76] In short, inequality of opportunity resulting in radically different life chances, drives pessimism about the future, erodes trust, and hence, social cohesion.[77]

Divided by class and political party

National opinion polls consistently show that people with less education and less money are less likely to trust others and their governments.[78] People who do not trust the government are less likely to trust one another.[79] In 1960, 58% of Americans indicated they trusted other people, but this declined to 34% by 2006. For the group referred to by the PEW Research Center as the "young millennials," that is, those in the 18–33 age range, levels of trust in others reached a low of 19% in 2014.[80] Another poll, conducted in 2013 by the Associated Press and GfK, an international polling firm, showed that 78% of Americans have little faith in the people they meet while traveling, indicating they trust them "just somewhat," "not too much," or "not at all." Seventy-five percent mistrust other drivers, bikers, or walkers. The numbers are also bad for those who scan our credit cards,

> Since 1940, income inequality has increased in every state in the nation.

those with whom we share information on social media sites, those people who prepare our food when we eat out, and those people who come into our homes to do work. When Americans were asked if they could trust the government in Washington to do what is right, 81% of Americans said they could do so only some of the time.[81] Why the growing mistrust in others and the government?

Jennifer M. Silva, a sociologist of culture and inequality, interviewed over 100 working-class twenty- and thirty-somethings in Lowell and Richmond, Virginia to try to understand what it means to come of age in a world of disappearing jobs, soaring educational costs, and social isolation. Those she writes about are the people:

> Bouncing from one temporary job to the next; dropping out of college because they can't figure out financial aid forms or fulfill their major requirements; relying on credit cards for medical emergencies; and avoiding romantic commitments because they can take care of only themselves. Increasingly disconnected from institutions of work, family and community, they grow up by learning that counting on others will only hurt them in the end. Adulthood is not simply being delayed but dramatically reimagined.[82]

People's level of optimism about economic growth has fallen. In 1987, 67% of the population believed that the possibility of economic growth was unlimited. This figure fell to 51% by 2012, driven down no doubt by the economic collapse of 2007/2008.[83] A more telling reason for the continued drop in levels of trust in others and faith in the government has been the steady increase in the Gini coefficient, the measure used for income inequality. *Income inequality has increased since 1940 in every state in the nation.*[84] The Gini coefficient was at its highest level in 1920, dropped with the Great Depression of the 1930s and has now reached levels similar to those in the 1920s. As we detailed in Chapter 2, wage levels and household incomes for the average American have been frozen in place or declined since the 1970s, while the income and wealth of the 1% climbed steeply.

A growing number of Americans give every indication that they believe the economic and political system is rigged. When people think a game is fixed, many simply sit down and refuse to play. Almost two-thirds of eligible voters sat out the vote in the 2010 midterm federal elections (only 38% voted) and even the excitement of the 2008 presidential election drew just over half of the electorate (57%). In the 2012 presidential race, where the choice was presented as one between big government and one in which social safety nets and taxes would be cut, the turnout was lower than in 2008 (56% in 2012).

While there is broad distrust of the federal government, there are wide differences in terms in terms of political party, gender, age, and education. Among Democrats, 28% trust the federal government always or most of the time, while only 10% of Republicans do. Only 3% of those who identify with the Tea Party trust the government all of the time, with 76% saying they trust it only some of the time and 20% indicating they never trust the government. Female college graduates trust the government (26%) more than male college graduates (15%) and among those

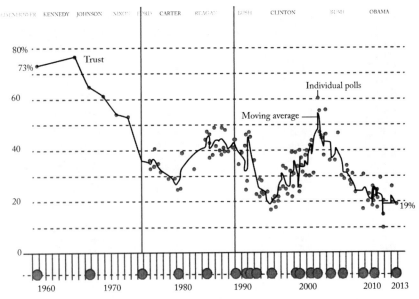

Figure 5.1 How Much of the Time Do You Trust the Government in Washington?
Source: "Public Trust in Government 1958–2014" Pew Research Center, Washington, DC, (November 2014). Retrieved from: http://www.people-press.org/2014/11/13/public-trust-in-government/.

who have not completed college men and women generally express low levels of trust (14% and 15% respectively.)[85]

Trust is not generated in the abstract. Trust in others and trust in government depends on specific economic, political, and social circumstances. As Figure 1 indicates, there is great variation from the time of Eisenhower's administration to Obama's. The decline in trust began with Nixon and was a product of Nixon's personality and the Watergate Trials, as well as the war in Vietnam. Trust continued to trend downward during the Carter administration, which saw gas prices skyrocket during the Arab oil embargo. Doubts about America's global hegemony increased with the Iranian hostage crisis, when a group of young Islamic revolutionaries overran the U.S. Embassy, took sixty Americans hostage, and held them for 444 days. They were released when Reagan was elected, who assured America that now all was well. Reagan's political success was due, argues the historian and journalist Rick Perlstein, to his ability to create a "cult of optimism"—the belief that America could do no wrong and that tomorrow would always be better. Yet it was under Reagan that conservatives developed and began to act on the mantra that government was the problem, not the solution to America's ills.[86] Trust slid down again during George H.W. Bush's presidency when he raised taxes, but spiked upward with the First Gulf War and the defeat of Saddam Hussein's forces in Kuwait. Clinton's presidency began on an upbeat note, driven by growing prosperity, but declined during the hearings about his infidelity and lying. Trust returned, temporarily, with George W. Bush's administration and his declaration that he would be a "war president," after the attacks on the Pentagon and the World Trade (Twin) Towers on September 11, 2001. As the war in Afghanistan and Iraq dragged on and the economy plunged, trust continued downward; it bumped temporarily upward with Obama's victory, only to slide again.

Clearly much distrust is the result of partisan rancor, but it is also due to the fact that many Americans, regardless of their political party, do not believe the government is meeting *their* needs. This is why trust has declined in European states—national governments are not perceived as meeting the needs of their citizens. In societies divided by wealth and inequality, we expect our candidates to win and to take care of us, whether we are in Haiti, Kenya, or the United States.

One of our own

The 2014 Democratic primary in New York pitted Charles Rangel, an African-American who had served in Congress since 1970, against a Dominican-American, Adriano Espaillat. Rangel had won previous races, in large part because his district was heavily African-American, but changing demographics had made the area more diverse. In an exit poll interview conducted by a National Public Radio reporter, a voter who self-identified as a Dominican-American indicated he had voted for Espaillat, saying, "It would be nice to have one of our own in office." Rangel won with 47% of the vote to Espaillat's 44%.

Loyalty to one's own kind—class or ethnic group—can shape people's perception of public institutions and level of trust. Detroit, Michigan's population is 83% African-American and was one of the hardest hit of all cities by the economic downturn in the fortunes of automobile manufacturers. Kwame Kilpatrick, an African-American, served as Detroit's mayor from 2002–2008 and was regarded as one of the most corrupt mayors ever to serve a major city; he was certainly Detroit's most corrupt mayor. Although other public officials in Detroit were guilty of extortion, bribery, and fraud, Kilpatrick was alone in being convicted on 24 felony counts, including mail fraud, wire fraud, and racketeering. He was sentenced to 28 years in prison, but this had little effect on levels of trust in local government. As Figure 5.2 clearly shows, the level of support among African-Americans for city government was at or above 80% before Kilpatrick went to jail, at which time the Governor appointed a manager for the city and it entered into receivership.

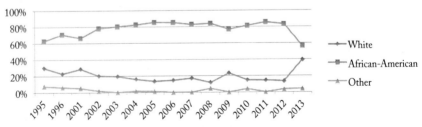

Figure 5.2 Trust in Local Government by Race in Detroit
Source: Data from the 1994–2013 Michigan State University's Institute for Public Policy and Social Research, "State of the State Survey." http://ippsr.msu.edu/soss/. Data compiled by Miles Allen McNall and used with his permission and that of Michigan State University.

As long as our own particularistic needs are met, and our candidate is in office, we tend to trust. According to Barry Hollander, professor of journalism at the University of Georgia, when people are asked who will win an election they predict their own candidate will. Surprise when he doesn't win erodes trust. As Hollander says:

> We have become more fragmented in our media diet and that leads to hearing what we want to hear and believing what we want to believe, despite all evidence to the contrary ... Our surprise in election outcomes makes us angry, disappointed and erodes our trust in the basic concept of democracy ... And that can threaten our trust in government.[87]

Hollander found that 78% of all Romney supporters in the 2012 election believed he would win, in spite of nearly all the polls showing that Obama would. Why did Romney supporters believe he would win? Because they talked to friends and family who agreed with them and because the majority of Romney supporters watched the Fox News Channel. The upshot was that when Romney lost, his supporters—including Fox viewers—expressed a loss of trust in the government. The polarization by ethnicity and political party in the United States is leading to an unwinding of the democratic project. The British historian, Niall Ferguson, has referred to this as the "great degeneration" now taking place among liberal democracies where institutions and laws have been bent to serve the interests of the few.[88]

Summary

What can we say about democracy, equality, and trust? Trust depends on equality and on the concrete experiences people have with their fellow citizens and with their governments. For trust, and by extension democracy, to flourish there must be open political and economic institutions. People cannot be excluded from participation based on irrelevant moral criteria, and all people must be treated as equal before the law. In this view, it is the job of the government to create good institutions that give rise to trust. Associational behavior does not by itself give rise to trust; trust gives rise to associational behavior and creates the conditions for democratic societies. *When human talent is squandered, inequities prevail, corruption deepens, and democracy fails to take root.* Human capital must be created, because it is human capital that allows people to participate actively in their own societies. The evidence is clear: people who are economically deprived, discriminated against on the basis of age, gender, or religion, do not trust. Without trust, we end up with countries like Haiti, Zimbabwe, or Rwanda.

Through a Sustainability Lens

All countries must prepare themselves to deal with the consequences of climate change. The challenges faced by some of the poorest countries are substantial. They are frequently plagued by civil wars, weak institutions, and surrounded by hostile neighbors.[89] They require the full development of human capital (the knowledge, the capacity and the freedom to act) if they are to make progress in solving problems related to social inequality. The University of Notre Dame has constructed a global-adaptation index (ND-GAIN) to assess the degree to which the countries of the world are vulnerable to the effects of climate change (drought, rising sea levels, severe weather, acidification of ocean fisheries, and so forth) and a country's readiness to improve resilience to related challenges.[90] Resilience in the index is a measure of the human resources and fiscal resources a society has to return to a previous state, after a major perturbation such as an earthquake, flood, or hurricane. In short, inequity is a factor militating against resilience.

Table 5.4 Readiness for Climate Change

Readiness Bottom Tier	Readiness Score	Readiness Top Tier	Readiness Score
North Korea	34.3	Japan	72.7
Afghanistan	35.9	U.S.	79.0
Burundi	38.7	Sweden	79.7
Central African Republic	39.6	Luxemburg	79.7
Eretria	39.8	UK	79.7
Chad	39.9	Ireland	79.8
Zimbabwe	40.1	Australia	80.0
Dem. Rep. of Congo	40.2	Netherlands	80.0
Sudan	40.6	Finland	80.8
Iraq	41.1	Switzerland	83.0
Togo	42.4	Denmark	83.4

Source: Notre Dame Gain Index. http://index.nd-gain.org:8080/index_main.py?tool_type=basic.

For example, out of 177 countries ranked, Haiti is the 158th country least likely to be able to deal with climate change and its consequences.

As Table 5.4 indicates, no country is completely ready for the effects of climate change, but those countries in the left-hand column are fully 100 years behind those in the right-hand column in terms of their readiness to cope with climate change and the consequences of climate change. None of the countries least prepared to deal with climate change have open political and economic systems. None are full democracies and some, like North Korea, fall very far from the standard of free and open societies.[91] None of these societies have effective governments; the rule of law does not operate within them; and their citizens tend not to trust one another. They maintain gross inequities, waste human resources, and fail to develop their citizens' capacity to deal with change.

Marcus King, director of research at the George Washington School of International Affairs, sees climate change as an *instability accelerant*.[92] That is, it will accelerate migration as people cross national borders in search of food and water. It will lead to political instability and the rise of terrorism as poor nations face a set of interrelated problems and fail to meet the needs of their citizens. As Stephen Cheney, retired Marine Corps Brigadier General, noted, there is a tight relationship between political disorder and climate change. "The massive forest fires in Russia in 2010 caused wheat prices to skyrocket around the world, particularly in the Middle East, and that helped sow the seeds of the unrest for the Arab Spring."[93]

We don't know what all of the future challenges will be as a result of the interplay between inequity and climate change. What we do know is that we must be prepared to *adapt to new circumstances and the best way to do that is to free up human creativity and talent*. What stands in the way is inequity. Inequity erodes trust, and right now America is headed in the wrong direction.

Notes

1 Jonathan A. Lassa. 2011. "Japan's Resilience to Tsunamis and the Lessons for Japan and the World: An Early Observation." Cambridge, MA: Harvard University Press. Accessed August 15, 2015 at: http://www.zef.de/module/register/media/b4d0_Japantsunami%20resilience31mar2011.pdf.

2 Martin Fackler. 2011. "Severed from the World, Villagers Survive on Tight Bonds and To-Do Lists." *New York Times*. March 23. Accessed August 15, 2015 at: http://www.nytimes.com/2011/03/24/world/asia/24isolated.html?pagewanted=all.

3 Carol Gluck. 2011. Cited in Susan Donaldson James and Russell Goldman, "Japanese, Waiting in Line for Hours, Follow Social Order after Quake." March 15, ABC News. Transcript accessed at: http://abcnews.go.com/Health/japan-victims-show-resilience-earthquake-tsunami-sign-sense/story?id=13135355#.UKvf7eRlEZ8.
4 Daniel P. Aldrich. 2010. "Fixing Recovery: Social Capital in Post-Crisis Resilience." *Journal of Homeland Security*. Accessed at: http//works.bepress.com/daniel_aldrich/7.
5 Daniel P. Aldrich. 2012. *Building Resilience: Social Capital in Post-Disaster Recovery*. Chicago, IL: University of Chicago Press.
6 U.S. Government, Central Intelligence Agency, "World Fact Book, Gini Index." https://www.cia.gov/library/publications/the-world-factbook/rankorder/2172rank.html.
7 Chad Stone, Danilo Trisi, Arloc Sherman, and Brandon Debot. July 14, 2015. A Guide to Statistics on Historical Trends in Income Inequality. Washington, DC: Center on Budget and Policy Priorities. http://www.cbpp.org/research/poverty-and-inequality/a-guide-to-statistics-on-historical-trends-in-income-inequality.
8 Rebecca Solnit. 2009. *A Paradise Built in Hell: The Extraordinary Communities that Arise in Disaster*. New York, NY: Viking, p.2.
9 Ibid., p.42.
10 Ibid., pp.34–35.
11 Ibid., p.23.
12 Klein. 2008. The Shock Doctrine. New York, NY: Macmillan/Picador.
13 Anastasia Moloney. 2014. "It's 2014: Why Are Haitians Still Living in Makeshift Tents?" Reuters and Women's News Network. Retrieved on August 14, 2014 at: http://www.haitian-truth.org/tens-of-thousands-of-families-stuck-in-haiti-camps-iom/.
14 National Public Radio, January 11, 2011, news report.
15 Randal C. Archibold. 2011. "Haiti Hopes to Shrink Capital, Revive Rural Areas." *The New York Times* (December 25).
16 Amnesty International. 2014. "Haiti: Failure to Deal with the Consequences of the 2010 Devastating Earthquake." Retrieved on August 14, 2014 at: http://www.amnesty.org/en/library/info/AMR36/002/2014/en; and Jacqueline Charles. 2014. "Haiti's Homeless Earthquake Victims Drop Significantly, but Worry Continues." April 8. *Miami Herald*. Retrieved on August 14, 2014 at: http://www.miamiherald.com/2014/04/08/4046270/haitis-homeless-earthquake-victims.html.
17 Jared Diamond. 2005. *Collapse: How Societies Choose to Fail or Succeed*. New York, NY: Viking.
18 Daron Acemoglu and James A. Robinson. 2012. *Why Nations Fail: The Origins of Power, Prosperity, and Poverty*. New York, NY: Crown, p.9.
19 Dominique Zéphyr, Abby Córdova, Hugo Salgado, and Mitchell A. Seligson. 2011. *Haiti in Distress: The Impact of the 2010 Earthquake on Citizen Lives and Perceptions*. Nashville, TN: Vanderbilt University Press. Accessed on August 15, 2014 at: http://www.vanderbilt.edu/lapop/haiti/2010-presentation-en.pdf. The countries compared are: Argentina, Belize, Bolivia, Brazil, Canada, Chile, Columbia, Dominican Republic, Ecuador, El Salvador, Guatemala, Guyana, Haiti, Honduras, Jamaica, Mexico, Nicaragua, Panama, Paraguay, Peru, Suriname, Trinidad and Tobago, United States, Uruguay, and Venezuela.

20 Ibid., p.40.
21 Ibid., p.xx.
22 Ibid., pp.44–46.
23 World Values Survey. 2014. "Data and Analysis" for 2014 series. Retrieved on August 15, 2014 at: http://www.worldvaluessurvey.org/WVSContents.jsp.
24 World Bank. 2014. Accessed on August 19 at: http://data.worldbank.org/country/nepal.
25 Askvik Steinar, Jamil Ishtiaq, and Tek Nath Dhakal. 2011. "Citizen's Trust in Public and Political Institutions in Nepal." *International Political Science Review*. 32(4): 417–437.
26 S. Mansoob Murshed and Scott Gates. 2005. "Spatial-Horizontal Inequality and the Maoist Insurgency in Nepal." *Review of Development Economics*. 9(1): 121–134.
27 Kimber Haddix McKay. 2014. Personal communication.
28 For a detailed review of the literature on trust and its relationship to the effectiveness of governments, see: Peri K. Blind. 2006. "Building Trust in Government in the Twenty-First Century: Review of Literature." Accessed on August 17, 2014 at: http://unpan1.un.org/intradoc/groups/public/documents/UN/UNPAN025062.pdf.
29 Francis Fukuyama. 1995. *The Social Virtues and Creation of Prosperity*. New York, NY: Free Press.
30 James S. Coleman. 1988. "Social Capital in the Creation of Human Capital." *American Journal of Sociology*. 94 Supplement: Organizations and Institutions: Sociological and Economic Approaches to the Analysis of Social Structure. pp.95–120.
31 Alexis de Tocqueville (1835/2000), *Democracy in America, Volumes I & II*. Translated and edited by Harvey C. Mansfield and Delba Winthrop. Chicago, IL: University of Chicago Press. Chapter 5, "On the Use that the Americans Make of Association in Civil Life." Available online at: http://www.press.uchicago.edu/Misc/Chicago/805328.html, p.1.
32 For a discussion of the negative consequences of social capital see Alejandro Portes. 1998. "Social Capital: Its Origins and Applications in Modern Sociology." *Annual Review of Sociology*. 24: 1–25.
33 Robert Putnam. 2002. *Bowling Alone: The Collapse and Revival of American Community*. New York, NY: Simon & Schuster. The concept of social capital first entered the research literature when the journalist and activist, Jane Jacobs introduced the notion that mixed-use urban neighborhoods had dense networks that lead to lower crime rates. Jane Jacobs. 1961. *The Life and Death of Great American Cities*. New York, NY: Random House. Pierre Bourdieu spelled out a theory of social capital in his 1972, *Outline of a Theory of Practice*. Cambridge, UK: Cambridge University Press and in his 1986, *Forms of Social Capital*. Accessed on August 19 at: http://marxists.org/reference/subject/philosophy/works/fr/bourdieu-forms-capital.htm.
34 Robert Putnam. 1994. *Making Democracy Work: Civic Traditions in Modern Italy*. Princeton, NJ: Princeton University Press. An excellent summary and critique of Putnam's *Making Democracy Work* (Ibid.) is by Carles Boix and Daniel N. Posner. 1996. "Making Social Capital Work: A Review of Robert Putnam's Making Democracy Work: Civic Traditions in Modern Italy." Cambridge, MA: Harvard, The Weatherhead Center for International Affairs, Paper 96-4. Available online at: http://www.wcfia.harvard.edu/sites/default/files/96-04.pdf. See also Margaret Talbot. 2000.

"Who Wants to be a Legionnaire?" (Review of Putnam's *Bowling Alone*). *New York Times Book Review.* June 25: 11–12.
35 Putnam, 1993: 81.
36 Putnam, 1993: 157.
37 Putnam, 1993: 177.
38 Edward E.C. Banfield. 1958. *The Moral Basis of a Backward Society*. Glencoe, IL: The Free Press. Though dated, this book sparked considerably controversy and still informs research on the question of how culture and history affect economic development, and the role social capital plays in allowing people to work together.
39 Carlo Conestabile. 1881. "The Land Question in Southern Italy." Accessed on September 6, 2014 at: http://archive.thetablet.co.uk/article/29th-january-1881/8/the-land-question-in-southern-italy-fourth-letter.
40 Shanker Satyanath, Nico Voigtländer, Hans-Joachim Voth. 2013. "Bowling for Fascism: Social Capital and the Rise of the Nazi Party." *National Bureau of Economic Research, Working Paper No. 19201*. Accessed on August 20, 2014 at: http://www.nber.org/papers/w19201.
41 Gavin Jones and James Mackenzie. 2014. "Special Report—How Italy became a Submerging Economy." *Reuters*. Accessed on August 20, 2014 at: http://www.reuters.com/article/2014/07/14/us-italy-economy-submerging-specialrepor-idUSKBN0FJ0QT20140714.
42 World Values Survey. 2014. Accessed August 20, 2014 at: http://www.worldvaluessurvey.org/WVSOnline.jsp.
43 This finding is well supported by the research literature. See, in particular, Jan Delhey and Kenneth Newton. 2002. "Who Trusts? The Origins of Social Trust in Seven Nations." Berlin: Social Science Research Center, FS III 02–402. Retrieved September 2, 2014 at: http://www.colbud.hu/honesty-trust/delhey/pub01.pdf.
44 For example, Eric Klineberg. 2013. "Adaptation: How Cities Can Be 'Climate-Proofed,'" *The New Yorker*. January 13: 32–37 has argued that the way to make cities resilient in the face of climate change is to create associations so that people can help one another. See also, Robert J. Sampson. 2012. *Great American City: Chicago and the Enduring Neighborhood Effect*. Chicago, IL: University of Chicago Press. Sampson studied deaths in the aftermath of Chicago's heat wave in the summer of 2005 and found that strength of community bonds determined survival rates. I would argue that it was the economic stability of the neighborhoods that serves as the explanation.
45 Scott G. McNall. 1974. *The Greek Peasant*. Washington, DC: The American Sociological Association Arnold and Carolyn Rose Monograph Series.
46 Pierre Bourdieu et al. 2000. *The Weight of the World: Social Suffering in Contemporary Society*. Palo Alto, CA: Stanford University Press. (Translated by Priscilla Parkhurst Ferguson et al.)
47 Ibid., p.363.
48 United Nations. *Human Development Report, 2014*. New York, NY: United Nations. Accessed on August 20, 2014 at: http://hdr.undp.org/sites/default/files/hdr14-report-en-1.pdf.
49 Ibid., p.168.
50 The figure is for gender equity alone, as an IHDI score is not available for Saudi Arabia.

51 Lansana Gberie. 2005. *A Dirty War in West Africa: The RUF and the Destruction of Sierra Leone*. Bloomington, IN: University of Indiana Press.
52 The idea of ethnic fractionalization driving conflict comes from James D. Fearon. 2003. "Ethnic and Cultural Diversity by Country." *Journal of Economic Growth*. 8(2): 195–222. The number of ethnic groups comes from the CIA World Fact Book, "Ethnic Groups." https://www.cia.gov/library/publications/the-world-factbook/fields/2075.html.
53 The Pearson r^2 for rule of law and the IHDI is .65, which means that without a rule of law inequity is a likely outcome. The data for calculating the r^2 comes from the UN's IHDI index and the data on corruption comes from the World Bank's good government index.
54 Freedom House Index. 2014. The Freedom House ranks each nation in the world on a scale of 1–7 for both civil liberties and political rights. I have combined the two scores, which range from 1–7, and averaged them. http://www.freedomhouse.org/.
55 World Bank. 2014. Corruption Index. Accessed on August 21 at: http://info.worldbank.org/governance/wgi/index.asp.
56 David Reynolds. 2014. *The Long Shadow: The Legacies of the Great War in the Twentieth Century*. New York, NY: W.W. Norton.
57 The measure for ethnic fractionalization comes from James A. Fearon's work. Accessed on August 21, 2014 at: http://info.worldbank.org/governance/wgi/index.asp. Data also come from the CIA Fact Book, accessed on August 21 at: https://www.cia.gov/library/publications/the-world-factbook/fields/2075.html.
58 PEW Research Center. 2008. "Where Trust is High, Crime and Corruption are Low." Accessed on August 29 at: http://www.pewglobal.org/2008/04/15/where-trust-is-high-crime-and-corruption-are-low/.
59 Taking, for example, the top four countries in terms of wasted human resources (Sierra Leone, Angola, the Central African Republic, and Guinea-Bissau), we see that they all have high scores on ethnic fractionalization. They are, in order, .76, .76, .79, and .82, making them among the most fractionated nations in the world and the ones that discriminate the most on the basis of ethnicity.
60 Andreas Wimmer, Lars-Erik Cederman, and Brian Min. 2009. "Ethnic Politics and Armed Conflict: A Confrontational Analysis of a New Global Dataset." *American Sociological Review*. 74(2): 316–337.
61 Halvard Buhaug, Lars-Erik Cederman, and Kristian Skrede Gleditsch. 2014. "Square Pegs in Round Holes: Inequalities, Grievances and Civil War." *International Studies Quarterly*. 58: 418–431.
62 Charles Tilly. 2007. Democracy. Cambridge, UK: Cambridge University Press.
63 World Bank. 2014. "The World Governance Indicators Project." Accessed on August 27 at: http://info.worldbank.org/governance/wgi/index.aspx#home. The specific dimensions assessed are; voice and accountability; political stability and absence of violence; government effectiveness; regulatory quality; rule of law; and control of corruption.
64 The r^2 for the IHDI and WGI is .72. In addition, there is also a strong and positive relationship between good government (WGI) and satisfaction with one's life (r^2 = .39).
65 For a discussion of how situational variables impact trust and a discussion of the relationship between trust and government institutions see: Michelle T. Kuenzi. 2008. "Social Capital and Political Trust in West Africa." *Afro-Barmoter, Working Paper No. 96*. Accessed on September 2 at: http://pdf.usaid.gov/pdf_docs/PNADL740.pdf. See also: Ignacio J. Martinez-Moyano et al. 2007. "Investigating

the Dynamics of Trust in Government: Drivers and Effects of Policy Initiatives and Government Action." Chicago, IL: Argonne National Laboratory. Accessed on September 2 at: http://www.dis.anl.gov/publications/articles/Trust_in_Government%202007.pdf.
66 When all measures of association were added together and run against levels of trust r^2 was only .03. Other correlations were trust and HDI (r^2 = .25); trust and satisfaction with one's economic lot (r^2 = .24); trust and personal income (r^2 = .31); trust and rule of law (r^2 = .23); and trust and the perception of the quality of government (r^2 = .21).
67 Ken Newton and Sonja Zmerli. 2011. "Three Forms of Trust and Their Association." *European Political Science Review*. 3(2): 169–200.
68 European Commission. 2012. "Public Opinion in the European Union." *Standard Eurobarometer, 78*. Accessed on August 21 at: http://ec.europa.eu/public_opinion/archives/eb/eb78/eb78_first_en.pdf.
69 OCDE. 2013. *Government at a Glance 2013*. Retrieved on September 2 at: http://www.oecd-ilibrary.org/governance/government-at-a-glance-2013_gov_glance-2013-en.
70 Bo Rothstein. 2005. *Social Traps and the Problem of Trust*. Cambridge and New York, NY: Cambridge University Press.
71 Jim Salter. 2014. "Police Protestors Clash Again in Ferguson." August 16. Retrieved on August 27 at: http://www.startribune.com/police-protesters-clash-again-in-ferguson/271345531/.
72 The summary of many of the comments were collated by Tom Kando, a sociologist, and posted on his European-American Blog. Accessed on August 27 at: http://european-americanblog.blogspot.com/.
73 PEW Research Center for the People & the Press. 2014. (August 18). Accessed on August 27 at: http://www.people-press.org/2014/08/18/stark-racial-divisions-in-reactions-to-ferguson-police-shooting/.
74 Jaeah Lee. 2014. "Exactly How Often Do Police Shoot Unarmed Black Men?" *Mother Jones*. August 15. Retrieved on August 27 at: http://www.motherjones.com/politics/2014/08/police-shootings-michael-brown-ferguson-black-men.
75 PEW Research Center. 2007. "Americans and Social Trust: Who, Where, and Why." Accessed on August 28 at: http://www.pewsocialtrends.org/2007/02/22/americans-and-social-trust-who-where-and-why/.
76 Eric Uslaner, quoted in Connie Cass. 2013. "Poll: Americans Don't Trust One Another." Associated Press. November 30. Accessed on August 27 at: http://www.usatoday.com/story/news/nation/2013/11/30/poll-americans-dont-trust-one-another/3792179/.
77 Eric M. Uslaner. 2012. *Income Inequality in the United States Fuels Pessimism and Threatens Social Cohesion*. Washington, DC: Center for American Progress Working Paper. Accessed on August 27 at: http://www.americanprogress.org/issues/economy/news/2012/12/05/46886/4-charts-that-show-how-rising-income-inequality-increases-pessimism/.
78 Calculated from the General Social Survey Cumulative Datafile, 1972–2012.
79 Tyler Schario and David Konisky. 2008. "Public Confidence in Government: Trust and Responsiveness." *Institute of Public Policy*. Columbia, MO: University of Missouri, p.2.
80 PEW Research Center. 2014. "Millennials in Adulthood." March 3. Accessed August 28, 2014 at: http://www.pewsocialtrends.org/2014/03/07/millennials-in-adulthood/.

81 The AP-GfK Poll. 2013. "A Survey of the American General Population (ages 18+). Accessed August 28, 2014 at: http://ap-gfkpoll.com/main/wp-content/uploads/2014/04/AP-GfK-March-2014-Poll-Topline-Final_SCIENCE.pdf.
82 Jennifer M. Silva. 2013. "Young and Isolated." *New York Times.* June 23: SR 7. See also Jennifer Silva. 2015. *Coming Up Short: Working-Class Adulthood in an Age of Uncertainty.* New York, NY: Oxford University Press.
83 Nick Bunker. 2012. "4 Charts that Show How Rising Income Inequality Increases Pessimism." December 5. Washington, DC: Center for American Progress. Retrieved on August 28, 2014 at: http:www.americanprogress.org/issues/economy/news/2012/12/05/468886/4-charts-that-show-how-rising-income-inequality-increases-pessimism/.
84 Michael Morrison. January 21, 2013. "Historical Gini Coefficients by State, 1916–2005."
85 PEW Research Center. 2013. "Trust in Government Nears Record Low, But Most Federal Agencies Are Viewed Favorably." Retrieved on August 28, 2014 at: http://www.people-press.org/2013/10/18/trust-in-government-nears-record-low-but-most-federal-agencies-are-viewed-favorably/.
86 Rick Perlstein. 2104. *The Invisible Bridge: The Fall of Nixon and the Rise of Reagan.* New York, NY: Simon & Schuster.
87 Barry Hollander. 2014. "The Surprised Loser: The Role of Electoral Expectations and News Media Exposure in Satisfaction with Democracy." *Journalism & Mass Communication Quarterly.* July 24.
88 Niall Ferguson. 2012. *The Great Degeneration: How Institutions Decay and Economies Die.* London: Penguin.
89 For a discussion of the development traps suffered by the poorest nations, see Paul Collier. 2008. *The Bottom Billion: Why the Poorest Countries are Failing and What Can Be Done About It.* London: Oxford University Press.
90 University of Notre Dame Global Adaptation Index. 2014. Accessed on August 27, 2014 at: http://index.globalai.org/.
91 The r^2 for the relationship between rule of law and readiness to deal with climate change is 0.75.
92 Quoted in Laura Henson. 2014. "Ready for Change: Notre Dame Launches Global Climate Change Adaptation Index." Washington, DC: The Wilson Center, New Security. Retrieved on September 1, 2014 at: http://www.newsecuritybeat.org/2014/01/ready-change-notre-dame-launches-global-adaptation-index/.
93 Stephen Chaney. 2014. Cited in Henson, "Ready for Change."

6

CORRUPTION AND SOCIAL INEQUALITY

Consider:

- In a run-up to the 2013 presidential election in Azerbaijan, stickers for the opposition proclaimed, "Enough! Enough corruption, enough monarchy, enough unemployment, enough stolen oil money, enough low-quality education and health services, enough disrespectful officials, and enough war ..."[1]
- Corruption is often present in "new" societies.
- Corruption is a management tool in nondemocratic societies.
- Corruption results when power is grounded in irrelevant moral criteria.
- Social inequality gives rise to corruption.
- Corruption erodes trust.
- Corruption is politically destabilizing.
- Corruption can unravel democratic institutions.
- Corruption robs future generations.

William T. Tweed (1823–1878), or as he was better known, "Boss" Tweed, ruled New York City's system of patronage and politics in the mid-nineteenth century. Tweed was "Boss" of the city's Democratic political machine, known as Tammany Hall. The "Tweed Ring" bribed state legislators, bought votes, fixed elections, encouraged judicial corruption, and stole perhaps as much as $3.6 billion (in today's dollars) from public coffers. Born into a family of modest means, Tweed joined the family's chairmaking business in his twenties. Shortly thereafter, like others aspiring to the middle class, he became a member of both the Masons and the Odd Fellows. He also joined another popular form of affiliation for young men, a volunteer fire company, and shortly thereafter he and some friends organized their own company—Americus Fire Company No.6. Tweed was chosen as its first foreman.

Before 1865, if a fire in New York needed to be put out, volunteers would rush to the scene pulling hand-powered water pumps. Fire brigades competed with one another to be first on the scene and first to hook up their hoses; sometimes buildings would burn down while the companies fought one another.[2] Membership in a brigade provided a connection with other like-minded men in a constantly changing urban environment and provided an opportunity for engagement and a connection to the world of politics.[3]

The link between the volunteer fire departments and the emerging political order was an important one. The companies sometimes grew out of urban gangs and often out of well-defined ethnic communities. Fire companies voted in blocks, and their votes—as was often true in nineteenth-century America—were frequently bought with beer, liquor, cash, or the promise of work.[4] Tweed delivered the votes from the Seventh Ward and rose quickly through the political ranks of the Democratic Party.

Republican reformers in the state capital, who were primarily Anglo-Saxon Calvinists and were vehemently opposed to the influx of Catholic, working-class immigrants into New York City, sought to limit their potential power. To do so, the Republicans needed to rein in the power of the Democrats in New York City government, who relied on the votes of these same groups. The Republicans decided to water down the influence of the New York Board of Supervisors by adding more members, half to be appointed by the mayor and half to be elected at large. This move backfired. Tweed and his cronies were appointed to the expanded Board and soon forced anybody doing business with the city to pay them a 15% surcharge, which went directly into to their pockets and into support for their political machines.

In 1869, Tweed's protégé, John Hoffman, became governor of New York and proposed a new charter for the city that took power away from the state commissions favored by the Republicans. The proposal passed in large part because Tweed paid $11 million (current dollars) in bribes to Republican legislators. By 1870, Tammy Hall candidates had successfully captured all fifteen positions for Alderman and gained complete control of the city's finances. Corruption deepened. Contractors working for the city were given specific instructions to inflate their bills, with the understanding that the "extra" would be divided between Tweed and his associates in Tammany Hall.

Tweed colluded with the financiers Jay Gould and James ("Big Diamond Jim") Fisk to take control of the Erie Railroad from Cornelius Vanderbilt, got a large block of stock, and was made a director of the company. He also acquired directorships in the Brooklyn Bridge Company, a local railway company, and the Harlem Gas Company. He wore a large 10.5 carat diamond stick-pin, dined lavishly at places like Delmonico's, and owned a mansion on Fifth Avenue. His conspicuous and garish consumption was beyond anything that a public salary could have supported, and everyone knew it.[5] Businessmen and politicians all wanted to know him and paid for the privilege of his company.[6] Tweed's undoing came when his dealings threatened the stability of the city's financial system and the interests of the city's elites.

The New York County Sheriff, James O'Brien, had evidence to expose the vast degree of Tammany Hall's corruption. He first tried blackmailing the Tammany Hall ring, but when that failed he went to the *New York Times* with his evidence, as did the county auditor, Matthew J. O'Rourke. Tammany Hall offered the *Times* $90 million (in current dollars) to sit on the evidence, but the *Times* went ahead with banner headlines of corruption, detailing the extent of the fraud. Millions of dollars in bonds had been sold to finance schemes that directly benefited Tweed and his allies. The extent of New York's debts rattled international investors who held millions of dollars worth of the city's bonds. The bankers and members of New York's financial community were provoked to act because they understood that if the city's credit collapsed, so would the city's banks and their fortunes. The elite created a reform committee to oversee all city expenditures, cut off Tammany Hall's sources of funding, and had

Tweed arrested in 1871. He eventually died in prison in 1878. Though Tweed was finished, Tammany Hall would remain a force in city politics for years.

Tweed's rise and fall is of interest to us now because of the historical conditions that allowed corruption to flourish. *Discrimination against people based on their ethnicity, nationality, and religion had the effect of opening an opportunity for the graft of Tammany Hall.* Do we find these same conditions operating today, both in the United States and in other nations?

Social Instability and the Rise of Corruption

Mid-nineteenth-century America was characterized by political and economic chaos. During the period of Tweed's dominance (1840–1870), New York City experienced rapid population growth, as did Chicago, Cincinnati, Milwaukee, and San Francisco. New York, however, dwarfed all others in size. In 1840 it was already the largest American city, with 312,000 inhabitants, by 1850 the number had grown to 515,000, and by 1870 the population neared 1 million (942,292). In 1870, the first time the U.S. Census asked people where they were born, 44.5% of all New Yorkers indicated they were foreign born, many of them recent arrivals. The population of the city had swelled in large part by Irish Catholics fleeing the Potato Famine of 1845–1852. By the 1850s the Irish made up 25% of the city's population. Many of these immigrants were from agricultural backgrounds, had limited skills, and no money. They could not afford to head west and take up homesteading. When they could find work it was in construction, working on roads or canals, or in the case of women, working as domestics or in mills.

> Social and economic instability gave rise to corruption in nineteenth-century America.

New York's immigrants, arriving in the mid-nineteenth century, found themselves crowded into shabby tenements and living in communities characterized by violence and crime. Those forced into slums, where diseases such as cholera, yellow fever, and tuberculosis were endemic, were feared by others, not just because they could spread disease to the "better" classes, but also because they were seen as potential revolutionaries. In cities like Boston, Philadelphia, and New York, the influx of low-skilled immigrants gave rise to anti-immigrant fervor, which was expressed as a narrow form of nationalism and racism.

The "know-nothing" movement of the 1840s portrayed the growing urban underclasses as a threat equivalent to the "Indian threat" faced on the frontier by pioneers and the U.S. Army. As the historian Richard Slotkin has argued, immigrant workers, Native Americans, and southern Blacks were all lumped together in the mind of nativists as members of a dangerous and potentially revolutionary class.[7] Irish Catholics were portrayed as a group of dangerous drunks. One cartoon by Thomas Nast (also responsible for today's image of Santa Claus) titled "The Usual Irish Way of Doing Things," depicted a drunken Irishman lighting a powder keg and swinging a bottle of liquor. The influx of Catholics, the nativists asserted, would lead to the takeover of the U.S. government, and the Pope would replace the president. This mishmash of ideas was summed up by nativists' stance against, "Rum, Romanism, and Rebellion."

> Irrelevant moral criteria played a significant role in nineteenth-century America in gaining access to political and economic resources.

In 1882, nativists passed legislation at the federal level to exclude certain categories of people. It was left up to immigration officials to turn away "any convict, lunatic, idiot, or person unable to take care of him or herself without becoming a public charge." The legislation was used at the time to turn away the poor, including pregnant or single women. In some cities and states, laws were passed to deny immigrants the vote and access to public education.

Nineteenth-century politics in many cities was a "winner-take-all" system, "all" being money, positions, and jobs. Loyalty was given to those who could deliver benefits. Tammany Hall became identified with immigrant communities and, given the Republican and "know-nothing" opposition to immigrants, became a powerful political force for the Democratic Party. Irish Catholic support for Tammany Hall and for the Democratic Party was ironclad. Tammany functioned much like a Catholic parish: Ward bosses took the place of Irish priests in making the rounds, assuring that problems were solved, and families were provided for. Contractors who got city jobs were expected to hire those who provided the votes. When New York established a professional police department in 1845, most of the new jobs it created went to Irishmen. Support from Irish voters meant that Tammany Hall would control Democratic Party nominations and patronage in the city from 1854 until 1932. In other words, because of structural social inequalities and because of discrimination, many were happy to accept the "honest" graft of machines like Tammany Hall.

Tweed's excesses were not an anomaly in the nineteenth century. The American state was weak and corrupt. A democratic state in which political elites were accountable, the state's policies transparent and capable of implementation, and the rule of law was applied equitably, did not yet exist. In late-nineteenth-century political contests it was not unusual for a politician to buy up newspapers and give editors instructions about how to build up their qualifications and knock down those of their opponents. This would also occur at the national level.

The two terms of President Ulysses S. Grant (1869–1877) were marked by scandals in seven separate federal departments, including the Navy, Justice, War, Treasury, Interior, State, and the Post Office Departments. Family and friends of Grant cabinet members received government appointments for which they seldom had the qualifications and exploited those positions for personal gain. It would take time, but eventually these high levels of corruption in the nineteenth century would lead to the implementation of a Civil Service system through which jobs could be allocated on the basis of demonstrated achievement and talent.

The road to democracy was uneven. Attempts to advance equality in the South were rolled back in the aftermath of the Civil War. White Southern Democrats fought back, sometimes with violence, to destroy what Reconstruction had done for African-Americans. Sharecropping, which grew out of attempts to control free labor, imposed significant economic burdens on both Black and poor White southern farmers. Midwestern farmers were also hard hit. They had brought about rapid growth across the prairies, plowing up hundreds of thousands of acres of virgin soil in the aftermath of the Civil War for grain production. Yet they found themselves at the mercy of railroad monopolies that charged ruinous rates for moving their crops to market.

Discontent in rural America was matched by that in the cities, where workers demanded living wages, a shorter work week, and relief from unsafe and unhealthy working conditions. They were fighting back against corrupt and antidemocratic efforts on the part of manufacturers, mining barons, and railroad magnates to drive down wages. Many discontented workers would join the Knights of Labor, one of the first and largest efforts to mobilize labor. Between 1850 and 1900 there were over fifty organized strikes in the United States. Cigar makers struck, as did miners, carpet weavers, textile workers, printers, carpenters, tailors, and railroad workers. Even cowboys struck. In 1883 cowboys in Texas struck at five ranches in order to prevent Eastern investors from industrializing ranching and taking away their jobs.

At the same time as the social and economic unrest on farms and in factories, "know-nothings" opposed immigrants, Protestants were turned against Catholics, immigrants were pitted against Blacks, and ethnic groups battled one another in urban America for jobs.[8] Clear class divisions had developed by the end of the nineteenth century, and power was increasingly concentrated in the hands of the few. Entrepreneurs like Andrew Carnegie (steel), Jay Gould (banking and finance), John D. Rockefeller (oil), and Cornelius Vanderbilt (railroads and shipping) began to build their fortunes. Western copper, gold, and silver barons also joined the ranks of the wealthy.

> Corruption is an adaptation to chaotic political and economic conditions.

By any number of measures, the United States was not a democratic society. Women would not win the voting rights until 1920 and, when they did, it was because upper- and middle-class white Anglo-Saxon males needed their votes to "control" immigrants and pass legislation abolishing the manufacture and sale of alcohol. African-Americans' voting rights would be severely restricted well into the twentieth century. Illegal land grabs were common on the frontier, and Native Americans were driven from their lands and onto reservations by the U.S. Army. Late-nineteenth-century America was an age of buccaneering capitalism, a growing concentration of wealth, and the exploitation of working men, women, and children.

A shift toward a more benign economic and political system, designed to dampen the impacts of capitalism on ordinary men and women, came with Theodore Roosevelt (1858–1919).[9] "T.R." instituted a progressive agenda and went to work breaking up monopolies, holding down railroad rates to help the farmers, and creating regulatory agencies to oversee the manufacture of food and drugs. He helped to check some of the greater abuses of unfettered capitalism and to check class conflict.

To take an idea from the anthropologist Marshall Sahlins, economic and political systems adapt to specific circumstances in culturally specific ways.[10] The corruption of Tweed was an economic and political adaptation to the ever-changing conditions of nineteenth-century New York. Graft and corruption worked to get the city's infrastructure built, and it had the added benefit of integrating potentially isolated ethnic communities into Democratic politics.[11] *But not all countries are making a transition to democracy, because inequality and corruption are holding them back from doing so.* Further, the United States seems to be sliding back toward some of the political and economic abuses of the nineteenth century (see Chapter 7, this volume). The social and economic costs of corruption are high.

Before turning to an analysis of how corruption and inequality are linked in contemporary societies, let me briefly summarize how they operated in nineteenth-century America, because many of the same factors explain corruption today.

There were a number of factors contributing to the rise of corruption in nineteenth-century America:

- Immigrants and workers were shut out of full participation based on irrelevant moral criteria including religion, country of origin, ethnicity, and class status.
- Dense social networks based on these criteria developed in New York City.
- Boss Tweed and Tammany Hall were able to build a political power base by integrating these groups into New York's evolving political system.
- At the same time, there were active attempts on the part of Nativists to discriminate against new arrivals, as well as workers, and to operate within closed economic and political systems that advantaged elites. This had the effect of strengthening organizations like Tammany Hall.

- There was political and economic turmoil brought on by the Civil War, the industrialization of the North, the failure of Reconstruction in the South, the rise of working-class movements, and cycles of economic boom and bust that affected everyone.

The Costs of Corruption

As the economist and former president of Claremont Graduate University Robert Klitgaard noted:

> Systemic corruption distorts incentives, undermines institutions, and redistributes wealth and power to the undeserving. When corruption undermines property rights, the rule of law, incentives to invest, and eventually economic and political development are crippled. In extreme cases, state institutions may become vulnerable to criminalization or capture by illegitimate groups seeking to expand their influence and power.[12]

We can think of many examples of contemporary nations that function in this manner. Systematic corruption is the norm in Russia (as it was previously in the Soviet Union). In the fifteen years since he first came to power in 2000, President Vladimir Putin has increased his hold on power, his friends have grown wealthy, and his enemies have been punished. The privatization of former state factories and oil production facilities has made billionaires out of those who are his cronies. Those who have opposed this consolidation of power have found themselves in jail, their resources seized.[13]

The type of corruption found in any given country varies greatly depending on its level of political and economic development and its culture. In countries with weak governments and low tax bases, public servants are often underpaid and engage in petty corruption to supplement their salaries. Once our family was held up was by the Mexican National Police, the *Federales*, on a back road in Baja, California. We came driving around the bend on a dirt road and were confronted by three policemen wielding rifles. We had, apparently, committed a traffic "crime." The crime was unspecified, but it was clear that for twenty dollars we would be allowed to continue on our way. We paid. Corruption of the police and military in Mexico has worsened since then, driven in part by the fact that opportunities to profit from collusion with drug traffickers is more profitable than simply collecting a salary from the state. In October of 2014, for instance, 43 activist students were rounded up by the police, and according to one theory, handed over to a drug gang to be murdered because they annoyed the mayor of the town and his wife, who were in league with the gang.[14]

Karachi is Pakistan's largest city, with a rapidly growing population that numbered around 24 million in 2014. People have streamed in from rural areas, seeking jobs in the expanding economy, but housing has not kept pace with population growth. People have expanded their homes without permits to accommodate newly arriving relatives. Developers put up houses with no electricity, water, or sewers on land they do not own. Owners are left to illegally tap electricity lines for power, dig their own sewers, and buy their water from delivery trucks. Garbage is usually just thrown into the narrow streets that separate homes. It is the job of the underpaid police to make sure none of this happens. However, officers have worked out a standard fee of $57 per lot to look the other way.[15]

Normative Corruption

Corruption can become normative in a society. Becoming a democracy is a process, as is becoming a systematically corrupt society. The political and historical circumstances that give rise to durable inequalities are the drivers of this process. There is a vicious cycle between social inequality and corruption. As a study by the International Monetary Fund revealed, regardless of the level of economic development:

> ... high and rising corruption increases income inequality and poverty by reducing economic growth, the progressivity of the tax system, the level and effectiveness of social spending, and the formation of human capital, and by perpetuating an unequal distribution of asset ownership and unequal access to education.[16]

The cycle works in both directions: *The greater the degree of income inequality, the more likely it is that a society is both undemocratic and corrupt.* And even though the economy may be expanding, the benefits may not help the poor or even the middle class.[17] In addition, in societies

> The greater the degree of economic inequality, the more likely a society is to be nondemocratic and corrupt.

with high degrees of inequality in wealth and income, people assume—rightfully—that their governments are corrupt and operate accordingly.[18] A number of Sub-Saharan African countries experience endemic corruption; it will be useful to look at two (Nigeria and Uganda) in order to better understand how the twin processes of inequality and corruption operate in the developing world and how *corruption reduces government's capacity to solve problems and weakens civic institutions.* Even though African economies have been growing, the benefits of growth have been highly concentrated so that after a decade of growth, little has changed for the average person.[19]

Nigeria

Nigeria captured public attention in April 2014 when nearly 300 schoolgirls were captured by the extremist Islamic group Boko Haram (whose name means, "Western education is evil"). The Nigerian army proved particularly inept in their initial attempts to find and rescue the girls. In some confrontations, soldiers simply ran away from the better-trained and better-equipped fighters of Boko Haram. Becoming a soldier in Nigeria requires paying a series of bribes. At each stage of the induction process, a form must be signed and payment must be given to an officer for his signature. Once they are admitted to the armed forces, recruits still need to buy some of their equipment. They need a rifle to complete basic training, but unlike soldiers in a Western army, they won't be given one. The usual tactic is to "rent" one from a regular soldier. To pay for the rifle the new recruit will use it to rob their fellow citizens. Once in the Army, and having paid for their weapons, they will rent it out to other aspiring soldiers, and the process of corruption continues.[20]

An anonymous corporal in the Nigerian Air Force wrote to complain that while he and the men in his unit live without any accommodations, vast sums of money were being spent on a golf club for the senior officers. Money for enlisted men's food and weapons is regularly being skimmed off by their officers.[21] The result has been an inability on the part of the government to mount an effective offensive against the insurgents of Boko Haram who are intent on establishing an Islamic caliphate in northern Nigeria.[22] Nigeria thus fails at fulfilling a critical function of government: It cannot protect its people. The newly elected president and former Army General, Muhammadu Buhari, has vowed to drive Boko Haram out of the country.

Nigeria is Africa's biggest economy, exceeding that of South Africa in 2014. Nigeria has the world's fastest-growing market for private jets as well as for champagne. In 2010, the equivalent of $25 million was spent by members of the Nigerian elite for 593,000 bottles of champagne. Luxury SUVs clog the streets of the capitol, Lagos, and the women of Nigeria's economic and political elites fly to Paris to have their hair done and to shop.[23] At the same time, 100 million, or 63% of Nigerians are destitute, living on less than $1.25 a day. If we take $2.00 a day per person as the measure of poverty, then the situation looks even worse, as 84.5% of the population live at or below the poverty line. Of the 175 countries ranked by Transparency International in terms of perception of corruption in 2013, Nigeria was among the thirty most corrupt.[24]

Nigeria is defined as a partial democracy by the Freedom House. It achieved its independence from Great Britain in 1960 but plunged into decades of civil war as democratically elected governments traded places with military dictatorships until 2010, when Goodluck Jonathan was elected president. The country's population is divided between 500 different ethnic groups with the three largest—Hausa, Igbo, and Yoruba—accounting for the majority. The northern part of the country is primarily Muslim and the south is Christian. When African colonies achieved their independence, one of the strongest institutions left behind by colonial powers was the military, often made up of recruits and officers from one ethnic group. Recruits and their officers formed tight trust networks, which were not easily integrated into the state.

> In Nigeria, appointments to high-level military, governmental, and economic positions are based on irrelevant moral criteria.

Whether a leader takes power through a coup or by a democratic election, he needs to assure the loyalty of the armed forces. High-level appointments in the military are, therefore, as much about politics as they are about national security. So, while national forces may be recruited from a wide spectrum of different ethnic groups and religions, the officers who control those forces are frequently appointed on the basis of their ethnicity and/or loyalty. Early in 2014, Goodluck Jonathan appointed new chiefs for the army, air force, and navy. His new Chief of Staff for the army was from the Niger Delta, the home of the President. As a result, Goodluck Jonathan was accused of ethnic favoritism by his opponents.[25]

Democratically elected presidents in post-colonial regimes have frequently had a difficult balancing act to perform; they need to assure the loyalty of the military in order to govern, and they need to provide the military, particularly the officer class, with benefits. Those benefits can include skimming the pay of their men, building elaborate quarters for themselves, or giving them control over natural resources or even core businesses.

As a legacy of colonialism, the militaries of many developing nations are tied to core countries such as the United States, France, or the United Kingdom. Officers have received training in the West, and often substantial military aid is provided to their nations. This can result in dual loyalties for the officer corps, meaning the president must balance the security needs of his or her own country against those of its Western sponsor. Another problem leaders of developing countries face is that their economies (based on mining, manufacturing, oil extraction, etc.) are either owned by core countries or controlled by them.[26] Foreign investors—whether from China, the United States, or any other core country—expect laws and policies to be crafted to benefit them, not the host country. In short, many of the tools needed to create a democratic government are taken away from leaders in emerging economies, and what grows out of these situations is corruption, because leaders act against the interests of their own citizens.

Corruption is endemic in Nigeria and is seen as permeating all levels of the government. A report offered by the Nigerian government's Independent Corrupt Practices and Other Related Offenses Commission detailed the corrupt behavior of the police.[27] Included were payoffs to the police to ignore the infringement of traffic laws, payoffs by organized criminals, receipt of money, or discounts for services rendered, pocketing money from the process of crime, giving false evidence to ensure dismissal of cases, and the actual perpetration of criminal acts. The Commission saw corruption as giving rise to political instability because the poor, who cannot afford to pay bribes and who are hurt the most by corruption, see their basic human rights violated and resent the rich for flaunting their corrupt gains.

Uganda

Uganda has many similarities to Nigeria although it is not an oil-rich nation. Close to 30% of its budget comes from foreign aid. Like Nigeria, it was a British colony. It is not yet a democracy and is a regarded as one of the world's most corrupt states, ranking 140th out of 175.[28] Yoweri Museveni has served as its president since 1986. Museveni, like other African leaders such as Robert Mugabe of Zimbabwe, rose to power as a result of his success as a guerrilla leader. The British had organized the colony's military so that two ethnic groups, the Lango and the Acholi, made up the army. When Major-General Idi Amin seized power from Milton Obote in a military coup in 1971, Amin began to fill top government positions with members of his own ethnic group, the Kakwa, as well as the Lugbara. Amin then began the systematic oppression, including rape, torture, and murder, of the Lango and Acholi peoples. Museveni, along with the Lango and Acholi and their allies, fled to Tanzania, from where he would eventually, with the help of the Tanzanian Army, launch a successful attack to overthrow Amin. The core of Uganda's National Resistance Army would prove loyal to Museveni and they would, under his military and political leadership, ultimately seize control of the Ugandan government in 1986. Shortly thereafter Museveni was declared president.[29]

The former guerrilla leader was seen by the *New York Times* as ushering in a new kind of politics in Africa: "the end of corrupt, strong-man governments."[30] Yet the opposite happened. Unrest continued as the new government dealt with both internal and external conflicts, some driven by religious differences. Rebel groups in the north, composed mostly of Muslims, opposed the national government, and Uganda became involved directly and indirectly in conflicts in Sudan, Kenya, Rwanda, and the Democratic Republic of the Congo. All of these conflicts led to a strengthening of the national armed forces; securing their loyalty led to corruption, as state institutions came to support the state, rather than the citizens. *The state was essentially privatized for the benefit of the political class and economic elites.*[31]

Human Rights Watch reported the fact that in 2012, millions of dollars from donor nations to help rebuild northern Uganda, which had been ravaged by twenty years of civil war, were stolen and funneled into private accounts. Previous donor funds to help in the fight against AIDS, tuberculosis, and malaria had also been taken. As Human Rights Watch noted, "Years of evidence indicate that Uganda's current political system is built on patronage and that ultimately high-level corruption is rewarded rather than punished."[32] Patronage politics necessitates giving voters something in return for their votes, just as happened with Tammany Hall. In the Nigerian elections of 2011, Museveni and his party spent the equivalent of $350 million in support of his campaign, money that came from state coffers.[33] In 2013, he lavished a new truck, minibus, fifteen motorcycles, and the equivalent of $100,000 in Ugandan currency on a young group of supporters.[34] Museveni's strategy for survival has been, as he has said, never to run away from his friends.[35] This has included the assurance that they will not suffer from using the state and its resources for their own private gains. A political class has captured the country and, though there are elections, corruption in Uganda has reduced democracy to the concept of "citizens electing their own dictators."[36] In 2015 the Freedom House characterized Uganda as "not free."[37]

Once a state *permits* corruption, those who hold positions of power rationalize their corruption as a form of "protecting" the state. Vladimir Putin uses the ideology of protecting "Mother Russia" to legitimize the crushing of civil society. This includes practicing discrimination against homosexuals and anybody else who deviates from a path of orthodoxy, including the feminist, punk-rock protest group, Pussy Riot. Members of this group were arrested after staging an unauthorized performance in Moscow's Cathedral of Christ the Savior. They were objecting to the Church's support for Putin during his election campaign. Putin claimed the band, some of whose members fled abroad to escape imprisonment, were a threat to the moral foundations of the nation.

> The concentration of political power leads to the concentration of economic power, which deepens economic inequality and gives rise to corruption.

In China, corruption is perceived as being a growing concern. In a 2013 poll conducted by the Pew Research Center, 53% of Chinese saw corrupt public officials as a problem.[38] Although China's new Premier, Xi Jinping, has launched an anti-corruption campaign, very few of the

5,000 plus who hold the rank of vice minister have been targeted (35 as of 2014). Cheng Li of the Brookings Institute has argued that it was expected that public officials would be corrupt. If you did not take bribes and give favors, you would not be regarded as trustworthy by Party officials and would not be promoted.[39] Wen Jiabao, who served as China's Premier from 2002 to 2012, is seen as responsible for China's rapid economic expansion. During his tenure, his relatives were estimated to have accumulated billions from shares in banks, factories, tourist resorts, and telecommunication and infrastructure projects. Family members were given government no-bid contracts and sometimes received financial support for their projects from state-owned companies.[40]

The concentration of economic and political power deepens economic inequality and gives rise to corruption. As noted earlier, corruption is costly to a society because it distorts incentives and allows people to grow rich through thievery and malfeasance.[41] *This in turn has the effect of generating political unrest.* The Arab Spring was precipitated by a 26-year-old Tunisian fruit vendor, Mohamed Bouazizi, who set himself on fire in front of the municipal building in Sidi Bouzid, the capitol city of the Sidi Bouzid Governorate in central Tunisia. A poor man, Bouazizi made his living peddling fruit from a cart. In order to stay in business, Bouazizi, like a number of other peddlers, was required to pay bribes to the police to stay open because they would not issue him a permit.[42] On the day he killed himself, an officer confiscated his wares because he did not have enough money to pay a bribe. His self-immolation on December 17, 2010 set off a wave of protests that would ultimately drive Tunisia's president, Zine El Abidine Ben Ali from power after twenty-three years in office. Tunisians had suffered for years from the usual a range of grievances relating to corruption: economic inequality, political oppression, a ruling party that served as a kleptocracy, a lack of jobs, and high food prices. After the 2011 revolution, 214 businesses, and assets worth USD $13 billion, which included 550 properties and 48 boats and yachts, were seized from Ben Ali and his relatives and friends.[43] Yet, although the Arab Spring took root in Tunisia, the promise of a democratic government has been forestalled by the rise of an increasingly authoritarian government.

The revolution in Tunisia sparked violent and nonviolent protests throughout North Africa and the Middle East. Three years after the Arab

Spring began, power had changed hands in Egypt, Libya, and Yemen, and there were uprisings in a number of other countries, including Bahrain, Sudan, Kuwait, Morocco, and Syria. Years of economic decline and high levels of unemployment led to dissatisfaction throughout the Middle East. In Egypt the call was for an end to the corruption of the Mubarak regime, which had concentrated economic and political power in the hands of his family, cronies, and the military. The World Bank calculated that in 2010 firms connected to Mubarak accounted for 60% of all business profits in the country, but only 11% of all employment.[44] This is a striking measure of the concentration of wealth and deep social inequality.

Before the revolution in Egypt, there had been a fourfold increase in the number of college graduates, one sign of a growing elite.[45] Inequality and its companion, corruption, create both physical and psychological distance between the rich and the poor. There is some evidence to suggest that people are more willing to cheat those who are subordinate to them and categorized as different from them. The bosses with 100 employees is more likely to take a greater percentage of the profits for themselves rather than share it with their workers, than are bosses with just one employee.[46] *Unequal societies cannot sustain democracy.*

> The power of corrupt regimes is grounded in the maintenance of durable inequalities.

The Worst of the Worst

Freedom House, as noted in Chapter 5, tracks the progress of 195 different nations toward democracy, as well as tracking any falling-away from this standard. They assess political rights using twelve criteria and civil rights using fifteen different measures. For example, under civil liberties they examine whether or not a country operates under the rule of law by asking these questions: Is there an independent judiciary? Does the rule of law prevail in civil and criminal matters? Are the police under civilian control? Is there protection from political terror, unjustified imprisonment, exile, or torture? Do laws, policies, and practices guarantee equal treatment of various segments of the population?

Ten countries out of 51 designated as "Not Free" by the Freedom House, were designated in 2015 as the "Worst of the Worst." Here we can see the tight links between a lack of democracy, corruption, and inequality.

These worst-rated countries represent a narrow range of systems and cultures. One—North Korea—is a one-party, Marxist-Leninist regime. Two—Turkmenistan and Uzbekistan—are central Asian countries, each ruled by dictators with roots in the Soviet period. Sudan is ruled by a leadership that has elements of both radical Islamism and a traditional military junta. The remaining worst-rated states are Equatorial Guinea, a highly corrupt regime with one of the worst human rights records in Africa; Eritrea, an increasingly repressive police state; Saudi Arabia, an absolute monarchy with severe social controls; Syria, a dictatorship in the midst of a bloody civil war; and Somalia, a failed state.[47]

All of the Worst of the Worst are by definition corrupt regimes; none are democratic. In all of them, judges, military officers, or "elected" officials, use their offices for economic gain. Corrupt regimes derive their power from the maintenance of durable inequalities, which may be religious affiliation in one country or ethnicity in another. Let us take the country regarded as the most corrupt and repressive of all nations—North Korea—to illustrate the point about irrelevant social criteria determining one's life chances.

The United Nations Human Rights Council inquired into human rights violations in the Democratic People's Republic of North Korea in 2013.[48] The North Korean state classifies and assigns people a social status based on their class and birth, which includes consideration of their political opinions and their religion. This system determines where people can live, the kind of accommodations they are allowed to have, whether they can go to school, how much and what kind of food they can have, and whom they can marry. The State imposes blatant discrimination on women in "order to maintain the gender stereotype of the pure and innocent Korean woman."[49] Freedom of movement is limited by the state assigning places to live and work. Only those of high status and politically loyal to the regime are allowed to live in the capitol city, Pyongyang. If one member of the family commits a crime, the entire family is banished to an undesirable region. People who try to flee are caught, returned, and subjected to persecution, torture, and prolonged and arbitrary detention.[50] North Korea retains a massive police force. Military spending, even when people are starving, receives priority. The State maintains power through control of information, webs of informants who turn in friends and family members suspected of disloyalty to the state, and by control over the means of violence.

China also uses irrelevant criteria in placing people in society. In China, Li Xue does not exist. She does not exist because she was born outside of the state's family-planning regulations that dictated a family could have only one child. The fine for ignoring the regulations was $800, but her parents could not pay that sum, which was more than their annual earnings. This means that Li has no legal identity because she does not have a household registration certificate. As a result she is not able to attend school, get a job, or get married. She filed suit against the government in her town but it was dismissed by the court, which claimed she had no legal basis for it.[51] After all, she doesn't exist. *What limits democracy is the use of irrelevant moral criteria for determining one's fate.*

Challenges to Democracy

Transitions to democracy are frequently a messy process and do not come about simply because a constitution modeled on that of the United States is written and adopted. A move toward democracy, as in the case of Egypt, can be undone by a military coup. A military coup in turn can be undone by free and democratic elections. The sociologist Charles Tilly has made the argument that a critical step in becoming a democracy is for autonomous trust networks to become integrated into the state.[52] Fire brigades were dense trust networks integrated into politics via Tammany Hall. Corrupt as those politics were, they provided an opportunity for people to practice democracy by voting and competing in the political arena to have their voices heard. Tilly argued that three things are essential for a democracy:

- Many autonomous trust networks, like volunteer fire companies, must be integrated into public politics.
- Public politics must be isolated from categorical inequities such as ethnicity.
- There must be a reduction in the autonomy of coercive power centers. Coercive power centers can be a military, as in the case of Egypt, Pakistan, or Thailand, or militias in countries like Libya, Iraq, or Syria.

These three conditions represent substantial challenges, especially when autonomous trust networks such as ethnic or tribal groups control the machinery of the state and the forces that brought them to power and keep them in power. At a minimum, democracies depend on the rule of law, on equality before the law, transparency, and not having the state captured by special interest groups. They must create and maintain open economic and political systems.

> Political and economic institutions in the United States are increasingly controlled by elites.

The Stanford political scientist Francis Fukuyama has argued that because of growing inequality, we may be seeing a reversal of the progress toward democracy in the United States. Concentration of wealth in the hands of a few has meant that political institutions are now captive to special interests that do not represent the social and economic diversity of the nation.[53]

As Robert B. Reich, Berkeley professor and Secretary of Labor under President Bill Clinton, 1993–1997, has noted, the boundless wealth of America's financial class elicits cooperation from those politicians who depend on it for campaign donations; the politicians toil in turn to implement policies favorable to that class.[54] The Pulitzer Prize-winning business reporter and *New York Times* columnist, Gretchen Morgenson and Joshua Rosner, an expert on the housing industry, traced the tight personal links between Wall Street banks, financial firms, the mortgage giants Fannie Mae and Freddie Mac, and the U.S. Treasury in *Reckless Endangerment: How Outsized Greed and Corruption Led to Economic Armageddon*.[55] They demonstrate how these links led to predatory lending practices, the issuing and marketing of subprime mortgages, and the financial collapse of 2007/2008.

In the 1990s, President Clinton's administration called for a strong partnership between the government and Fannie and Freddie to stimulate home buying by providing subsidies. About one-third of the government subsidy was retained by Fannie, rather than being used to give borrowers lower rates on their home loans, thus allowing James Johnson, head of Fannie Mae from 1991 to 1998, to "earn" around $100 million. Some of Fannie's profits were channeled to academics to write position papers outlining the benefits of Fannie's activities; other resources were used to organize bankers and real estate brokers to lobby on Fannie's behalf. Fannie also channeled money to Congressional campaigns and provided patronage positions for relatives and former Congressional staff members.

This gave Fannie free rein to underwrite more loans, regardless of the risk, increase their profits, and without the public knowing it, increase the risk to American taxpayers. Robert Reich outlined what happened:

> A company called Countrywide Financial became Fannie's single largest provider of home loans and the nation's largest mortgage lender. Countrywide abandoned standards altogether, even doctoring loans to make applicants look creditworthy, while generating a fortune for its co-founder, Angelo R. Mozilo. Meanwhile, Wall Street banks received fat fees underwriting securities issued by Fannie and Freddie, and even more money providing lenders like Countrywide with lines of credit to expand their risky lending and then bundling the mortgages into securities they peddled to their clients.[56]

Goldman Sachs knew the securities they were marketing were shaky and used its own money to bet against these bundled securities, making huge profits when the market collapsed. The tight links between government and Wall Street created conditions where risky behavior was simply ignored or even encouraged.

Robert Rubin, who had spent 26 years at Goldman Sachs and served as U.S. Secretary of the Treasury under Clinton in 1995–1999, pushed for repeal of the Glass-Steagall Act that—since the Great Depression—had prevented the merger of commercial and investment banks. As Morgenson and Rosner make clear, this policy change had been sought by Sanford Weill of the Travelers Group so that Travelers could merge with Citicorp. The merger in 1998, worth over $70 billion, was one of the largest in financial history. When Rubin stepped down from the Treasury, he became Vice Chairman of the merged corporation, Citigroup. He earned more than $100 million in the ensuing decade, as the company stepped up the issuing of mortgages. The company collapsed in the crisis of 2007/2008 and, like other banks and insurance companies deemed "too big to fail," was bailed out by the U.S. government.

Martin Gilens, a professor of political science at Princeton, has demonstrated in unequivocal terms that we are bearing witness in the United States to the takeover of the state by the rich.[57] Looking at literally thousands of proposed policy changes and the degree of support for them among poor, middle-class, and affluent Americans, he found that when the preferences of low- and middle-income Americans differ from those of the affluent, there is no relationship between policy outcomes and the desires of the less affluent. The affluent get their way. This situation held even before the 2010 decision by the U.S. Supreme Court in the *Citizens United* case that corporations and unions could give unlimited amounts of money to political action committees (PACs). The Court's decision exacerbated the problem of money influencing both the outcome of elections and the policies that are crafted by the state. In addition, there were 11,761 registered lobbyists in Washington, DC, in 2014, whose purpose was to sway members of Congress. Collectively, they spent on average more than $3 billion a year in 2008 through 2014 for this purpose.[58]

Business groups do not always get their way, but there is a systematic and unending effort to shape economic and political policy to benefit the few rather than the many. As the political scientists Jacob Hacker and Paul Pierson have argued in their *Winner-Take-All Politics*, inequality is driven by highly efficient organizations designed to craft public policies to benefit the wealthy. For example, attempts to moderate the explosive pay of CEOs by, among other things, honest accounting that would require corporations to list the stock options they give to their CEO's to boost their pay was fought by legions of businesspeople. Hedge fund managers have been allowed to treat the income they receive from investors as investor income, which means that some of the richest people in America pay no more than 15% on what they earn (the capital gains rate).[59] In short, what we are witnessing is a closure of political and economic systems, which is characteristic of nondemocratic and corrupt regimes.

Corruption takes place on many levels and assumes many different forms. There is the petty corruption of the police in Uganda, who supplement their salaries by taking bribes, or that of the Afghan police, who routinely seize the cars, trucks, and motorcycles of those who commit a traffic offense and fail to pay a bribe.[60] And there is the grand corruption that takes place in America's health care system and military. In an article in the Journal of the American Medical Association, Daniel M. Berwick and Andrew D. Hackbarth estimated that Medicare and Medicaid fraud costs taxpayers as much as $98 billion a year, and up to $272 billion across the entire health care system.[61] In the devastation wrought by Hurricane Katrina in 2005, no-bid contracts were given to those with ties to the government, and defective trailers were knowingly purchased that leaked formaldehyde into the air breathed by their inhabitants.[62] In conjunction with the decision by the United States to begin an air war against the Islamic State in the fall of 2014, a $7.2 billion contract was signed without fanfare for private contractors to carry out and coordinate global intelligence support five years into the future. Under its terms, 21 companies, led by Booz Allen Hamilton, BAE Systems, Lockheed Martin, and Northrop Grumman will compete to fully integrate intelligence, security, and information systems around the world.[63] Here, without bribery, extortion, or embezzlement, individuals derive private benefits from the positions they hold. The fact that many senior military officers secure high-level appointments in defense firms after their retirement encourages the use of weapons systems they champion. The management of war and intelligence by private contractors reduces citizen participation in discussions about the wisdom of expanding such ventures and their cost to the society.

Attempts to control the judiciary by the wealthy have gained traction in recent years. During the administration of George W. Bush, several U.S. attorneys were dismissed. It was alleged that the dismissals were aimed at preventing them from investigating Republican politicians. When the affair was investigated by the inspector general of the Justice Department, he concluded that the dismissals were arbitrary, flawed, and politically motivated. Interference in the justice system by business interests is also becoming common.

The novelist and attorney John Grisham focused on the purchase of justice by wealthy corporations in *The Appeal*.[64] The story begins in Mississippi with two small-town lawyers winning a large settlement, $3 million for wrongful death and $38 million in punitive damages, for their client Jeannette Baker, whose husband and young son died from cancer. The cancer was caused by carcinogens that "Krane Chemical" had knowingly allowed to pollute the town's water supply. A billionaire stockholder of Krane vows to do whatever is needed to overturn the verdict, including having the verdict overturned by the Mississippi Supreme Court. As Mississippi elects its Supreme Court Justices, a firm is employed to defeat a justice up for re-election who is known to favor the underdog. A hand-picked candidate is showered with money for his campaign and defeats the incumbent. The case goes to the supreme court and the winning candidate sides with the corporation, overturning the jury's award of $41 million to the plaintiff.

We wish this were complete fiction, but the story was inspired by an actual case in West Virginia. Massey Coal had lost a $50 million verdict in a fraud lawsuit brought by another coal company. The CEO of Massey, Don Blankenship, appealed the decision to the West Virginia Supreme Court of Appeals. He then contributed $3 million to help Charleston lawyer Brent Benjamin defeat an incumbent justice on the court of appeals. Benjamin won and, three years later, when Massey's appeal reached the court, Benjamin was asked to recuse himself, because of Blankenship's support for his campaign. He refused to step aside and Massey's appeal was upheld. (In 2014, Blankenship was indicted for the routine violation of federal mining and safety laws that led to the death of 29 miners. He said the charges were politically motivated.)

By 2014, 38 states were electing their supreme court justices. These races, which are supposed to be "nonpartisan," have drawn money from groups *outside of the states in which the races are held.* The U.S. Chamber of Commerce for example, funded successful campaigns to install pro-business justices in North Carolina, Michigan, Ohio, and Mississippi.[65] In the 2014 election for Montana's supreme court, a national Republican group ran ads trying to oust an incumbent state supreme court justice who was up for re-election. The Republican group was just one of three groups spending money to unseat the incumbent. Most of the money was coming from outside the state with the purpose of creating "a more stable and business-friendly" supreme court in Montana.[66] The challenger lost. We are, however, witnessing the degeneration of the very institutions—political, economic, and judicial—that are essential for the maintenance of a democratic society.

Summary

When Boss Tweed offered immigrants a hand up in exchange for their votes, he used graft as a tool of management. A growing city needed an infrastructure—water lines, streets, sewers, and schools. City contractors needed to hire those who voted for Tammany Hall's candidates and they needed to give those voters jobs. Tweed got rich in the process but ended up in prison when the magnitude of his corruption became a problem for the city's WASP bankers and financiers.

The United States was still struggling to realize the values embodied in the Constitution; it was not yet a fully democratic nation, and discrimination based on gender, religion, and ethnicity was common. The aftermath of the Civil War saw both political and economic corruption deepen in the South as a backlash against Reconstruction. During Grant's administration corruption was the order of the day at both the national and state level. Boomers rushed West, driving Native peoples off their lands, and justice was sometimes administered in territories by vigilante groups even into the twentieth century. At the same time, inequality was taking root. Manufacturing cartels formed to increase profits and oil and railroad monopolies were forming. Workers had few protections against rapacious bosses as unions were slow to form.

The costs of corruption in any historical period are high, although corruption is most likely to occur when a national government is weak and unable to ensure equality before the law, is unable to incorporate diverse trust networks into the body politic, and where coercive power centers thrive. Nineteenth- and twentieth-century America fit the same profile as many of those countries that are today struggling to become full democracies. *Corruption and inequality create a vicious cycle in which each worsens the other.* The concentration of wealth in the hands of a few allows them to capture a nation's political and economic institutions, which allows them to use the resources of the state to protect and magnify their wealth. Corruption channels wealth into the hands of the elite, stifles economic growth, and causes the civic sector to wither as people are shut out of their own societies. If the magnitude of corruption is significant enough it can serve as an underlying cause for rebellion, civil war, and the ultimate collapse of a nation.

Yet civil wars do not provide a clear path from a dictatorship to a democracy, as is evident in the case of a number of nations. A civil war might involve the mobilization of specific trust networks— ethnic groups. These trust networks, if they are successful in capturing state power, are unwilling to share the power they have acquired. Civil war can concentrate power in the hands of military and paramilitary forces. A civil war can increase the likelihood that irrelevant moral criteria will be the defining factor in terms of whether or not people have access to their nation's resources, as was the case in Nigeria and Uganda.

One-party states like China, Russia, and North Korea are infected with corrupt institutions because they have closed economic and political systems. In the case of China and North Korea one's party status serves as the irrelevant moral criteria by which access is granted and in Russia it is granted on the basis of loyalty to Vladimir Putin. But *regardless of how corruption comes about it clearly creates endemic social inequality and destroys democracy.*

We can see at the present time that those very principles upon which a democracy is founded are being challenged by growing degrees of inequality, which allow state policies to be crafted so that they benefit a select few. Institutions which are supposed to guarantee the rule of law are now the target of those who want judges to make decisions favorable to the increased accumulation of wealth and power. Democracy can roll forward or backward driven by equality or inequality.

Through a Sustainability Lens

What has corruption and inequality got to do with sustainability? There are five ways it is crucial. First, sustainability is about community, about learning to live within the biophysical constraints of the planet. Corporations that seek to maximize profit at the expense of all else play an antisocial role in society. They behave in a way that is fundamentally corrupt. As experts on the problems of inequality, Richard Wilkinson and Kate Pickett, have noted that corporations

> ... use their huge advertising wealth, media and political influence, to counter evidence of risk coming from scientific research and to fight any legislative attempts to reduce risk. They pack regulatory systems with people who will defend their interests, they spend huge amounts on lobbying politicians ... And, on top of it all, the whole business effort, with its sophisticated marketing and advertising, still aims to maximize sales and consumerism even when we know carbon emissions have to be reduced ... to save us from the worst effects of global warming.[67]

Oil and gas companies have funded climate deniers and skeptics to assert that "the science was uncertain," and that humans were not the drivers of climate change. These campaigns of deceit have proven to be effective and divisive: a majority of Americans express the opinion that climate change is a naturally occurring event, not caused by humans.[68]

Second, and related to the notion of community, is the fact that corruption has a moral dimension. In virtually all societies that suffer from endemic corruption people describe it as wrong, and those who engage in it as cheaters. To the extent that we are robbing future generations by using up multiple planets to maintain our current style of life, we are engaging in corrupt behavior. We rob future generations by imposing upon them crushing debts to pay for our current lifestyles. If we do not reverse these trends, each future generation in the United States will be responsible for an additional 17 to 24% of national debt.[69] Those who ignore the needs of other humans and future generations contribute to the development of corrupt societies, or worse.

Third, corruption destroys the civic sector which is essential for crafting local, national and international solutions to the problem of climate change. People must have practice coming together in order to change political and economic institutions and to affect government policy. When the Soviet Union disintegrated in the face of demands for democracy and economic reform the long-term outcome—because there was no civic sector—was not democracy in Russia, but an oligarchy.

Fourth, corrupt regimes are often propped up by violence. Military and paramilitary forces, as well as police and prisons, are a way to control populations. These institutions—prisons and armies—are a drain on the economy of any country, and they destroy human capital. Unfortunately, the countervailing forces are not organized political parties or unions that would serve as checks on corruption; rather they are often criminal gangs. Mexico with its closed economic and political system and violent drug cartels is an example. Sometimes even unions stand in the way of reform. Political patronage in Mexico has, until recently, looked remarkably the same as that practiced by Boss Tweed. In 2013 lawmakers finally passed legislation to end the corrupt practice of union bosses selling classroom teaching jobs and pocketing the money at the expense of the students. As *The Washington Post* reported, Mexico spends a greater share of its public funds on education than most developed nations but produces the lowest academic achievement levels, and less than half of all students finish high school. Heads of teacher unions, who receive high salaries, have seldom taught and even drug lords have ended up on the teacher payrolls.[70]

Corruption in all cases challenges the rule of law, which is fundamental for the creation of democratic and sustainable societies. Even when war is not used to control an aggressor's population it distorts the economy. Depending on when you wish to begin the countdown, either with the first Gulf War of 1990 or the bombing of Afghanistan that began on October 7, shortly after September 11, 2001, the United States has been engaged in constant warfare for over a decade. War is not sustainable: not just because of the trillions of dollars spent, but because the longer war continues, the more the policies that guide it derive from and are consolidated by the elites who benefit economically.

Finally, inequality and corruption have psychological effects. We compare ourselves to others. In modern western societies we frequently seek to feel "better" through consumption. We "need" large houses, big cars, and new clothes, just as Nigerians "need" to have champagne, private planes, and luxury SUVs to be like the western elites to which they compare themselves. Greedy rulers and elites generate envy. We see other people "living large," and often want to be like those people. None of these behaviors generate the conditions for a sustainable society in which a notion of community, rather than competition dominates. No vision of a sustainable society leaves room for corruption and inequality.

Notes

1 David M. Herszenhorn. 2013. "Fairness an Issue, Even after Azerbaijan Votes." *The New York Times*. October 9. Accessed on February 16, 2014 at: http://www.nytimes.com/2013/10/10/world/asia/fairness-an-issue-even-after-azerbaijan-votes.html?_r=0.
2 New York Fire Museum (website). "Post-Revolution: 1786–1865." Accessed on September 3, 2014 at: http://www.nycfiremuseum.org/history_post_revolution.cfm; see also Edwin G. Burrows and Mike Wallace. 1999. *Gotham: A History of New York City to 1898*. New York, NY: Oxford University Press.
3 Charles Tilly. 2007. *Democracy*. New York, NY: Cambridge University Press, p.85.
4 Richard F. Bensel. 2004. *The American Ballot Box in the Mid-Nineteenth Century*. New York, NY: Cambridge University Press.
5 Kenneth D. Ackerman. 2005. *Boss Tweed: The Corrupt Pol Who Conceived the Soul of Modern New York*. New York, NY: Carroll & Graf.

6. Pete Hamill. 2005. "'Boss Tweed': The Fellowship of the Ring." *The New York Times, Sunday Book Review*. March 27. Retrieved on September 4, 2014 at: http://www.nytimes.com/2005/03/27/books/review/027HAMILL.html.
7. Richard Slotkin. 1998. *The Fatal Environment: The Myth of the Frontier in the Age of Industrialization*. Norman, OK: Oklahoma University Press.
8. Susan Olzak. 1989. "Labor Unrest, Immigration, and Ethnic Conflict in Urban America, 1880–1914." *American Journal of Sociology*. 94(6): 1303–1333.
9. Lane Kenworthy. 2014. *Social Democratic America*. New York, NY: Oxford University Press.
10. Marshall Sahlins. 1963. "Poor Man, Rich Man, Big Man, Chief: Political Types in Melanesia and Polynesia. *Comparative Studies in Society and History*. 5(3): 285–303.
11. Terry Golway has made the argument that Tammany Hall gave rise to American Democratic politics. Terry Golway. 2014. *Machine Made: Tammany Hall and the Creation of American Politics*. New York, NY: Liveright.
12. Robert Klitgaard. 2006. "Introduction: Subverting Corruption." *Global Crime*. 7(3–4): 299–300.
13. Karen Dawisha. 2014. *Putin's Kleptocracy: Who Owns Russia?* New York, NY: Simon & Schuster.
14. Tim Johnson. 2014. "Mexico Confronts Reports that Police Helped Massacre 43 Students." McClatchy News Service, October 7. *The Missoulian*, A-7.
15. Steve Inskeep. 2011. "Cities Beyond the Law." *The New York Times*. December 4: SR 4.
16. Sanjeev Gupta, Hamid Davoodi, and Rosa Alonso-Terme. 1998. "Does Corruption Affect Income Inequality and Poverty?" Washington, DC: IMF Working Paper/98/76.
17. Eric Chetwynd, Frances Chetwynd, and Bertram Spector. 2003. "Corruption and Poverty: A Review of Recent Literature." Washington, DC: Management Systems International, p.3; see also Raymond Fisman and Edward Miguel. 2009. *Economic Gangsters: Corruption, Violence, and he Poverty of Nations*. Princeton, NJ: Princeton University Press.
18. Jong-Sung You and Sanjeev Khagram. 2005. "A Comparative Study of Inequality and Corruption." *American Sociological Review*. 70: 136–157.
19. Boniface Dulani, Robert Mattes, and Carolyn Logan. 2013. "After a Decade of Growth in Africa, Little Change in Poverty at the Grassroots." *Afrobarometer, Policy Brief No.1* Retrieved on October 14, 2014 at: http://www.afrobarometer.org/files/documents/policy_brief/ab_r5_policybriefno1.pdf.
20. Global Security. 2014. "Nigerian Army." Retrieved on October 14, 2014 at: http://www.globalsecurity.org/military/world/nigeria/army.htm.
21. Anonymous. 2014. "Corporal of Air Force on Corruption in Nigerian Military." *Information Nigeria*. September 3. Retrieved on October 6, 2014 at: http://www.informationng.com/2014/09/corporal-of-air-force-on-corruption-in-nigerian-military.html.
22. Nathaniel Allen, Peter M. Lewis, and Hilary Matfess. 2014. "The Boko Haram Insurgency, by the Numbers." *Washington Post*. October 6. Retrieved on October 6, 2014 at: http://www.washingtonpost.com/blogs/monkey-cage/wp/2014/10/06/the-boko-haram-insurgency-by-the-numbers/.
23. Diversity Affluence. 2013. "Africa, Africa's Elite, Conspicuous Luxury Consumption." Retrieve on October 7, 2014 at: http://www.diversityaffluence.com/blog20130130africa-africas-elite-conspicuous-luxury-consumption/.

24 Transparency International. 2014. "2013 Data Set." Retrieved on October 7 at: http://www.transparency.org/research/cpi/overview.
25 Max Siollun. 2014. "Making Sense of President Jonathan's New Military Appointments." Max Siollun at WordPress. Accessed on October 8 at: http://maxsiollun.wordpress.com/2014/01/20/making-sense-of-president-jonathans-new-military-appointments/.
26 This insight was provided by Michael Schwartz in a private communication. February 19, 2015.
27 Independent Corrupt Practices and Other Related Offenses Commission. 2008. "Report at the Police Service Commission Retreat." Accessed on October 7, 2014 at: http://www.psc.gov.ng/files/Combating%20Corruption%20in%20the%20Nigeria%20Police.pdf.
28 Transparency International. 2015. "Corruption by Country, Uganda." Accessed on August 27 at: https://www.transparency.org/country/.
29 Yoweri Museveni. 1997. *Sowing the Mustard Seed: The Struggle for Freedom and Democracy in Uganda*. Oxford, UK: Macmillan Education; see also: Ondoga Ori Amaza. 1998. *Museveni's Long March from Guerrilla to Statesman*. Kampala, Uganda: Fountain Publishers.
30 James C. McKinley Jr. 1997. "New African Leader Stands Tall in African Order." *New York Times*. June 15. Retrieved on October 7, 2014 at: http://www.nytimes.com/1997/06/15/world/uganda-leader-stands-tall-in-new-african-order.html.
31 Robert Klitgaard. 2006. "Introduction: Subverting Corruption." p.302.
32 Human Rights Watch. 2013. *"Letting the Big Fish Swim:" Failures to Prosecute High-Level Corruption in Uganda*. New Haven, CT: Allard K. Lowenstein International Human Rights Clinic, Yale Law, p.2.
33 Ibid., p.15.
34 *HumanIPO*. April 24, 2013. "Ugandan President's Sack of Money." Retrieved on October 13, 2014 at: http://www.humanipo.com/news/5465/Ugandan-presidents-sackofmoney-causes-uproar-on-social-media/.
35 Human Rights Watch. 2013. "Letting the Big Fish Swim:" p.16.
36 International Political Forum. 2013. "Uganda and the Culture of Corruption." Retrieved on October 14 at: http://internationalpoliticalforum.com/uganda-and-the-culture-of-corruption/.
37 Freedom House. "Freedom in the World, 2015." Retrieved on August 26 at: https://www.transparency.org/country/.
38 Pew Research Center. 2013. "Inflation, Corruption, Inequality Top List of Chinese Public's Concerns." Retrieved on October 6, 2014 at: http://www.pewresearch.org/fact-tank/2013/11/08/inflation-corruption-inequality-top-list-of-chinese-publics-concerns/.
39 Cheng Li and Tom Orlik. 2014. "China's Corruption Crackdown More Than Factional Politics." Retrieved on October 8, 2014 at: http://www.brookings.edu/research/interviews/2014/07/31-corruption-crackdown-factions-li; and, *The Economist*. 2014. "Because We're Worth It: How and Why Lofty Ideologies Cohabit with Rampant Corruption." July 12: 55–56.
40 David Barboza. 2012. "Billions in Hidden Riches for Family of Chinese Leader." *New York Times*. October 25. Retrieved on October 8, 2014 at: http://www.nytimes.com/2012/10/26/business/global/family-of-wen-jiabao-holds-a-hidden-fortune-in-china.html?pagewanted=all&_r=0.

41 Moisés Naim. 2014. "The Problem with Piketty's Inequality Formula." *Atlantic*. May 27. Retrieved on October 13, 2014 at: http://www.theatlantic.com/international/archive/2014/05/the-problem-with-pikettys-inequality-formula/371653/.
42 Peter Beaumont. 2011. "Mohammed Bouazizi: The Dutiful Son Whose Death Changed Tunisia's Fate." *Guardian*. Accessed on October 13, 2014 at: http://www.theguardian.com/world/2011/jan/20/tunisian-fruit-seller-mohammed-bouazizi.
43 *The Economist*. 2014. "Crony Capitalism: Friends in High Place." October 11: 74.
44 Ibid.
45 Peter Turchin makes the argument that corruption leads to regime collapse, and one signal of pending collapse is the growth in number of elites and their competition with one another. Peter Turchin. 2007. *War and Peace and War: The Rise and Fall of Empires*. New York, NY: Penguin Group.
46 Laura Spinney. 2011. "The Underhand Ape." *New Scientist*. November 5: 42–45.
47 Freedom House. 2013. "Freedom in the World, 2013," p.6. Accessed on September 12, 2014 at: http://www.freedomhouse.org/.
48 United Nations General Assembly, Human Rights Council. 2014. *Report of the Commission of Inquiry on Human Rights in the Democratic People's Republic*. New York, NY: United Nations. Available online at: http://www.ohchr.org/EN/HRBodies/HRC/CoIDPRK/Pages/ReportoftheCommissionofInquiryDPRK.aspx.
49 Ibid., p.8.
50 Ibid., p.9.
51 *The Economist*. 2014. "Fighting for Identity." May 17: 43.
52 Charles Tilly. 2007. Democracy.
53 Francis Fukuyama. 2014. *Political Order and Political Decay: From the Industrial Revolution to the Globalization of Democracy*. New York, NY: Farrar, Straus & Giroux. See also; Niall Ferguson. 2012. *The Great Degeneration: How Institutions Decay and Economies Die*. London: Penguin Books.
54 Robert B. Reich. 2011. "Getting Away with It." *New York Times Book Review*. May 29: 9.
55 Gretchen Morgenson and Joshua Rosner. 2011. *Reckless Endangerment: How Outsized Greed and Corruption Led to Economic Armageddon*. New York, NY: Times Books/Henry Holt & Company.
56 Robert Reich. May 27, 2011. "Washington and Wall Street: The Revolving Door." Review of Gretchen Morgenson and Joshua Rosner, (2011), *Reckless Endangerment*. New York, NY: Times Books/Henry Holt. *Sunday Book Review, New York Times*. Retrieved on August 27 at: http://www.nytimes.com/2011/05/29/books/review/book-review-reckless-endangerment-by-gretchen-morgenson-and-joshua-rosner.html?_r=0.
57 Martin Givens. 2012. *Affluence and Influence: Economic Inequality and Political Power in America*. Princeton, NJ: Princeton University Press.
58 Open Secrets. 2015. Accessed on September 15, 2014 at: http://www.opensecrets.org/lobby/.
59 Jacob Hacker and Paul Pierson. 2010. *Winner-Take-All Politics: How Washington Made the Rich Richer and Turned Its Back on the Middle Class*. New York, NY: Simon & Schuster.
60 Azam Ahmed. 2013. "Police Corruption Turns Off Afghans." *New York Times*. February 18. Reprinted in *The Sacramento Bee*. February 18, 2013, p.A6.

61 Donald M. Berwick and Andrew D. Hackbarth. 2012. "Eliminating Waste in U.S. Health Care." *Journal of the American Medical Association.* 307(14): 1513–1516.
62 Naomi Klein. 2007. *Shock Doctrine: The Rise of Disaster Capitalism.* New York, NY: Knopf.
63 Tim Shorrock. 2014. "Who Profits from Our New War? Inside NSA and Private Contractors' Secret Plans." *Salon.* September 24. Retrieved on October 14, 2014 at: http://www.salon.com/2014/09/24/heres_who_profits_from_our_new_war_inside_nsa_and_an_army_of_private_contractors_plans/.
64 John Grisham. 2008. *The Appeal.* New York, NY: Doubleday.
65 Bill Buzenberg. 2013. "Justice for Sale in State Supreme Court Elections?" *Center for Public Integrity.* Retrieved on October 14, 2014 at: http://www.publicintegrity.org/2013/06/13/12829/justice-sale-state-supreme-court-elections.
66 Charles S. Johnson. 2014. "Independent Groups Raise Profile of Race." *Missoulian.* October 8: A1,8.
67 Richard Wilkinson and Kate Pickett. 2014. *A Convenient Truth: A Better Society for Us and the Planet.* London: The Fabian Society, p.46.
68 Pew Research. 2014. "Climate Change: Key Data Points from Pew Research." Accessed on October 16, 2014 at: http://www.pcwresearch.org/key-data-points/climate-change-key-data-points-from-pew-research/.
69 Alan J. Auerbach, Jagadeesh Gokhale, and Laurence J. Kotlikoff. 1991. "Generational Accounts: A Meaningful Alternative to Deficit Accounting." Washington, DC: National Bureau of Economic Research, Working paper #3589. Available online at: http://www.nber.org/papers/w3589.
70 Nick Miroff. 2013. "Mexican Lawmakers Pass Education Overhaul." *Washington Post.* Retrieved on October 17, 2014 at: http://www.washingtonpost.com/world/the_americas/mexican-lawmakers-pass-education-overhaul/2013/09/04/ce459d1c-1583-11e3-961c-f22d3aaf19ab_story.html.

7

NARRATIVES OF POWER: HOW THEY DRIVE INEQUALITY

Consider:

- The stories we tell matter, because they shape action.
- We are hardwired for narratives.
- Some narratives cannot be reconciled with others.
- A narrative of market fundamentalism is driving social policy.
- The social contract between employer and employee is under attack.
- The social costs of low-wage jobs are significant and borne by the entire society.
- The American state continues to expand by increasing expenditures for social control while decreasing expenditures for social welfare.
- Narratives of power and control allow corporations to escape the human and environmental costs of their actions.

When Ronald Reagan was running for President in 1976 he told the same story about welfare cheaters at virtually every campaign stop. According to Reagan, "There's this woman in Chicago. She has eighty names, thirty addresses, twelve Social Security Cards ... She's got Medicaid, [she's] getting food stamps, and she is collecting welfare under each of her names. Her tax-free cash income alone is over $150,000 ($630,000 in 2014 dollars)." The story, though false, resonated with many white, working-class voters who assumed that those getting welfare did not deserve it and were simply scamming the system because they did not want to work. Though Reagan never used the term "welfare queen," it entered the American lexicon during his successful campaign for the presidency. "Welfare queens" became a stereotype for Black women who had children out of wedlock in order to use the AFDC (Aid to Families with Dependent Children) money intended to provide assistance for their children to buy drugs; also, they had no work ethic.

> Attacks on social welfare often have a racist undertone and focus on eliminating social safety nets for the "unworthy."

An irony, however, is that during the time Reagan was campaigning for office, the majority of welfare recipients were white women. Nevertheless, so powerful was Reagan's story about welfare queens that many voters came to associate receiving welfare with being Black and lazy. Attacks on social welfare have a racist undertone and focus on eliminating social safety nets for the "unworthy." Reagan was running against Lyndon Johnson's Great Society programs and tapping into growing class and ethnic resentment.

The Great Society Versus the Free Market

When President Kennedy was assassinated in 1963, Lyndon Johnson, former majority leader of the Senate and a master politician, assumed the presidency and began to implement an agenda of American exceptionalism: The Great Society Program. In a speech at the University of Michigan, Johnson laid out his vision of what a Great American Society would look like. He noted that Americans had labored for a century to "settle and subdue" a continent. But, now, the challenge would be to use the nation's wealth "to enrich and elevate our national life and advance the quality of American civilization." He told his audience:

> The Great Society is a place where every child can find knowledge to enrich his mind and to enlarge his talents. It is a place where leisure is a welcome chance to build and reflect ... It is a place where the

city of man served not only the needs of the body and the demands of commerce but the desire for beauty and the hunger for community. It is a place where man can renew contact with nature. It is a place that honors creation for its own sake and for what it adds to the understanding of the race. It is a place where men are more concerned with equality of their goals than the quantity of their goods.[1]

Johnson mixed familiar religious language with the American idea that education can solve social ills and his own evolving notions about the need for racial equality. Major new spending programs focusing on education, medical care, urban problems, and transportation were launched. Yet the growing cost of the war in Vietnam caused divisions within the Democratic Party and Congress over funding the Great Society.

Anti-war protests paralleled marches and riots by African-Americans demanding equality before the law. Race riots in Chicago and Detroit and attempts to register Black voters in the South, led to a fissioning of the Democratic Party and the loss of the solid Democratic South. The 1960s would see members of the working class from industrialized northern cities (traditionally Democratic) and white Southerners of all classes joining the ranks of the Republican Party. The reason for the shift was resentment and racism. Poverty became politicized.

In his 1981 inaugural address president Ronald Reagan laid out in simplistic terms what he perceived to be the difference between a liberal and a conservative, or free-market, agenda. He argued that "government is not the solution to our problem; government is the problem." He added that "It is my intention to curb the size and influence of the federal establishment ..." He scorned the bureaucratic elites in Washington who, he claimed, had created the nation's crises. "From time to time, we have been tempted to believe that a society has become too complex to be managed by self-rule, that government by an elite group is superior to government for, by, and of the people."[2] However, as the conservative Mises Institute calculated, by the end of his second term, Reagan had tripled the Gross Federal Debt from $900 billion to $2.7 trillion and taxes had increased.[3] Sometimes a good story is better than reality.

By the time Reagan assumed the Presidency in 1981, conservative think tanks had been created to challenge "leftist" ideology and roll back the "socialist" gains of the Great Society. Reagan also came into office during a period of hyperinflation, when interest rates stood at 18%, which meant few could afford to buy a home. Growth in real income of the American worker had stagnated; the OPEC (Organization of the Petroleum Exporting Companies) oil embargo of 1973–1974 had caused a fourfold increase in the price of gas, and American hostages were being held by the Iranians. Even worse for some was the notion that women, like minorities, wanted equality. The Equal Rights Amendment, introduced in Congress in 1972 to guarantee women equal treatment in all spheres, failed to meet its deadline for ratification in 1982. Johnson's vision of a Great Society was no longer plausible to many.

In its place came market fundamentalism, which at its core was an attack on the Great Society programs. The welfare queen stood in as a proxy for all of those—usually minorities and women—who were imagined to be getting something they did not deserve. The Great Society programs were seen as an attack on the values of hard work and individualism. The narrative of market fundamentalism that was embraced by corporate leaders, politicians, and some academic economists lead to a war on unions, the erosion of the social contract between worker and employer, and to challenges to the simple notion that people should be paid a living wage for their work. This narrative continues to find robust support among donors and organizations who have crafted legislation and wooed legislators at both the state and national levels to eliminate financial and environmental regulations, weaken the power of public sector unions, and reduce the social safety nets for those most in need. Decisions by the Supreme Court have made it easier to fund such campaigns and to hide the identity of those organizations and individuals who are providing the money. The steady drumbeat of "jobs, jobs, jobs," has deafened many to the fact the jobs created are often low-wage jobs. The message of standing on one's own two feet, not needing government assistance, and accepting any job regardless of what it paid were echoed in the 2012 Presidential elections.

Mitt Romney said to a group of supporters that no matter what he said or did, 47% of the American people were going to vote for Obama. They were the "47% … who are dependent on government, who believe that they are victims, who believe that the government has a responsibility to care for them, who believe that they are entitled to health care, to food, to housing, you name it." These people were not Romney's responsibility because, as he said, "I'll never convince them they should take personal responsibility and care for their lives."[4]

Romney's running mate, Paul Ryan (congressman from Wisconsin), echoed and reinforced the message that people had a choice: They could be dependent on government or be responsible, self-reliant individuals. In criticizing the Obama administration, Ryan said: "None of us has to settle for the best this administration offers—a dull ... journey from one entitlement to the next, a government-planned life, a country where everything is free but us." He went on to add that people needed to think for themselves and define happiness for themselves, because that is the American Dream. "That's freedom, and I'll take it any day over the supervision and sanctimony of central planners."[5]

Ryan's message, among other things, was an attempt to underscore the idea that success or failure in life was due to individual effort alone and that less government was better than more. These are the two core principles of neoliberal economic theory (see Chapter 4, this volume).

There are reasons why this narrative has traction in the United States, besides the money put behind campaigns to further it. It also has traction because for many Americans it represents a story that they've been told and up until recently has made sense: If you work hard you can succeed. It is also grounded in our Puritan religious heritage, which says that if you fail, it is entirely your fault. Poverty is punishment for our sins. Yet there is an evolving alternative narrative that may carry equal weight and is one of the reasons for the political and ideological divisions that exist in American society.

At the Democratic National Convention, President Barack Obama told the delegates that the choice for America in the 2012 election was between two different visions for the future—Democratic and Republican. "Ours," he said, "is a fight to restore the values that built the largest middle class and the strongest economy the world has ever known." He went on to argue that the promise that hard work would pay off, that everyone should get a fair shot, and that everyone would play by the same rules was now being threatened. In place of this promise was a Republican plan to boost the economy by instituting "another round of tax breaks for millionaires."[6]

One could argue that Obama's narrative was the more powerful in 2012, as he was returned to office. Win or lose, though, all candidates know they must have a convincing story to tell or they will not be successful. We need stories to help us make sense of the world, and we need them to envision a path to the future.

Hardwired for Narratives

Humans are *hardwired to create narratives* and *hardwired to attribute causes to empirical events*. In *The Believing Brain*, Michael Shermer, a science writer, describes our brains as pattern-seeking belief engines.[7] That means we are predisposed to see patterns, even if there are none, and to attribute them to knowing agents, after which our brains seek out information to confirm what we "know" and ignore information that contradicts the beliefs we have formed. As Shermer says, "We form our beliefs for a wide variety of subjective, personal, emotional, and psychological reasons in the contexts of environments created by family, friends, colleagues, culture, and society at large; after forming our beliefs we then defend, justify, and rationalize them with a host of intellectual reasons, cogent arguments, and rational explanations."[8]

> Humans are hardwired to create narratives.

The stories we tell to make sense of the social world we inhabit can be benign or have terrible consequences. We tell stories about the poor, the homeless, bankers, corporate executives, men, women, and children. If we have had no contact with the homeless, we might not see them as people down on their luck, but rather develop a story that portrays them as too lazy to get a job. If we have struggled to find a job ourselves, our views and our stories would probably be different. If our home was repossessed by the bank because we lost our job and could not pay the mortgage, we might craft stories about heartless bankers and corporations who care nothing for the "little man." In 1974, when the Hutus in Rwanda were encouraged to think of their Tutsi brothers and sisters as "cockroaches" by the government and urged to exterminate them, the story had terrible consequences. As the neuropsychologist Michael Gazzaniga has confirmed, the stories we tell matter, help to reconcile the information available to us, and create a unified sense of self.[9]

Storytelling also lights up our brains. A story with strong emotional content and one in which we identify with the characters releases oxytocin, the so-called "love" hormone. Researchers have found that the greater the amount of oxytocin released, the more likely we are to trust the story teller.[10] Drew Westen, professor of psychology and psychiatry at Emory University, has argued in *The Political Brain: the Role of Emotion in Deciding the Fate of the Nation*, that if we are going to tell a story, we need to do so with passion and conviction, and the story needs to follow a particular structure.[11] Stories our political leaders tell us are like the stories and folktales we tell our children. They "orient us to what is, what could be, and what should be"; they orient us to their world views. Westen reasons that our brains evolved to "expect" stories with a particular structure, with protagonists and villains, a hill to be climbed, or a battle to be fought. Stories are how we transmit our values.

There is both an upside and downside to collective narratives. A strong narrative can bring people together for a common purpose, while the lack of a narrative that charts a course of action can sow confusion. As the writer George Packer has noted, when America was attacked by terrorists flying planes into the Twin Towers on 9/11 (September 11, 2001), we could not formulate a unifying story about it. A crime had been committed by a small group of militants attached to some group we knew little about. We were surprised and faced with something new and confusing.[12] In the face of this confusion, we were asked by President Bush to go shopping; others would later be asked to fight the wars in Iraq and Afghanistan. We do not have a national narrative for explaining such conflicts, identifying how they should be solved, or what the role of all Americans should be; we have lost one of the powerful narratives for integrating a nation around the need to solve common problems. What we do have is a struggle over competing narratives about such issues as the need to provide robust social safety nets, the extent to which a free-market can solve social ills, and whether or not we are doomed to spend our lives trapped by the social conditions into which we were born. The story we choose to believe depends a lot on what we already believe.

Ignoring Inconvenient Truths

We all know the story of Paul Revere, the American hero who, late in the evening on April 18, 1775, set off on his horse to warn the colonial militia of an impending attack by the British army. In June of 2011, the political figure Sarah Palin told a crowd of supporters that Paul Revere was actually riding to warn the British, letting them know we were going to be free, and that

> The more certain we are of our facts, the more likely we are to be wrong.

we were armed. When it was pointed out to her that she got the story backwards, she unsuccessfully tried to assert that her version of history was the correct one. But what is most intriguing is that her supporters went to the Wikipedia site that tells about Revere's ride and tried to edit it to be consistent with Palin's interpretation of history. The editors at Wikipedia quickly stepped in to prevent a revision of history.

One of the problems with political stories is that we reject facts that do not square with our previous beliefs. In fact, *our brains are a threat to democracy*. In the words of the political scientists Brendan Nyhan and Jason Reifler, they "backfire" when presented with a contradiction; that is the brain's way of dealing with cognitive dissonance. Over and over again we find that ideas that do not fit our preconceptions get rejected, if not immediately, then later, as might happen in a bad organ transplant.[13]

The misinformed are often those who hold the strongest positions, which means they are even harder to budge. In a study reported in 2000, the political scientist James Kuklinski of the University of Illinois and his colleagues asked participants about their views on welfare (for instance, what percentage of the federal budget was spent on welfare, how many people were enrolled in welfare program, how many of those enrolled were Black, and what the average payout was). This oft-cited study showed that over half of all respondents thought they got all the answers correct, when only about 3% of respondents got more than half of the answers right. The *more* confident respondents were in their answers, the *more* likely they were to have gotten them wrong.[14] The narrative of the welfare cheat developed in the 1960s and 1970s has had great staying power. It is clear that whether or not a story conforms to empirical facts is irrelevant. What is relevant is whether or not it resonates with what people want to believe and with their emotions. This underscores a point about *all narratives: they strip away complexity and make it seem as though there are simple solutions to problems.*

One example of a simplifying narrative is that of market fundamentalism: the notion that all social ills can be resolved by allowing free markets to operate unfettered by restraint or regulations. Taxes are always bad because, as the fundamentalists argue, individuals will always spend money more wisely than the government. Likewise, private firms can provide services more efficiently than the government. Assistance should not be provided to those in need, because they will lose their incentive to work.[15] Everything becomes an opportunity to privatize and create more "efficient" social services. This narrative has recently led, in the United States, to development of private prisons, the private monitoring of parolees, and the outsourcing of defense work to private contractors, to name just a few of the consequences. It is a narrative that argues for a shrinking of social safety nets and an expansion of social controls.[16] The problem is, we don't have a counternarrative that resonates with enough people about how democracies work and what leads to their unwinding. Let us examine who is behind such efforts and what their consequences are.

The War on Unions

As I will argue in this chapter, middle- and working-class Americans have been on the losing end when it comes to the development and support of public policies that protect their wages, working conditions, and benefits (p.181 ff.). In addition, there has been an all-out assault on unions, with a narrative that claims they limit people's right to work, are a drain on the taxpayer, and that the pensions of union members are out-of-line with those of workers in the private sector. Further, public school teachers, whose unions protect them with tenure, are blamed for the lack of student achievement, rather than blaming the impoverished backgrounds from which the students come. A primary reason for the attack on unions is, of course, that they have historically provided significant funding for Democratic Party candidates. However, a weakening of unions increases inequality.

My first well-paying summer job after high school was working at the Crown Zellerbach Paper Mill in West Linn, Oregon. By working an entire summer I was able to save enough money to pay for a year of college. As a temporary employee filling in for those who were either sick or on vacation, my wages were by no means at the top of the scale. But the union I was required to join, The International Brotherhood of Pulp, Sulfite, and Paper Mill Workers, was intent on not allowing a low-wage class of employees to develop within the mill. Their goal was to raise everyone's wages.

Many of the regular adult employees, whose sons and daughters I had gone to school with, had been at the mill for their entire working careers and had done well. They owned homes, raised families, had money left over for hobbies like fishing and hunting, and sometimes had saved enough to buy vacation property. The same was true for employees of the United Auto Workers (UAW) in Michigan. Their wages were high enough that they, too, enjoyed what we think of as solid, middle-class prosperity. They bought homes, sent children to college, paid the doctor and dentist out of pocket, saved a little for retirement, and some built small vacation homes in upstate Michigan. More important, perhaps, is the fact that union wages made Detroit one of the wealthiest cities in America during the 1950s and 1960s. Unions enhanced overall prosperity, not just for workers but also for the communities in which they were situated. The logic of this is clear. More money to spend means that property values go up, car sales are stimulated, and schools, roads, and infrastructure are built, giving rise to jobs beyond those directly tied to the union.

> Unions help to reduce both racial inequality and economic inequality.

There are well-documented bonuses to being a union member. Ben Casselman, a *Wall Street Journal* reporter, estimated that in 2011 the median private-sector union member made "878 dollars a week compared to 716 dollars for nonmembers, a nearly 23% premium."[17] Lawrence Mishel and his colleagues at the Economic Policy Institute calculated that in 2011, those covered by a collective bargaining agreement made 13.6% more than those workers who were not covered by such an agreement. The gains of union membership were even more significant for specific categories of workers. Unionized men received a 17.3% wage bonus for being union members, while the bump for women was less, just 9.1%. (To put this in perspective in terms of dollars and cents, union men got $1.24 more per hour and union women got $0.67 more than nonunion men and women.)[18]

Unions have helped to reduce racial inequalities in wages, if not those based on gender.[19] Those African-American men who were union members received in 2011 an average wage of $2.60 an hour more than non-union workers and Hispanic men fared even better at $3.44 an hour. Union members of all races were also 28.2% more likely to have health, retirement, and paid leave benefits than non-union workers. (Once this figure is adjusted for size of business, occupational position, type of industry, and so forth, the benefit is still substantial at 17.5%.)[20] As the Economic Policy Institute has noted, unions reduce overall wage inequalities most for those at the bottom and middle of the wage scale. There are only small wage gains (2.2%) to be had for white collar and college-educated workers who are union members. "These two factors—the greater union representation and the larger union wage impact for low- and middle-wage workers—are key to unionization's role in reducing wage inequalities."[21] Even though the benefits of membership are substantial, union membership has continued a long, downward slide since the 1960s.

Fifty years ago almost 35% of the American labor force was unionized. It has now dropped to a historic low of 11.3%, rivaling the membership figures of the Great Depression.[22] The most precipitous drop in union membership occurred among those employed by the private sector (now 6.7%), while the numbers for those employed in the public sector (teachers, state and municipal workers, police and firemen) has held steady at around 35%. The Bureau of Labor noted that even with the drop in the number of workers joining unions, there was still a wage bonus for union workers. "In 2013, among full-time wage and salary workers, union members had median ... weekly earnings of $950, while those who were not union members had median weekly earnings of $750,"[23] a difference of about $10,000 a year.

One odd thing about the drop in union membership is that the drop has occurred while the American people have continued to support labor unions. Drew DeSilver of the PEW Research Center noted that in 1987, 59% of people in the South, 65% of those in the West, and 74% of those in the Northeast and Midwest viewed unions favorably. In 2012, these figures had changed somewhat with the South at 60%, the West at 64%, and the Midwest dropping to 65%, and the Northeast also trending down from 1987.[24] But the majority of Americans still support unions. So, why have they fared so poorly?

Kris Warner, writing for the business newsletter *Bloomberg*, draws our attention to Canada, a country that has gone through many of the same challenges as the United States—globalization, technology, and a shift of manufacturing to low-wage areas elsewhere in the world. One might expect then that if unions were weakened by all of these trends, the same pattern—falling union membership—would emerge in both countries. But the obverse is true. Beginning around 1960, union membership in Canada began a slow, steady, upward climb and now stands around 30% of the workforce, while membership in the United States, as noted, has dropped to about 11%.[25] The differences are due to labor law and public policy. *Corporations and their lobbyists have been more successful in the United States than in Canada in shaping labor law to their satisfaction.*

Canada has no right-to-work laws while, at present, there are 24 states in the United States that do. The term "right-to-work," doesn't mean that everybody has a right to work; it is a statute that prohibits unions and employers from requiring employees covered by a union contract to pay for representation. This means, for example, that if you worked in an automobile manufacturing plant represented by the UAW and the state passed a right-to-work law, you could opt out of paying union dues. Michigan, the home of the UAW, passed such a law in 2012, claiming that it would be "good for business." The preponderance of right-to-work states are in the South and are also among those with Republican governors and legislatures.

A second difference between Canada and the United States is the way in which unions can be formed. In Canada the process is a short one. In most provinces, workers can sign a card indicating they want to form a union; if a majority favors it, that is all that needs to be done. In other provinces, cards are signed, a petition is sent to the labor board, and an election is held in 5–10 working days after the petition is received by the labor board, leaving little time for countermobilization by employers. In the United States, the time between when a petition is submitted and an election is held can stretch out for months, with negative consequences for union organizers. (The National Labor Relations Board in the United States is trying to make our system more like that of Canada, but House Republicans have vowed to defeat any such attempt.)

Finally, bargaining after a union is formed also differs in the United States and in Canada. Canada has first-contract arbitration to resolve differences that arise during initial negotiations. A mediation and conciliation process is available to both employers and employees and if it fails, then an arbitrator or panel will impose a contract. In the United States, organizers must mobilize a campaign and if successful, then enter into bargaining that, if unsuccessful, can lead to strikes and extended periods of unemployment for the workers.

Unions in the United States have, not surprisingly, mounted vehement arguments against "right-to-work" laws, seeing them as a precipitating a "race to the bottom," leading to lower wages for workers in a given industry, as well as worse safety and health regulations. Business interests, on the other hand, have argued that such laws spur economic growth.[26] The National Right to Work Legal Defense Foundation and the National Right to Work Committee have spent millions of dollars on lobbying state legislatures. Their goals are clear. The National Right to Work Foundation claims on its website that "No force is inflicting more damage on our economy, citizenry, and cherished democracy than the union bosses."[27] SourceWatch has identified four of the several foundations involved in these efforts. The first is Castle Rock, founded by the Coors family, which has a long history of anti-union activity. Next is the Olin Foundation, which teams up with Coors, as well as with Richard Mellon Scaife, to "create a chain of anti-environmental, pro-business, legal advocacy organizations."[28] The Jaquelin Hume Foundation, named for the California businessman and Reagan supporter who made his fortune with dehydrated garlic and onion, funds union-busting activities. Finally, there is the Roe Foundation, whose founder, Thomas Roe, also founded the State Policy Network, a group with the purpose of working state-by-state to promote free-market principles and to militate against unions, environmental regulations, and tax increases. (This agenda has been taken up by ALEC [American Legislative Exchange Council], which is discussed below.)

The South has stood out as the most anti-union area in the country, and for years has offered itself as a haven to multinational corporations and others seeking out sites with low wages and few, if any, unions. States such as Alabama, Mississippi, South Carolina, and Tennessee have all offered substantial tax incentives to firms such as Volkswagen, Boeing, Toyota, Hyundai, Honda, BMW, Nissan, and Michelin to locate in their states. If you are an automobile worker, a job in one of the auto plants pays well by southern standards. The starting pay at the Volkswagen planet in Tennessee was around $17 an hour in 2014, soon rising to $19 an hour. Compare that to what a unionized UAW worker at a northern Ford or GM's Detroit plant makes: around $26–28 an hour. A 2002 report by the Moore School of Business at the University of South Carolina indicated that the decision by BMW to open a plant in the United States provided substantial economic benefits to the state.[29] Nevertheless, with all these efforts by southern states to improve their economic circumstances, the South still lags behind the rest of the country in terms of income and wages.

For example, the U.S. Census Bureau's most recent figures reveal that the average per capita income in the United States is $28,051; the median household income is $53,046, and the percentage of people living below the poverty line is 14.9%. In Tennessee it is 17.3%, in South Carolina it is 17.6%, in Louisiana 18.7% are below the poverty line, and in Mississippi the figure is 22.3%. The median per capita income in all of these states is below the U.S. average.[30] As a result jobs have flowed from the North to the South, where wages are lower and environmental regulations are weak or seldom enforced.

The UAW has seen the South as a place to grow their membership. They picked what they thought would be an easy target—the Volkswagen plant in Chattanooga, Tennessee. A majority of workers had signed cards indicating they wanted a union, and Volkswagen had pledged neutrality, noting that if the UAW was successful they would work with them to set up a works council—a common practice in Germany where labor and management collaborate to achieve higher productivity. The idea of works councils generated some controversy because, according to U.S. labor law, a union would need to be in place before a labor council could be formed.[31] Volkswagen's response was that union and corporate responsibilities could be negotiated immediately if the union won the vote.

The reaction by business and political leaders to the possibility of the UAW setting up shop in the South was swift and intense. Billboards went up claiming that Detroit's fiscal woes and collapse were due to the

UAW. Tennessee's governor, Bill Haslam, as well as U.S. Senator Bob Corker, claimed the union would make the plant less competitive and hurt the state and the city. Haslam also noted that if the UAW was successful, automobile parts manufacturers would not want to locate in Tennessee. Senator Corker claimed to have inside knowledge that if the UAW won the vote, Volkswagen would not expand its Chattanooga plant and further claimed that if the UAW was defeated VW would expand the plant and start making SUV's in Tennessee instead of Mexico. The President of the Chamber of Commerce added his voice, stating that a union vote would make it difficult for Chattanooga to pursue economic development. The state senator representing Chattanooga, Bo Watson, warned that the Republican-controlled legislature would be unlikely to provide any further tax subsidies to VW if the UAW vote was successful. The UAW lost the vote by 712 to 626. Bob King, who had led the UAW effort, blamed the defeat on Republican lawmakers and their anti-union threats.[32] Some of those who voted against unionization said it was because unions would be bad for the community. They provided as examples the textile mills that had moved to Asian countries, where wages are cheaper and the foundries, which had been closed and moved abroad because the owners did not want to address environmental concerns. The irony of the textile mills and foundries having been located in the South because wages were cheap and then closed and moved elsewhere because they were even cheaper was lost on some of the workers who opposed the union. In the South, an anti-union culture and politics influenced the outcome of the vote.

> Attacks on unions are politically motivated and not driven by economic necessity.

The historic gains that unions made in the past across the country are being deliberately rolled back with consequences for equality. The economic downturn beginning in 2007/2008 provided the initial impetus needed by Republican-controlled legislatures to start the rollback. Attacks were directed at public-sector union employees, arguing that their pensions and health benefits were too generous, they were retiring too early, they were making more than people in the private sector, and so forth. They were described as society's "haves" by conservative politicians. The intent was to turn public sentiment against public employees but not against police and firefighters, as they tended to vote Republican; some of the arguments about the need to "check pension abuse" were that the money saved could then be used to hire more police and firefighters.

The most dramatic action taken to roll back public sector union benefits took place in Wisconsin, when Scott Walker, a Republican conservative, was elected governor in November of 2010. Citing a state budgetary crisis, Walker introduced what became known as Act 10. Act 10 severely restricted the ability of public employee unions to bargain collectively. It bars "public-sector unions from bargaining over pensions, health coverage, safety, hours, sick leave, or vacations. All they can negotiate is base pay, and even that is limited."[33] Any raise for public sector employees cannot exceed inflation, and any raise must be approved by the legislature. Under these circumstances, why would you pay union dues? The answer given by 60% of Wisconsin's previous public sector union members was you would not. As a result, the Wisconsin State Employees' Union budget has dropped from $6 million a year to $2 million, which means it has far fewer resources to put into trying to change things. Act 10 was not passed without controversy. When it was introduced, crowds of up to 100,000 union supporters jammed into the State Capitol building in Madison, but they were unsuccessful in making their case and the bill was signed into law in March of 2011. Union supporters then mounted a recall campaign, which led to donations for both sides flowing in from around the country. Walker survived. In 2015, he proposed cutting the budget of the state university system by $300 million, capitalizing on the idea that universities are bastions of liberal academics who don't work hard enough, fail to provide their students for the world of work, and are a burden on taxpayers.[34]

Act 10 had real consequences for union members, as the *New York Times* labor-relations correspondent, Steven Greenhouse, has noted. The Act gave public officials throughout Wisconsin the ability to freeze wages, raise the retirement age, and demand increased contributions to employee health and pension benefits. Some state agencies demanded that their employees contribute 12% to their health care costs. A 12% increase in paying for health benefits translates into a 12% pay cut, which meant that some of the low-wage government workers had to seek second jobs.[35] There may be good reasons for requiring state and municipal employees to contribute more to their retirement funds and their health plans, because some of these plans are woefully underfunded. But that was not the goal of the efforts in Wisconsin and the efforts it has spawned in other states; the effort is clearly to limit the power of unions to bargain on behalf of their employees and to reduce the resources available to unions, especially teacher's unions, to support the political campaigns of liberal politicians. Here, again, is an example of how politics is being used to erode the security of middle-class jobs in a systematic and determined manner.

The proof that the attacks on unions were politically motivated and not driven by budgetary necessity has been provided by the University of Oregon economist, Gordon Lafer.[36] Governor Walker claimed that Act 10 was necessary because "our people are weighed down paying for a larger government" and "we can no longer live in a society where the public employees are the haves and taxpayers who foot the bills are the have-nots."[37] Virtually all states were hard hit by the budgetary downturns that began in 2007/2008, but state-level financial crises were not related to the number of unionized public employees. In fact Texas, the state that had *no* public unions because they were prohibited, had the largest of the deficits, totaling $20 billion for a two-year period. The fiscal crisis was, in those states with Republican governors and controlled by Republican legislatures, used to diminish government services. Arizona's governor proposed eliminating health insurance for 300,000 people, some of whom were in the middle of chemotherapy. Texas eliminated 10,000 teaching jobs and cut the funding for full-day pre-kindergarten for 100,000 at-risk children. Ohio and Pennsylvania also cut back full-day pre-kindergarten, and in 2012–2014 the Philadelphia school district eliminated 5,000 teachers, reading coaches, librarian, nurses, counselors, and support staff. Thirty-one schools were closed, and Philadelphia teachers had their contract suspended in 2014.[38] All of these actions put at risk the neediest members of society.

The Erosion of the Social Contract

Income inequality is driven by the decline of union jobs and the changed nature of work in developed countries. David Weil, who became the U.S. Wage and Hour Administrator in the U.S. Department of Labor in 2014, has argued that the employer-employee relationship has become fractured.[39] There is a deep divide not just between temporary and part-time workers and their employers but also between those caught up in subcontracting, franchising, third-party management, and outsourcing. The "independent" contractors who deliver packages to our homes or offices may wear a company uniform, but they are frequently paying for all of their benefits—health insurance, Social Security taxes, and retirement fund (if they have anything is left over to put in it). The technician sent out by the cable company to hook up your television set or telephone is in all likelihood an independent contractor. The maids who make up the beds in hotel rooms are not working for Hilton but for a company that Hilton contracts with to have their rooms cleaned. The security guard standing in the lobby of the bank is hired not by the bank but by a private security company with which the bank has contracted.

Fifty years ago things were not this way. Large employers took care of their employees, providing good wages and benefit packages that covered the medical expenses of a worker and his or her family, and provided a pension that assured a decent retirement. The worker of the 1950s

> The decline in union membership may be good for business, but it is not good for the body politic.

was not receiving public assistance. But that model, as Weil convincingly documents, does not generate maximum profit. What does work for investors now is for companies to shed their role as direct employers and outsource to smaller companies that are fiercely competitive and that in turn must drive down worker wages to stay in business. This is a story about a shift in political power, about the relentless drive by free-market ideologists to turn all employment into temp work.[40] Work is thus degraded and wealth transferred from workers to shareholders. *The social contract, which binds people together for a common purpose, is being destroyed and along with it the foundations of democratic society.*

Large corporations with union employees frequently use the threat of moving elsewhere to gain concessions. The aerospace giant, Boeing, has plans to build a new plane, the 777X, an updated version of the 777. Over twenty states entered a bidding war by offering tax incentives, free land, and developed infrastructure to get Boeing to abandon its plans to manufacture the plane in Seattle. Boeing has agreed to stay put, but only on the condition that unionized employees make significant concessions, which included freezing their pensions. Though local union officials had urged a rejection of the contract, because of the loss of benefits, it passed with 51% of the vote out of 23,900 votes cast. Workers, fearing for their jobs and under pressure from their national union and Washington State political officials, voted to give Boeing what they wanted. These concessions were asked for during a period of significant profitability for Boeing, though Boeing said the cuts were necessary to be competitive with other airline manufacturers in the future.[41]

A decline in union membership means a decline in the social capital that comes from participation in dense networks that increase levels of social capital and levels of trust necessary for political engagement. A decline in union membership is also a strain on social safety nets because of lower wages. Nonunion workers in the restaurant business and in retail and grocery outlets such as Walmart often need assistance from state and federal programs to make ends meet. Clare O'Connor, a writer for the business magazine *Forbes*, reported that because of their low wages, Walmart employees cost the taxpayers $6.2 billion a year in food stamps, Medicaid, and subsidized housing.[42] As a result of negative publicity, Walmart agreed to pay their employees $9.00 an hour beginning in 2015. The hamburger chain, McDonald's, realizing that most of its workers could not make ends meet with what they earned at their job, provided a resource line that explained to callers how to get public assistance to pay their heating bills and how to get food stamps.[43] McDonald's even had a website called McResources (before they took it down) that explained to workers who were having trouble stretching their food budget that if they broke their food into smaller pieces and ate them more slowly they would feel less hungry.[44] Some restaurant workers don't even get the federal minimum wage.

The Debate over the Minimum Wage

In September of 2014, the Oakland Raiders football team agreed to pay ninety of their cheerleaders $1.25 million to settle a lawsuit that alleged they were underpaid or had faced lengthy delays in receiving what they were due.[45] The Tampa Bay Buccaneers were sued by one of their cheerleaders, Manouchcar Pierre-Val, who claimed she was paid no more than

$2.00 an hour when all of the time she was required to work was accounted for.[46] Other teams were also being sued by their cheerleading squads for unfair labor practices. Whether intentional or not, the owners of the franchises were engaging in a form of wage theft—not paying the federal minimum wage of $7.25 an hour. However, if the cheerleaders had been working for tips, like a waitress or waiter, the owners would only have had to pay them $2.13 an hour, the assumption being that if there was a shortfall in the total of $7.25 an hour, it would be made up by the employer. If tips are shared with busboys and the kitchen employees, it means those employees are "tipped" employees and the employer need pay them no more than $2.13 an hour. It gets even worse in some states.

> The debate over the minimum wage has taken on some of the same characteristics as the debate over global warming.

In 2011 Maine legislators passed a law that declared tips were a "service charge" and not tips. Therefore, if the bill listed a service charge, it was not a tip, it did not belong to the workers, and it could be pocketed by the employers.[47] Workers under 20 years of age may be paid as little as $4.25 an hour during the first 90 *consecutive* days of employment. This means, as you might guess, that employers can lay somebody off for a few days, "rehire" them, and go on paying $4.25 an hour. Workers with disabilities can also be paid far less than the minimum wage. In a facility in Maryland, run by a nonprofit organization, workers with developmental disabilities are paid as little as 25 cents an hour. The nonprofit says their workers are learning valuable skills and the self-respect that comes from having a job. Others would argue this is exploitation.[48]

The debate over whether or not the federal minimum wage should be raised has taken on some of the same characteristics as the debate over global warming. Facts don't matter when they don't fit into people's preconceived ideas about how the world works. Narratives that are not borne out by the facts are mounted to discredit the work of main stream economists.[49]

John Schmitt, a senior economist at the Washington, DC, Center for Economic and Policy Research has detailed how the Employment Policies Institute (EPI), a leading employers group that opposes an increase in the minimum wage, set out to discredit the authors of a well-known study on the relationship between raising the minimum wage and jobs gained or lost as a result.[50] The EPI is a nonprofit created by Rick Berman, whose firm lobbies on behalf of the restaurant, hotel, alcoholic beverage, and tobacco industries. Its website lists "five things you didn't want to know about the minimum wage." For example, it claims that a 10% increase in the minimum wage would mean that teen employment would drop by 4.6–9.0%; that increases in the minimum wage would inversely affect Hispanic and Black teenagers, who would lose their jobs; and that the average family income of those earning the minimum wage in 2009 was over $48,000 a year, well above the official poverty level of $24,000 for a family of four.[51] The first two examples are simple conjecture and the third is simply not true. The EPI has even speculated that raising the minimum wage would cause some students to drop out of high school to take these "good" jobs. The research supporting each of these claims comes from work the EPI itself paid for and published.

The EPI began its attack in 1995 to discredit what is known as the Card-Krueger study. David Card and Alan Krueger, two respected Princeton economists, published a study based on an analysis of what happened when New Jersey raised its minimum wage in 1992 by 19% and neighboring Pennsylvania did not. Standard theory predicted New Jersey would lose jobs, but nothing like that happened. In fact, there was a slight increase in the number of jobs in New Jersey, implying that raising the minimum wage could actually create economic growth and prosperity. The counterattack to these findings was originated by the EPI. The Institute provided two economists, David Neumark and William Wascher, with a set of data for analysis that, when they ran the data, showed that employment dropped in New Jersey, contrary to what the Card-Krueger study revealed. The EPI and Berman placed editorials in numerous business journals denouncing the "fraudulent" data and analysis by Card-Krueger.

The attack on their colleagues was so vitriolic that Neumark and Wascher, who had been paid by EPI, decided they needed to take a closer look at their own conclusions. In a later version of their study they noted that the data they had been provided by the EPI may have been "falsified so as to undermine [Card and Krueger's] results."[52] And in fact, when they collected their own data, it yielded the same results as Card and Krueger, namely that raising the minimum wage did not lead to job loss.[53]

Nevertheless, the battle continues to determine which narrative—the one saying that raising the minimum wage will create jobs and prosperity, or the one saying it will not—is correct.

Despite this, most Americans are clear that they believe an increase in the minimum wage to $10.10 an hour is warranted. Celinda Lake, a pollster, reported that nearly 75% of all likely voters in 2014 supported increasing the minimum wage to $10 and indexing it to inflation.[54] In addition, voters who were polled supported raising the minimum wage regardless of gender, age, level of education level, race, region, or political leanings. Lake and her colleagues found some expected relationships, such as Democrats demonstrating 91% overall support and 79% strong support, as opposed to Republicans, of whom 51% were generally supportive with 41% opposed to an increase. Women, particularly blue-collar women, African-American women, and Latinas, were the most supportive, probably because they are more likely than men to be in low-wage jobs. Even Southern women, in a heavily Republican and conservative region, were supportive (67%).

People continued to be supportive when they were presented with the opposition's argument: "Some people say that we cannot afford to force a 38% increase in minimum wage costs on job creators. It will hurt our ability to compete economically and the added labor costs will be passed on to the rest of us. The last thing we need is more government regulations on small businesses. It will only slow job growth and hurt the people it's supposed to help."[55] Against an argument posed in this extreme way, 71% still supported an increase.

> The evidence suggests that an increase in the minimum wage has no effect on employment.

Adding their voices to those who support a minimum wage increase were 600 economists, including seven recipients of the Nobel Prize and eight past presidents of the American Economic Association, who wrote to the President and to congressional leaders in 2014 urging action. Their recommendation was to raise the minimum wage by 95 cents an hour for three years in a row and then index it to inflation. As they noted, "The increase to $10.10 would mean that minimum-wage workers who work full-time, full year would see a raise from their current salary of roughly $15,000 to roughly $21,000." This, they suggested, would provide higher wages for 17 million workers by 2011 and have positive economic spillover effects, boosting economic growth. As for those who would benefit, the vast majority would be "adults in working families, disproportionately women, who work at least twenty hours a week and depend on these earnings to make ends meet." They summed up their report by noting, "In recent years there have been important developments in the academic literature on the effect of increases in the minimum wage on employment, with the weight of evidence now showing that *increases in the minimum wage have had little to no effect on the employment of minimum wage workers, even during times of weakness in the labor market.*"[56]

The Center on Wisconsin Strategy (COWS), a liberal think tank at the University of Wisconsin, saw nothing but positive outcomes if the minimum wage were raised to $10.10. Some 234,000 Wisconsin children would see their family's income rise and 404,000 workers being paid less than $10.10 an hour would see an increase in their wages. In total, 587,000 workers would be affected. Of this total, 57% of them would be women, 87% would be older than 20; and 64% of them would be in families with incomes below $60,000 a year.[57]

The controversy over just exactly what the minimum wage would do was sharpened when the Congressional Budget Office (CBO) offered its analysis in February of 2014 of the bill to raise the minimum wage that was introduced by Senator Harkin of Iowa. While the CBO agreed with the analysis offered by Harkin that the bill would lift people out of poverty, they noted that it would result in 0.3% fewer jobs overall. The headline on Fox News was, "Increase will cost jobs." The spokesman for Republican House Speaker John Boehner said, "With unemployment Americans' top concern, our focus should be on creating—not destroying—jobs for those who need them the most."[58] President Obama's Council of Economic Advisors, relying on the same data as the 600 economists who signed the letter urging an increase, pointedly noted that it would have no such effect on jobs. They also reaffirmed their position that raising the minimum wage would have significant positive effects, would give 16.5 million workers a boost in pay, and lift close to a million of them out of poverty.[59] Heidi Shierholz and David Cooper, of the liberal Economic Policy Institute, noted that the CBO had not used their own data to arrive at the conclusion that there would be a 0.3% reduction in jobs but instead relied on old published literature that claimed a slight relationship between job loss and raising wages.[60] They reaffirmed the fact that the CBO, the Council of Economic Advisors, and leading economists all concurred that low-wage workers would be helped by this action. So if so many were for raising the minimum wage, why didn't it happened?

No one lives under the delusion that the minimum wage is sufficient for anybody, let alone a person helping to support others, to participate in any meaningful sense in the society of which they are a part. If they have a child, they can't pay for any enrichment activities for that child, and they struggle to pay their rent and utilities. A person in a minimum waged job has virtually no rights compared to those of management. If someone doesn't like $7.25 an hour, the position of management is, "find another job."

It is neither fair nor reasonable to pay people the current minimum wage. Why? If the minimum wage had kept pace with inflation since 1968, it would now be $10.63 an hour. If labor productivity had been factored in, it would have been $18.28 in 2013.[61] What this means is that management, not labor, has benefited from the rising productivity of workers—both low- and high-wage—across the board. As an example, if you buy a hamburger at Wendy's, McDonald's, or Burger King, you will see a small group of very busy employees filling orders. It usually takes 3–4 minutes during rush hour to complete an order because everything is automated. Who benefits from the gains in worker productivity? In a word: management. In 2013 the CEO of Walmart earned $8,371,057. A worker earning $7.25 an hour, who worked forty hours a week and worked 52 weeks a year would earn $15,080. This would mean they would have to work 555 years full-time to earn as much as the Walmart CEO did in one year.[62] The United States is an outlier among developed nations in terms of providing safety nets but also in terms of the minimum wage. Australia, a prosperous country, has a minimum wage the equivalent of over USD $15 an hour. Canada, France, Germany, New Zealand, Ireland, and France, among others, all have higher guaranteed hourly wage rates than does the United States.[63] The reason this is true is that these countries have chosen through their political systems to enact policies that allow their citizens to develop the human capital they need to succeed and to participate in the societies in which they live.

Some cities and states have mounted initiatives to raise the minimum wage, and some employers are responding positively to such attempts. In June of 2014, the city of Seattle raised the local minimum wage to $15.00 an hour, double the Federal minimum wage. The California legislature passed a law in 2014 that will raise the minimum wage to $11 an hour in 2015 and to $13 an hour by 2017. The California Chamber of Commerce labeled the bill a "job killer" and argued that it would hurt California economically and lead to fewer restaurants, shops, and less hiring.[64] One of the Republicans voting against the bill noted that the minimum wage was not meant to be an entry-level job, saying that the minimum wage is for "kids, who need summer jobs." Florida, Indiana, and Mississippi have put in place laws banning local governments from increasing the minimum wage. In 2011, New Hampshire legislators simply abolished the state's minimum wage.[65] Who doesn't want people to participate in their own societies by earning a living wage?

> Attacks on labor and employment standards have been driven by a powerful coalition of anti-union forces.

The Political War Against Equality

The economist Gordon Lafer has argued that the "attacks on labor and employment standards have been driven by a powerful coalition of anti-union ideologues" who are supported by a coalition made up of traditional corporate lobbies such as the Chamber of Commerce and the National Association of Manufactures, as well as the Koch Brother's-backed Americans for Prosperity founded in 2000.[66] Americans for Prosperity declares it has three goals: (1) to cut taxes and government spending "to halt the encroachments of government in the economic lives of citizens," (2) to remove unnecessary barriers to entrepreneurship, and (3) restore fairness to our judicial system.[67] Translated this means, to cut corporate taxes, to eliminate all regulations, especially those concerning the environment, and to limit the power of trial lawyers to sue corporations.

The efforts of these groups are coordinated nationally by ALEC. ALEC is a national network that brings together upward of 2,000 state legislators with the executives of large corporations such as Walmart, Kraft Foods, Exxon Mobil, Coca-Cola, AT&T, Verizon, and Koch

Industries, as well as some from tobacco and pharmaceutical companies, to write business-friendly legislation. Corporations pay membership fees that, among other things, pay the expenses of the legislators to attend exclusive retreats. The cookie-cutter legislation developed at these retreats is then introduced by ALEC participants on a state-by-state basis, and ALEC corporate sponsors put money behind efforts to pass such legislation. Common Cause has estimated that over the last decade, ALEC's corporate sponsors have invested $370 million in state elections and been successful in passing 100 laws modeled on their legislation.[68]

One piece of ALEC's model legislation is the "Living Wage Mandate Preemption Act," which would repeal all "living wage" mandates and prevent localities from establishing a starting minimum wage. They want legislatures to declare that starting wage laws are detrimental to business because "Local variations in mandated wage rates threaten many businesses with a loss of employees to areas that require higher mandated wages rates [and] threaten many other businesses with the loss of patrons to areas that allow lower mandated rates." An earlier version of this legislation claimed that those who hold minimum wage jobs don't really need the money because they come from "middle-income families with other significant sources of income." ALEC also noted that "three-fourths of all economists agree that minimum wage laws reduce job opportunities, that only a small percentage of the workforce is actually employed at the minimum-wage level, that when tips are taken into account many restaurant workers earn more than the minimum wage, and that higher wages make it difficult for employers to hire those who need job experience, such as teenagers."[69] ALEC has also crafted proposed legislation that opposes linking minimum wages to the Consumer Price Index.

ALEC has model legislation to fight crime called the "Swift and Certain Sanctions Act." The unwitting might think the legislation, as worded, would help to solve the problem of crime. ALEC wants states to have the power to "deliver swift, certain, and proportionate responses to violations of probation and parole." To help communities get people to comply with the terms of their parole, ALEC proposes a range of sanctions, "including, but not limited to, electronic supervision tools, drug and alcohol testing or monitoring, day or evening reporting centers, restitution centers, ... secure or unsecure residential treatment facilities or halfway houses, and short-term or intermittent incarceration."[70] This represents the privatization of incarceration and parole and subsidizes those who sell ankle bracelets, monitoring services, drug and alcohol testing, and private treatment facilities.

ALEC also wants to turn all public lands over to the individual states to "grow the economy and create high-paying jobs." ALEC's "Resolution Demanding that Congress Convey Title of Federal Public Lands to the States" is driven by cattle ranchers who do not want to pay grazing fees, developers, and timber companies. More timber needs to be harvested, according to ALEC, because al-Qaeda has published a story about "the opportunity to burn down our national forests—causing billions of dollars in damage and destroying our watersheds for decades—with only a few matches." The solution: Cut down more trees to reduce the potential for fires.[71] Transferring public lands to the states would bankrupt many western states. That's actually a goal of this legislation, because the only way states could pay for the management of public lands would be to raise taxes, a nonstarter, or to sell and lease large tracks of land to developers, including oil, gas, timbre, and mining companies.[72]

Mounting attacks on unions, public sector employees, and the development and backing of corporate-sponsored legislation has been made easier by the *Citizens United* decision of the U.S. Supreme Court, which declared that corporations were citizens and thus could contribute to campaigns and political action committees. The Court opened the floodgates to donations even further in its 2014 decision, *McCutcheon v. Federal Election Commission*. That decision struck down caps on what any individual may contribute to all federal candidates. Money thus becomes a form of free speech. One of the dissenting justices in the 5/4 decision, Justice Stephen G. Breyer, wrote, "Where enough money calls the tune the public will not be heard."[73] At least it is not just wealthy conservatives who attempt to influence the legislative agenda. The billionaire Tom Steyer put up $50 million of his own money in an attempt to elect candidates with strong environmental records in 2014.[74]

We might assume that money does not matter and that voters will be savvy enough to make the right decisions, or the ones that will help them the most, when they go to the polls. But what if they cannot even vote? In 2013 the Supreme Court by a 5–4 vote overturned a key section of the Voting Rights Act of 1965. The Act required that lawmakers in states with a history of discrimination against minority voters get federal permission before changing voting rules. Writing for the majority, Chief Justice Roberts claimed that the country had changed and that federal protection was no longer needed. Almost immediately, fifteen predominately southern states set out to impose restrictions on voters by implementing voter ID laws, cutting the days and hours for voting, ending same-day registration, and purging voter rolls. ALEC provided model legislation for voter ID laws. Critics of these laws noted they would discriminate against low-income voters, young people, and minorities, all of whom were more likely to vote for Democrats than Republicans. The State of Texas created new voter restrictions for the 2014 elections that were struck down initially by a lower federal court but eventually upheld by the U.S. Supreme Court. The lower court judge, Nelva Gonzales Ramos, issued a 143-page ruling, explaining that upward of 600,000 voters, most of them Black and Latino, could be refused the right to vote because they lacked acceptable identification. Voter ID laws in Texas amounted to a new form of poll tax. While a college-identification card would not get you into the polling booth in Texas, a concealed weapons permit would.[75]

Incompatible Narratives

The narrative of free-market fundamentalism comes most sharply into focus in the United States, although it appears in muted form in Great Britain and other Western European countries. It is a narrative that argues if we could only shrink government then everything could go back to the way it was in the 1950s. The irony, as already noted, is that government has continued to grow whether under liberal or conservative administrations. One cause of the growth has been the social control functions of the government—an expansion of prisons, of half-way houses, of police forces, and the military. At the same time, those government functions that create both human and social capital such as expenditures on education have shrunk. For example,

> The narrative of free-market fundamentalism is incompatible with a narrative of sustainability.

California institutions of higher education have seen their share of the state general fund budget shrink over the last two decades at the same time as that for prisons has grown.

One of the most relentless efforts to discredit the expansion of social safety nets has been the attacks on the Affordable Care Act, or Obamacare. James Sherk of the conservative think tank the Heritage Foundation has asserted that Obamacare will wreck the economy. Businesses, he said, will have to pass the costs of health insurance onto their workers through lower wages and by lowering the number of hours worked. Some low-income workers might even cease working full-time because by working less than 40 hours a week you could make almost as much as you would working full-time once after-tax and after-health care premiums were taken into account. Sherk feared for the larger economy. This reduced "labor supply will also hurt the broader economy. Fewer workers and fewer jobs mean less wealth in the economy."[76] The message that government interference is always costly and that the market, left to itself, can resolve the nation's ills has been a consistent conservative theme since Reagan's term in office. What has changed is the money and influence being used to implement this agenda.

There is a competing narrative that suggests what the agenda of free-market capitalism increases poverty and social inequality. Robert Reich, professor of public policy at Berkeley and former Secretary of Labor under President Clinton, has said that rather than confronting poverty by extending jobless benefits, and supporting a minimum wage, conservatives are spreading three fictions about poverty. First, there is the argument that economic growth will reduce poverty. The evidence, however, differs. Since the late 1970s, the economy has grown by 147% per capita but little of this growth has trickled down to the working and middle classes, whose incomes have stagnated. What has happened is a greater concentration of wealth among top income earners. Second is the notion that jobs alone will reduce poverty. The problem with this argument is that since the bounce back from the recession of 2007–2014, job growth has been primarily in low-paying industries such as retail and fast food. One-fourth of all working Americans are now working in jobs paying below what a full-time worker needs in order to live above the poverty line for a family of four. Third is the notion that if only people were more ambitious they could escape their miserable circumstances. There is little evidence to support the notion that people are poor because they lack ambition. What they lack is an opportunity that begins with good schools. As Reich says, "America is one of only three advanced countries that spends less on the education of poorer children than richer ones."[77] Republicans argue that any discussion about inequality smacks of class warfare, while Democrats argue that the discussion must be framed in terms of fairness, equal opportunity, and a chance for upward mobility. Sixty percent of Americans agree, according to the Pew Research Foundation, that the nation's economic system unfairly favors the rich.[78] But that has not translated into economic and political policies that benefit the majority of citizens. Often those most affected by inequality don't vote and second, when pressed, they believe little needs to change.

> Narratives connect the past and present and are used to help sort out morally confusing and ambiguous situations.

One might dismiss such divisive narratives as mere white noise but narratives matter because they help us make sense out of the confusing world in which we live. *Narratives are the way we connect the past and present and narratives are used to help sort out morally confusing and ambiguous situations.* And once we invest in a narrative we seek out friends, acquaintances, and information to reinforce it.

One narrative we operate with is the narrative of American exceptionalism, which has had the consequence of the U.S. serving as the world's policeman and spending trillions on our military forces. In a May 2014 address to the graduating class of West Point, President Obama told the graduates that the United States had the best fighting force in the world.

> Our military has no peer ... And when a typhoon hits the Philippines, or schoolgirls are kidnapped in Nigeria ... it is America that the world looks to for help. So, the United States remains the one indispensable nation.
>
> Here's my bottom line: America must always lead on the world stage. If we don't, no one else will. The military ... is, and always will be, the backbone of that leadership ... The United States will use military force, unilaterally if necessary, when our core interest demand it.[79]

President Obama went on to note that we needed to fight terrorism throughout the Middle East, ramp up our support for those fighting the regime of Assad in Syria, and strengthen democratic institutions throughout the world. He added that he believed "in American exceptionalism with every fiber of my being." This was clearly a political speech but it is a narrative that resonates with many Americans.

Few Americans compare their own situation to that of the citizens of other democracies, and when we do listen we hear a stream of invective from conservative news sources that European social democracies are broken. Data published by the Pew Research Center showed that in 2014, 81% of Americans felt that the United States was either the greatest country in the world (28%) or one of the greatest (53%). Democrats (25%) and Independents (25%), however, were less likely than Republicans (37%) to agree that America was the greatest country, or one of the greatest. Comments posted on Center's website suggested the view of American exceptionalism was not shared worldwide. A foreign writer, commenting on American's belief that their nation is #1, said, "It's things like this that make everyone else laugh at Americans for being clueless about the rest of the world."[80]

Nationalism is clearly an important framing device or story for how Americans understand their society but it is a narrative that has negative consequences. Nationalism causes people to be blinded to the problems in their own society (such as poverty, discrimination, and the degradation of the environment) and to the conditions that give rise to it (such as the buying of both elections and politicians). Further, as noted, the rhetoric of American nationalism or exceptionalism assumes that individuals create their own fortunes and misfortunes and should live with the consequences. The narrative of American exceptionalism, which assumes we can go anywhere, pay any price, and solve any problem, has not been applied or appropriated to develop solutions that will allow its own citizens to participate in the society in which they live. There is not yet have a national narrative that makes it possible to craft the political policies that open up our institutions and provide equal opportunities to develop each person's talents. Today's dominant narrative is one that legitimates the concentration of wealth and the socialization of the costs of doing so. The reason an alternative narrative has not developed is because there has been a concerted effort to leave us with one moral tale: You are on your own. This narrative of hyper-individualism is not one that includes the growth of human or social capital.

Summary

America experienced significant economic growth in the post-war years and throughout the 1950s. Good jobs were available in manufacturing and in white-collar jobs. There was a social compact between workers and employers that assured people would have health benefits for themselves and their families, wages decent enough so that a worker could buy a home, raise a family, and plan for a comfortable, if not extravagant, retirement. Building on prosperity and hope for the future, Lyndon Johnson used his considerable political skills to push through legislation that was focused on creating an equal society in which everyone regardless of their gender, ethnicity, or wealth would have a fair chance at a decent life. The war in Vietnam, race riots, and a push for women's rights led to the growth of the modern conservative movement that championed free-market fundamentalism. Today, conservative groups have waged a war on equality by attempting to weaken unions, disenfranchise voters who don't support their causes, and undermine legislation that would create a living wage. As a result, the issue of social equality has risen to the top of the agenda for an increasing number of Americans.

Through a Sustainability Lens

A profit narrative stands in opposition to one of the fundamental values of sustainability: community. It does so because the constant global search for ever cheaper labor ultimately beggars individual workers and, by extension, limits their ability to participate in their communities, or even create a community. Trust, which is essential for the creation of true communities, is a victim of structured inequality and the narrative that both creates and legitimates it. A narrative crafted around American exceptionalism and the virtues of the free market has limited attempts to create a "green" economy and to limit the buildup of CO_2 in the atmosphere. Opponents have claimed that regulations would hurt families by raising energy prices and costing them jobs. A response to such a narrative could be one that talks about CO_2 buildup as being a threat to national security, as in fact the military currently does.[81]

A sustainability narrative must be broadened to include more than discussions about the environment. It must embrace and it must make it clear how sustainability creates a pathway to justice and equity. It cannot use scare tactics, because there is overwhelming evidence that people are not moved to action by them.[82] They can in fact backfire. The more we talk about extreme weather events, the more likely people are to see them as acts of God.[83] What does work is focusing on solutions that people are aware of, like the use of more natural gas and nuclear energy, even though these are vehemently opposed by some environmentalists.[84]

A sustainability narrative needs to embrace fundamental values that relate to people taking care of one another. Many mainstream religious denominations embrace this as a core value that must be realized in practice. A sustainability movement and narrative must stand for justice, freedom, safety, security, good health, family, and strong, vital, robust, and enduring communities. Most of all, it needs to create vision of what a sustainable future will look like. As I said at the outset, stories connect the past and the future. So far our collective stories have focused on what we as individuals can do, rather than what we can do together. The story must change.

Notes

1. Lyndon Baines Johnson. May 22, 1964. The Great Society Speech. Ann Arbor, MI. Retrieved on October 31 at: http://www.americanrhetoric.com/speeches/lbjthegreatsociety.htm.
2. Ronald Reagan. 1981. "First Inaugural." Washington, DC. Retrieved on October 30 at: http://www.reaganfoundation.org/reagan-quotes-detail.aspx?tx=2072.
3. Sheldon L. Richman. 1988. "The Sad Legacy of Ronald Reagan." *The Free Market* 6(10): 1–2. Retrieved on October 30, 2014 at: http://mises.org/freemarket_detail.aspx?control=488.
4. David Corn. 2014. "Mitt Romney's Latest Excuse for His 47 Percent Remarks Is a Doozy." *Mother Jones*. September 30. Retrieved on October 27, 2014 at: http://www.motherjones.com/politics/2014/09/mitt-romney-latest-excuse-47-percent-remarks.
5. Paul Ryan. 2012. "Republican National Convention Speech." *The Washington Post*. August 29. Retrieved on October 27, 2014 at: http://www.washingtonpost.com/politics/paul-ryan-republican-convention-speech-excerpts/2012/08/29/f245c6b6-f21f-11e1-a612-3cfc842a6d89_story.html.
6. Barack Obama. 2012. "President's Democratic Convention Remarks." *Washington Post*. September 6. Retrieved on October 27, 2014 at: http://www.washingtonpost.com/

politics/dnc-2012-obamas-speech-to-the-democratic-national-convention-full-transcript/2012/09/06/ed78167c-f87b-11e1-a073-78d05495927c_story.html.
7 Michael Shermer. 2012. *The Believing Brain: From Ghosts and Gods to Politics and Conspiracies—How We Construct Beliefs and Reinforce Them as Truths.* New York, NY: St. Martin's Press.
8 Ibid., p.5.
9 Michael S. Gazzaniga, *The Mind's Past.* Berkeley: University of California Press, 1998; Michael S. Gazzaniga. 2005. "Forty-Five Years of Split-Brain Research and Still Going Strong." (Review) *Nature Reviews Neuroscience.* 6(8): 653–651; Steven Pinker, *How the Mind Works.* New York, NY: W.W. Norton, 1997; Nichole K. Speer, Jeremy R. Reynolds, Khena M. Swallow, and Jeffrey Zacks, "Reading Stories Activates Neural Representations of Visual and Motor Experiences." *Psychological Science.* 2008 (Vol 20, 8): 989–999; Jessica Marshall, "Gripping Yarns." *New Scientist.* February 12, 2011: 45–47; Paul Zak, Robert Kurzban, and William T. Matzner, "Oxytocin is Associated with Human Trustworthiness." *Hormones and Behavior.* 2005 (48): 522–529; Paul Zak, Robert Kurzban, and William T. Matzner, "The Neurobiology of Trust." *Annals of the New York Academy of Sciences.* 2004. 1167: 224–227.
10 Ibid; see in particular, in the previous footnote the articles by Jessica Marshall, "Gripping Yarns," and the one by Paul Zak, et al., "The Neurobiology of Trust."
11 Drew Westen. 2007. *The Political Brain: The Role of Emotion in Deciding the Fate of the Nation.* New York, NY: Perseus Book Group; and Drew Westen. 2011. "What Happened to Obama?" *New York Times, Sunday Review.* August 7, pp.1, 7.
12 George Packer. 2011. "Coming Apart: After 9/11 Transfixed America, the Country's Problems Were Left to Rot." *New Yorker.* September 12, p. 67.
13 Brendan Nyhan and Jason Reifler. 2010. "When Corrections Fail: The Persistence of Political Misperceptions." *Political Behavior.* 32(2): 303–330.
14 James H. Kuklinski, Paul J. Quirk, Jennifer Jerit, David Schwieder, and Robert Rich. "Misinformation and the Currency of Democratic Citizenship." *Journal of Politics* 62(3), August, 2000: 790–816.
15 For an extended discussion of how liberals helping Blacks causes them to fail, see Jason L. Riley. 2014. *Please Stop Helping Us: How Liberals Make It Harder for Blacks to Succeed.* New York, NY: Encounter Books.
16 It has been contested by the Nobel Laureates Joseph Stiglitz and Paul Krugman, among others.
17 Ben Casserman. 2012. "Closer Look at Union vs. Nonunion Workers' Wages." *Wall Street Journal.* December 17. Accessed on February 24, 2014 at: http://blogs.wsj.com/economics/2012/12/17/closer-look-at-union-vs-nonunion-workers-wages/.
18 Lawrence Mishel, Josh Bivens, Elise Gould, and Heidi Shierholz. 2012. *The State of Working America.* 12th ed. Economic Policy Institute. Accessed February 23, 2014 at: http://stateofworkingamerica.org/files/book/Chapter1-Overview.pdf.
19 Gender differences in union wage benefits are primarily a factor of the type of industry. More men than women are employed in manufacturing, which is where the high-wage union jobs are concentrated.
20 Lawrence Mishel. 2012. "Unions, Inequality, and Faltering Middle-Class Income." Economic Policy Institute, Table 2. Retrieved on August 29 at: http://www.epi.org/publication/ib342-unions-inequality-faltering-middle-class/.
21 Ibid., Table 5.

22 U.S. Bureau of Labor Statistics. 2014. "Union Members Summary." Accessed on February 24, 2014 at: http://www.bls.gov/news.release/union2.nr0.htm.
23 Ibid.
24 Drew DeSilver. 2014. "American Unions' Membership Declines as Public Support Fluctuates." Pew Research Center. Accessed on February 24, 2014 at: http://www.pewresearch.org/fact-tank/2014/02/20/for-american-unions-membership-trails-far-behind-public-support/.
25 See also W. Craig Riddell. 1993. "Unionization in Canada and the United States: A Tale of Two Countries." In David Card and Richard Freeman, eds., *Small Differences that Matter: Labor Markets and Income Maintenance in Canada and the United States*. Chicago, IL: University of Chicago Press, pp.109–148.
26 The evidence about whether or not "right-to-work laws" create job growth is mixed. There is evidence that job growth has occurred in the South, where most states have such laws, but these are usually jobs that pay less than similar jobs in other areas of the country.
27 National Right to Work Legal Defense Foundation. Accessed on February 24, 2014 at: http://nrtw.org/.
28 SourceWatch. Accessed on February 24, 2014 at: http://www.sourcewatch.org/index.php?title=National_Right_to_Work_Legal_Defense_Foundation.
29 Moore School of Business. 2002. "The Economic Impact of BMW on South Carolina." Accessed on February 24, 2014 at: http://mooreschool.sc.edu/UserFiles/moore/Documents/Presentations%20&%20Studies/2002%20BMW.pdf.
30 Accessed on February 24, 2014 at: http://www.census.gov/.
31 Steven Greenhouse, 2014. "V.W. Workers in Tennessee to Vote on Union." *New York Times*. February 3. Accessed on February 24 at: http://www.nytimes.com/2014/02/04/business/volkswagen-workers-in-tennessee-to-vote-on-union-membership.html?_r=0; Steven Greenhouse. 2014. "Volkswagen Vote is Defeat for Labor in South." *New York Times*. February 14. Accessed on February 24, 2014 at: http://www.nytimes.com/2014/02/15/business/volkswagen-workers-reject-forming-a-union.html; Erik Schelzig and Tom Krisher. 2014. "Union Drive Falls Short Amid Culture Clash in Tennessee." February 15. Retrieved on February 24, 2014 at: http://www.denverpost.com/breakingnews/ci_25149975/uaw-falls-87-votes-short-major-victory-south; Melanie Trottman and Siobhan Hughes. 2014. "Unions Struggle to Regroup after Stinging Loss in South." *Wall Street Journal*. February 18: 1–2.
32 Steven Greenhouse. 2014. "Defeat of Auto Union in Tennessee Casts Its Plans into Doubt." *New York Times*. February 16: 19.
33 Steven Greenhouse. 2014. "The Wisconsin Legacy." *New York Times*. February 23: Business, 1, 4.
34 Julie Bosman. 2015. "2016 Ambitions Seen in Walker's Push for University Cuts in Wisconsin." *New York Times*. February 16. Accessed on February 21, 2014 at: http://www.nytimes.com/2015/02/17/us/politics/scott-walker-university-wisconsin.html?_r=0.
35 Ibid.
36 Gordon Lafer. 2013. *The Legislative Attack on American Wages and Labor Standards, 2011–2012*. Washington, DC: Economic Policy Institute Briefing Paper.
37 Ibid., p.10.
38 Ibid., pp.13–14. See also, Claudio Sanchez. 2014. "In Crisis, Philadelphia Public Schools Revoke Teachers' Contract." *National Public Radio transcript*. October 16.

Accessed on October 27, 2014 at: http://www.npr.org/2014/10/16/356728021/in-crisis-philadelphia-public-schools-revoke-teachers-contract.
39 David Weil. 2014. *The Fissured Workplace: Why Work Became So Bad for So Many and What Can Be Done to Improve It.* Cambridge, MA: Harvard University Press.
40 Robert Kuttner. 2014. "Why Work Is More and More Debased." *The New York Review of Books.* October 23, pp.53–54.
41 Phuong Le. 2014. "Local Labor Influence Takes Hit in Boeing Contract." *Associated Press*, January 5. Retrieved on October 30, 2014 at: http://www.twincities.com/breakingnews/ci_24844823/boeing-machinists-ok-contract-tied-777x.
42 Clare O'Connor. 2014. "Walmart Workers Cost Taxpayers $6.2 Billion in Public Assistance." *Forbes.* April 15. Retrieved on October 29, 2014 at: http://www.forbes.com/sites/clareoconnor/2014/04/15/report-walmart-workers-cost-taxpayers-6-2-billion-in-public-assistance/.
43 Emily Jane Fox. 2013. "McDonald's Helps Workers Get Food Stamps." *CNN Money.* October 24. Retrieved on October 29, 2014 at: http://money.cnn.com/2013/10/23/news/companies/mcdonalds-help-line-workers/index.html.
44 Alexander Abad-Santos. 2013. "McDonald's Tip to Its Hungry Employees: Break Your Food into Smaller Pieces." *The Wire/Atlantic.* November 19. Retrieved on October 29 at: http://www.thewire.com/business/2013/11/mcdonalds-tip-its-hungry-employees-break-your-food-pieces/355293/.
45 Eric M. Johnson. 2014. "Raiders Agree to Pay $1.25 Million to Cheerleaders Suing Over Unfair Pay." *Reuters.* Retrieved August 15, 2015 at: http://www.reuters.com/article/2014/09/05/us-usa-cheerleaders-raiders-idUSKBN0H002S20140905.
46 Elaine Silvestrini. 2014. "Bucs Sued by Former Cheerleader Over Pay." *The Tampa Tribune.* May 19. Accessed on October 27, 2014 at: http://tbo.com/news/crime/bucs-sued-by-former-cheerleader-over-pay-20140519/.
47 Gordon Lafer. 2013. "Legislative Attack on American Wages and Labor Standards, 2011–2012." Emphases added.
48 Alison Knezevich. 2014. "Subminimum Wage for Disabled Workers Called Exploitative." *Baltimore Sun.* June 14. Retrieved on October 27, 2014 at: http://articles.baltimoresun.com/2014-06-14/news/bs-md-subminimum-wage-20140614_1_disabled-workers-subminimum-wage-low-paying-jobs.
49 Economic Policy Institute. 2014. "Over 600 Economists Sign Letter in Support of $10.10 Minimum Wage. Presented to President Obama, Speaker Boehner, Majority Leader Reid, Congressman Cantor, Senator McConnell, and Congresswoman Pelosi. Retrieved on February 25, 2014 at: http://www.epi.org/minimum-wage-statement/.
50 John Schmitt. 2001. "Cooked to Order." *The American Prospect.* Retrieved on February 25, 2014 at: http://prospect.org/article/cooked-order.
51 The Enterprise Policy Institute. 2014. "Minimum Wage." Accessed on February 25, 2014 at: http://www.epionline.org/.
52 John Schmitt. 2001. "Cooked to Order." *The American Prospect.* Retrieved on February 25 at: http://prospect.org/article/cooked-order.
53 For a more nuanced view of the effects of minimum wages see David Neumark and William Wascher. 2008. *Minimum Wages.* Cambridge, MA: MIT Press.
54 Celinda Lake, Daniel Gotoff, and Alex Dunn. 2014. "Public Support for Raising the Minimum Wage: Findings from a Survey of 805 Likely 2012 General Election Voters

Nationwide." Washington, DC: Lake Research Partners. Accessed on February 25, 2014 at: http://nelp.3cdn.net/0be1c6315f2430afa6_arm6bq9wu.pdf.
55 Ibid., p.10.
56 Economy Policy Institute. 2014. "Over 600 Economists Sign Letter in Support of $10.10 Minimum Wage." Accessed on January 14, 2014 at: http://www.epi.org/minimum-wage-statement/.
57 Center on Wisconsin Strategy (COWS). February 2014. "Raising the Minimum Wage to $10.10 per Hour in Wisconsin." Accessed on February 26, 2014 at: http://www.cows.org/.
58 Alan Fram. 2014. "Budget Office: Increase Would Lift Pay, Cost Jobs." *The Missoulian*. February 19, 2014. A5.
59 Council of Economic Advisors. 2014. Accessed on February 25, 2014 at: http://www.whitehouse.gov/blog/2014/02/18/congressional-budget-office-report-finds-minimum-wage-lifts-wages-165-million-worker.
60 Heidi Shierholz and David Cooper. February 20, 2014. "CBO Report Shows Low-Waged Workers Would Be Better Off with a Minimum Wage of $10.10." Washington, DC: Economic Policy Institute. Accessed on February 24 at: http://www.epi.org/blog/cbo-report-shows-wage-workers-minimum-wage/.
61 *New York Times, Editorial*. February 9, 2014. "The Case for a Higher Minimum Wage." SR: 10.
62 AFL-CIO, 2014. *Executive Pay Watch*. Retrieved on August 29 at: http://www.aflcio.org/Corporate-Watch/Paywatch-2014.
63 OECD. Accessed on February 25, 2014 at: oecd.org.
64 Melody Gutierrez. 2014. "Bill Passes to Push California's Minimum Wage to $13 an Hour." *San Francisco Chronicle*. May 30. Accessed on October 27, 2014 at: http://www.sfgate.com/bayarea/article/Bill-passes-to-push-California-s-minimum-wage-to-5514974.php.
65 Corey Robin. 2014. "The Republican War on Worker's Rights." *The New York Times*. May 18. Retrieved on October 27, 2014 at: http://opinionator.blogs.nytimes.com/2014/05/18/the-republican-war-on-workers-rights/.
66 Gordon Lafer. 2013. "Legislative Attack on American Wages and Labor Standards, 201–2012." Washington, DC: Economic Policy Institute, p.8.
67 Americans for Prosperity. Home page. Retrieved on October 27 at: http://americansforprosperity.org/.
68 Common Cause. 2009. "Legislating Under the Influence of Money." June 24. Accessed on October 27 at: http://www.commoncause.org/press/press-releases/legislating-under-the-influence.html; see also Center on Media and Democracy, "ALEC Exposed." Accessed on October 27, 2014 at: http://www.alecexposed.org/wiki/ALEC_Exposed.
69 ALEC. 2014. "Living Wage Mandate Preemption Act." Accessed on October 27, 2014 at: http://www.alec.org/model-legislation/living-wage-mandate-preemption-act/.
70 ALEC. 2014. "Swift and Certain Sanctions Act." Accessed on October 28 at: http://www.alec.org/docs/ALEC_Swift_and_Certain_Sanctions_Act.pdf.
71 ALEC. 2014. "Resolution Demanding that Congress Convey Title of Federal Public Lands to the States." Accessed on October 27, 2014 at: http://www.alec.org/model-legislation/resolution-demanding-that-congress-convey-title-of-federal-public-lands-to-the-states/.

72 Martin Heinrich. 2014. "The Land Grab Out West." *The New York Times.* October 26, 2014. Retrieved on October 27 at: http://www.nytimes.com/2014/10/27/opinion/the-land-grab-out-west.html?_r=0.
73 Cited in Clyde Haberman. 2014. "The Cost of Campaigns." *New York Times.* October 19. Retrieved on October 30, 2014 at: http://www.nytimes.com/2014/10/20/us/the-cost-of-campaigns.html?_r=0.
74 Jim Rutenberg. 2014. "Money Talks." *New York Times Magazine.* October 19. 26–33, 51.
75 Associated Press. October 18, 2014. "Supreme Court Allows Texas to Use Voter ID Law in November." Retrieved on October 30, 2014 at: http://www.npr.org/2014/10/18/357117516/supreme-court-allows-texas-to-use-voter-id-law-in-november.
76 James Sherk. 2014. "Unhealthy to the Economy: How the Affordable Care Act is Killing Jobs." The Heritage Foundation. *Missoulan.* February 11: B4.
77 Robert Reich. 2014. "The Three Biggest Right-Wing Lies about Poverty." October 13. Reich's blog retrieved on October 30, 2014 at: http://robertreich.org/post/88708262000.
78 Jackie Calmes. 2014. "Obama Moves to the Right in a Partisan War of Words." *New York Times.* February 4: A11.
79 President Barack Obama. 2014. "Full Transcript of President Obama's Commencement Address at West Point." *Washington Post*, May 28. Retrieved on October 31, 2014 at: http://www.washingtonpost.com/politics/full-text-of-president-obamas-commencement-address-at-west-point/2014/05/28/cfbcdcaa-e670-11e3-afc6-a1dd9407abcf_story.html.
80 Alec Tyson. 2014. "Most Americans Think the U.S. Is Great, but Fewer Say It's the Greatest." Pew Research Center, July 2. Retrieved on October 31, 2014 at: http://www.pewresearch.org/fact-tank/2014/07/02/most-americans-think-the-u-s-is-great-but-fewer-say-its-the-greatest/.
81 United States Department of Defense. 2014. *2014 Climate Change Road Map.* Washington, DC: Department of Defense.
82 Scott G. McNall and Andy Szasz. 2014. "Teaching Climate Change." TRAILS. Washington, DC: American Sociological Association.
83 P. Sol Hart and Erik C. Nisbet. 2009. "Boomerang Effects in Science Communication: How Motivated Reasoning and Identity Cues Amplify Opinion Polarization about Climate Mitigation." *Communication Research.* Published online on October 29, doi: 10.1177/0093650211416646.
84 Ted Nordhaus and Michael Shellenberger. 2014. "Global Warming Scare Tactics." *The New York Times.* April 8. Retrieved on October 31 at: http://www.nytimes.com/2014/04/09/opinion/global-warming-scare-tactics.html.

8
REBOOTING CAPITALISM TO CREATE A RESILIENT FUTURE

Consider:

- We must create both human and social capital to have a sustainable future.
- Complex systems are fragile and require substantial amounts of human and material energy to stabilize them.
- We must prepare for shocks we cannot anticipate and be prepared to adapt constantly to changed environmental, social, and economic circumstances.
- We can build the future we want even if we don't know precisely what that future will look like.
- Innovation and creativity have been central to getting us where we are and will be central to getting us where we want to go.
- We live in an 80/20 world where things work for only 20% of the population.
- Any strategy that tries to use inequity as success, as a stabilizing force, or a driver of innovation will be a loser.
- The greater the inequity, the greater the effort needed to sustain the status quo.
- Economic growth alone will not meet basic human needs.
- All societies must move in the direction of inclusivity.

Linda Tirado, author of *Hand to Mouth: Living in Bootstrap America*, explains what it is like to be poor.[1] At the time she wrote, she was a mother with two children and a husband who was an Iraq war veteran. She was carrying a full load at college and working two jobs. She got up at 6 a.m. to go to school, then to work, then to pick up the children after work, then her husband, then to home where she had a half-hour to get ready for her second job, which ended at midnight. Studying for classes meant she sometimes did not get to bed until 3:00 a.m. She was always tired and she smoked, even though she knew it was bad for her health.

> You see, I am always, always exhausted. It's a stimulant. When I am too tired to walk one more step, I can smoke and go for another hour. When I'm enraged and beaten down and incapable of accomplishing one more thing, I can smoke and feel a little better, just for a minute.[2]

There was no leisure time in Tirado's world, and health was a luxury for the rich. Tirado suffered a number of indignities in the different jobs she held, including sexual harassment, no health benefits, no sick time, no vacation time, scars on her arms from the burns she received using a restaurant's deep-fat fryers, no scheduled breaks, and absolutely no respect. Speaking for herself and for others in similar service jobs, she says:

> In exchange for all that work we're doing, and all our miserable working conditions, we're not allowed to demand anything in return. No sense of accomplishment or respect from above, or job security ... Being poor while working hard is ... crushing. It's a living nightmare where the walls just never stop closing in."[3]

Taking a step back to the Chapter 1, where I identified a set of basic human needs common to all societies, very few of them are being met for those struggling to make a living through low-wage work. Those needs were subsistence, protection, affection, understanding, participation, leisure, creation, identity, and freedom.[4] (Other cultures will have different words for these needs, but the needs remain fundamentally the same.) In Tirado's case there was no time for leisure, no time for creativity, and no freedom to innovate. She received no understanding or acknowledgment for a job well done from her employers or from the larger society. Those who are shut out of participation in any society because they are poor, members of the "wrong" ethnic group, or of the wrong religion or gender cannot realize their full human potential and cannot develop the human and social capital necessary for dealing with the problems we have outlined: climate change, energy poverty, and global inequality. By either creating or embedding durable inequalities, such as income, in our society we not only waste human talent, we inevitably create the conditions for our society to fail.

> By embedding durable inequalities in a society, we inevitably create the conditions for it to fail.

Where Are We Headed?

We are somewhere on a downward slope that will eventually lead to environmental, social, and economic collapse. We don't know exactly where we are on this slope but we know we have problems that must be solved soon. The rise and fall of nations and empires whether Han, Mayan, Ottoman, or Roman is old news, so we want to be cautious when it comes to predicting the impending collapse of Western democracies. However, a 2012 study sponsored by the National Aeronautics and Space Administration looked at civilizations over the past 5,000 years and identified a clear pattern. Advanced, complex systems are susceptible to collapse for two basic reasons: unsustainable resource exploitation and the unequal distribution of wealth.[5]

The paper's authors note that elites are responsible for collapse both because of their overconsumption of resources and because of the economic stratification that results from the concentration of wealth. Over the centuries there are three possible patterns that emerge. First, for a long time civilization appears to be on a sustainable path with a small number of elites; but, as elites grow in numbers, so does their consumption of food surpluses and natural resources. The result is that commoners, or the poor, experience famine and the society eventually collapses. A second scenario is a speeded-up version of the first, where resource extraction leads to a higher environmental depletion rate, the poor's standard of living declines even faster, and eventually the elite follows in their stead. Once again society collapses. A third scenario is one in which some members of society recognize impending collapse, but elites, who are insulated from its immediate effects, resist change and eventually the system collapses.

As the authors point out, we could change the outcome or the path we are on, but to do so there would need to be political and economic changes that address resource exploitation and the distribution of wealth. As for technology saving us from ourselves, the authors are quick to note that:

> Technological change can raise the efficiency of resource use, but it also tends to raise both per capita resource consumption and the scale of resource extraction so that, absent policy effects, the increases in consumption often compensate for the increased efficiency of resource use.[6]

Creating fuel-efficient cars might mean we decide to drive them further. Others have also noted that new technologies lead to a higher consumption of energy and natural resources.[7]

All complex societies must solve problems, but every solution makes the society more complex. As the American anthropologist and historian Joseph Tainter has argued, with each new level of complexity we must spend ever greater amounts of resources or energy solving the problem, with the result that eventually collapse follows.[8] Tainter defines complexity as follows:

> Complexity is generally understood to refer to such things as the size of a society, the number and distinctiveness of its parts, the variety of specialized social roles that it incorporates, the number of distinct social personalities present, and the variety of mechanisms for organizing these into a coherent, functioning whole. Augmenting any of these dimensions increases the complexity of a society.[9]

By way of illustration, a hunter-gatherer society has perhaps a dozen or more distinct roles, while modern European societies have upwards of

20,000 different occupational roles. As a society becomes more complex, "it expands its investment into such things as resource production, information processing, administration, and defense."[10] But each new investment to solve a problem yields diminishing returns.

> As a society becomes more complex, each investment to solve problems yields diminishing returns.

Tainter used the case of Ancient Rome to illustrate the links between energy (the consumption of natural resources, human energy, or wealth), complexity, and the declining return on investment. The early Roman economy was based in agriculture, powered by solar energy, and was relatively egalitarian. When Rome was sacked by Gauls early in the fourth century BCE, a new problem emerged: Rome needed to protect its population. To solve this problem, a standing army was formed. There were other emerging problems. A growing population required a more complex state to solve problems of sewage disposal and the transportation of water for drinking, public baths, and farming. With a growing state and army, Rome needed new energy sources. Energy to keep this system running was simply taken from others. For a long time, complexity was sustained through a strategy of "loot and pillage."

Rome conquered and appropriated the resources of the people it subjugated. These resources or energy included agricultural products, precious metals (gold, silver, gems), and human labor in the form of slaves or the soldiers who were conscripted. But Rome's "loot and pillage" strategy had its limits. First, the Romans ran out of lands to conquer or goods to appropriate, and second, they needed to provide administrative services and security to the lands they had conquered. This in turn meant creating large standing armies that needed to be paid and creating new administrative classes for managing cities such as Constantinople (Istanbul) and regions as far removed as Great Britain. One solution they came up with for this problem, how to pay for it all, was to began the systematic debasement of their currency.

In addition, taxes were raised to confiscatory levels on farmers, while the wealthy were able to avoid taxes. "While peasants went hungry or sold their children into slavery, massive fortifications were built, the size of the bureaucracy doubled." In addition, Germanic tribes were bribed with gold to remain docile. Hyperinflation followed currency debasement, some peasants gave up farming and fled, divisions between rich and poor grew, and eventually the Empire collapsed. Complexity, coupled with inequality and a lack of energy (human and material), led to a reduction in the ability of the state to respond to evolving crises.

There are, of course, parallels in modern society. The countries of Sub-Saharan Africa, Latin America, or Russia that depend on natural resources such as oil or precious metals to prop up their economies and that have growing wealth and income gaps have the potential to devolve into political and economic chaos. They will need to spend more and more resources to maintain temporary stability.

Donella Meadows et al. provided examples of this "law" of diminishing returns in their classic book, *Limits to Growth* (revised 2004).[11] To raise world food production during the "Green Revolution" of 1951–1966 by one-third, expenditures on tractors increased by 63%, those on fertilizers by 145%, and on pesticides by 300%. Meadows, Randers, Meadows and Berhman argue that these kinds of expenditures are simply unsustainable, because there are limits to how much fertilizer, pesticides, and herbicides can be used to boost food production. In addition, the solution to the problem of needing to produce more food per acre creates other problems such as nitrate pollution of rivers and lakes and the collapse of bee colonies because of increased pesticide use. There are many other unsustainable activities whose costs continue to escalate, while return on investment falls.

The United States spent close to 20% of the entire Federal budget in 2014 on the armed forces, an amount far greater than that spent by any other nation. According to the Congressional Budget Office, if defense spending continues at its current rate, by 2020 the government will have paid $1 trillion in *interest* to borrow the money to sustain this technologically sophisticated force. Government borrowing drives up the interest rate for everyone, including those paying for a home mortgage. Estimates of what it has cost the United States to fight wars in Iraq, Afghanistan, and Pakistan between 2002 and 2014 vary, but one study by the Watson Institute for International Studies at Brown University suggests it may be as high as $4.4 trillion.[12]

To get to this total, the Watson Institute included not just the Pentagon's cost for deploying and equipping troops but also the money the State Department spent on hiring private contractors to provide security, as well as the money the State Department and the United

States Agency for International Development (USAID) spent on construction and redevelopment aid to rebuild what had been destroyed. Added, too, was $19 billion in military aid to Pakistan, the $29 billion it cost to mobilize the National Guard, the $135 billion for medical care and benefits to Iraq and Afghan war veterans, and the projected costs ($754 billion) of what will be incurred for future medical care and benefits for war veterans. Not yet accounted for are the costs and resources needed for checking the forces of the self-declared Islamic State.

War has become increasingly expensive, and complex, with less return on investment. One British estimate is that once civilian casualties are subtracted out, the number of enemy combatants killed who might have caused harm to either the United States or to European nations is extremely low.[13] Of course, the goal of these wars was not about economics but about national security and the desire to bring democracy to Iraq and Afghanistan. There are, however, serious disagreements about whether this was the best way to achieve these goals.[14] The point is that problem solving (eliminating terrorism) becomes more and more problematic as a society becomes more and more complex.

A National Security Agency (NSA) PowerPoint slide disclosed by Edward Snowden exposed some of the complexity of the security state. In order to prevent a terrorist attack, the NSA, CIA, or MI5, will deploy all of the tools at their disposal—including the use of drones and electronic surveillance. In terms of collecting information, the PowerPoint slide indicated that the stated goal of the NSA is to "Collect It All," "Process It All," "Partner It All," "Sniff It All," and "Know It All."[15] It is not just the NSA that is collecting information. Eric Schmidt, Google's chief executive, said, "We know where you are. We know where you've been. We can more or less know what you're thinking about."[16] The costs of maintaining complexity in this case is high and not just in terms of economic costs. The monitoring of all civilian communication is potentially a threat to a democratic society.

There is an upward spiral in terms of the energy needed to solve each new problem. Health care in the United States is, on a per capita basis, the most expensive in the world. In 2014, medical costs totaled $2.9 trillion, or $9,255 for every person in the country. Yet, people who live in less wealthy societies such as Costa Rica, where health care costs are under $1,000 per capita, live longer and healthier lives. The increased sophistication of medical care, its complexity, and its cost yield lower rates of return in developed nations than in the developing world. Chlorinating the water supply and providing mosquito nets yield a greater return on investment than an MRI (magnetic resonance imaging) machine that costs $3 million and requires an expensive suite to house it. As an article in the *New England Journal of Medicine* explained, costs in health care keep going up because productivity keeps going down. This is because more and more people are employed in health care professions—lowering productivity—with no real change in health outcomes.[17] In a field related to medicine, pharmaceuticals, increasing investments in research have also yielded declining marginal returns. The solution: buy other companies. Now, instead of spending hundreds of millions developing new drugs, some large pharmaceutical companies seek out and acquire smaller firms whose research results seem promising. The pharmaceutical giant, Merck, acquired Cubist Pharmaceuticals in late 2014 for $8.4 billion because of Cubist's development of new antibiotics. Google, Facebook, and Microsoft also continue their growth through acquisition, as opposed to in-house research and development.

> The greater the degree of inequality in any system, the greater the amount of energy needed to maintain it.

Complexity, Energy, and Inequality

All complex organizations require massive amounts of energy to maintain stability.[18] And, *the greater the degree of inequality in a system, the more the energy required to maintain it. Complexity does not stimulate economic growth; it does so only when it is subsidized by energy in the form of natural resources.* To quote Tainter, "Fossil fuels made industrialism, and all that flowed from it (such as science, transportation, medicine, employment, consumerism, high-technology war, and contemporary political organization), a system of problem solving that was sustainable for several generations."[19] If energy is the basis of cultural complexity, and if each problem creates higher complexity and higher costs with diminishing returns on investment, this has obvious implications for sustainability.[20]

Why? Because it would mean that we cannot solve problems going forward without more energy.

Here I want to create a deeper understanding of energy use in human systems. Energy comes in many forms and all life forms depend on it. For instance, we individual humans are unstable biological systems heavily dependent on energy use. We require an enormous number of calories (energy) to stay alive and keep our brains active. This does not make us unique, because (as noted above) energy needs are high in all complex systems.

There is a tight relationship between system complexity and energy use. The engineer and systems theorist, John Doyle and his colleagues, have demonstrated that in seeking to develop robust systems, we increase complexity.[21] To keep a telephone switching system, a power grid, or one of the Mars Rovers up and running, we have increased system complexity. This is done by creating redundant and backup systems, each of which requires additional energy. For example, the data centers on which banks, social media centers, government agencies, and drug companies rely use over 30 billion watts of electricity annually, equivalent to the output of 30 nuclear power plants. Most of this energy is wasted, because it is estimated that only 6 to 12% is used for computing purposes. The rest is used to keep the centers on standby to deal with potential power surges or other unanticipated problems.[22]

These observations about how complex systems waste energy can be applied to any country that has experienced extended turmoil or a natural disaster. Consider the use of the energy (as I have defined it) needed to maintain inequalities in South Africa. In the 1970s, when conflicts between Whites and Blacks intensified, it is estimated that Whites controlled or received almost 90% of all income in the country. By any measure, a system in which 10% of a population receives 90% of the income and controls virtually all resources is an unstable system.[23] The cost of maintaining this inequality was staggering, and it escalated as the African National Congress (ANC; Nelson Mandela's party) waged war against South Africa's army and mercenaries from other countries. Even though the ANC was victorious, there are still significant income gaps between Blacks and Whites. As a result, Blacks receive most of their income through government transfers.[24] South Africa still has one of the highest rates of income inequality in the world.[25] The result is that significant amounts of human energy and capital continue to be invested and wasted in an inherently unstable system.

Most readers will remember the devastation New Orleans experienced when Hurricane Katrina struck in 2005. To help New Orleans recover from Katrina, many outside sources of energy (in the form of capital, material goods, and human effort), were brought to bear. The Army Corps of Engineers spent millions on rebuilding and reinforcing levees; charitable organizations like the Red Cross raised resources for residents; and though it was insufficient and often ineffective, the Federal government provided money for temporary housing, relocation, and rebuilding. In short, massive amounts of energy were devoted to trying to restore a city that had tipped from one state to another. New Orleans was not resilient, nor had it built the capacity to be so. Before the storm hit, ecosystems had already been degraded, there was significant income inequality, local government was corrupt, and the economy was not diverse, as it depended primarily on tourism and oil. External resources were, therefore, essential to rebuild the city. Even though the response may not have been sufficient, the hurricane hit a state that was part of the wealthiest nation in the world. In some poor countries, there would have been no help.

> Complex systems are fragile to unknown shocks.

Complex systems are designed to withstand *known* shocks. Diesel generators stand by to power up a data center if the power goes out, because power failures are a known occurrence. They are not designed to withstand the devastation that would be caused by a suicide bomber. The Fukushima reactors that melted down were "protected" from potential tsunamis by sea walls, and back-up generators were available to assure the reactors continued to function in the event of a power failure. The Japanese had done everything they could to guard against known shocks. But the magnitude of earthquake and the ensuing tsunami were not predicted and not prepared for. All backup systems were destroyed. *Complex systems become fragile and susceptible to system failure especially with shocks that were not envisioned in the system design or those shocks to which an evolving system has not been exposed.* They can "break," and break catastrophically, as they did in the case of the Fukushima or the Chernobyl disasters.

One of the best known examples of a failure to anticipate shocks came with the building of the Great Wall of China, which once stretched for 4,300 miles. Its first sections were built out of mud bricks and date to 481–221 BCE during the Warring States Period, when they were erected as a barrier against northern nomadic tribes. The wall was never particularly effective militarily for two reasons. First, segments of it could be flanked and, second, those portions erected by literally millions of conscripts, including peasants, soldiers, and criminals, crumbled because of shoddy workmanship as well as natural disasters and earthquakes. The economic and human costs of building the wall were incalculable, but we know it led to higher taxes and it weakened the larger society it was designed to protect, largely because resources went to building the wall instead of being used to improve the lives of ordinary people living on the "right" side of the wall. This should sound familiar.

> You cannot guard, build, or design for unknown shocks.

The United States has determined for political and security reasons that it will strengthen its borders by, among other things, building a wall and tightening security at entry points. It is worth enumerating, if only briefly, some of the ways in which illegal immigrants from Mexico, as well as Central and South America, have found their way over the border. They have come by train, boat, by swimming, and by walking across dangerous desert terrain. And those are only a few of the way people have worked to beat the system. Photographs from U.S. Customs agents are revealing. One man tried to cross by disguising himself as a large piñata. Some illegal immigrants have crossed by disguising themselves as the seat of a car, pulling the upholstery over themselves and sitting in the passenger's seat. Depending on their size, some have been fitted into suitcases; some come stuffed into false compartments in the bottom of the trunk, or in the space behind the rear seat. Spaces have also been created between the dashboard of the car and the engine compartment; one person was even hidden in a modified "glove" compartment. Others have been buried in loads of fruit and vegetables or nailed inside shipping containers until they were safely over the border. And still others have made it over the border by walking around the fence, tunneling under, or simply digging a shallow hole at the bottom and wiggling through. Entrepreneurs on the Mexican side of the border have rented ladders, at $30, for climbing to the top of the wall and usually a confederate with a ladder is waiting on the other side of the wall, alerted by cell phone that someone is coming. Compare this solution to the $70 million cost per mile for the wall. Each time the Border Patrol devises a new solution to prevent crossing, creative people find new ways to get across.. The point is that *you cannot guard, build, or design for all known shocks* or all ways of getting over a barrier. There will always be new and unanticipated ways around it.

My friend, the biophysicist George Basile of Arizona State University, has noted that in the world of physics, the farther any complex system is pushed away from the surrounding systems—that is, the more extreme and far from equilibrium a system is moved—the more fragile it becomes to new shocks and the more difficult it becomes to maintain, requiring ever more energy. Put another way, the more unequal the parts of a system are, the greater the amount of energy needed to maintain stability. Think here about the cost of maintaining our prison systems, which supposedly "solve" the problem of crime. In 2014, over $100 billion was spent on locking up people in jails or prisons. Or, think about the costs involved in preventing acts of terrorism at home and abroad. Or, think about what it costs in wasted human potential when basic human needs are not met. Inequality has real economic costs. Thus, *the greater the degree of inequality in a system, the greater the degree of fragility, and the greater the amount of energy required to maintain it.* This may run to infinity, meaning that no matter how much energy we devote to a complex system, it will eventually evolve into another state. This holds true for both human and physical systems.

As the economist and Nobel Prize winner Kenneth Arrow has noted, *those countries with high rates of consumption will use vast amounts of energy, generate waste, and use up natural resources. As a result they are more vulnerable to external shocks (natural disasters, as well as economic ones) than others.*[26] The constant depletion of natural capital makes a system more vulnerable to "natural" and inevitable shocks such as hurricanes, tsunamis, and earthquakes and, by extension, makes them even more susceptible to the shocks that climate change will bring. The devastation of Hurricane Katrina in 2005 was due in large part to the fact that mangrove swamps and other natural barriers that could have cushioned the storm surge had been removed for housing developments.

A similar way of thinking about shocks was developed by the statistician and risk analyst Nassim N. Taleb in *The Black Swan*.[27] Finding a Black Swan is a rare event; Black Swans were once thought not to exist because they did not exist in Great Britain. (Now that they have been discovered in Australia, you can buy one on eBay for $1,200.) Taleb used the analogy of the Black Swan to illustrate the point that the sudden presence of such a bird can cause us to rethink completely our assumptions about the world. Black Swans are those things which are both unpredictable and have a huge impact on us. Taleb offers as these examples of "Black Swans": the growth of the Internet, the invention of the personal computer, World War I, the breakup of the Soviet Union, and the attacks of 9/11. After one of these events, we develop elaborate theories to explain these surprises. We now know, for example, that those who flew planes into the World Trade Center and the Pentagon had entered the country in advance, and that part of the team had received training on how to fly the kind of plane they hijacked. Now, after the fact, those attending flight schools are heavily screened. But even if we can explain these anomalous events and protect against similar ones from happening, we cannot predict what the next big event will be. Therefore, we must focus on developing robustness or resilience.

Resilience

The concept of resilience was developed by ecologists to describe the processes by which biological systems change. There are several ways the concept is used. One way is to measure how long it takes a system that has been disturbed to return to a previous state. A second way is to measure the magnitude of shock a system can absorb before it is transformed into a new stage, and, finally, there is the extent to which a system is self-regulating and can evolve to a new and "better" state. An ecologist might be interested in the length of time it takes for grasslands to recover after they have been heavily grazed or how long it will take the ecology of the Gulf Coast to recover from the Horizon oil spill of 2010. The concept is useful as a planning tool for managing ecosystems,

> Resilience systems are ones prepared to adapt constantly to new conditions and unknown shocks.

but in order to apply it to human systems, I want to make one important modification. No system can ever really return to its original state. That's not how nature or evolution works. Therefore, planning should be geared toward the fact that all systems will experience *unpredictable* shocks (terrorist attacks, hurricanes, tsunamis, nuclear explosions, financial disasters, or the outbreak of a pandemic). *The only thing that one can predict with certainty is that there will be shocks to a system.* The need, then, is to think about how to build resiliency into social systems that will allow them to *adapt* continually to changing political, economic, and social circumstances.

The concept of resilience recognizes that all systems are interconnected. As systems theorists such as James Lovelock and Lynn Margulis have noted, all interconnected systems must "learn," that is, have the capacity to change, or they will collapse.[28] Active living systems are characterized by self-organization, by interdependence and diversity. As the sustainability researcher Merlina Missimer and her colleagues have said, these characteristics are important because they lead to the resilience and adaptability of a system, meaning the system can survive even if the internal and external conditions change.[29] In sum, *a resilient society is* one that learns constantly, is open to connectivity and new ideas, and thereby anticipates and is *stabilized by change.* However, we need guideposts to determine whether or not we are moving toward or away from this goal. Here the concept of sustainability is useful.

Sustainability

A widely accepted definition of sustainability was adopted in 1987 by the United Nations General Assembly. The report, *Our Common Future,* spelled out what this meant: "Sustainable development is development that meets the needs of the present without compromising the ability of future generations to meet their own needs."[30] The report underscored the importance of meeting the needs of the world's poor first and "extending to all the opportunity to fulfill their aspirations for a better life." The problem of poverty needed to be attacked because: "a world in which poverty is endemic will always be prone to ecological and other catastrophes."[31] The report

> The changes needed to solve linked environmental and social problems will require political muscle and will.

also recognized that much of the world's economic activity had profound impacts on the biosphere, because it drew on raw materials from forests, soils, seas, and waterways. The crises of the world—energy, environmental, and developmental—were all seen as linked. It was noted that the solutions proposed would be painful, because they would require changing how those in the developed world consumed and used raw materials and energy. Change would require political will and muscle to bring these linked problems to heel. But many observers avoided the full implications of the report, believing that, without incurring pain or changing how we lived, human needs, economic growth, and protection of the environment could be balanced. Thus, embedded within the idea of sustainability was a massive contradiction, perhaps best summed up with the mantra of "people, planet, profit"—the idea that you could maximize profit, still protect the environment, and still meet basic human needs.

We could shop our way to a "green" world in this version of the future, although this is in point of fact impossible. Or, if we were entrepreneurial, we could help companies make money by going "green." Clearly there have been benefits for large organizations to learning how to better conserve resources. Walmart, for example, has figured out that if they are going to continue to have products to sell in the future, then the goods must come from sustainable or renewable resources. When Home Depot found out they were the biggest seller of lumber in the United States, they started buying lumber from sustainable forests so they would have lumber to sell in the future. China is trying to deal with the problem of air pollution by encouraging the use of solar panels, building wind turbines, and rushing forward with the building of nuclear power plants. Conservation is a good thing, but it will not get us where we need to be. China, as we noted earlier, is now witnessing growing inequality within the country. To manage this problem they will need even more energy.

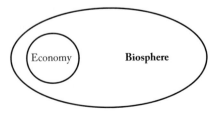

Figure 8.1 The Economy Is a Subset of the Biosphere.

As I noted when discussing complexity, often the answer to a problem is to increase complexity, which requires the complexity to be subsidized by some form of energy. To date, that energy has been primarily fossil fuels. So, one step to moving forward would be to ensure that all management decisions were based on whether or not the solution can be subsidized by a renewal form of energy (biomass, wind, solar, geothermal, wave motion, and so forth.) What this does is to make clear that *the economy is a subset of the biosphere and not the other way around.* Take the problem of getting from one place to another (transportation) and the number of solutions it has generated. When a donkey was hitched to a cart, the donkey needed hay and grain to keep going. When trucks and cars were invented as more efficient means of moving things around, they required fossil fuels. Further, the trucks and cars required roads and local, state, and federal agencies to build them, taxes to support them, as well as gas stations, garages, parts stores, parking lots, truck stops, and car washes. A simple problem (transportation) got complicated very quickly, and every new stage required the use of more energy.

Now imagine that we were trying to solve the problem of transportation by using only renewable resources. Well, we already solved this problem. Barges were once floated down navigable waterways, and sailing ships once traversed the globe. True, it meant things took a longer time to deliver, but that's not the point. The point is we solved a transportation problem by using renewal energy sources. We went with what worked. Once the steam engine, powered by coal or wood, was invented, the world became more complex and more energy dependent. Today, somebody who wants to buy a car as a means of transportation has a variety of options: big, small, or midsized; powered by hydrogen fuel cells, all-electric, or a hybrid that uses gas and electricity. There is the old standby, of course: one fueled by gasoline or diesel fuel. If I bought an all-electric Tesla, I could recharge it in the parking lot of the Best Western hotel, which is about a mile from our house. None of these forms of transportation, however efficient, are in themselves sustainable because their manufacture requires the use of irreplaceable natural resources.

The Natural Step, an organization committed to using the principles of science to help create a sustainable future, has identified four conditions that must hold if we are to create a sustainable society that can persist over generations and is far-seeing enough not to undermine the biosphere on which it depends.[32] Here are the things science tells us we *cannot* do.

- A society that mines and disperses materials at a rate faster than they are re-deposited back into the Earth's crust will not be sustainable.[33]
- A society that produces artificial substances at a rate faster than they can be broken down by natural processes, if they can be broken down at all, will not be sustainable.
- A society that physically degrades natural resources at a rate faster than they are replenished, or completely destroys those resources, will not be sustainable.
- A society that undermines the ability of people to meet their basic needs will not be sustainable.

I know of no nation-state or community that has avoided all of these perils, though many are making progress. To take just the first standard, reducing energy demand, using renewable energy sources, favoring compact development over sprawl, providing public transportation, and minimizing the use of petrochemical fertilizer and herbicides in food production all reduce the impact of materials being used up at a "rate faster than they are being re-deposited back into the Earth's crust."

The science has been developed to the point that we know what we should *not* do, and we know that we need to use the principles of sustainability in making management decisions. To be clear about what I mean by management: it involves looking at each problem in terms of how it could be solved in a sustainable fashion. Management of problems also recognizes that because things continually change, we need to actively manage them. No problem is solved forever. We also need to know whether or not our actions are moving us toward or away from a vision of sustainability. And to do this we need a pretty clear understanding of the kind of world we want to create. What would that be?

Guideposts to the Future

Let us return to where we began in Chapter 1. Imagine for a moment that you have not yet been born and you have no idea whether or not you'll be born a boy or girl, rich or poor, black or white, or even what country you will be born in. Do you want your life chances determined by something over which you had absolutely no control? I would hope your answer would be the same as mine, if not, this has been a long journey through dense material for nothing. But let's assume you agree with me. Now what?

As a next step, let's agree we want to be born into a democratic society. We know that democracy exists only when certain conditions are met: People must be treated as equal before the law and there must be an effective government that can execute the wishes of the governed and meet the needs of its people as the people define them. Further, its political and economic systems must be open as opposed to closed. We know that durable inequalities based on gender, religion, race, ethnicity, and nationality erode trust—the foundation on which a democracy exists. We would not want to live in a society in which selected trust networks—clans, tribes, or religious groups—were embedded in the workings of the state and others were excluded.

We would not want to be born into a corrupt society where we would be caught up in a never-ending spiral of corruption-feeding inequity and inequity-feeding corruption. We know that poverty is pain and humiliation, and we know the negative, long-term social consequences that come from trapping people into the social positions into which they were born. Therefore, we would not want our parents' income, jobs, or levels of education to determine our future. We would probably not want our government to develop policies on the basis of who had the most money to use in lobbying the government to pass specialized legislation and laws that privileged the few.

If we had to work for a living, which 99% of humanity does, would we want to work in unsafe environments or have no protection against employers who tried to harass or exploit us? Would it be fair to receive a wage that was so low we could not participate fully in our society? Would we want to live in a society where we could not afford medical or dental care when we needed it? Again, if we want to live in a truly sustainable society, the answer should be, "No!"

We'd also probably want a society focused on forgiveness rather than retribution. If we made some really bad mistake, would we not want the option to redeem ourselves? Would we want a society that built prisons as a first line of defense in dealing with crime and deviance, or one that worked to prevent crime in the first place by developing human capital and giving people opportunities to use their talents? And yes, there will always be greedy and sociopathic people in every society, but they really are in the minority and we should not organize our social institutions under the assumption they are in the majority.

You could probably add to this list those institutions and principles you would want to take into the future with you. What is important is to assess all social policies in terms of whether they take us closer to or further away from the kind of world we want to inhabit.

Rules of Resilience

I have painted with very broad strokes some new ways to think about a set of interconnected problems. I have suggested that the concepts of resilience and sustainability, coupled with our knowledge of how systems function, how energy and inequality relate, and how trust serves as the glue that can either retard economic and political growth or provide the foundations for it, can be of help in determining how to allocate scarce resources both within and among nations. Planning for sustainability can, and must be, based on our knowledge of the known world. Social systems operate with the same set of rules as biophysical systems, but with an important difference. *We choose the rules that govern the system*; we can, in the end, decide what we want. Achieving sustainability, solving problems of inequality, and meeting future energy needs are a *planning problem*. Of course they represent huge challenges if people are divided by class, religion, gender, or ethnicity. Nevertheless, based on the discussions we have had to this point in this book, it is possible to identify some of the *rules for resilience* that might make this task easier, or might increase the probability of success.

Resilience of a nation and community ...

• depends on inclusiveness or the elimination of durable inequalities, for example, those things over which we have no control or that determine whether or not our human needs are met.	All complex systems operate with the same rules, but in human systems we can choose the rules that govern the system.

- depends on trust and on the reality that a government acts to increase the openness of its political and economic systems and meet the human needs of all its citizens.
- depends on the ability to actively identify, adjust, and *manage* economic, social, and political problems.

Creativity and the ability to manage problems ...

- depends on human capital, that is, the knowledge and skills to act.
- requires the elimination of barriers to action.
- requires permission to act or the development of a robust civic sector.

Adaptation ...

- requires that all problems should be managed or solved by the use of renewable resources.
- is limited by biological constraints.
- requires that individuals and groups be given the freedom to act, as well as the human and social capital to do so.

Equity ...

- is essential for maintaining complex social systems, because it lowers energy costs.
- is essential, since inequity will lead to system collapse due to the unsustainable costs of maintaining it.
- must be a goal of all social systems.

> We are the wild card in creating a sustainable future.

Trust ...

- depends on the effectiveness of a government and its ability to meet the human needs of all its citizens.
- depends on equity; inequity lowers the level of trust.
- depends on the rule of law.
- is essential for system resilience.

Creative Adaptation

The wild card in getting to the kind of future we want is us—our passion for the problems we face and our ability to manage the problems. We are not without examples of how adaptation works in organizations. Creative adaptation, coupled with our knowledge of the rules of resilience and the principles of sustainability, is the strategy we need for going forward.

"Thank God we didn't drop the baby," said the Coast Guard flight mechanic, William Williams.[34] The Coast Guard had been given the task of rescuing people stranded in the aftermath of Hurricane Katrina, which struck New Orleans on Monday, August 29, 2005. The force of the hurricane, with winds of up to 125 miles an hour, created a surge of water that topped the city's levees, leaving 80% of the city flooded at depths of up to 20 feet and leaving 50,000 citizens trapped.

Williams and a trainee were using a hoist to lift a man and a baby, no more than 3 or 4 weeks old, off a rooftop. The man was frightened.

> I'm hosting him up, hoisting him up, and before he even got to the cabin he's trying to get out of the basket and I'm pushing on the top of his head because if he gets out he's going to fall, and we're at 150 feet so obviously he's going to die. Then he sat back down and just hands me the baby from underneath the aircraft and I've got one hand on the hoist button and one on the cable. So, I'm trying to get him in and he's trying to hand me the baby so I had to drop the hoist thing, grab the baby, and I'm like, "Please God don't ..."[35]

The trainee grabbed the baby and everyone was safe. The rescue operation and many others like it were successful because everyone on board—the pilot, the trainee, the flight mechanic, and the swimmer—worked together as a team focused on just one thing: rescuing people. They also had to innovate constantly. Sometimes the swimmer would "simply" pluck people off a roof and put them in a hoist to be winched up to the helicopter. Crews encountered people who were disabled and needed special help. At other times, swimmers found they needed to chop through the roofs of buildings and homes to free people trapped inside. Because the axes carried on board the helicopters were too small, crews borrowed axes from the firemen and, when those weren't available, they went to Home Depot and bought every ax and wood saw they could find. They did not ask for permission; they just did it. Everyone had a clear understanding of what the goals were and did not need elaborate instructions about what to do. Captain Mueller outlined the instructions he gave to one of his lieutenants: "I can't tell you what you're going to be doing exactly, but when you get there you're going to understand what needs to happen ... So you go there and do the best you can and we'll send you everything we can."[36] This organizational strategy can be summed up as "We trained you; you know what the goal is; you figure it out, because we can't anticipate everything."

The Coast Guard operates with what they officially refer to as, "The Principle of On-Scene Initiative." What this means is that central command determines what the mission is, but those in the field are given permission to act. As Vice Admiral Allen explained, this can-do attitude was exemplified in New Orleans by "pilots flying at night through power lines, rescue swimmers swinging axes on rooftops, or a deck hand [or a] buoy tender commandeering buses to evacuate victims."[37] Such flexibility is essential for success because the organization operates in an environment with many moving parts and unknowns. In responding to Katrina there were an almost limitless number of factors at play. They not only had to keep aircraft flying and repaired; they had to supply food and water to the people they rescued; deal with armed aggressors; rescue fishermen who tried to ride out the storm; help with the cleanup of oil spills; and feed and supply their own crews. They modeled adaptability in dealing with new and unknown challenges. And they were one of the few organizations that did. Others would fail dramatically, as they stuck to tried-and-true ways of doing things.

For example, the local police were ineffective in maintaining order and made matters worse by shooting unarmed civilians. Evacuation was haphazard, and many were unnecessarily trapped in their homes. Local officials gave confusing and conflicting reports about where to go to seek shelter and what shelter there was proved to be inadequate. The federal government was slow to respond to the needs of the people. The Report of the Select Bipartisan Committee to Investigate the Preparation for and Response to Hurricane Katrina was scathing in its criticism of local, state, and federal governments, the New Orleans Police Department, the Department of Defense, the Department of Homeland Security, and the Federal Emergency Management Agency (FEMA).

The Committee found it difficult to understand why all of the agencies in question were overwhelmed and why their response was so disorganized, given the fact that all of the agencies involved had participated one year prior to Katrina in a virtual planning exercise called "Hurricane Pam." The exercise assumed, among other things, that many people would not evacuate the city (and many did not prior to Katrina, because they did not have the means to flee); more than 500,000 buildings would be destroyed; 1,000 shelters would be needed; ships and helicopters would be needed to rescue people; and 97% of all communications would be down.[38] This is almost exactly what did happen, although the virtual exercise did not take into account or anticipate the toxic brew of sewage, chemical and oil spills that would be churned up by the storm and dropped on top of people and their homes. Why didn't the agencies take into account the findings of the planning study? Because they did not think a disaster of that magnitude would actually happen. This meant that when the storm hit most agencies were woefully unprepared, leaving many residents of the city feeling helpless.

Patricia Thompson, an evacuee, said:

> We were abandoned. City officials did nothing to protect us. We were told to go to the Superdome, the Convention Center, the interstate bridge for safety. We did this more than once. In fact, we tried them all for every day for over a week. We saw buses, helicopters and FEMA trucks, but no one stopped to help us. We never felt so cut off in all our lives. When you feel like this you do one of two things, you either give up or go into survival mode. We did the latter. This is how we made it. We slept next to dead bodies, we slept on streets at least four times next to human feces and urine. There was garbage everywhere in the city. Panic and fear had taken over.[39]

There are several points to make about differential responses to Katrina and its aftermath, and how they relate to a world in which inequity has taken root. As noted, the Coast Guard was effective in carrying out their rescue mission because that is one of the things for which they are trained and, of critical importance, people had permission to act on their own to deal with changing and novel conditions. The Coast Guard had what I have referred to as both substantial human capital (knowledge and skills) and social capital (a dense network on which captains and crew could rely).

One of the major problems faced in New Orleans and other areas hard hit by the storm was communication and coordination. The Department of Homeland Security (DHS) and FEMA, which is part of DHS, were heavily criticized for their inability to coordinate activities before the storm hit and in its aftermath. Coordination would have been difficult given the severity of the storm but it was impeded by an organizational structure that undercut innovation and adaptation. I cannot squeeze onto this page the entire organizational chart for DHS, or the many agencies that fall under its jurisdictions but let me give you an idea of the organizational challenge. (Please Google it.) The DHS alone has thirty separate heads of divisions, which include the U.S. Coast Guard, FEMA, the Secret Service, Customs, and so forth. FEMA, just one division of the DHS, has

> We tend to plan on the basis of past events, rather than future ones, and we are reluctant to decentralize because we don't trust others to solve problems.

36 separate offices and administrators, along with 10 more regional coordinators. Added to the mix in New Orleans were nonprofits like the Red Cross trying to help; private corporations like Walmart shipping supplies; Carnival Cruise Lines providing housing for first responders, and the presence of National Guard troops. In evaluating this mish-mash of efforts the Select Committee suggested adding additional levels of bureaucracy to assure that things would work more smoothly the next time there was a natural disaster. Fortunately this suggestion was not implemented but it represents a problem with much of our planning efforts in a complex and dynamic world.

We tend to plan on the basis of past crises, and we want to centralize rather than decentralize our response to them. We are reluctant to decentralize because we don't automatically trust people to figure out how best to respond to unanticipated events, though they do it all the time.

Hurricane Sandy, in 2012, caused billions in damages in the Caribbean and along the East Coast of the United States. New York City experienced flooded streets, tunnels, and subways, and power outages from the storm. The city, in response to both Sandy and to rising sea levels, is laying out plans for the next big storm. They include building a network of levees, planting oyster beds and reefs to buffer storm waves, and creating parks with "upland knolls" where people could sunbathe, garden, farm or take refuge in the event of flooding.[40] This is planning for the last event, when the next event could be a prolonged heat wave, water shortage, ice storm, or heavy snow fall.

Centralized planning does not necessarily meet the needs of people most affected by a catastrophe. The Japanese government budgeted $148 billion in response to the March 2011 tsunami and the meltdown of nuclear reactors at Fukushima. According to the government's own reports, one year after the disaster about 25% of this money was spent on unrelated projects, including subsidies for a contact-lens factory, whaling "research," aircraft and fighter-pilot training, and prison vocational training, among other things. The idea was to stimulate economic growth as part of the recovery effort, which it did not. As for the 340,000 people evacuated from the area around Fukushima or who had homes destroyed by the tsunami, they were still living in temporary shelters more than a year-and-a-half after the disaster. Critics of the government's slow response noted that the resources should have been allocated to provincial governments where locals could participate in reconstruction efforts.[41]

The example of experts in Tokyo deciding on the problem that needed to be solved—boost the economy, rather than rebuild based on local needs—is counter to how the natural world works. As the University of Arizona marine biologist, Rafe Sagarin, has explained, most natural organisms have a decentralized organizational structure that allows them to adapt to new circumstances. His favorite example, the octopus, has a centralized brain that "trusts" its sensors, or individual tentacles, to observe the world, detect problems, and come up with solutions to those problems. It can hide from predators because it has color-changing cells in its epidermis that allow it to maintain different colors over its body depending on the background it is moving over. (We humans also have independent sensors such as our white blood cells that mobilize to fight infections of all kinds.)

Octopuses are also smart in addition to being adaptable. They learn from their changing environments. Researchers studying them in laboratories have found that they will frequently pull off the sensors placed on them to test their brain activity; they will crawl out of their tanks to find food elsewhere in the laboratory and then scurry back to their tank. In the ocean they will use found objects like the halves of coconut shells to create their own armor. Octopuses are amazing but the lesson is not about the octopus. As Sagarin argues, the lesson we want to learn is that species survival, including ours, depends not in planning for the future based on the past, and not spending our time and energy trying to predict what the next disaster will be and planning for that. The lesson is to be open to constant learning and adaptability.

We need to understand that if people are given the resources, knowledge, and freedom to act they can solve an unlimited set of problems. We are self-organizing and problem solving creatures. When the Twin Towers were struck on September 11, 2001, thousands of people were stranded on the island of Manhattan. Some, fleeing smoke and debris actually jumped in the water and tried to swim away. But in less than 9 hours, it is estimated that 500,000 New Yorkers were rescued by ferries, tug boats, party boats, ferries, fishing boats, and yachts. The captain of the Staten Island Ferry James Parese said he had never seen so many boats come together in his lifetime. "One radio call and they just all came together." If a woman in a wheelchair needed to be lifted over the fence on the water's edge to get in to one of the boats, people helped. If people were stranded on ledges by the water, they were picked up. Nobody was left behind. And all of this happened without coordination.[42] We can count on one another, if we know what the problem is, and we have the human and social capital to manage it.

Solutions

Any solution to the problems of climate change, energy poverty, and inequality must include the goal of increasing individual human capital so that people can be full participants in their own societies. People also need the freedom and the ability to make their own choices about the kind of world in which they wish to live, and to develop their full human potential to solve problems unique to their communities and nations. All humans must have the freedom and civic space to act in order

> Human creativity and ingenuity will be critical in solving emergent problems.

to create a sustainable and resilient future. Human creativity and ingenuity will be essential to develop the knowledge needed to balance social, economic, and environmental needs. The challenges in accomplishing these goals will necessarily be different in the developing countries of the world than in the advanced industrial economies of the West. For example, in Sub-Saharan Africa progress must continue to be made on improving the health of mothers and their children, dealing with widespread hunger, and eliminating easily and inexpensively preventable diseases such as malaria. Dealing with endemic political and economic corruption will require organizations such as the World Bank and NGOs to assure aid is directed to improving human capability and not enriching entrenched elites. In the advanced industrial world growing gaps in income and wealth must be addressed, as it will need to be in emerging countries such as Brazil, China, and India.

We do not know precisely what the future will look like, or what new challenges or crises will emerge. We haven't even yet begun to solve or manage the ones we know about—war, energy poverty, climate change, and problems of inequity. *We need to prepare for resilience, or the ability to adapt constantly.* A benign future is not a given unless we act to make it so.

Where does the future of a country like the United States lie? Will our future devolve to that of our southern neighbor, Mexico? Or will we act on the basis of the knowledge we have to create a fair and democratic society? We do not want Mexico's closed political, economic, or social systems. The killing of 43 students who were attending a teacher's college in a rural Mexican town in 2014, highlighted some of Mexico's many problems. The students were murdered because the mayor of the town told the police, who had deep connections to a drug gang, to "take care of things" when the students came to town to protest against the conditions at their school. The killings highlighted the endemic political

> Social inequality stands in the way of creating and maintaining a democratic society.

corruption, the huge gaps between wealth and poverty, and the violence that plagues the daily lives of all Mexicans. Lack of economic opportunity, corruption, and inequality limit the ability of the Mexican state and its citizens to solve the problems a modern state must confront. What would it take to make things different in a country like Mexico, or what will we need to do to create and maintain our own resilient and democratic society?

Solutions Unique to the United States

As the richest nation in the world, and one with growing inequities that are potentially destabilizing, it is important to identify those factors that serve as a brake on citizens participating in the democratic project. Democracy, as I've argued, is not a given; it must constantly be created and revived. What stands in our way is inequity and being shut out from our society based on irrelevant moral criteria: how much money we have, where and to whom we were born, or what our gender, ethnicity, or religion is. Yawning gaps between income and wealth have become one more in the list of durable inequities; something over which most have little control. Inequity erodes trust and, to quote Tocqueville, "shuts people up in the habits of their own hearts."[43] This in turn erodes social capital or civic capacity—the ties that bind us together in pursuit of common efforts. What could we do better? *And above all, what would enhance people's capacity to act on their own behalf and therefore that of others?* The larger answer is that we need to change politics and policies. *We should make no mistake about the challenges faced in creating resilient societies and a sustainable future. They are political challenges.*

Taxes

Virtually every book that treats the problem of inequity ends up arguing that we need to raise taxes on those with high incomes, tax the actual wealth people have, or reduce the amount of wealth that can be passed on from one generation to the next without paying taxes.[44] The government, whether state or national, needs resources to implement programs on behalf of all its citizens and to use those resources in a manner that is perceived to be *fair*. However, as pointed out in earlier chapters, there has been a systematic attempt by American conservatives to "starve the beast." The phrase, attributed to a staffer for President Reagan, seeks to reduce the government's capacity to serve the needs of its citizens by limiting tax revenue. The argument about whether to tax or not is seldom grounded in what works for the common welfare. As one of the world's most influential economists, Joseph E. Stiglitz, has argued, preferential tax treatments undermine the efficiency of the economy.[45]

For example, when the $1 trillion Farm Bill was passed in 2014, "savings" were realized by cutting $8 billion for SNAP (formerly the Food Stamp Program), which meant a cut of ninety dollars a month to recipients and denial of assistance to about 3.8 million low-income people. The bulk of the benefits went to large corporate farms and provided continued subsidies for corn, wheat, rice, cotton, and tobacco crops. The modest savings in the Farm Bill were extracted from the needy. There is a cognitive disconnect in terms of our system of taxes because very often the same people who argue for cutting safety nets like the food stamp program, unemployment insurance, or universal health care, are also those who support growing the military, already the largest in the world.

Given the facts about income inequality even the conservative columnist, George Will, has changed his mind about taxes. *Surely it is time to give earners on the lower rungs of the ladder of upward mobility a boost by cutting their payroll taxes. This can be paid for by ending the nonsense of taxing at the low capital gains rate [15%] the income that fabulously wealthy hedge fund managers call 'carried interest.*[46] He had other suggestions that included capping the amount of mortgage interest that could be deducted and other forms that I showed benefited only a small slice of the American public. The problem, as he noted, was that every single Congressman has wealthy people in their districts, bankers, and so on, who will object mightily to tax reform.

> Hard work is no guarantee of success.

There are other ideas that have been floated, such as extending the Earned Income Tax Credit further up the income ladder and indexing it to the average per capita income. Whatever the solution proposed for making the system fairer, it will require a concerted and bipartisan political effort to accomplish.

Wages

The majority of those living in poverty are working, which means that people are poor because their jobs don't pay them enough, not because they don't want to work. The poor are not different from you or me in terms of human needs. We all want respect and a sense of accomplishment. Yet, as the Urban Institute has noted, 50% of all Americans will live in poverty at some point in their lives. Escaping poverty is difficult. The majority of those who do will become poor again in five years.[47] *Working hard is no guarantee you will get ahead.*

The solution to the problems of low-wage workers is not just to raise the minimum wage, which can be as low as $2.13 an hour for waiting tables, but to make the Federal minimum wage the same in all states, raise it to $15 an hour, as some municipalities are now doing, and link it to increases in the Consumer Price Index. Period! It can be phased in, but we need to let go of the myth that those working minimum-wage jobs are teenagers or married members of a household trying to pick up a few extra dollars. They are trying to make a living. Also, we need to end the myth that any "able-bodied" person can get work.

Will there be enough work?

Related to the problem of wages is the matter of whether or not there are actually enough jobs for the people who want to work. Though an economic recovery was celebrated in Washington, DC, in 2014, the actual number of jobs created each month, around 300,000, was lower than during the 1960s, when there were only half as many Americans as there are today. In the 1960s, only 5% of men between the ages of 25 and 54 did not work; today that figure is around 16%. There are areas of the country where more than 25% of men are not working. These areas tend to be where mines or natural resources have played out, as in states like West Virginia and Kentucky, Indian reservations, or in cities like Cleveland and Detroit. The reasons people don't work vary considerably and include being retired, disabled, going to school, or not able to find work. Being out of work, though, could become the new normal.

As I noted in Chapters 3 and 4, Marx thought that capitalism would create the seeds of its own destruction, but he also believed capitalism would usher in a new era of plentitude. He thought that the efficiencies of capitalism and the labor-saving inventions it spawned would mean we would no longer need to work long hours to meet our basic needs. The irony, though, is that technology and the efficiencies of the market may simply take away our jobs and give rise to greater inequality. The Nobel economist Joseph A. Stiglitz has argued that inequality is driven by, among other things, globalization and automation.[48] Because of globalization, American workers have found themselves unable to compete against low-wage labor from China and India. Good, high-paying jobs in manufacturing that require only a high school education are gone. What is left is work in the trades that cannot be easily outsourced such as welding, carpentry, or plumbing and low-wage service work. Automation may even imperil some service work. One Silicon Valley hotel now has a "bellhop" robot that will carry your bags to your room. (I assume this means we will no longer have to tip the bellman.)

Advances in artificial intelligence means that machines can now learn. IBM's machine, Watson, is now helping people do a number of jobs, but as Watson learns we may not need salespeople, chefs, paralegals, radiologists, or booking agents. If I buy shoes on Zappos or goods using a Google search, the entire process is automated. As Google perfects cars that need no drivers, then I won't need a taxi cab driver. I'll dial in, note where I want to go, and a driverless car will soon appear to take me to my destination. Google's co-founder, Larry Page, has suggested that we cut the work-week to four days so that as technology displaces workers, people can still find employment.[49] American workers are falling behind their European counterparts in terms of training for jobs that are likely to be enhanced by technology, as opposed to being replaced by technology. So, at a minimum we need a national policy focused on retraining those displaced by technology and programs to cushion the transition from a manufacturing economy to one driven by technology. *But we need people to propose these new policies and show up and vote for them.*

Voting

Poll after poll shows that Americans have lost faith in their government and its ability to solve problems that are important to them. Discouragement and apathy were evident in the number of voters, only 36.3% of those eligible, who went to the polls in the midterm elections of 2014, the lowest number since 1942 when we were in the middle of a world war. Yet in order to create the capacity for civic action (social capital), people need to participate in the political activities of their country. There are 22 nations where voting is mandatory and universal, usually beginning with age 18. If you fail to vote in Australia, the fine is $20; not much, but something of an incentive. All of those countries that have mandatory voting laws are constitutional democracies, although some, like the Democratic Republic of the Congo, fall far from the standard of what we think a democracy should be. In other words, mandatory voting does not automatically create democracies. Nevertheless, the argument here is that voting should be made mandatory because of concerted attempts to limit voter rights in the United States to those most likely to vote anyway, that is, older white people with money. Mandatory voting would push back against attempts to disenfranchise some members of the population and make the outcomes of elections more democratic, which is to say, based on the "will of the people." And one should be automatically registered to vote when they reach the age of 18.

> Mandatory voting and automatic voter registration on turning 18 could push back against attempts to disenfranchise some members of the population and make the outcomes of elections more democratic.

Money and politics

We would all like our political candidates to win, but at what cost? The expenditures in the 2014 midterm elections for the Senate and the House totaled almost $4 billion. The costs of the 2012 Presidential election, which pitted the winner, President Barack Obama, against his Republican challenger, Mitt Romney, were $2.6 billion. Unaccounted for in the total were the hundreds of millions of dollars in "shadow" money spent by unidentified organizations and individuals to promote their respective candidates. The Super PAC American Crossroads and its nonprofit cousin, Grassroots Policy Strategies (Crossroads GPS), were created by the GOP strategist Karl Rove and others. They are estimated to have spent $158 million in the campaign on electioneering "communications." The Koch brother's organization, Americans for Prosperity, spent $35 million.[50] These sums add up to staggering amounts of money donated to both Democratic and Republic candidates; and donors often want something in return. That's not surprising, but it means that politicians at all levels are always faced with the daunting prospect of raising increasing amounts of money to get elected and making commitments to donors.

There have been consistent attempts to limit money in politics. One of the most notable was the Bipartisan Campaign Reform Act of 2002, also known as the McCain-Feingold Act, named for its two sponsors, John McCain, the Republican Senator from Arizona, and Russ Feingold, the Democratic Senator from Wisconsin. McCain explained in his 2003 autobiography that:

> By the time I became a leading advocate of campaign finance report, I had come to appreciate that the public's suspicions were not always mistaken. Money does buy access in Washington, and access increases influence that often results in benefiting the few at the expense of the many.[51]

The Act, which was signed into law by the first President Bush, was intended to limit the amount of "soft money" in campaign financing and to limit advocacy ads or electioneering communications. (Soft money is money donated to support general political activities, rather than a particular candidate and is not subject to regulations that govern how much can be contributed to a political campaign.) The larger goal was to eventually get to the point where campaigns would be funded from the public purse with strict limits set on how much each candidate could spend. The law was attacked almost immediately. Senator Mitch McConnell of Kentucky, now the majority leader of the Senate, claimed it was unconstitutional. Eventually the Supreme Court would strike down in 2010 significant portions of the McCain-Feingold Act. The Court's reasoning was: "If the First Amendment has any force, it prohibits Congress from fining or jailing citizens, or associations of citizens, for simply engaging in free speech."[52] Thus, money and free speech have become equated. The solution to this complication may require a constitutional amendment.

Redistricting and open primaries

How could we avoid some of the polarization that now characterizes our political system? Should primary elections be open and competitive so that the "best" man or woman wins? Thomas Brunell, a political science professor at the University of Texas at Dallas, has argued that we should structure districts so that they are packed with like-minded voters so they will be satisfied with the outcome of an election, instead of having some who are disappointed.[53] This is pretty much what has happened. Whether it is a Democrat or Republic running for the House of Representatives, very few races are competitive, because the lines of the congressional districts have been drawn to privilege one party over the other.

In 2008, California voters passed the Voters First Act in spite of stiff opposition from the leaders of the entrenched Democratic and Republican parties in Sacramento. The fear of party leaders and incumbents was that many districts would no longer be "safe." The act gave to the voters, not the legislators, the power to both redraw U.S. congressional district boundaries according to the U.S. Census and the maps for legislative districts within California. The Commission was composed of fourteen members who were able to agree by votes of 12–2 and 13–1 to approve respectively the congressional district and state legislative district maps. After several court challenges in California the matter was settled. Californians did not stop there. Through the referendum process that bypasses the State Assembly and Senate, they also instituted a "top two" primary. Thus, regardless of party affiliation, the top two vote-getters now run against each other in the general election. This, coupled with the Commission's redrawing of maps, has resulted in significant turnover and in intra-party races. It also means that parties need to run toward the center, which is where most voters are clustered, rather than to the extremes. The State of Ohio has taken similar steps. In late 2014 it initiated a bipartisan plan to redistrict in order to make races more competitive.[54]

> Social inequality drives up the costs of social control.

Prisons

The United States has more people locked up behind bars than any other nation. With 5% of the world's population, we have 25% of all prisoners. One of the points I made earlier in the chapter was that complex and unequal systems drive up the need for energy to maintain these inequalities. In the case of prisons, *inequity is helping to drive up expenditures for social control*. Prisons are costly. In 2014, $74 billion was spent to lock people up. The average cost, per year, to house someone in a minimum security Federal prison is $21,006 and $33,930 for high security lockup. As many have noted, it would be cheaper to send everyone to a public university than put them in prison. Prisons are big business. The publically traded Corrections Corporation of America and GEO, formerly the Wackenhut Correction Corporation, together generated more than $3 billion in revenue in 2014.

Prisons also represent bad social policy with lasting consequences for those classified as felons and for the society at large. Bad policy began in 1971 with President Richard Nixon's "war on drugs" and with the subsequent rise of state governments following suit with harsh sentences. People were sent to prison for fifteen years to life for using or dealing drugs, whether their crime was cocaine, marijuana, or heroine. The amount of drugs in their possession was irrelevant. Numerous studies have also demonstrated that justice is not blind.[55] When all other things are equal in terms of the nature of the crime committed, those who are from the minority community or are poor are far more likely to be locked up than their well-off white counterparts. Federal mandatory sentences for other crimes, put in place in an effort "to get tough on crime," have reduced judicial discretion in setting sentences. No other democratic nation follows our model of punishment over rehabilitation. The result is that once an American is finally released from prison, he or she may end up back in prison within a short time. The solution: Reform our prisons and sentencing guidelines to bring them in line with European nations. They have a smaller percentage of their population in prison, spend less on incarceration, and see fewer of them return to prison. Second, make it easier for convicted felons, once released, to expunge their records so they can get jobs. As it now stands, many are forever shut out of gainful employment.

Unions

Make it easier, not harder, for workers to form unions. Unions not only provide protections for workers, they also generate social capital or networks of trust that make it easier for people to act collectively for other purposes. In Canada, workers in most provinces have the option of a card-check certification. If a majority of workers sign in support of unionizing, the employer is required by law to recognize the union. On the other hand, in the United States, if an employer does not recognize the union, employees must file a petition demonstrating support for a union, and then hold a vote. This delay, usually more than a month, means the employer can mobilize opposition to the union, sometimes claiming that if employees vote for a union, the plant will be closed.[56]

The importance of this rule to employers and employed was highlighted in 2014 when President Obama sought to appoint his nominee to the National Labor Relations Board. Failing in his attempt to get Congress to approve his nominee, he made a recess appointment and was rebuked by the Supreme Court for doing so. In December 2014, the Board split along party lines with three Democrats voting for legislation that would make it easier to form unions while the two Republicans on the Board voted against doing so. The leaders of the House and Senate have vowed to roll back this ruling.

There are many other needed protections for workers as employers increasingly move people from full-time to temporary or contract positions, ensuring they have no rights. Virtually everyone working in the cleaning industry, in a department store, in a franchise outlet or restaurant, delivering packages, and so on, is an at-will employee. It means they have absolutely no rights and can be terminated from employment at any time and for any reason. Employers like the flexibility. Workers, unless their civil rights are violated, have no legal recourse. Other nations do better. In the UK, France, Italy, Germany, Japan, and other industrialized nations employers must show good cause to terminate an employee. Which system would you rather work under?

Universal early childhood education

The benefits of early childhood education extend well into adulthood. Researchers from the University of Minnesota followed 1,400 children up to age 25 who had been enrolled in pre-kindergarten through third grade classes that provided intensive instruction in reading and math, along with frequent educational field trips. The children's parents received job skills training, parenting skills training, and participated in their children's education. The children who participated in this program were more likely to go to college, have higher income levels, and were less likely to end up in prison or to use drugs than those in a control group who did not receive these services.[57]

A related study by Flavio Cunha and James J. Heckman (a Nobel laureate in economics) found that an early investment in the education of disadvantaged children pays high dividends by improving not only their cognitive ability but also traits like sociability, motivation, and self-esteem.[58] These investments need to be made early, even *before* kindergarten. That is because by the age of 5, when most children in the United States start kindergarten, more than half of all poor children do not have the math, reading, or behavioral skills to benefit from kindergarten.[59] The evidence is clear. If we fail to make investments in the early education of disadvantaged children, very few will be able to make up for these educational deficits later in life, with the result that the entire society suffers. But even here, where the evidence seems so compelling, we find political divisions in doing what is right.

With the beginning of the new 2015 legislative session in Montana, the Republican State House Speaker, Austin Knudsen, said that his party would oppose the Democratic Governor's proposal to spend $37 million on early childhood education. His reason was that "children don't benefit over time."[60] Several studies have shown that after these early interventions, most poor children end up where they started—behind the children of middle- and upper-class parents. But the reason they do is clear: they are still stuck in poverty. Other studies have clearly demonstrated that helping children succeed is a long-term effort, which cannot end with kindergarten.[61]

Other options to improve human capital and enhance the ability to act

This could be a very long list. Many have argued the need for universal health insurance, modeled along the lines of Medicare. Because more and more employees are at-will, they are not eligible for unemployment insurance. They should be. Paid vacation time and paid parental leave should also be available. All of these things, and many like them, would make this a much more productive society.

> It is time to "reboot," because our current social, political, and economic systems do not work for the majority of the world's people.

Rebooting Capitalist Society

This work has not been some thinly disguised argument in support of a socialist economy. It is an argument in support of social democracy, a strategy that evolved in the early twenty-first century as a way to improve capitalism.[62] Free schooling, the building of infrastructure, the creation of social safety nets, and health care are all seen as ways to enhance human capacity and economic productivity. Capitalism has its virtues and in its unrelenting drive for efficiency has given some of us inexpensive clothing, food, lights that work when we turn them on, and consumer goods we never imagined would or could be invented. But it does not work for at least 80% of the world's population and does not work for the vast majority of the American population. It does not work when wealth and income are concentrated, or when environmental costs are externalized and when air and water are treated as "free" goods. Capitalism, as its godfather Adam Smith stated, requires checks and balances. Further, it needs to meet the needs of all the planet's inhabitants, not just those who live in wealthy countries.

Do we want to live in a society that squanders human and material resources and thereby limits the options for future generations to meet their needs? I hope not. But what we are doing now, in terms of degrading the environment and heating up the planet, cannot be sustained. To solve the interlocking problems of energy poverty, inequality, and climate change we will need to count on human creativity and our ability to solve problems. To do that, we must maximize human capital. We know how to do this and the solutions are at hand. Now we need the political will to act.

Here is where we can learn from those who have studied revolutions, rebellions, and social movements. As we know from history, nothing is inevitable. Once, the Divine Right of Kings, or the idea that the King was accountable only to God and not the will of the people, was the law of the land in England. Then people grew tired of this oppression and staged a revolution (1649–1660). The French did likewise (1787–1799).[63] In each country citizens were basically *"rebooting" their societies*, or starting over, with a *new* set of laws and principles to make their societies more inclusive and to dampen the power of wealth and privilege.

There were a number of factors that came together and contributed to the success of these revolutions. The sociologist Jack Goldstone identified three destabilizing factors in both countries. First, neither state could meet its financial obligations any longer. Second, there was growing disaffection among squabbling elites. And third, there were a growing number of disaffected groups who were not integrated into the state. All of these factors were exacerbated by rapid population growth that deepened hunger and provided the push that ultimately made the English Revolution a success. In short, in Goldstone's view timing, or the conjunction of these events, was everything.[64]

Another social movement theorist, William Gamson, argued that whether or not a social movement was successful depended on its organizational structure. Did it have the means to deal with setbacks, a leadership group, and resources to keep going?[65] A successful social movement or revolution requires both a strong organization and it needs to seize the moment, as Charles Tilly has pointed out.[66]

Right now the conditions that Goldstone identified are present. We have disaffected populations. In the United States, during the depth of the 1997–1998 economic crisis, 72% of Americans said they believed that hard work could result in riches. By 2014, this number had dropped to 64%. It is anyone's guess how far it will continue to drop. In an interview conducted by the *New York Times* a retired worker in Ohio said, "The decks have been stacked against not only the lower class but also the lower middle class."[67] As I noted in Chapters 5–7, citizens feel the government is ineffective at meeting their needs. The majority stand outside a political system captured by elites. We have also increased complexity to the point where each new problem is solved with diminishing returns on investment. Clearly something must change. Whether it does or not will depend, just as it did during the English and French revolutions, on a willingness to "reboot."

It seems obvious to you and me why we would want to change how we are doing things. However, to build a case with others it might be useful to compare the United States to other developed democracies. Further, it might be interesting to know that the rest of the developed world thinks we are crazy.[68] Why? We do not have universal health care; we have more people in prison per capita than any other country; we have thousands of lobbyists shaping our laws and battalions of tax lawyers writing legislation to assure their clients can protect their wealth and pass it on to the children; we continue to interfere in women's health issues; we don't have universal free preschools; we don't provide paid parental leave; our CEO's are paid 300 to 400 times what the average worker makes; 150 years after the Civil War African-Americans are still discriminated against; we spend trillions of dollars on military adventures that have destabilized nations and entire regions without bringing peace or an end to terrorist activities; we have growing extremes of wealth inequality; we contribute far more than our fair share to the buildup of greenhouse gases in the atmosphere; and many Americans don't accept the findings of science. This seems a lot to change. It is.

In rebooting we would not want to jettison the values that made capitalism possible. As I explained in Chapters 3 and 4, capitalism grew out of the Enlightenment and the values of the Enlightenment are ones to embrace. Reason as opposed to received wisdom, secularism, political freedom, and the concept of private property, have all contributed to social and economic progress. Science, too, arose during the Age of Enlightenment and systematic reasoning slowly gave rise to a deeper understanding of the physical world including ourselves. Science will be critical to helping us find solutions to the challenges we know about, as well as those we cannot anticipate.

Any successful attempt to "reboot" capitalism and manage the problems of energy poverty, inequality, and climate change must of necessity be a multifaceted and long-term effort. But multifaceted does not mean fractured. One goal cannot be pursued at the expense of others. Those who want to stop the burning of coal *must* propose and work for solutions that will include job placement and retraining activities for those who lose their jobs. Other nations have done it.

Where might we start? We could start with the ideals expressed in the Constitution to "promote the general Welfare and secure the Blessings of Liberty to ourselves and our posterity." Or we could turn to the Declaration of Independence[69] as our starting point:

> We hold these truths to be self-evident that all men are created equal, that they are endowed by their Creator with certain unalienable Rights, that among these are Life, Liberty, and the pursuit of Happiness ... That whenever any Form of Government

becomes destructive of these ends, it is the Right of the People to alter or abolish it, and to institute new Government, laying its foundation on such principles and organizing its powers in such form, as to them shall seem most likely to affect their Safety and Happiness.

Whether we turn to the Declaration of Independence or the Constitution, the goal would be to measure our current laws and policies against these principles. Do they lead to a promotion of the general good or not? It is contrary to the ideals on which the country was founded to have 80% of your life chances determined by the family into which you were born. The Constitution and the Declaration hold significant symbolic value for many citizens, especially notions about freedom. We need a strong and consistent narrative grounded in the ideals expressed in the country's founding documents, and we need to use the principles of sustainability and resilience laid out earlier in the chapter in crafting forward-looking policies.

We need reminders that those people President Obama referred to as "clutching their Bibles and guns" have reasons not to see the world the same way you or I might. They may not, for example, see the government as particularly effective in terms of meeting their needs, or they may believe that if somebody is deriving benefits, it is not them. They may argue against "big government," even though these same people derive benefits from public schools, roads, fire protection, and so forth. Cultures of defiance have evolved in opposition to both state and federal government.

There are cultures both in the United States and elsewhere that *fundamentally reject modernism*. Modernism—the wedding of secularism, democracy, and capitalism— crushes traditional societies and erodes "nonrational" values that revolve around personal autonomy, freedom, family, religion, and community. Yet these values remain important not only to a large segment of the American population but also to cultures around the world. *The excesses of capitalism erode the Enlightenment values that gave rise to it.* Part of the pushback against modernism and capitalism involves acting out "freedom" in sometimes bizarre ways. Why do people ride motorcycles without helmets when they can get away with it?

Gamble away their money? Get drunk? Shoot wolves? Run down game with their snowmobiles? It may be the only kind of freedom they have under neoliberal capitalism. So, when we wonder why people don't protect the environment or don't vote their "real" class interests or buy into the arguments of conservative free-market politicians, part of the answer is that this is their idea of freedom.

The concept of freedom must be part of any narrative that seeks to propose alternatives to our current circumstances. To be free must mean to be fully human and to be able to celebrate and create real communities. Yet the concept of freedom has been appropriated by advertising agencies and corporations so that we are "free" to consume their products, whatever they might be and no matter how destructive they might be. We are "free" to explore nature in an SUV. The concept of freedom needs to be taken back to mean, in part, "promote the general Welfare."

Those of us who embrace just part of the concept of sustainability (care for the environment) will find ourselves in conflict with those who need work. We speak about the dignity of good work and the importance of people having good jobs. But coalitions of workers and environmentalists have been difficult to forge. In an earlier chapter I quoted the chair of the Crow Nation, Old Coyote, who said that "the war against coal is a war against the Crow." Environmentalists in Montana, Oregon, and Washington are fighting to prevent the shipping of coal from the Crow reservation to power plants in China, without providing any answer to the Crow's economic needs.

For another example, the Keystone XL Pipeline had, as of January 2015, been discussed and debated for close to a decade. For environmentalists, the pipeline was symbolic of a world fueled by fossil fuel and argued that its construction would be the last straw in a looming climate disaster. Those who favored the pipeline, such as Fox Media, argued that it would create upwards of 20,000 jobs. A report from Cornell University's Global Labor Institute came up with very different numbers. It calculated that the pipeline would create no more than 6,000 jobs and many would include existing Keystone employees and contractors. Only 10–15% of the temporary workforce would be American.[70] Yet it was the message of the Republican Party and Fox Media that gained traction with the public. Sixty-one percent of Americans favored the pipeline's construction, while only 27% opposed it. Among Republicans, 84% favored its construction; 61% of Independents favored it; and among Democrats, 49% were in favor of its being built. Big oil and energy companies keep winning the sustainability argument because of its focus on their jobs.

ExxonMobil issued a 2015 Energy Report that detailed the growing need for fossil fuels,[71] correctly noting that world's energy needs will increase because of new energy demands for growing populations. To save people from having to live in abject poverty, "they need electricity ... They need fuel to cook their food on that's not animal dung ... They'd love to burn fossil fuels, because their quality of life would rise immeasurably," along with their health and that of their children. Note how this debate has been framed.[72] If we really care about the future of the impoverished, we will let the exploration for oil and natural gas go on everywhere—in the Gulf, in the Arctic, anywhere we can find it. Just as in the case of jobs we see a narrative being crafted that poses human needs against those of the environment. This is a false choice.

Science itself has been appropriated to shore up arguments about why fossil fuels are here to stay. For years climate deniers have argued that climate change and global warming were a hoax. Claims were made that scientists were not certain, that their results were in doubt, and that it was too soon to come to any conclusions that would lead to any action. For example, Roger H. Bezdek, president of an energy-consulting firm, argued in an Op-Ed piece that CO_2 is actually good for us. He explains that photosynthesis depends on CO_2 and that "the more CO_2 there is in the air, the better plants grow." Based on such reasoning, his company, in a report for the American Coalition for Clean Coal Electricity, "found that the benefits of carbon dioxide to all of us are far greater than its costs."[73]

Rebooting capitalism, then, will be a massive challenge, because it involves rejecting a free-market ideology that is fueling social inequality, eroding democracy and wrecking the environment. At the same time, we want to embrace the ideas of the Enlightenment and the idea of reason. Reason and science are essential for managing the problems that confront us now and in the future. It needs to be made crystal clear that science is not just another ideology from which we can pick and choose which facts we want to accept and which we want to reject. We need to draw on our Constitution to revive a discussion about what is meant by equality of opportunity and what this means for fairness. We need to use a narrative that resonates with people; one in which community, family, and the rights of the individual are paramount.

There are endless ways to create a fair, democratic, and sustainable society. But first, we need to agree that that's what we must do. That may be the hardest step, because there are people who really do want to take it all—all the money, all the natural resources, all the power. How do we deal with that? The most efficient way is through politics and policy. Environmental laws and regulations were not passed out of the kindness of politician's hearts, but because people mobilized to get them passed. We must mobilize now to keep them; there are members of the Senate and the House who want to roll them back. They are determined that public lands, our air, and our water should be up for grabs. They want to roll back challenges to the free market and remove regulations on Wall Street. What can you or I do and what do you say to the person on the elevator who believes the system we now have works?

The Elevator Speech

- European social democracies are not a mess. They don't restrict your freedom. People are happy. They even have health care for everybody.
- People living in countries where people have less money than we do live longer and happier lives. Think about that.
- Learn to distinguish between your wants and your needs.
- Pay attention to the ways other people have needs that are not being met.
- Read both the *Wall Street Journal* and the *New York Times* for a month and then answer the question: Is the game rigged?
- Nobody can "take it all," because the systems on which we depend for life will collapse.
- Vote. Get others to vote.
- All politics is compromise. Stop voting for politicians who vow to never compromise.
- Get involved in an organization committed to changing something, no matter what it is.

- Everyone needs respect and everyone needs to be able to participate in the societies in which they live.
- Solve the social, economic and environmental problems in your own backyard first. Then, if you have time left over, focus elsewhere.
- Ask yourself how power happens. How do people acquire ideological, political, economic, and military power and how do they keep it?
- We will not get to where we need to be by recycling cans and bottles or eating organic vegetables. We need to *recycle our values*.

Notes

1. Linda Tirado. 2014. *Hand to Mouth: Living in Bootstrap America*. New York, NY: G.P. Putnam's Sons.
2. Ibid., p.xvii.
3. Ibid., p.25.
4. Manfred Max-Neef. 2014. "Fundamental Human Needs." *Wikipedia*. Retrieved on December 31, 2014 at: http://en.wikipedia.org/wiki/Fundamental_human_needs.
5. Safa Motesharrei, Jorge Rivas, and Eugenia Kalnay. 2012. "A Minimal Model for Human and Nature Interaction."
6. Ibid., p.7.
7. Richard F. York, Eugene A. Rosa, and Thomas Dietz. 2003. "STIRPAT, IPAT, and ImPACT: Analytic Tools for Unpacking the Driving Forces of Environmental Economics." *Ecological Economics*. 46(3): 351–365.
8. Joseph A. Tainter. 1988. *The Collapse of Complex Societies*. New York, NY: Cambridge University Press; see also Charles Tainter. 1996. "Complexity, Problem Solving, and Sustainable Societies." In Robert Costanza, Olman Segura and Juan Martinez Altier, eds, *Getting Down to Earth: Practical Applications of Ecological Economics*. Washington, DC: Island Press. The paper is available at: http://dieoff.org/page134.htm.
9. Tainter. 1996, "Complexity, Problem Solving."
10. Ibid.
11. Donella H. Meadows, Dennis L. Meadows, Jorgen Randers, William W. Behrens III. 1972. *Limits to Growth*. New York, NY: Universe Books.
12. Watson Institute for International Studies. 2014. "Costs of War." Providence, RI: Brown University Press. Retrieved on December 16, 2014 at: http://costsofwar.org/article/economic-cost-summary. See also: Joseph E. Stiglitz and Linda J. Bilmes. 2008. *The Three Trillion Dollar War: The True Cost of the Iraq Conflict*. New York, NY: W. W. Norton.
13. See James Meek's 2014 review of four books on the war in Afghanistan. "Worse than a Defeat." *London Review of Books*.
14. Ed Dolan. 2013. "Ten Years on, New Estimates of the Economic Costs of the Wars in Iraq." Retrieved on December 16 at: http://www.economonitor.com/dolanecon/2013/03/18/ten-years-on-new-estimates-of-the-economic-cost-of-the-wars-in-iraq-and-afghanistan-2/.
15. Cited in David Cole. 2015. "Must Counterterrorism Cancel Democracy?" *New York Review of Books*. January 8: 26–28.

16 *The Economist.* 2015. "Robber Barons and Silicon Sultans." January 3. Retrieved August 15, 2014 from: http://www.economist.com/news/briefing/21637338-todays-tech-billionaires-have-lot-common-previous-generation-capitalist.
17 Robert Kocher and Nikhil R. Sahni. 2011. "Rethinking Health Care Labor." *New England Journal of Medicine* 365: 1370–1372.
18 A number of these insights come from work I did with my colleague and friend, George Basile. See our collective piece: Scott G. McNall and George Basile. 2013. "Challenges in Creating Resilient and Sustainable Societies." In Stephan A. Jansen, Eckhard Schröter, and Nico Stehr, eds., *Fragile Stability: Stable Fragility.* Wiesbaden, Germany: Springer.
19 Tainter. 1996. "Complexity, Problem Solving." p.14.
20 Ibid., p.13.
21 John Doyle and Marie Csete. 2011. "Architecture, Constraints, and Behavior." *Publications of the National Academy of Science.* 10(1073): 1–7; Fiona Chandra, Gentian Buzi, and John C. Doyle. 2011. "Glycolytic Oscillations and Limits on Robust Efficiency." *Science.* 333: 187–192; David L. Alderson and John C. Doyle. 2010. "Contrasting Views of Complexity and Their Implications for Network-Centric Infrastructures." *IEEE Transactions on Systems, Man, and Cybernetics.* 40(4), July: 839–852.
22 James Glanz. 2012. "Power, Pollution, and the Internet." *New York Times.* September 22. Retrieved on December 31. 2014 at: http://www.nytimes.com/2012/09/23/technology/data-centers-waste-vast-amounts-of-energy-belying-industry-image.html?pagewanted percent3Dall&_r=0.
23 It is also the case that a system can appear stable but may be in a state of transition to a more stable and more equitable state, or the reverse—more unstable and more inequitable. The problem is identifying where a system is on the curve.
24 Servaas van der Berg and Megan Louw. 2003. "Changing Patterns of South African Income Distribution: Towards Time Series Estimates of Distribution and Poverty." Paper presented at the Conference of the Economic Society of South Africa. September 17–19. The paper is available online and is useful for its detailed analysis of sources and changes in income. It also clearly demonstrates the difficultly of answering questions about an emergent middle class, and the development of the economy.
25 See the Gini coefficient for South Africa, which measures income inequality. Retrieved on July 12, 2012 at: http://data.worldbank.org/indicator/SI.POV.GINI/.
26 Kenneth Arrow, Bert Bolin, Robert Costanza, Partha Dasgupta, Carl Folke, C.S. Holling, Bengt-Owe Jansson, Simon L. Levin, Karl-Göran Mäler, Charles Perrings, and David Pimentel. 1995. "Economic Growth, Carrying Capacity, and the Environment." *Science.* 268: 520–521.
27 Nassim Nicholas Taleb. 2010. *The Black Swan: Impact of the Highly Improbable,* 2nd ed. New York, NY: Random House.
28 See, for example, James Lovelock. 2006. *The Revenge of Gaia: Why Earth is Fighting Back—and How We Can Still Save Humanity.* Santa Barbara, CA: Allen Lane.
29 Merlina Missimer, Karl-Henrik Robèrt, Görman Broman, and Harald Sverdrup. 2010. "Exploring the Possibility of a Systematic and Generic Approach to Social Sustainability." *Journal of Clean Products.* 10: 1016.
30 Gro Harlem Brundtland. 1987. *Our Common Future.* New York, NY: The United Nations, p.41. Retrieved on December 16, 2014 at: http://www.un-documents.net/our-common-future.pdf.

31 Ibid., p.16.
32 The Natural Step. 2014. Retrieved on December 16 at: http://www.naturalstep.org/.
33 City of Madison, Wisconsin. 2014. They have adopted the principles of The Natural Step and provide examples of how these can be implemented. Retrieved on December 16, 2014 at: https://www.cityofmadison.com/Sustainability/naturalStep/index.cfm.
34 Scott Price. 2005. *A Bright Light on the Darkest of Days: The U.S. Coast Guard's Response to Hurricane Katrina.* Washington, DC: U.S. Coast Guard. Scott Price was the Deputy Historian for the Coast Guard and his report is based on first-hand accounts and interviews of participants; see also "The Select Bipartisan Committee to Investigate the Preparation for and Response to Hurricane Katrina." 2006. *A Failure of Initiative.* Washington, DC: U.S. Government Printing Office.
35 Ibid., pp.21–22.
36 Ibid., p.40.
37 Ibid., p.52.
38 Select Bipartisan Committee. 2006. *A Failure of Initiative.* p.81.
39 Select Bipartisan Committee. 2006. *A Failure of Initiative.* p.6.
40 Alan Feuer. 2014. "Building for the Next Big Storm." *New York Times.* October 26: 28–29.
41 Elaine Kurtenbach. 2012. "Japan Used Rebuilding Money on Unrelated Projects." *Associated Press,* October 31. Retrieved on December 11, 2014 at: http://bigstory.ap.org/article/japans-rebuilding-money-spent-unrelated-jobs.
42 Katharine Herrup. 2011. "Boatlifters: The Unknown Story of 9/11." Reuters, September 9. Retrieved on December 11, 2014 at: http://blogs.reuters.com/katharine-herrup/2011/09/09/boatlifters-the-unknown-story-of-911/.
43 Alexis de Tocqueville. 1835 (1999). *Democracy in America,* Vol.1. New York, NY: Signet.
44 See, e.g.: Lane Kenworthy. 2014. *Social Democracy in America.* New York, NY: Oxford University Press; and Thomas Piketty. 2014. *Capital in the Twenty-First Century.* Cambridge, MA: Harvard University Press.
45 Joseph A. Stiglitz. 2011. "Of the 1 percent, by the 1 percent, for the 1 percent." *Vanity Fair.* May. Retrieved on December 22, 2014 at: http://www.vanityfair.com/society/features/2011/05/top-one-percent-201105.
46 George Will. 2014. "The Cheerfulness of Coming Tax Reform." December 16. *Missoulian.* p.B4.
47 Signe-Mary McKernan, Caroline Ratcliffe, and Stephanie R. Cellini. 2014. "Transitioning in and Out of Poverty." Washington, DC: Urban Institute. Retrieved on December 17, 2014 at: http://www.urban.org/publications/411956.html.
48 Joseph A. Stiglitz. 2012. *The Price of Inequality: How Today's Divided Society Endangers Our Future.* New York, NY: W.W. Norton.
49 Claire Cain Miller. 2014. "As Robots Grow Smarter, American Workers Struggle to Keep Up." *New York Times.* December 15. Retrieved on December 22, 2014 at: http://freerepublic.com/focus/f-news/3238688/posts.
50 Center for Responsive Politics. 2014. Retrieved on December 18, 2014 at: http://www.opensecrets.org/news/2012/10/2012-election-spending-will-reach-6/.
51 John McCain and Mark Salter. 2003. *Worth the Fighting For: The Education of an American Maverick, and the Heroes Who Inspired Him.* New York, NY: Random House.

52 Citizens United v. Federal Election Commission, 558 U.S. (2010). Retrieved on August 28 at: https://supreme.justia.com/cases/federal/us/558/08-205/.
53 Thomas Brunell. 2012. *Redistricting and Representation: Why Competitive Elections Are Bad for America.* New York, NY: Routledge.
54 Trip Gabriel. 2014. "In a Break from Partisan Rancor, Ohio Moves to Make Elections More Competitive." *New York Times.* December 21, A25.
55 Ronald Weitzer. 1996. "Racial Discrimination in the Criminal Justice System: Findings and Problems in the Literature." *Journal of Criminal Justice.* 24(4): 309–322.
56 Alan Barber. 2012. "Labor Rights in Canada and the United States." Washington, DC: Center for Economic and Policy Research. Retrieved on December 18, 2014 at: http://www.cepr.net/index.php/press-releases/press-releases/labor-rights-in-canada-and-the-united-states.
57 Arthur J. Reynolds, Judy A. Temple, et al. "School-Based Early Childhood Education and Age-28 Well-Being: Effects of Timing, Dosage, and Subgroups." *Science.* 333 (6040): 360–364.
58 Flavio Cunha and James J. Heckman. 2010. "Investing in Our Young People." Cambridge, MA: National Bureau of Economic Research.
59 Julia Isaacs. 2012. "Falling Behind Before the First Day of School: The School Readiness of Poor Children." Washington, DC: The Urban Institute. Retrieved on December 22 at: http://blog.metrotrends.org/2012/08/falling-day-school-school-readiness-poor-children/.
60 Martin Kidston. 2014. "Resource Extraction, Charter Schools, Tax Relief Top GOP Agenda." *Missoulian.* December 30: A1,4.
61 For a summary and reference to these studies see: Ron Haskins. 2014. "Social Programs that Work." *The New York Times.* December 31. Retrieved on January 2, 2015 at: http://www.nytimes.com/2015/01/01/opinion/social-programs-that-work.html?_r=0.
62 Kenworthy. 2014. *Social Democracy in America.* p.8.
63 There are a number of ways of dating the English and French Revolutions, as they extended over several years. Some date the English Revolution as beginning in the First Civil War of 1647–1649 driven by tensions over religious freedom. Others date he beginning of the Revolution in 1649 when Charles I was executed. There was a continued back-and-forth between the old ruling classes and those who advocated for new ideas, such as the right of private property and personal freedom. The French Revolution also did not take place with one event but evolved over several years with a constant clash but evolving clash between parties with rival political and economic interests. The larger point, however, is that in both cases people were able to transform the very nature of their societies by making them more inclusive. They rebooted their societies, hanging on to those values and ideas they valued at the same time as they embraced new ones.
64 Jack Goldstone. 1993. *Revolution and Rebellion in the Early Modern World.* Berkeley: University of California Press.
65 William Gamson. 1975. *The Strategy of Social Protest.* Belmont, CA: Wadsworth.
66 Charles Tilly. 2003. *States, Parties, and Social Movements.* Boulder, CO: Paradigm.
67 Andrew Ross Sorkin and Megan Thee-Brenan. 2014. "Many Feel the American Dream Is Out of Reach, Poll Shows." *The New York Times.* December 10. Retrieved on January 2, 2015 at: http://dealbook.nytimes.com/2014/12/10/many-feel-the-american-dream-is-out-of-reach-poll-shows/.

68 Ann Jones. 2015. "Is This Country Crazy?" January 11. TomDispatch.com. Retrieved on January 12, 2014 at: http://www.tomdispatch.com/post/175941/tomgram:_ann_jones,_answering_for_america/.
69 United States Government Archives. "Declaration of Independence." Retrieved on August 28 at: http://www.archives.gov/exhibits/charters/declaration_transcript.html.
70 Cornell University, Global Labor Institute. 2015. "Employment Facts: The Keystone XL Pipeline." Retrieved on January 12, 2014 at: http://priceofoil.org/content/uploads/2011/09/CU_KeystoneXL_090711_FIN2.pdf.
71 Exxon-Mobil. 2015. *The Outlook for Energy: A View to 2040*. Retrieved on January 12, 2014 at: http://corporate.exxonmobil.com/en/energy/energy-outlook/download-the-report/download-the-outlook-for-energy-reports.
72 Michael T. Klare. 2015. "Carbon Counterattack." *TomDispatch.com*. Retrieved on January 8, 2014 at: http://www.tomdispatch.com/post/175940/tomgram percent3A_michael_klare percent2C_perpetuating_the_reign_of_carbon/.
73 Roger H. Bezdek. 2015. "Carbon Dioxide, Despite the EPA's Word Games, Is Profoundly Earth-Friendly." January 11. *Missoulian*. E6.

INDEX

absolute mobility 43–44
absolute poverty 5
absolute surplus value 82
Acemoglu, Daron 122–3
Act 10, Wisconsin 207–8
adaptation 249; creative 250–5
affluence *see* wealth
Affordable Care Act 220
Africa: and good governments 143; resource allocation based on tribal and ethnic groupings 8
African-Americans: experience with the judicial system 146; wages of union members 201–2
African National Congress (ANC) 238
Aftershock (Reich) 95
Aldrich, Daniel 117
ALEC 216–19
Alexander VI, Pope 68
al-Sisi, Abdel Fattah 3
Amazonian basin and outmigration 65
American Crossroads 261
American exceptionalism 221–3
Americans for Prosperity 216, 261
Amin, Idi 173

amoral familism 131
Angola 140
Anti-Corn Law League 79
Appeal, The (Grisham) 182–3
Apple (company) 106
Arab Spring (2010–2011) 21, 175
Aristide, Jean-Bertrand 122
Arrow, Kenneth 241
Asian countries losing face 9
associations: impacting economy and democracy 129–30; not influencing trust and democracy 143–4
automation driving inequality 260
autonomous trust networks 178–9
autonomy, need for 7

Bacon, Francis 69
Banfield, Edward 131
basic human needs 4–6, 231–2; being met by economic systems 65
Basile, George 241
Believing Brain, The (Shermer) 197
Bell, Daniel 100
belonging, sense of 18, 20
Ben Ali, Zine El Adbidine 175

Bengal Famine of 1943 8
Benjamin, Brent 183
Berbers, discrimination against 17
Berman, Rick 212
Bernstein, William 72
Berwick, Daniel M. 182
Beyoncé 37
Bezek, Roger H. 272
Big Diamond Jim 162
Bipartisan Campaign Reform Act of 2002 262
Birth of Plenty, The (Bernstein) 72
Black Death 67
Black Swan, The (Taleb) 242
Blankenship, Don 183
Blow, Charles M. 17
Boccaccio, Giovanni 67
Boehner, John 214
Boeing 209–10
bonding social capital 126, 128
border crossing from Mexico to the United States 240–1
Boss Tweed 160–3, 167, 183–4
Botswana 140
Bouazizi, Mohammed 175
bounded rationality theory 19
Bourdieu, Pierre 134
Bowling Alone (Putnam) 129
Breyer, Stephen G. 218
bridging social capital 126, 129–33, 135
Britain's changes in degree of wealth 33
Brosnan, Sarah 12
Brown, Michael, shooting death of 145–6
Buffett, Warren 42
Buhaug, Halvard 142
Bush, George H. W. 149
Bush, George W. 48, 106, 149

Calvinism influencing growth of capitalism 72–3
Calvin, John 72–3
campaign donations 85, 261–2; by corporations 218
Canada and union membership 203
capability approach to meeting human needs 8, 19
capital: concentration of 93; human 19, 30, 101, 125, 135–9, 152, 255–66; overaccumulation 94; social 19; transformation of the form of 94
capital gains tax 41
capitalism 12–13; addition to growth 92, 93; causing inequality 101–6; consolidation and centralization of markets 93; crises of 91–95; degrading ecosystems 64–66, 86, 106–9; falling rate of profit 91–92; finding buyers in other countries 93; and globalization 109–10; growth due to Calvinism 72–73; improving the economy 259–60; increasing poverty and social inequality 220; and inequality 63–87; influence on culture 98; originating from the Enlightenment 66, 71–73; to produce profit 92–93; rebooting 267–73; resilience of 95–97; as response to feudalism 66; role of government 98–100; state 110; survival of 97–101; views of Adam Smith 75–77; views of David Ricardo 77–79; views of Karl Marx 80–85
Capitalism, Socialism, and Democracy (Schumpeter) 97
Card, David 212
Card-Krueger study over minimum wage 212
Carnegie, Andrew 34, 43, 166
Carter, Jimmy 149
Casselman, Ben 201
Castle Rock 204
caste system and distrust 124
categorical inequalities 11, 12–13
Catholic Church during the Enlightenment 68

Center on Wisconsin Strategy (COWS) 214
Central African Republic 7; corruption and inequality 139–40
CEOs as top income earners 36–38
Chad and corruption 139–40
Chang, Leslie T. 83
charter schools 50
cheerleading squads suing over unfair labor practices 210–11
Cheney, Stephen 153
Chetty, Raj 44
childhood education, early 265–6
China: class impacting marital patterns 50–51; climate change and poverty 54–55; corruption in 174–5, 185; decline in poverty 33; dictatorships 142; economy of 34; income inequality 39–40; irrelevant criteria for placing people in society 178; and renewable energy resources 244; reversing democracy 3
Citizens United v. Federal Election Commission 85, 181, 218
civic associations 126–7; and the Nazi party 132
civic cooperation related to social capital 129–30
civic nation 140
Clark, Gregory 44
class 14; background impacting marital patterns 50–52; division in the U.S. 166–7; loyalty to 150
climate change 22, 186; impact on the poor 111–12; linked to poverty and affluence 54–56; readiness for 152–3; related to political disorder 153
Clinton, Chelsea 14
closed economy 11, 13
closed political structure 11, 13
Coca-Cola 93
cognitive dissonance 199
Coleman, James 125
college graduation rates 47

colonization resulting in income inequalities 73–74
commodities, value of 80–81
community 223; collective commitment of 117–18; resilience of 248–9
competitive advantage theory 77
complexity and increased energy requirements 237–42
Condition of the Working Class in England (Engels) 96
Conestabile, Carlo 131
Congressional Budget Office (CBO) 214–15
contractors, independent 209
Cooper, David 214
Corker, Bob 206
Corn Laws 78–80
corporations donating to political candidates 218
corruption: costs of 168–9; effects of 186–7; in health care system and military 181–2; and low trust 142; negatively correlated with democracy 139–40, 176–8; normative 169–76; rise of and social instability 163–8; and social inequality 138–40, 160–87
countries *see also* specific ones: comparison of student performances 46–47; destabilized by illegal immigration 10, 35; treating citizens equally 3; wealth and income gaps between 33–35
Crassus, Marcus 34
creative adaptation 250–5
creative destruction 97
creativity to manage problems 249
crime and low trust 142
cult of optimism 149
Cunha, Flavio 266

Dawisha, Karen 39
democracy: associated with membership in associations 128–9; based on trust 126–7; and capitalism 96; challenges to 178–

83; countries lacking 176–8; destroyed by social inequality and corruption 185; and ethnic fractionalization 141; and high levels of trust and engagement 144; impacted by inequality 52–53, 85, 138–40; improving 257–66; lack of support in Haiti 123; liberal 110; necessity for meeting human needs 21; negatively correlated with corruption 139–40; negatively correlated with inequality 139; not influenced by participation in associations 143–4; reversal of rights 3; and trust networks 142–3

Democratic People's Republic of North Korea *see* North Korea

Democratic Republic of Congo 74–75

democratic societies 2–3; meeting subjective needs 8; right to satisfaction of universal human needs 7; and working together for the common good 125

Democrats 161, 165, 221; trust in the government 146, 148; view on poverty 17; vision for the future 196

Demoura, Antonio 134–5

Department of Homeland Security (DHS) 253

Der, Ziem 30–31

developing countries *see also* specific ones: basic needs of 4–5; graft and corruption 13

development index of society 108

Dickens, Charles 96

Dinka in conflict with Nuer 10–11

disaster: planning 253–4; response by Haiti 120–4; response by Japan 115–18; social inequality affecting response to 118–20

discrimination 9; ethnic and political unrest 142

divine right of kings 68, 70

division of labor 76

Downey, Robert Jr. 37

Downton Abbey Syndrome 102

Doyal, Len 7
Doyle, John 238
durable inequalities 10, 21–22
Duvalier, Francois 122
Duvalier, Jean-Claude 122

early childhood education 265–6
earned income tax credit (EITC) 42
ecology 111–12; impacted by capitalism 106–9
economic crisis of 2007–2008 96
economic growth: and cutting taxes on the wealthy 41–42; decreasing optimism in 147–8; and rate of return on capital 104–5
economy: and capitalism 65, 78–79, 92–93, 97–112, 259–60; of China 34; closed 11, 13; commodity based 94; driven by associational behavior 130; and environmentalism 244–6; and Italy 130–3; and labor 204, 218–20; and role of associations 129–30; role of government in stimulating 99–100; of the world 73–74
education: cost of educating a child shifted to individual family 47–49; inequality of 45–50, 53; negatively impacted by poverty 50
educational achievements gap 45–46
Egypt: reversing democracy 3; revolution in 21, 176
Eisenhower, Dwight 159
elite panic 118–20
Ellison, Larry 38, 104
employer-employee relationship changed due to outsourcing 208–9
employment and effect of increase in minimum wage 211–15
Employment Policies Institute (EPI) 211–12
Endless Crisis, The (Foster and McChesney) 93
End of History, The (Fukuyama) 110

endogamy 14
energy: renewable resources 244–6; requirement for nations 108; use increased with system complexity 238–42; use in the world 54–55
energy capture factor 108
energy poverty 22, 54–55
Engels, Friedrich 96
England and growth of capitalism 72
Enlightenment 66–73; and capitalism 66, 71–73
entrepreneurs as top income earners 37
environmentalism 271–2; and the economy 244–5
equality: and coalition of anti-unionists 216–19; education 46; racial 194; and trust and social capital 124–6; women 195
Equal Rights Amendment 195
Equatorial Guinea's corrupt regime 177
equity 249
Eritrea's corrupt regime 177
Espaillat, Adriano 150
Essay on the Principle of Population, An (Malthus) 77
estate taxes 43
ethnic fractionalization and absence of the rule of law 140–2
ethnicity: discrimination and political unrest 142; and divisions in society 128; homogeneity and trust 142; with inequality reduces trust 142; loyalty to 150; tensions 10–11
ethnic nation, rise of 140–3
exceptionalism, American 221–3
exchange value 81
exclusion, sense of 18, 20
exploitation: of the periphery 73–75; of production and distribution 12

fairness 10, 11–12
fair society: being a just society 2; defined 2–3

falling rate of profit 91–92, 94
family structure influencing social mobility 52
Fannie Mae 179–80
Farm Bill 258
Feingold, Russ 262
Ferguson, Niall 151
financial collapse of 2007/2008 179–80
financialization of capital 94–95
First and Second Treatise of Government (Locke) 70
Fisk, James 162
Ford, Henry 98
fossil fuels 272
Foster, John Bellamy 93, 94
fraternal organizations and trust 127–8
Freddie Mac 179–80
freedom: to achieve well-being 7, 8; concept of 271; lack of and inequality 138–9
Freedom House 3
free-market 76–77, 194–5
Friedman, Milton 81
Fukushima 116, 239, 254
Fukuyama, Francis 110, 179
Funston, Frederick 119

Gamson, William 268
Gates, Bill 43
Gazzangia, Michael 197
gender as basis of inequality 10, 12, 17
General Electric 106
General Theory of Employment, Interest, and Money (Keynes) 98
genocide caused by religious and ethnic tensions 10–11
Germinal (Zola) 96
Gilens, Martin 181
Gini coefficient 40, 53, 101, 118, 147
Gini, Corrado 101
global-adaptation index for climate change 152–3

globalization: and capitalism 109–10; driving inequality 260
Gluck, Carol 117
Goldin, Claudia 46
Goldstone, Jack 267–8
Goodwin, William 71
Gough, Ian 7
Gould, Jay 162, 166
government: dependency on 219–20; distrust in 146–9; and free-market 194–5; lack of dependency on 193, 195–6; linked with Wall Street 179–80; policy and social mobility 44; resilience of 248–9; role during the scientific revolution 70; role in a stimulating a economy 99–100; and trust 132, 143
Goyal, Piyush 54
graduation rates from colleges 47
Grant, Ulysses S. 165
Grassroots Policy Strategies 261
Great Britain and their wealthy 39
Great Famine of 1317 67
Great Society Program 193–5
Great Transformation, The (Polyani) 97
Great Wall of China 240
green economy 244–6
greenhouse gas emissions (GHGs) 54–55
Greenhouse, Steven 207
Grisham, John 182

Hackbart, Andrew D. 182
Hadenya 117
Haiti: lack of support for democracy 123; lack of trust 124; social inequality resulting in corruption and mistrust 120–4
Hand to Mouth: Living in Bookstrap America (Tirado) 231
Hargraeves, James 106
Harvey, David 95
Haslam, Bill 206
Hayek, Friedrich 98–99, 111
health care system: corruption in 182; costs 236–7

Heckman, James J. 266
hedonism 100
Henry, James 40–41
Henry VIII, king of England 68
Herzer, Dierk 41
Hesse, Daniel R. 38
high-status groups 19–20
Hispanics and wages of union members 202
historical memories 11, 133–4
history, revising 199
Hobbes, Thomas 70
Hoffman, John 162
Hollander, Barry 151
human capital 19, 30, 101, 125, 152; being human in a society 4; costs of being human in a society 7–8; improving 257–66; increasing individual 255–6; increasing level of 135–6; loss of 136–9
Human Development Index (HDI) 136
human needs 4–12; for autonomy 7; basic 4–6, 231–2; capability approach 8; classification of 4, 6; failure to meet through discrimination 8–9; for health 7; Maslow's hierarchy of needs 4; objective 6; protection 6–7; subjective 6, 8; subsistence 5, 6; universal 6, 7
human rights violations in North Korea 177–8
hunger as component of poverty 30
Hungerford, Thomas 41
Hurricane Katrina 239, 241–2; responding to 250–3
Hurricane Sandy 254

illegal immigration destabilizing a country 10, 35
Illinois curbing labor unions 13
immigration: illegal destabilizing country 10, 35; opposition to 164–6
income: influencing educational achievements 45–46; and poverty 29; top 1% earners 36–40

income inequality 101–4, 201–2, 208–9, 258; increased cost in maintaining 238–9; increase in 52–53, 147–8
inconvenient truths, ignoring 198–200
independent contractors 209
India: British Colonial 8; climate change and poverty 54; decline in poverty 33
individualism 195–6; *versus* the state 99
industrial class 78
industrialization's negative impact 96
inequality *see* social inequality
Inequality-Adjusted Human Development Index (IHDI) 136
inequity 101, 257; caused by capitalism 101–6; and economic crisis of 2007–2008 96; *versus* inequality 9–10
information technology 108
instability accelerant 153
International Brotherhood of Pulp, Sulfite, and Paper Mill Workers 200–1
Ireland's corporate tax rate 106
Irish Catholics, discrimination against 164–5
irrevocable trust 43
Italy's differences in economy and civic cooperation 130–3

Jacker, Jacob 181
James, LeBron 36
Japan's response to natural disasters 115–18
Jaquelin Hume Foundation 204
Jiaboa, Wen 175
Jihad to gain autonomy 8
Jinping, Xi 174
jobs, availability of 259–60
Jobs, Steve 43
Johnson, James 179–80
Johnson, Lyndon 193
Jonathan, Goodluck 171–2
Judt, Tony 52
just society being fair 2

Kanter, Rosabeth Moss 19
Katz, Lawrence 46

Kenya's discrimination by elected officials 11
Kerry, John 11
Keynes, John Maynard 98, 110
Keystone XL pipeline 271–2
Kilpatrick, Kwame 150
King, Bob 206
King, Marcus 153
Kirn, Walter 19–20
Klein, Naomi 119
Klitgaard, Robert 168
Knights of Labor 166
know-nothing movement 164, 166
Knudsen, Austin 266
Koch, Charles 85
Koch, David 85
Kornrich, Sabino 45
Kristof, Nicholas 55
Krueger, Alan 212
Kuklinski, James 199

labor as a commodity 80–81
labor movement 12–13, 166
labor power 81–83
labor theory of value 71, 81
labor time 92
Lafer, Gordon 216
Lake, Celinda 213
Landes, David 72
landlords as parasites 78
languages, multiple and ethnic fractionalization 140
Lazzarini, Sergio 110
Leopold II, king of Belgium 74–75
Leviathan (Hobbes) 70
Lewis, Al 100
liberal democracy 110
Li, Cheng 175
Limits to Growth (Meadows) 235
living wage 19, 217
Living Wage Mandate Preemption Act 217
Llanos, Angélica Navarro 56
Locke, John 70
losing face in Asia 9
Lovelock, James 243

low-status groups 18–20
Lundberg, Shelly 51
Luther, Martin 68

Madison, Angus 33
Malawi and poverty 31–32
Malthus, Thomas 77–78
Mankiw, N. Gregory 43
Marcos, Ferdinand 13
marginal productivity theory 100
marginal tax rate 41
Margulis, Lynn 243
market fundamentalism 195–6, 199–200, 219–21
markets, consolidation and centralization of 93
marriage: influencing social mobility 50–52; rationale for 51–52
Marshall, George 55–56
Martelly, Michel 122
Marx, Karl 4, 71, 77, 80–86, 259; criticism of capitalism 91–93, 99
Maslow, Abraham 4
Maslow's hierarchy of needs 4
Masonic Brotherhood 127–8
Massey Coal 183
Max-Neef, Manfred 6
McCain-Feingold Act 262
McCain, John 262
McChesney, Robert W. 93, 94
McConnell, Mitch 262
McCutcheon v. Federal Election Commission 218
McKay, Kimber Haddix 124
Meadows, Donella 235
Medina, Jennifer 15
Mettler, Suzanne 48
Mexico's corruption 186–7
microagressions 9
micro-inequities 9
Middle East's religious and ethnic tensions 10
Milanovic, Branko 34, 104

military: corruption in 182; support of 221–2, 235–6
millennials and trust 146
minimum wage 19; debate over raising 210–16, 259
Mishel, Lawrence 201
Missimer, Merlina 243
mobility in society 43–45, 50–52
modernism 270
Monroe Doctrine 74
Moore, Jason 109
More, Thomas 68–69
Morgensen, Gretchen 179
Morris, Ian 87, 107
Mubarak, Hosni 13, 21, 176
Mugabe, Robert 173
Muller, Jerry 109
Musacchio, Aldo 110
Museveni, Yoweri 173–4

narratives: incompatible 219–23; of power 192–224; simplifying 199–200
Nast, Thomas 164
nationalism 222–3; due to anti-immigrant fervor 164–6
National Right to Work Committee 204
National Right to Work Legal Defense Foundation 204
Nation at Risk, A (Reagan) 49
Natural Step 245–6
Nazi party and civic associations 132
necessary labor time 92
neoliberal economic theory 99–100, 196
Nepal's level of distrust 124
Netherlands' changes in degree of wealth 33
Neumark, David 212
Newton, Isaac 69
New Zealand's labor movement 13
Nigeria 7; inequality and corruption 170–2
Nixon, Richard 149, 264
No Child Left Behind Act (2002), 48
Nogales, Arizona 122–3

Nogales, Mexico 122–3
normative corruption 169–76
Norris, Frank 96
North Korea: corruption in 185; lack of democracy in 177–8
Nuer in conflict with Dinka 10–11
Nussbaum, Martha 8
Nyhan, Brendan 199

Obama, Barack 85, 149, 196–7, 221–2, 261, 265
Obamacare 220
objective needs 6
O'Brien, James 162
Olin Foundation 204
open primaries 262–3
Operation Uphold Democracy 122
opportunity hoarding 11, 13
O'Rourke, Matthew J. 162
overproduction of goods 92–94
overseas operations as tax shelters 106
oxytocin improving trust 198

Packer, George 198
Page, Larry 260
Palin, Sarah 199
Paradise Built in Hell, A (Solnit) 118
Parese, James 255
patriarchal societies and lack of autonomy 8
Pepsi 93
Perlstein, Rick 149
Philippon, Thomas 94
physiological stage in hierarchy of needs 4
Pickett, Kate 185
Pierre-Val, Manouchcar 210
Pierson, Paul 181
Piketty, Thomas 39, 102, 104–6, 111
Pinker, Steven 2
police shootings, fatal 145–6
political action committees (PACs) 181
political unrest caused by corruption 175
politicians being influenced by the wealthy 179–83

politics: and corruption 160–5; linked with volunteer fire departments 161; and monetary donations 261–2; rejecting facts contradictory to beliefs 199
Pollak, Robert 51
Polyani, Karl 97, 111
population growth theory 77–78
poverty 53, 243, 259; absolute 5; being painful and humiliating 26–28; consequences of 30–32; decline in 33; as driver of climate change 54–55; energy 22, 54–55; extreme 32; impacting getting an education 50; leading to distrust 146; multidimensional 29; nature of 28–32; reducing 220–1; relative 5–6; self-reinforcing 16–17; varying among countries 29–30; views on causes of 17–19
predestination 73
price markup 94
primaries, open 262–3
Principia Mathematica (Newton) 69
prison reform 263–4
private property 70–71
production 12, 14, 65–66, 76–79, 91–94; social relations of 84–85
profit: distribution of 82–84, 86; falling rate of 91–92, 94; increasing in capitalism 81–83; producing 92–93
protection as a human need 6–7
public lands being turned over to states 218
public sector union benefits 207
purchasing power parity (PPP) 34
Putin, Vladimir 168, 174, 185
Putnam, Robert 129–30, 143

race: as basis of inequality 10–11, 12; division in the U.S. 145–6; equality 194; inequality in wages 201–2; riots 194
racism due to anti-immgrant fervor 164–6

Ramos, Nelva Gonzales 219
Range, Frederike 11
Rangel, Charles 150
rate of return on capital and economic growth 104–5
Rawls, John 2
Reagan, Ronald 49, 99, 192–5
Reardon, Sean F. 45
Recept Tayyip Erdogdan 3
redistricting voting areas 262–3
Reich, Robert 95, 179, 180, 220–1
Reifler, Jason 199
relative mobility 44
relative poverty 5–6
relative surplus value 84
religion as basis of inequality 10, 12
rent-control in New York 9
Republicans 106, 194, 221; corruption 161–4, 183; trust in the government 146, 148; against unionization 206–7; view on poverty 17; vision for the future 196
resilience 242–3, 250–7; rules of 248–9
"Resolution Demanding that Congress Convey Title of Federal Public Lands to the States," 218
Reynolds, David 140
Ricardo, David 71, 77–79, 86, 92, 100, 103
rich *see* wealthy
Ridgeway, Cecilia 15
right-to-work laws 203–4
Road to Serfdom, The (Hayek) 99
Robinson, James 122–3
Rockefeller, John D. 166
Rodrik, Dani 36
Roe Foundation 204
Roe, Thomas 204
Rogers, Deborah 10
Rome, ancient and its collapse 234–5
Romney, Mitt 85, 151, 195–6, 261
Roosevelt, Theodore 166–7
Rosner, Joshua 179
Rothstein, Bo 20, 144

Rove, Karl 261
Rubin, Robert 180
rule of law 138–9, 179; absent with ethnic fractionalization 140–2
Russia: corruption in 168, 185; reversing democracy 3; wealthy in 39
Rwanda 7
Ryan, Paul 196

Saez, Emmanuel 38
Sagarin, Rafe 254–5
Sahlins, Marshall 167
Said, Jamac 35–36
Salter, Jim 145
San Francisco earthquake of 1906 119
Satyanath, Shanker 132
Saudi Arabia's corrupt regime 177
Scaife, Richard Mellon 204
Schmidt, Eric 236
Schmitt, John 211
schools: charter 50; elite 49
Schumpeter, Joseph 97
Schwartz, Michael 10
scientific revolution 69–73
Second Treatise of Government (Locke) 70
security, increased complexity in maintaining 236
self-actualization stage in hierarchy of needs 4
Sen, Amartya 8
Sennett, Richard 17
separation of church and state 70–71
September 11, 2001 attack on the World Trade Center 198
Sherk, James 220
Shermer, Michael 197
Shia in conflict with Sunni 10
Shierholz, Heidi 214
Shock Doctrine (Klein) 119
shocks: planning for 243; susceptibility to 239–1
Sierra Leone 136–7; corruption 139
Silva, Jennifer M. 147

Simon, Herbert A. 19
Sinclair, Upton 96
Slim, Carlos 34
Slotkin, Richard 164
Smith, Adam 71, 75–77, 86, 92, 267
Snowden, Edward 236
social capital 19, 257; creating 126–9; decline in 210; dependent on impartial politics 144; fragility of 134–6; impacted by civic cooperation 129–30; linked to wealth 129; provided by fraternal organizations 128; and trust 125; types of 126
social contract, erosion of 52–53, 208–10
social democracy 267
social discontent 165–6
social inequality: affecting people's response to disasters 118–24; based on status 15–20; and capitalism 63–87, 109; categorical 11; costs of on society 16–17; and democracy 138–40, 176–8; driven by globalization and automation 260; durable 10, 21–22; economic reinforced by social power 85; erodes trust 124–5, 130–3, 142; global among countries during colonization 73–74; growing 1; impacted by uncontrolled factors 43–44; in income 201–2, 208–9, 258; increased by concentration of power 175; increases loss of human development 136–9; increasing or declining globally 32–36; *versus* inequities 9–10; maintaining 12–13; nature of 1–22; negatively correlated with democracies 139; requiring increased energy to maintain 237, 241; and status 13–20; views on increase in 17–19
social instability and rise of corruption 163–8
social mobility 43–45; impacted by marital patterns 50–52; influenced by family structure 52

social networks as a form of capital 127–8
social power reinforcing economic inequality 85
social relations of production 84–85
social stratification 14
social suffering 134–5
society: being human in 4–5, 7–8; collapse of 232–3; development in phases 107–8; fully active in 5–6, 15; increased complexity of 233–4; increased expenditures in solving problems 234–7; just society being fair 2; resilience in 242–3; sustainable 245–6; unstable due to unmet human needs 7, 10
socioeconomic status of parents and their children 44–45
soft money in campaign financing 262
Solnit, Rebecca 118
Somalia 35, 36; corruption 177
South Africa maintaining income inequalities 238–9
South Asia's extreme poverty 32
Southeast Asia's extreme poverty 32
Southern United States and lack of unions 204–5
South Sudan and ethnic tensions 10–11
sports and media stars as top income earners 36–37
Springsteen, Bruce 37
state capitalism 110
State Policy Network 204
status: derived from associations with others 19; to maintain inequalities 13–20
status groups 14–15; self-regulating 19–20
Sterman, John 54
Steyer, Tom 218
Stiglitz, Joseph E. 100, 102, 258, 260
storytelling 197–8
student performance 46–47
subjective needs 6, 8
Sub-Saharan Africa's extreme poverty 32–33

subsistence needs 5, 6
Sudan's corrupt regime 177
Sunni in conflict with Shia 10
surplus labor time 92
surplus value, increasing 92
sustainability 22; and capitalism 86–87, 111–12; corruption and social inequality 185–7; defined 243; incompatible with free-market fundamentalism 219–20; and inequity 152–3; influenced by wealth and income 54–56; narrative 223–4; and need for increased energy 237; and renewable energy resources 244–6; and social inequality 22; of the society over time 245–6
Swift and Certain Sanctions Act 217–18
Swift, Taylor 37
Syria 7; corruption 177

Tainter, Joseph 233, 234, 237
Taleb, Nassim N. 242
Tammany Hall 160, 162, 164–5, 167
tariffs 79
taxes: debate about cutting taxes on the wealthy 41–4; estate 43; reform 157–8
teachers pressured to teach to mandated tests 48–49
Thatcher, Margaret 99
Theory of Justice, A (Rawls) 2
"The Principle of On-Scene Initiative," 251
Thompson, Patricia 252
Tilly, Charles 10, 12, 142, 178, 268
Tirado, Linda 231
Tocqueville, Alexis de 126, 128, 257
top two primary 263
Townsend, Joseph 78
Townsend, Peter 5
trust 223, 249; of a community 115–18; correlated with ethnic homogeneity 142; declining in the U.S. 144–51; dependent on equality 124–5; fostered by fraternal organizations 127–8; and government institutions 143; grows from engagement 126–7; historical conditions generating low levels 133–4; irrevocable 43; lack of due to poverty 146; lack of in governments 146–9; lack of in Haiti 124; lack of in low-status groups 20; loss by inequality 137–8; low and high corruption and crime 142; low with ethnic fractionalization and lack of law 140–2; in national governments 144; not influenced by participation in associations 143–4; and social capital 125
trust networks 142–3, 178–9, 184
truth, ignoring 198–200
Tunisia, revolution in 175
Turkey reversing democracy 3
Turkmenistan's corrupt regime 177
Tweed, William T. 160–3, 167

Uganda's inequality and corruption 173–4
unions: aid in forming 264–5; attacks on 216–19; benefits 206–8; inability to increase in the South 205–6; lack of in the South 204–5; membership 129, 200–4
United Auto Workers (UAW) 201, 205–6
Universal Declaration of Human Rights (1948), 3
universal human needs 6, 7, 231
urbanization 108
U.S.: class division 146–9, 166–7; corruption in 160–8; declining trust with political institutions and others 144–51; labor movement in 13; political party division 148–9; racial divide 145–6; relative poverty in 6; reversal in progress toward democracy 179; support of the military 221–2, 235–6; wealthy in 36–39
use value 81

INDEX

Uslander, Erik M. 146
Utopia (More) 68–69
Uzbekistan's corrupt regime 177

value: of goods 92; impacted by status 15; increasing surplus 92
Vanderbilt, Cornelius 166
Vietnam: and defining poverty 29–30; dictatorships 142
violence: caused by inequality and political discrimination 142; and corruption 186
Vogel, Kenneth 85
Volkswagen and unionization 205–6
Vollmer, Sebastin 41
Voltaire 71
volunteer fire departments linked to politics 161
voter ID laws 219
Voters First Act 263
voting becoming mandatory 261
Voting Rights Act of 1965 219

wages: inequality reduced by union membership 201–2; raising minimum wage 210–16, 259; and supply of workers 78
Walker, Scott 207, 208
Wallerstein, Immanuel 73
Wall Street linked with government 179–80
Wal-Mart effect 77
Wal-Mart going green 244
Wapner, Paul 112
war: on drugs 264; to gain autonomy 8
war-making capacity 108
Warner, Kris 203
Wascher, William 212
Watson, Bo 206
Watt, James 106
wealth: concentration of a few 34, 102–4, 220, 232; distribution in the U.S. 38; as driver of climate change 55; gap 36–43, 101; gap between countries 34–35; gap during the Enlightenment 68; of individuals 38; inherited 45, 103; linked to social capital 129; U-shaped distribution trend 38–39
Wealth and Poverty of Nations, The (Landes) 72
Wealth of Nations, The (Smith) 75–76
wealthy: controlling the judiciary 182; having advantages in the educational system 45–46; increased concentration of 34, 102–4, 230, 232; influencing politics 179–83; shifting money offshore 40–41
Weber, Max 14, 72–73, 85, 127–8
Weil, David 208
Weill, Sanford 180
welfare attacks 193
welfare cheat 199
welfare queen 193, 195
Westen, Drew 198
Why the West Rules – For Now (Morris) 107
Wilkinson, Richard 21, 185
Will, George 258
Williams, William 250
Winfrey Oprah 37
Winner, Andreas 142
Wisconsin eliminating bargaining rights 13
women: equality 195; inequality of 10, 12, 17
Woods, Tiger 37
workers and wages 78
world system, rise of 73–75

Zafirovski, Milan 72
Zola, Émile 96
Zuckerberg, Mark 43
Zucman, Gabriel 38, 39, 41

# Taylor & Francis eBooks

Helping you to choose the right eBooks for your Library

Add Routledge titles to your library's digital collection today. Taylor and Francis ebooks contains over 50,000 titles in the Humanities, Social Sciences, Behavioural Sciences, Built Environment and Law.

Choose from a range of subject packages or create your own!

Benefits for you
- Free MARC records
- COUNTER-compliant usage statistics
- Flexible purchase and pricing options
- All titles DRM-free.

Benefits for your user
- Off-site, anytime access via Athens or referring URL
- Print or copy pages or chapters
- Full content search
- Bookmark, highlight and annotate text
- Access to thousands of pages of quality research at the click of a button.

 Free Trials Available
We offer free trials to qualifying academic, corporate and government customers.

eCollections – Choose from over 30 subject eCollections, including:

Archaeology	Language Learning
Architecture	Law
Asian Studies	Literature
Business & Management	Media & Communication
Classical Studies	Middle East Studies
Construction	Music
Creative & Media Arts	Philosophy
Criminology & Criminal Justice	Planning
Economics	Politics
Education	Psychology & Mental Health
Energy	Religion
Engineering	Security
English Language & Linguistics	Social Work
Environment & Sustainability	Sociology
Geography	Sport
Health Studies	Theatre & Performance
History	Tourism, Hospitality & Events

For more information, pricing enquiries or to order a free trial, please contact your local sales team:
www.tandfebooks.com/page/sales

 | The home of Routledge books | www.tandfebooks.com